Understanding Language Series

Series Editors: Bernard Comrie and Greville Corbett

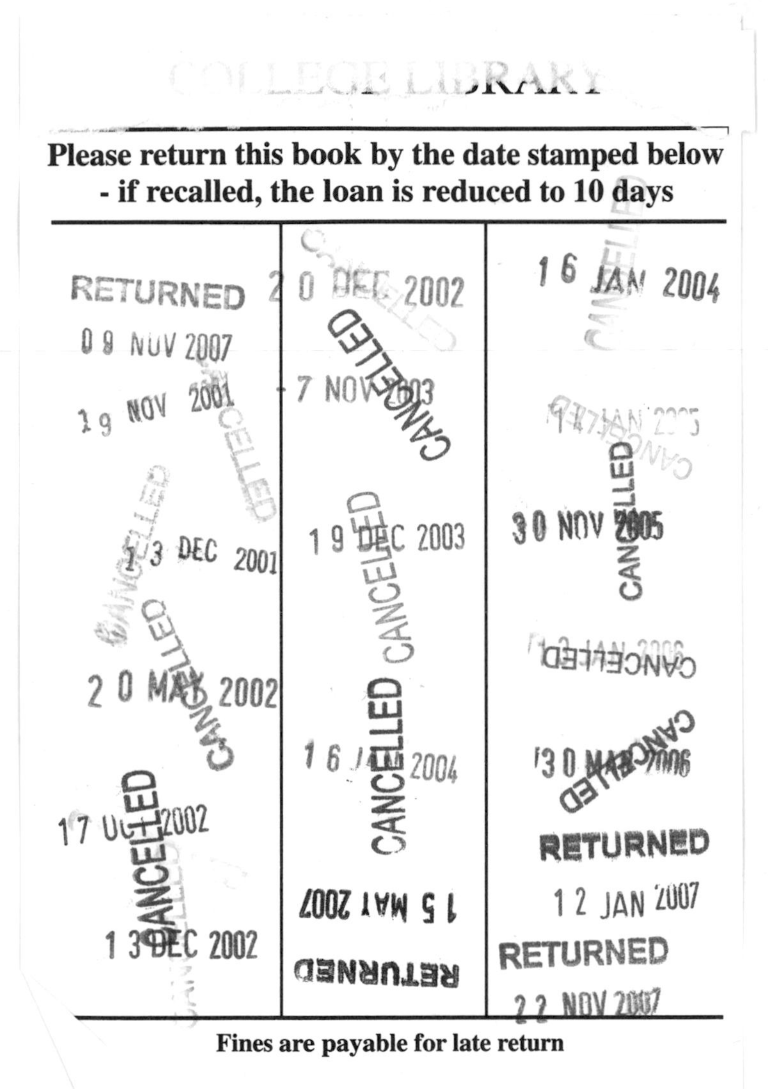

ALSO IN THE *UNDERSTANDING LANGUAGE* SERIES

PUBLISHED:

UNDERSTANDING PHONOLOGY
Carlos Gussenhoven and Haike Jacobs

UNDERSTANDING SYNTAX
Maggie Tallerman

FORTHCOMING:

UNDERSTANDING TEXT AND DISCOURSE
Jan-Ola Östman and Tuija Virtanen

UNDERSTANDING SEMANTICS
Bernd Kortmann and Sebastian Löbner

Understanding Pragmatics

Jef Verschueren

A member of the Hodder Headline Group
LONDON • NEW YORK • SYDNEY • AUCKLAND

First published in Great Britain in 1999 by
Arnold, a member of the Hodder Headline Group,
338 Euston Road, London NW1 3BH

http://www.arnoldpublishers.com

Co-published in the United States of America by
Oxford University Press Inc.,
198 Madison Avenue, New York, NY 10016

British Library Cataloguing in Publication Data
A catalogue record for this book is available from the British Library

Library of Congress Cataloging-in-Publication Data
Verschueren, Jef.
Understanding pragmatics / Jef Verschueren.
p. cm. -- (Understanding language)
Includes bibliographical references (p.) and index.
ISBN 0–340–64624–1. -- ISBN 0–340–64623–3 (pb)
1. Pragmatics. 2 Linguistics. I. Title. II. Series.
P99.4.P72V47 1998
306.44--dc21 98–22271
CIP

ISBN 0 340 64624 1 (hb)
ISBN 0 340 64623 3 (pb)

2 3 4 5 6 7 8 9 10

Production Editor: Rada Radojicic
Production Controller: Priya Gohil
Cover Design: Terry Griffiths

Typeset in 11/12 pt Times by Photoprint Typesetters, Torquay, Devon
Printed and bound in Great Britain by MPG Books Ltd, Bodmin, Cornwall

Contents

Part III Topics and trends

That is the essence of science:
ask an impertinent question,
and you are on the way
to the pertinent answer.
(Jacob Bronowski 1973: 153)

There is no reason to be compromising
about what I call good reductionism.
It is simply the commitment to non-question-begging science
without any cheating by embracing mysteries or miracles at the outset.
(Daniel C. Dennett 1995: 82)

Acknowledgements

The author and the publisher would like to thank the following for permission to use copyright material in this book:

Guinness Limited for the beermats on page 171. The GUINNESS Word is a registered trade mark of Arthur Guinness & Son (Dublin) Limited;

Les Éditions Albert René for drawings from the ASTERIX adventures on page 21 © 1998 – Les Éditions Albert René/Goscinny – Uderzo;

Virgin Trains for the editorial on page 145 (consisting of a letter addressed to Virgin Trains Travellers, signed by Richard Branson) from HotLine magazine, Autumn/Winter 1997.

Every effort has been made to trace copyright holders. Any rights not acknowledged here will be acknowledged in subsequent printings if notice is given to the publisher.

Preface

This book is an attempt to meet a double challenge. The first, and not the least, is to present a coherent theoretical framework in terms of which most of what is known today about the pragmatics of language, i.e. language use, can be reflected upon and further explored. The second challenge is to keep the presentation elementary, usable as a textbook, accessible both to students with a basic linguistic background and those more skilled in the sciences of language, and open to scholars in other academic fields which stand to gain from a deeper insight into the ways in which language 'works'. The demands of innovation and initiation, however, are only seemingly contradictory. At the level of abstraction that motivates my choice of epigraphs, they clearly converge. Impertinent questions, those that have to be asked to push the limits of insight and knowledge, are rarely the most sophisticated ones. Assuming that language use is a cognitively, socially and culturally anchored form of behaviour, the question that will guide our search for theoretical coherence in the field of linguistic pragmatics is simply this: 'What do people do when using language?' Similarly, satisfactory answers usually involve a fair degree of demystification. The general question, therefore, will be gradually reduced to subsidiary questions that lend themselves to responses based on empirical observation. Recourse to a 'black box', or a *deus ex machina*, will be carefully avoided.

There is no shortage of pragmatics textbooks today. Restricting myself to those available in English and bearing 'pragmatics' in their title or subtitle, we find – in chronological order – Leech (1983), Levinson (1983), Green (1989), Blakemore (1992), Mey (1993), Grundy (1995), Thomas (1995) and Yule (1996). Dozens should be added if we were to list those in other languages, those avoiding the label 'pragmatics' though dealing with the same range of usage phenomena, or collective volumes. All of them, however, restrict their theoretical or their empirical scope, or both. They tend to focus on a somewhat random set of phenomena, including deixis, implicature, presupposition, speech acts, conversation, and the like. Cognition is brought in regularly, but only for theory-specific purposes. Social and cultural factors fail to be accounted for systematically; a chapter on 'societal pragmatics' may be added as if it were an afterthought. Thus, trying to pull together different topics and orientations in a principled way, this book does not have immediate precursors.

A project like this is not conceived and completed in one breath. Barring an even earlier attempt at theory formation in pragmatics (Verschueren 1978a) as well as earlier attempts at 'organizing' the field by means of a bibliographical effort (Verschueren 1978b, with five annual supplements 1978–1982 in the *Journal of Pragmatics*) and participation in the organization of a conference on *Possibilities and limitations of pragmatics* (in Urbino on 8–14 July 1979) and in the setting up of the book series *Pragmatics & Beyond* (John Benjamins, 1979 onwards), the present enterprise has at least a 14-year history. A first outline of the ideas underlying this book was presented during the workshop, *Between semantics and pragmatics*, held at the Inter-University Center for Postgraduate Studies in Dubrovnik on 7–18 May 1984. Its basic tenet, the quest for coherence in the field of pragmatics, subsequently led to the organization of the *International Pragmatics Conference* in Viareggio on 1–7 September 1985 (the first in an ongoing series), the establishment of the *International Pragmatics Association (IPrA)* in 1986, the production of a more comprehensive pragmatics bibliography (Nuyts and Verschueren 1987), the teaching of courses on theory formation in pragmatics (University of Antwerp), the publication of a working document sketching the basic structure of a general pragmatic theory (Verschueren 1987), of a variety of articles on aspects of the same (Verschueren 1994, 1995), and of the *Handbook of pragmatics* (Verschueren *et al.* eds. 1995).

All of these endeavours imply a high degree of indebtedness to numerous colleagues. In particular I wish to thank: Jacob Mey, for encouraging the preparation of my very first contribution to pragmatic theory for the *Journal of Pragmatics* (and for later taking me on as review editor, a capacity in which I learned further tricks of the trade in interaction with Hartmut Haberland and Ferenc Kiefer); Herman Parret, for inviting me to join forces to organize the Urbino conference (with Marina Sbisà) and to start the *Pragmatics & Beyond* series; Svenka Savić and Johan van der Auwera, for giving me the opportunity to present some embryonic ideas during the Dubrovnik lectures; Marcella Bertuccelli Papi, Jan Blommaert, Jan Nuyts, and Jan-Ola Östman for taking those ideas seriously enough for me to pursue them further (Marcella later co-organized the Viareggio conference, Jan N. co-produced the pragmatics bibliography and co-founded IPrA, both Jan N. and Jan-Ola were one-time co-teachers in the 'theory formation' course at the University of Antwerp, and both Jan B. and Jan-Ola are – with Chris Bulcaen – still co-editors of the ongoing *Handbook* project); Ann Verhaert, without whose constant support and labour (free at first, underpaid ever since) none of the organizational work would have been possible; Jan Blommaert, Frank Brisard, Chris Bulcaen, Helge Daniëls, Sigurd D'hondt, Gino Eelen, Jürgen Jaspers, Luisa Martín Rojo, and Michael Meeuwis, for their critical attention during long periods of collaboration at the IPrA Research Center and for comments on earlier versions of this book. Though it is impossible to weigh individual contributions, it is only fair to draw attention to Michael Meeuwis' merciless and unrelenting stabs at my poor terminology which, I think, have greatly influenced the conceptual clarity of what I am trying to present, and to Gino Eelen's special gift for pointing out, with embarrassing accuracy, where I was falling into the traps I am warning against – a problem that may still persist here and there. Many others have contributed to varying degrees by commenting on a first draft: Jannis Androutsopoulos, Bert Bultinck, Pol Cuvelier, Thorstein Fretheim, John Gumperz, Annick De Houwer, Cornelia Ilie, Geert Jacobs, Alexandra Jaffe, István Kecskés, Manfred Kienpointner, Li Wei, Tom Naegels, François Némo, Srikant Sarangi, Rachida Senoussi, Tom De Smet, Ludwina Van Son, Khalid Touzani, Rod Watson, Zhang Shaojie. Also, this may be the proper place to acknowledge, once and for all, intellectual indebtedness to Louis Goossens, who first introduced me to a functional perspective on language, and to Charles Fillmore, John Gumperz, George Lakoff, and John Searle who helped me to refine it during several years of interaction at the University of California, Berkeley.

The work leading towards the writing of this book was supported by the Belgian National Fund for Scientific Research (NFWO/FKFO), a Belgian government grant (Federale Diensten voor Wetenschappelijke, Technische en Culturele Aangelegenheden, IUAP-II, contract number 27), and the University of Antwerp. The actual writing was started during an unforgettable stay at the Bellagio Study and Conference Center (8 February to 8 March 1997), granted by the Rockefeller Foundation and – with equal merit – by Ann, who took on the full burden of a sizeable family meanwhile. My co-residents at the Bellagio Center provided most useful examples (usually unwittingly), inspiration and discussion.

Further thanks are due to Bernard Comrie and Greville Corbett for inviting me to write this book and for their unfailing editorial attention ever since. Finally, I wish to thank Mouton-de Gruyter, the American Anthropological Association, and John Benjamins for their permission to re-use some examples and analyses from Verschueren (1989a, 1995b, and 1995d/1995e, respectively).

Because of the restricted size of this book, extensive comments on the literature as well as long lists of references have been avoided. Its more advanced readers are therefore advised to use it in conjunction with *A comprehensive bibliography of pragmatics* (covering most of the literature, though only up to 1985) and especially the *Handbook of pragmatics* (providing succinct but detailed descriptions of traditions, methods, and topics, and containing additional reference lists).

Jef Verschueren
31 March 1998

Introduction

At the most elementary level, **pragmatics** can be defined as *the study of language use*, or, to employ a somewhat more complicated phrasing, *the study of linguistic phenomena from the point of view of their usage properties and processes*. This base-level definition does not introduce a strict boundary between pragmatics and some other areas in the field of linguistics, such as discourse analysis, sociolinguistics, or conversation analysis. Yet it is rarely disputed, and when thinking through its logical consequences it has interesting implications for the way in which pragmatics is to be situated in the science of language in general. The following sections will be an attempt to do so.

0.1 *Linguistics of language resources: components of a linguistic theory*

Linguistics is traditionally divided into *component disciplines* such as phonetics, phonology, morphology, syntax and semantics. Each of those is related to a specific *unit of analysis*. Thus phonetics and phonology deal with speech sounds. **Phonetics** does so by identifying constituent parts of a continuous stream of sound, as elements in a universal repertoire from which all languages use a selected subset and outside of which there are only non-linguistic sounds (e.g. audible yawning or sneezing); either the physical properties of the sounds are focused on (acoustic phonetics), or their manner of production in the vocal tract (articulatory phonetics), or their reception (auditory phonetics). **Phonology** studies the way in which speech sounds form systems which enable speakers of a given language to agree on when two strings of sounds (the production of which can be infinitely varied) are basically the 'same'; when looked at in this way, mere sounds become 'phonemes', the basic building blocks for meaningful language units such as morphemes and words. **Morphology**, then, investigates 'morphemes' (such as *dis-*, *en-*, *chant*, *-ment*, *neighbour*, *-hood*), the minimal linguistic signs in the sense that they are the minimal units carrying a conventional meaning or contributing conventionally to the meaning of larger units, and the ways in which they combine to form words (such as *disenchantment* or *neighbourhood*); thus there is a basic distinction between morphemes that can themselves occur as separate words, i.e. free morphemes (such as *chant* or *neighbour*), and those that have no choice but to combine with others to form words, i.e. bound morphemes (such as *dis-*, *en-*, *-ment* and *-hood*, the latter happening to have the same form as the free morpheme *hood*). Words or 'lexical items' are those units of analysis which, carrying a conventional meaning, either as free morphemes or as combinations of morphemes, can combine with each other along a syntagmatic dimension, placing words in a linear order in accordance with language-specific rules to form sentences. **Syntax** studies such sentence-formation processes. **Semantics**, finally, explores the meaning of linguistic units, typically at the level of words (lexical semantics) or at the level of sentences, whether or not they correspond to simple propositions (such as *The bird ate the worm*) or to more complex structures (as in *John saw the bird eat the worm* or *John says he thinks the bird ate the worm*).

All of these endeavours share a focus on *language resources*, i.e. the ingredients that make up a language as a tool that people use for expressive and communicative purposes. Since language is highly structured, both formally and in terms of form–meaning relationships, units of analysis can be identified, thus leading to a manageable division of labour as outlined above. But where does pragmatics come in? Is there a comparable task to be found that would place pragmatics in the same contrast set?

0.2 *Linguistics of language use: the pragmatic perspective*

As is implied in the base-level definition with which we started this Introduction, pragmatics cannot possibly be identified with a specific unit of analysis, so that it cannot partake in the division of labour associated with the traditional components of a linguistic theory. Clearly, the linguistic phenomena to be studied from the point of view of their usage can be situated at any level of structure or may pertain to any type of form–meaning relationship. The question is: How are the language resources used? Therefore, pragmatics does not constitute an additional component of a theory of language, but it offers a different *perspective*. This book will have to explain precisely what that perspective entails.

There are no doubt units of linguistic structure that lend themselves more readily to a pragmatic investigation than to resource-oriented explorations. This is the case for most supra-sentential units such as texts, conversations, or discourse in general. The reason is that these are typical *products* of *putting resources to use*. On the one hand, they involve an expansion of the range of resources itself. For instance, beyond sounds, words and sentences, there are argumentation patterns, styles, genres and the like. On the other hand, the latter cannot even be defined outside a usage context. But there are definitely *no* linguistic phenomena, at any level of structure, that a pragmatic perspective can afford to ignore. Let us try to illustrate this briefly.

Take the level of speech sounds. When a linguistic anthropologist discovers that members of a certain community adapt the phonological system of their language to whether or not they are communicating with other members of the same group, this observation bears on a usage phenomenon and is therefore fundamentally pragmatic, though situated at a structural level that is unmistakably the province of phonology (see section 4.2.1). It is not even necessary to go to exotic data to come to similar conclusions. Most speakers of languages with a significant degree of dialectal variation, who have grown up with a local dialect but who were socialized into the use of a standard variety through formal education, will find that the language they use sounds quite different depending on whether they are in their professional context or speaking to their parents or siblings. Usage variation of this type does not stop at the sound level: morphological, lexical and even syntactic choices may be involved as well.

Going to the morpheme and word levels, there are pragmatic restrictions on and implications of aspects of derivational morphology (the way in which free morphemes, such as *speak*, and bound morphemes, such as the prefix *un-* and the suffix *-able*, can be combined to form the word *unspeakable*), of compounding (the word-formation process which expands the vocabulary by creating new words such as *boathouse* out of the separately existing *boat* and *house*), and even of inflectional morphology (the way in which the forms of words change in accordance with grammatical variables such as tense, number, gender, case and the like).

Consider the derivational relationship between *grateful* and *ungrateful*, *kind* and *unkind*, *lawful* and *unlawful*. The reason why this relationship is not reversed, with a basic lexeme meaning 'ungrateful' from which a word meaning 'grateful' would be derived by means of the negative prefix *un-*, has everything to do with a system of social norms which emphasizes the need for gratefulness, kindness, lawfulness and the like. Norms or standards can also be of a more conceptual nature: 'familiarity' is the conceptual standard that determines the emergence of a pair, such as *familiar* and *unfamiliar*, leaving the possibility of a monomorphemic equivalent for the 'negative' pole of the contrast set, viz. *strange*, but precluding the creation of a pair such as *strange* (in the sense of 'strange') versus *unstrange* (in the sense of 'familiar') – except as an individual's willful act for specific rhetorical purposes. Normativity can be such that logic is completely disregarded: it must be the case that objects which can be 'fastened' are seen to be 'normally' in a 'fastened' state; otherwise it is hard to explain why *unloosen*, which must have crept into the English language inadvertently, does not have the meaning 'fasten' but is in fact synonymous with *unfasten*. Another derivational process which usually requires a pragmatic account is the formation of diminutives (see Dressler and Barbaresi 1994).

Compounding is a process guided by pragmatic principles and restrictions related to interpretability and the availability of context. A compound such as *house tree*, for instance, would be less likely to occur as a description of 'a tree between two houses' than in the sense of 'a tree standing close to (or inside) a house'. The reason is that it would require a higher amount of specific contextual information to ensure successful interpretation. Similarly, a creative compound such as *the apple-juice seat* requires a very specific shared context (with, for instance, a seat in front of which a glass of apple-juice has been placed) to be produced at all (see Downing 1977). Moreover, the very shape of certain more conventional compounds is often the product of fundamentally pragmatic processes. When two aeroplanes nearly collide in mid-air, the term *near miss* (where both elements separately stress the fact that the planes did *not* hit each other) is greatly preferred over *near hit* (which would emphasize the dire consequences of what almost *did* happen).

Grammatical choices of morphemes are also subject to pragmatic constraints. Just consider the recent changes in socio-political awareness which have made it harder to interpret the generic use of the personal pronoun *he* (referring to any human being, male or female) in a gender-neutral way.

Turning to syntax, it should be clear that the same state of affairs can be described by means of very different syntactic structures: *John broke the figurine*, *The figurine was broken by John*, *The figurine was broken*, *The figurine got broken*. Though roughly equivalent at first sight, these forms of expression have very different usage conditions. To point out just one aspect for the sake of illustration, note the progressive reduction of emphasis on the person responsible for the breaking of the figurine, which starts with the full passive formula that still includes mention of the agent, John, and which ends with a formula that may even suggest complete absence of (or ignorance about) any responsibility. Another usage aspect involved is the speaker's assessment of whether it is more relevant to the hearer to be told something about John (in which case the sentence is more likely to start with *John*) or about the figurine (in which case *The figurine* will more easily be chosen as the subject).

At the level of word meaning, the domain of lexical semantics, as soon as a word gets used, more has to be taken into account than what would normally be regarded as its 'dictionary meaning'. In a simple sentence such as *The door opened*, the verb *open* may have different meanings, depending on physical properties of the context. Without access to further information, we know that in order for *The door opened* to be an appropriate description of an event, the door must have opened either automatically or by someone hidden from the speaker's view. This means that, for there to have been a human agent, he or she cannot have been on the same side of the door as the speaker. This possibility is excluded completely, moreover, if the door is a transparent one. Many words cannot even be understood unless aspects of world knowledge (sometimes called 'encyclopedic knowledge') are invoked, a process which makes the accessibility of meaning gradable: most people today can be assumed to interpret the term *non-smoking section* without difficulty; also a *topless district* is not too hard to interpret, though it requires knowledge about city areas with a high concentration of establishments for (predominantly male) entertainment where scantly dressed hostesses or performers are the main attraction; a newspaper article with *mental midwives* in its title, however, cannot really be understood until after reading the article, which describes patients in a *mental hospital* (another term which requires institutional knowledge) assisting a fellow patient when giving birth.

Usage-related aspects of sentential or propositional meaning, also requiring world knowledge and contextual information, produce many different interpretations of the same simple reference–predication structure such as *The X is on the Y*, e.g. *The cat is on the mat* (typically invoking a horizontal position, the cat being supported by gravity), *The painting is on the wall* (a vertical position, the painting being supported by any type of artificial attachment as a remedy against gravity), *The fly is on the ceiling* (also horizontal, but with *on* taking a meaning that would have to be labelled *under* if the speaker's perspective were not to intervene, and with the fly being supported by suction pads) and *The painting is on the ceiling* (where *on* no longer suggests an existential distance between X and Y, the paint having been applied directly to the ceiling, so that the issue of 'support' is made irrelevant). The sentence level also takes us back to the area of syntactic structures, to which a pragmatic perspective was already shown to be relevant. It also reintroduces the level of speech sounds as soon as we pay attention to prosody and intonation patterns. Varying the intonation of *It's cold in here* may turn the expected statement meaning into a question (probably not to be interpreted as a real question but as an expression of disagreement with the content of the proposition), a complaint and (perhaps more indirectly) a request to turn up the heating.

Why do we describe all these phenomena (and many more to be introduced later) as 'pragmatic'? This is a direct consequence of the uncompromising acceptance of the definition of pragmatics as the study of language use. Maybe this can be clarified by acknowledging a radical return to the wide definition originally proposed by the founding father of pragmatics, Charles Morris (1938). Morris distinguishes between syntax, semantics and pragmatics in terms of three correlates: signs, the objects to which signs are applicable, and sign users or interpreters. Syntax studies the relationship of signs to other signs; semantics deals with the relations of signs to the objects to which signs are applicable; and pragmatics studies whatever relations there are between signs and their users or interpreters (see also section 9.1). Without identifying it in the way I have done so far by distinguishing between the linguistics of language resources and the linguistics of language use, Morris's approach already implies the recognition of an entirely different dimension touched upon by pragmatics. Thus he observes the following:

> Syntactical rules determine the sign relations between sign vehicles; semantical rules correlate sign vehicles with other objects; pragmatical rules state the conditions in the interpreters under which the sign vehicle is a sign. *Any rule when actually in use operates as a type of behavior, and in this sense there is a pragmatical component in all rules.* (1938: 35; italics added)

More than half a century later, we could not have expressed this idea better.

0.3 *Pragmatics and interdisciplinarity*

A pragmatic perspective, as tentatively described and illustrated above, is by definition interdisciplinary. Or, to quote Morris again:

> By 'pragmatics' is designated the science of the relation of signs to their interpreters. [. . .] Since most, if not all, signs have as their interpreters living organisms, it is a sufficiently accurate characterization of pragmatics to say that it deals with the biotic aspects of semiosis, that is, with all the psychological, biological, and sociological phenomena which occur in the functioning of signs. (1938: 30)

Linguistic pragmatics studies people's *use of language*, a form of *behaviour* or *social action*. Thus the *dimension* which the pragmatic perspective is intended to give insight into is *the link between language and human life in general.* Hence, pragmatics is also *the* link between linguistics and the rest of the humanities and social sciences.

Having said this, we must also observe that pragmatics is not only situated outside the contrast set to which phonetics, phonology, morphology, syntax and semantics belong; neither does it fit into the set of interdisciplinary fields such as neurolinguistics, psycholinguistics, sociolinguistics and anthropological linguistics. Each of these fields has its own *correlational object* in relation to which language is studied: oversimplifying a little, **neurolinguistics** tries to reveal the neurophysiological bases and processes of speaking and listening (and whatever can go wrong in this domain), **psycholinguistics** studies the relationships between language and the mind in general (a task to subareas of which certain brands of **cognitive linguistics** are also devoted), **sociolinguistics** is concerned with the ways in which social relationships, statuses, patterns, and networks interact with language structure and use, and **anthropological linguistics** is devoted to the relationships between language(s) and culture(s). Just as it was impossible to assign a basic unit of analysis to pragmatics, it is impossible to identify a specific correlational object. Pragmatics is concerned with the full complexity of linguistic behaviour. From that perspective, there is no way of addressing, for instance, issues of cognition without taking society and culture into account, nor are there ways of addressing issues of culture abstracted from their cognitive underpinnings and implications. When looking at the work done under the interdisciplinary labels, actual research practice indeed shows a serious degree of thematic as well as methodological overlap. By the same token many aspects of what we will present in this book as pragmatics, would fit comfortably under one or more of the interdisciplinary labels. There is no reason to see this as a problem. Many forms of research require clear self-imposed restrictions to push the limits of our understanding. The main function of linguistic pragmatics in the academic landscape of the language-related sciences could be, then, to make sure that there is a point of convergence for the various interdisciplinary undertakings, a global picture against which the overall relevance of more specific efforts can be measured and from which the need for specific lines of investigation will emerge. At the same time, pragmatics could function quite effectively as the latch connecting what we have called the linguistics of language resources with the interdisciplinary fields mentioned here.

Summing up, we can now further specify **pragmatics** as *a general cognitive, social, and cultural perspective on linguistic phenomena in relation to their usage in forms of behaviour* (where the string 'cognitive, social, and cultural' does not suggest the separability of what the terms refer to). Thus the question of how language resources are being used rephrases itself as: How does language function in the lives of human beings?

0.4 *Meaningful functioning of language*

Whatever else can be said about the functioning of language, there is no doubt that it is fundamentally 'meaningful'. Language is the major instrument in attempts to construct meaning in a world which does not have meaning in itself. This lofty claim not only bears on the elevated level of a philosophical quest for sense in life. Many examples in this book will show that the generation of meaning is a low-level everyday type of occurrence to be found wherever language is used. Thus the (individual) choice between *John broke the figurine* and *The figurine got broken* is not inconsequential, nor is the (conventionalized) choice between *near miss* and *near hit*.

Before continuing, a note on terminology is in order. Instead of the more commonly used term 'meaning construction' (or its verb equivalent 'constructing meaning'), this book will refer to the meaningful functioning of language in general as **meaning generation**. In contrast to 'construction' and 'construct', the term 'generation' and the verb 'generate' do not necessarily focus on the active (and, by extension, predominantly conscious) involvement of the language producer. Because of its potential for being used intransitively (as in *Under the right circumstances, electricity generates spontaneously*), 'to generate' (and hence the nominalized 'generation') allows for both the language user's active contribution to the processes under discussion and for their more spontaneous activation beyond the direct control of a language user's intentionality. Why this is an important nuance will be clarified later (especially in section 1.3 and Chapter 6). Whenever a selective focus is needed, we will distinguish between **meaning construction** (or 'constructing meaning', emphasizing agentivity) and **meaning emergence** (or 'emerging meaning', emphasizing processes that involve a lower degree or less salient type of agentivity or consciousness), as different aspects of **meaning generation** (or 'generating meaning').

In section 0.2 earlier in this chapter we have repeatedly referred to meaning in relation to context. It is one of the traditional, and maybe the most widely accepted, delimitations of pragmatics to contrast it directly with semantics by saying that the latter deals with context-independent meaning while the former investigates meaning in context. The 'meaningful functioning' of language envisaged by our approach to pragmatics, however, is not restricted to a 'meaning in context' which can simply be added on to another level of meaning adequately studied in semantics. Just imagine having to separate the non-contextual and the contextual meaning of *I'm tired*. For one thing, this is virtually impossible. Moreover, even trying to do so would violate the perspective view of pragmatics and reintroduce it into the contrast set of the traditional components of a linguistic theory. More importantly, however, such a stance would ignore the fact that pragmatics deals with *a different* ***type*** *of 'meaning'*, which allows us for instance to speak even about the 'meaningfulness' of choices between phonological systems, as illustrated. *Meaning in context*, no doubt, belongs to that type of meaning, but does not exhaust it. Nor does it necessarily turn 'meaning' into the dynamic notion it must be to help us grasp what goes on in language use. More often than not, treatments of pragmatics as the study of meaning in context, whilst allowing for the variability of the meanings of linguistic forms, simply add context as a parameter of stability at a different level.

Having introduced the notion of 'functioning', a few words need to be said about the kind of *functionalism* involved. What is *not* meant is the *functionalism of the system* which is already to be found in traditional linguistic structuralism and which is at times quite mechanistic. The premises of structuralism included the view of language as an autonomous system in which all elements are functionally related to each other and derive their significance entirely from the functional relationships with other elements. Thus the phonemes /f/ and /v/ form a functional contrast in English, distinguishing such words as *few* and *view*. And while /p/, /b/ and /f/ are all functional in English (as in *pin*, *bin* and *fin*), some languages may allow for free variation between /p/ and /b/ or between /b/ and /f/, whereas other languages such as Quechua multiply the number of functional contrasts by distinguishing between /p/, /p^h/ and /p'/. This type of functionalism is characterized by an internal contradiction: the functional principle that is said to operate within the language system is not applied to language as a phenomenon amongst other phenomena, since it is seen as autonomous. Pragmatics, on the other hand, emphasizes the functional relatedness of language with the other facets of human life. By not recognizing the full significance of this, structuralist functionalism often remains mechanistic and allows for (restricted aspects of) meaning to come in only sideways, whereas pragmatics gives it a central role – though we should be careful not to attribute an identical attitude to all structuralists.

This book will also avoid a functionalism oriented at the identification of ***functions*** of language, viewed as links between formal systems and their use. Without ignoring the need for generalizable explanations (as illustrated, for instance, in 7.1), pragmatics ought to focus straightforwardly on the *functioning* of language in actual contexts of use.

0.5 *An infinite task?*

The tasks of pragmatics, as emerging from the orientation and delimitation outlined so far, are wide-ranging indeed. Fears of uncontrolled expansion far beyond the limits of what could be called 'linguistic' are, therefore, not entirely without grounds. Usually, however, as will be illustrated in the course of the following explorations, a practical cut-off point is not too difficult to find. For instance, it is perfectly legitimate for a pragmatic analysis to relate my saying *John has red hair* to its typically expected association with my belief that John has red hair (unless this interpretation is barred by specific known conditions of utterance). However, it would not be the task of pragmatics to probe into my reasons for believing that John has red hair, unless this would be necessary for an understanding of other aspects of the discourse my utterance fits into.

Moreover, the suggestion that pragmatics is a *perspective*, 'the linguistics of language use' in its most general sense, ought to be taken literally. As a perspective it is all-encompassing. And a description of that perspective is feasible, as this book will try to demonstrate. For the practice of 'doing pragmatics', however, it is quite acceptable and often necessary to select research foci which justify their own topical and methodological boundaries – without losing sight, of course, of the wider frame of reference.

0.6 *Summary and further reading*

We have made a distinction between:

- *The linguistics of language resources*, consisting of the traditional components of a linguistic theory (phonetics, phonology, morphology, syntax and semantics), each of which has its own unit(s) of analysis.
- *Interdisciplinary fields of investigation* (such as neurolinguistics, psycholinguistics, sociolinguistics, anthropological linguistics), each of which has its own extra-linguistic correlational object(s).

In contrast to those, **pragmatics** was presented

- As *the linguistics of language use*.
- Having neither its own unit(s) of analysis nor its own correlational object(s).

- Constituting *a general functional (i.e. cognitive, social and cultural) perspective* on language.
- With as its topic of investigation *the meaningful functioning of language* in actual use, as a complex form of behaviour that *generates meaning*.
- And serving, within the realm of the language-related sciences, as a point of convergence for the interdisciplinary fields of investigation and as a latch between those and the components of the linguistics of language resources.

It is particularly important to remember that **meaning**, as a defining feature of what pragmatics is concerned with, is not seen as a stable counterpart to linguistic form. Rather, it is dynamically generated in the process of using language.

Though the perspective sketched in this introduction is not elaborated elsewhere in the pragmatic literature, many discussions are to be found of the definition of the field, a careful reading of which may make the present position easier to understand. In particular, the introductory chapters to Levinson (1983) and Davis (1991) are useful. For an extensive discussion of why the 'component view' of pragmatics is thought not to be tenable, see Verschueren (1985b). Early formulations that come close to what we call a 'perspective view' are found in Weiser (1974) and Haberland and Mey (1977), as will be shown later (in Chapter 9). For an earlier systematic attempt to approach language use in terms of meaning generation (or, in their terms, meaning construction) see Grunig and Grunig (1985). Outside the traditional pragmatic literature (see Coulter 1991 and Lee 1991) interesting discussions can be found which point at the inseparability of the cognitive, the social and the cultural – all of which must combine in a pragmatic perspective.

0.7 *Preview*

This book will have to demonstrate that the broad view of pragmatics adopted does not at all lead to vagueness, a property often attributed to it, but that it enables us to approach different aspects of language use in a quite coherent manner. The once-popular 'waste basket' view of pragmatics (Bar-Hillel 1971), assigning to pragmatics the task of dealing with whatever syntax and semantics could not properly cope with, will be radically left behind.

The book is organized in three parts and nine chapters. Part I, 'The pragmatic perspective', explains the idea of pragmatics as a general functional perspective on (any aspect of) language, i.e. as an approach to language which takes into account the full complexity of its cognitive, social and cultural functioning. To that end, Chapter 1,

'Language and language use', will review a wide range of phenomena studied previously under the label of pragmatics, explaining why their interrelatedness and the restricted treatment they have so far received lead almost necessarily to the more global perspective we are adopting. Chapter 2, 'Key notions', will then return to the question 'What do people do when using language?' or 'What is it to use language?', to introduce the primary observations on which a pragmatic theory will have to be built. It will be suggested that using language consists in the continuous making of linguistic choices (both in speaking and in interpreting), and that this 'making of choices' can be understood in terms of three hierarchically related notions: 'variability' as the property of language determining the range of possible choices; 'negotiability', implying that the choices are not mechanical but guided by flexible principles and strategies; and 'adaptability' as the property of language which enables human beings to make negotiable choices from a variable range of possibilities in such a way as to satisfy communicative needs. It will be shown how fundamental these notions are, and have been implicitly if not explicitly, to an understanding of the phenomena introduced in Chapter 1.

Part II, 'Aspects of the meaningful functioning of language', will offer the building blocks for an understanding of pragmatics as a coherent field of inquiry. Using 'adaptability' as the starting point, it will demonstrate that four aspects of the meaningful functioning of language can be distinguished that any pragmatic theory, description or explanation has to take into account. To each of them, a chapter will be devoted. Chapter 3, 'Context', will identify contextual correlates of adaptability, including all the ingredients of a communicative setting which communicative choices have to be interadaptable with. A wide range of examples will be given of the types of contextual elements constraining language use. It will be argued that, in spite of the apparent limitlessness of the range of potentially relevant phenomena, 'context' is not a vague notion since contexts are themselves generated (as choices made from the infinite range of possibilities, for specific instances of language use) and this generation process can be linguistically traced. Chapter 4, 'Structure', situates the meaningful functioning of language in relation to the different structural layers of adaptability. Since the making of linguistic choices takes place at all possible levels of structure that involve variability of any kind, pragmatic processes can be related to any level of structure, from sound feature and phoneme to discourse and beyond, or to any type of interlevel relationship. In this chapter, a wide range of favourite pragmatic topics – supplementing those already introduced in Chapter 1 – will be reviewed. In Chapter 5, 'Dynamics', the actual processes of 'making choices' will be accounted for, allowing for the fundamental negotiability involved. It will be shown how communication principles and strategies are used in the making and negotiating of choices of production and interpretation. Chapter 6, 'Salience', considers the fact that not all choices are made equally consciously or purposefully, that some are automatic while others are highly motivated. This chapter is concerned with different manners of processing in the medium of adaptability, the human 'mind in society'. It is with reference to this issue that the distinction between explicitly communicated meaning and implicit information will take on special relevance.

Part III, 'Topics and trends', has two goals. First, Chapters 7 and 8 are intended to explain, with reference to two types of specific research questions, how the described aspects of the meaningful functioning of language can be handled in practice. Whereas Parts I and II are more theoretical, the first two chapters of Part III will be more methodological, addressing also the issue of what counts as evidence in pragmatics. Chapter 7, 'Micropragmatic issues', will discuss some examples that are to be situated at the micro-level of face-to-face communication or at the level of linguistic 'details'. Chapter 8, 'Macropragmatic issues', will explore wider societal communicative processes. Second, Chapter 9, 'The pragmatic landscape', will point out current trends and historical connections. This final chapter is basically conceived as a guide for further study. It will point at some current 'theories' of pragmatics, and an explicit link will be made with some 'formative' traditions, the main idea being that pragmatics certainly did not appear in a vacuum.

Part I

The pragmatic perspective

Introduction

The following two chapters are intended to explain the idea of pragmatics as a general functional perspective on (any aspect of) language, i.e. as an approach to language which takes into account the full complexity of its cognitive, social and cultural functioning. Linking this book to established traditions, Chapter 1 reviews a wide range of phenomena studied previously under the label of pragmatics. It also explains how closely they are interrelated and how accidental the resulting distinctions are, so that taking a more global perspective seems wise at this point in the development of the field. Chapter 2 returns to the basic question 'What do people do when using language?' or 'What is it to use language?' Some elementary observations are presented which lead to the key notions required to construct a coherent theory of pragmatics. In contrast to Chapter 1, Chapter 2 is short, but theoretical. Familiarity with the theoretical premisses, however, is essential to put the remainder of this book in its proper perspective.

1

Language and language use

Our first task is to establish a clear link with the research questions and traditions that are commonly associated with the label 'pragmatics'. To that end, we start with two examples of actual language use. The first is an extract from a dinner conversation at the Rockefeller Foundation's Study and Conference Center in Bellagio, Italy (the names of the interlocutors have been changed; as in later examples, bold type indicates stressed syllables). The second is the opening sentence of the editorial introduction to *The world in 1996*, published by *The Economist* at the end of 1995 in a series of annual publications of the same type.

(1) 1. Debby: Go anywhere today?
2. Dan: Yes, we went down to Como. Up by bus, and back by hydrofoil.
3. Debby: Anything to see there?
4. Dan: Perhaps not the most interesting of Italian towns, but it's worth the trip.
5. Debby: I might do that next Saturday.
6. Jane: What do you mean when you say per**haps** not the most interesting of Italian towns?
7. Jack: He means **cer**tainly not the most interesting . . .
8. Dan: Just trying to be polite . . .

(2) 1996 will be a year of prosperity and peace.

In relation to these perfectly ordinary pieces of discourse, representing types which we encounter frequently every day, some of the more common topics that pragmatics has traditionally explored are first pointed out (section 1.1). I will then ask whether these 'common topics' can be as neatly separated as would seem at first sight, and it is suggested that they simply have so much in common that there are good reasons to stop using them as individual focal points for the organization of a book on pragmatics (section 1.2). A further explicit link with the literature will be made by discussing one of the major points of dispute, the issue of 'intentionality', with which any theory of pragmatics will have to come to terms (section 1.3). At the end of this first chapter are a few introductory words about the manifold categories of language use which make up linguistic behaviour (section 1.4).

1.1 *Common topics in pragmatics*

1.1.1 Deixis

Utterances relate to a real world – or what is perceived as such – in at least two different ways. The relationship can be descriptive, as when *by bus*, *cathedral*, and *silk* in (1), or *prosperity* and *peace* in (2) refer to aspects of reality in the realms of transportation, religion, commodities, social conditions and group interaction. This type of reference has usually been left in the province of semantics. It has already been hinted (in section 0.2 on page 5) and will further be demonstrated (in section 4.2.4) that pragmatics also has interesting things to say in this area. A second type of relationship, however, which has been dealt with under the label of pragmatics for many years, bears on the positioning of an utterance **in** a surrounding reality (which it may at the same time be **about**). One of the first phenomena that scientific considerations of language use could not ignore was this 'anchoring' of language in a real world, achieved by 'pointing' at variables along some of its dimensions. This phenomenon is called **deixis**, and the 'pointers' are **indexical expressions** or **indexicals**. There are essentially four *dimensions* involved: time, space, society (in particular the interlocutors), and discourse (the ongoing linguistic activity).

Markers of **temporal deixis** include *today* in (1)1., the past tense of *went* in (1)2., *next Saturday* in (1)5., *1996* and the future tense of *will be* in (2). Note that variables along the time dimension – and any other dimension, as will be clear soon – have no absolute values. Even to determine the **deictic centre**, the point of reference from which the dimension is looked at (typically *now* where time is concerned), information is needed about the **deictic context**. Thus the meaning of *today* in (1)1., which might seem quite unambiguous (*today* being at least quite 'proximal' in comparison with the more 'distal' *next Saturday* in (1)5.), cannot be precisely understood without knowledge about the time of speaking. For one thing, one would have to know the date to give full temporal substance to *today*. Apart from that, it is important to know that the conversation took place at dinner time, so that it is reasonable to assume that *today* refers to a stretch of time that is already past and that the elliptical phrase can be completed as *Did you go. . . .* Without the contextual knowledge, (1)1. could as well have been a question about planned activities for a future part of the day (though in that case the more likely elliptical form would have been *Going* . . ., short for *Are you going* . . ., since *Will you go* . . . is a less common form to ask about immediate future plans). Similarly, even though *1996* in (2) is a very conventionalized expression for referring to a specific period of time, and though its being combined with future time reference in *will be* indicates that the deictic centre must be either before 1996 or relatively early in that year, a selection from these two possible interpretations cannot be made with certainty until we know that the text from which the sentence was taken was published at the end of 1995. Deictic expressions can never be taken at face value. Thus there is no automatic or mechanistic link between choices of tense and temporal anchoring points: the simple present in *do* and *say* in (1)6., and in *means* in (1)7., all refer to a past act, albeit a very recent past, and albeit an act with wider implications of 'meaning'; the same could be said of *trying* in (1)8., though this may be interpreted as an elliptical past continuous as well as a present continuous. Without a certain degree of interpretive flexibility and freedom of choice in utterance production, communication would cease already at this elementary level.

Spatial deixis is marked by *go* and *anywhere* in (1)1., *went*, *down to*, *Como*, *up*, and *back* in (1)2., and *there* in (1)3. The discourse itself does not indicate the deictic centre, the Bellagio Study and Conference Center, which is only accessible through knowledge of the real-world context. But a contextually unambiguous *here* is obviously assumed. The choice of the verb *go* (in contrast to *come*) indicates movement away from a spatial point of reference, typically either located with the speaker(s) (as in this conversation), or with the people the discourse is about. Therefore it is clear that *Como* cannot be the place where the conversation is taking place, which is further underscored by the 'distal' indexical marker *there* in (1)3., which is coreferential with *Como*. The relativity of spatial deictic expressions is abundantly clear in (1)2. The choice of *down to* in *we went down to Como* may be primarily motivated by a geographic orientation which traditionally places locations to the south lower on maps than locations to the north; Como is indeed situated south of Bellagio. Another parameter that may be involved is the location of the Bellagio Study and Conference Center on top of a hill, while Como is situated at the level of Lake Como. Such parameters may combine and interfere with each other in various ways, or their relevance may be cancelled altogether (since, after all, we are dealing here with conventionalized forms of expression which preserve only an elementary link with their spatial origins). It is not predictable, therefore, whether *down to* would still be used if Como would be situated to the north of the deictic centre but lower, or to the south and higher; most probably, however, it would not be used if it were both to the north and higher.

Interestingly, *down to* and *up* refer to exactly the same direction in (1)2. Nothing in the meaning of the sentence would be changed if *up* were to be replaced by *down*. The reason why *up* can appear without contradiction, however, is that there is a shift in **deictic perspective**. Whilst the deictic centre remains the same, *down to* was mainly motivated by more or less 'objective' spatial properties (leaving the 'relational' work to *go*), whereas *up* functions as one standard (though not irreplaceable) pole of a 'relational' contrast set, meaning 'away from the deictic centre' in opposition to *back*. In example (2) the absence of any specific spatial indexicals indicates that the described state of affairs is seen as quite general, the location being 'everywhere'. This interpretation is contextually supported by the title of the publication from which the sentence was taken, *The world in 1996*.

Social deixis anchors language into its immediate interactional context of use. This process includes, at its most elementary level, what is usually called **person deixis**. Face-to-face communication involves a number of social actors whose roles underlie the basic three-fold distinction between first person, the deictic centre along the social dimension, second person or addressee, and third person or 'others'. All three are activated in (1): an omitted *you* in (1)1., *we* in (1)2., *I* in (1)5., *you* twice in (1)6., and *he* in (1)7. Again, the usage of such forms is not without its intricacies. This conversation involves the same four people, with one person talking in each turn and the other three forming the audience. A small shift in deictic perspective, however, can turn the same person, Dan, into a second person *you* in (1)6., and into a third person 'outsider' *he* in (1)7., where Dan is obviously still one of the people being addressed. To understand the use of *we* in (1)2. it is useful to know that Dan and Jane are husband and wife, and that they have taken the trip together (a fact which makes (1)6. more challenging for Dan than if someone else would have asked the same question, and which is not simply inferrable from (1)6.). In general, *we* is an indexical with quite a range of uses. In (1)2. it is an 'exclusive *we*' because it excludes the direct addressee whose question is being answered. In a sentence such as *We should go to Como some day*, uttered as a suggestion, the addressee is included within the scope of *we*, which can therefore be called an 'inclusive *we*'. *We* may also be a 'ceremonial' substitute for *I*, as in much academic writing (just as Julius Caesar, pushing things a bit further, managed to reserve *he* for describing his own feats). And *we* may even come to replace *you* as in a doctor's *How are we feeling today?* In example (2), no person deixis is available at an explicit level at all, which is not uncommon in written communication.

Also included in the domain of social deixis, and often involving pronoun choices, is a phenomenon that may be called **attitudinal deixis** (usually simply called 'social deixis' in contrast to 'person

Plate 1.1 (From: Goscinny and Uderzo 1973: *Asterix: The mansions of the Gods*. London: Hodder Dargaud, p. 5)

deixis'): the use of indexical expressions which signal aspects of social status and/or forms of respect, whether or not grounded in 'objective' status. Typical examples are the choices available in many languages between formal and informal second-person forms of address, such as *tu* versus *vous* in French, *du* versus *Sie* in German, *jij* versus *U* in Dutch, *tú* versus *Usted* in Spanish. Also included under this label are the elaborate systems of 'honorifics', or expressions (not only pronouns but also vocative expressions, titles of address and the like) indicating higher status, available in numerous languages.

Finally, once produced, discourse itself also provides a dimension for anchoring utterances. **Discourse deixis** is involved whenever a form of expression points at earlier, simultaneous, or following discourse. Thus *there* in (1)3. points back at *Como* in (1)2., *that* in (1)5. refers to the *going down to Como* brought up in (1)2., and *you mean . . . you say* in (1)6., *He means* in (1)7., and *trying to be polite* in (1)8. all refer back to the utterance made in (1)4. A somewhat special case is *there* in (1)3. because in addition to being discourse-deictic it is also 'anaphoric' since it shows 'coreference' with *Como* in (1)2.: both expressions refer to the same reality outside of the discourse. Discourse deixis may also be of a 'self-referential' or 'reflexive' kind, as when the expression *in this book* is used in this book, or when I say *This is what she sounded like* while imitating the voice of the person I am talking about. A 'projective' kind of discourse deixis is to be found when I announce my telling of a story by saying *I would like to tell you this story about. . . .* And projection and self-reference are combined in *This book will explain. . . .* (This kind of phenomenon will be dealt with at length later, in sections 3.3.2 and 6.4.1, when the topic of contextual cohesion and indicators of metapragmatic awareness, respectively, are approached.)

1.1.2 Speech acts

When Debby says *Go anywhere today?* (in (1)1.), she **does** something. What she does is called 'asking a question'. Interest in this type of act, structurally corresponding to sentences and called **speech acts**, has been one of the basic ingredients of pragmatics for a long time. The concept was introduced by the philosopher John Austin. In his own search for ways of coping with language as a form of action (in reaction to logical positivism, which did not accept meaning outside the realm of what could be tested for its truth or falsity), he first made a distinction between 'constative' and 'performative' utterances. In this dichotomy, constatives, such as *we went down to Como* in (1)2., are utterances in which something is *said* which can be evaluated along a dimension of truth. Performatives, on the other hand, are utterances, such as *Go anywhere today?* in (1)1. (or, to take examples closer to his own, *I promise to go to Como* or *I baptize this ship the Lago di Como*), in which something is *done* which cannot be said to be true or false but which can be evaluated along a dimension of 'felicity'. Thus *Go anywhere today?* is not felicitous as a question unless Debby is interested in Dan's response; *I promise to go to Como* is not felicitous unless I intend to go to Como and commit myself to doing so; *I baptize this ship the Lago di Como* requires my being authorized to perform the christening of this ship. Soon, however, Austin realized that such neat distinctions are problematic. If Dan's short-term memory is impaired and he does not really remember what he did earlier today, there would be something infelicitous about *we went down to Como*, even if he got it right by accident. Equally troublesome are examples such as (2), where *1996 will be a year of prosperity and peace* has the structure of a simple constative, but where an evaluation as to truth or falsity could not be undertaken until a year later, and where felicity would demand the author to be in a position to know enough about the world to make some kind of authoritative prediction.

Austin's conclusion was simple: all utterances contain both constative and performative elements; they are all sayings and doings at the same time. To capture the implications of this intuition, he replaced the constative–performative terminology by a three-fold distinction: 'locutions' are acts *of* saying something (the uttering of the string of sounds *I promise to go to Como*, containing a proposition, or the constative aspect of the speech act); 'illocutions' are what is done *in* saying something (in saying *I promise to go to Como* I make a promise); and 'perlocutions' are what is done *by* saying something (by saying *I promise to go to Como* I make you count on my going to Como). Leaving terminological details aside, we can see that it is at this point that John Searle takes over with his speech act formula **F(p)**, where 'F' stands for **(illocutionary) force**, the action side of every speech act, and 'p' for **proposition**, the content side of the speech act (consisting of a reference and a predication).

Searle systematized Austin's intuitions about felicity with the proposal that for a proper definition of every type of speech act four kinds of conditions, all necessary and together sufficient, should be specified. Thus for (2), *1996 will be a year of prosperity and peace* to be a felicitous prediction, the following conditions should hold:

- Propositional content condition: specification of a future state of affairs.
- Preparatory condition: the speaker/writer has adequate information to form a 'valid' opinion about the future state of affairs.
- Sincerity condition: the speaker/writer believes that the future state of affairs will indeed be as described.
- Essential condition: the utterance counts as an act committing the speaker/writer to the likelihood of the future state of affairs to be as described.

Or for (1)3., *Anything to see there?*, to be a felicitous question, the following should hold:

- Propositional content condition: none.
- Preparatory condition: Debby has reason to believe that Dan can give information about Como.
- Sincerity condition: Debby wants Dan to give information about Como.
- Essential condition: the utterance counts as an attempt to get Dan to give an answer providing information about Como.

As will already be clear from these two examples, actual usage has a tendency to play fast and loose with such conditions. Example (2) may serve a largely rhetorical effect, making it immune to criticism along the dimensions stipulated by the felicity conditions. As for (1)3., its major function may be to sustain a relatively unfocused conversation (a phenomenon generally known as 'phatic communion'; see Senft 1995), so that the less-than-informative response in (1)4. may be perfectly satisfactory. But that does not make (2) and (1)3. any less of a prediction or a question, respectively. At the same time, however, this does not necessarily invalidate the proposed analysis, since it may represent notions in terms of which communication, in a given community, is habitually conceptualized.

In addition to the analytical apparatus in terms of necessary and sufficient conditions, which may be more 'prototypical' within a specific community than 'necessary and sufficient' (even within the same community; see section 4.3), orthodox speech act theory also suggests that all speech acts, in any language anywhere in the world, fall into five categories:

1. Assertives (e.g. statements, such as *We went down to Como*): expressing a belief, making words fit the world, and committing the speaker to the truth of what is asserted.
2. Directives (e.g. requests, such as *Please, go down to Como with me*, or orders, such as *Go down to Como tomorrow!*): expressing a wish, making the world fit the words, and counting as an attempt to get the hearer to do something.
3. Commissives (e.g. promises, such as *I promise to go to Como*, or offers, such as *We offer you the job of official tourist guide for the city of Como*): expressing an intention, making the world fit the words and counting as a commitment for the speaker to engage in a future course of action.
4. Expressives (e.g. apologies, such as *I'm terribly sorry*, or thanks, such as *We greatly appreciate what you did for us*): expressing a variety of psychological states, having no direction of fit between words and world, and simply counting as expressions of a psychological state.
5. Declarations (e.g. baptizing, abdicating, declaring war): not expressing any psychological state, making both the words fit the world and the world fit the words, and the point of which is to bring about a change in (institutional) reality.

Let me make just two brief remarks about this classification of speech acts, which is without a doubt the most influential one ever proposed. First, the categories are by no means mutually exclusive. Actual language use contains many types of acts which, taking the classification seriously, would have to be called hybrids. Take, for instance, threats of the type *If I ever see you with my sister again, I'll kill you*, which are at the same time directive (intended to change someone's behaviour) and commissive. Second, the classification is entirely based on three dimensions of variation (psychological state, 'direction of fit' and 'illocutionary point'); choosing other dimensions as a starting point (such as relative strength, as between suggesting and insisting; or differences in status relations between speaker and hearer, as in the difference between asking and ordering) would lead to different classifications. More remarks will have to be made later (see section 4.3).

A few more speech act notions have to be introduced for later reference. First there is the distinction, already made by Austin, between **explicit performatives** and **primary performatives**. Explicit performatives (simply, and somewhat confusingly, called 'performatives' in later usage) are speech acts of the type *I promise to go to Como* or *I baptize this ship the Lago di Como*, which contain verbs such as *promise* and *baptize* in the first-person singular present indicative active, describing the kind of act that is being performed (see also section 7.1.2). All other forms of utterance, such as *I'll go to Como* (said with the same 'promise' meaning), are primary performatives (also called, somewhat misleadingly, 'implicit performatives'). Note that explicit performative formulae are instances of what we have described earlier (in 1.1.1) as discourse deixis of the self-referential type. The **performative verbs** involved (a subcategory of a wider range of **speech act verbs**, many of which cannot be used performatively, such as *threaten*) belong to the range of **illocutionary force indicating devices** (or **IFIDs**), which also include the sentence type (see the next paragraph), certain adverbs (e.g. *frankly, seriously, briefly, confidentially*; see also section 6.4.1), aspects of word order, stress and intonation. (It is because of the role which these other IFIDs play as explicit markers of illocutionary force, that it is misleading to label all 'primary performatives', in contrast to 'explicit performatives', as 'implicit performatives'.)

Finally, it is usually assumed that the major sentence types – serving as IFIDs – have a typically associated **literal force**: an assertive force for declarative sentences, a question force for interrogative sentences and a directive force for imperative sentences. When this pattern is broken, as in *Can you call me a taxi?*, which is literally a question about the addressee's ability to call a taxi but which functions as a request to do so, the label **indirect speech act** is used. In a case like this, the 'primary illocutionary point' is that of a request: the utterance counts as an attempt to get the hearer to call a taxi. The illocutionary point that defines the literal force, that of a question (which makes the utterance count as an attempt to get confirmation about the hearer's ability to call a taxi), is secondary at best.

1.1.3 Implicit meaning

If pragmatics looks at language as a form of action anchored in a real-world context, or what is perceived as such, one of the most immediate consequences is that it must pay attention to types of meaning that go beyond what is 'given' by the language form itself, or what is literally 'said'. In other words, a range of meanings emerging from the contextually embedded action character of speech, which could be captured under the general term **implicit meaning**, becomes the inevitable topic of investigation. Three things are involved: the impossibility of complete explicitness, conventional linguistic means to cope with that impossibility, and strategies to exploit it in generating meaning.

The impossibility of complete explicitness

Just imagine what Debby would have to say to clarify in completely explicit linguistic terms what she means when asking *Go anywhere today?* in (1)1. She could try the following:

> Assuming that we are sitting close enough together for you, Dan, having normal hearing capabilities and a workable knowledge of English, to understand me, I am addressing you. I also assume that we share some knowledge about where we are, and why we are here. I mean: I assume that you know that I know that you know, etc. Further, I guess that you, like me, do not want us to sit here silently but that we both want to interact socially and sociably by means of a conversation. Since we also share the knowledge that it is now dinner time, that the main part of the day is over, and that during a day like this there are many things one can do, a basic option being either to remain here or to leave, it seems reasonable for me to start a conversation by asking whether you went somewhere today. So I am asking you: 'Did you go anywhere today?' And I would very much appreciate it if you could say something in response to that question.

No matter how elaborate this attempt is, the new phrasing still leaves more implicit than it is able to make explicit. The world of unexpressed information which an utterance carries along is called **background information**. Sometimes it also goes under the name **common knowledge** or **common ground**, because it must be assumed to be shared – to a certain degree – by utterer and interpreter. And because such assumptions involve recursive and mutual embeddings (I know that you know that I know, etc.), the term **mutual knowledge** is also often used. I will usually employ only 'background information' or 'background assumptions', terms which avoid claims about the actual or even assumed 'sharing' of the information in question. Needless to say, whatever term is used, the implicit meaning it covers is not a fixed entity but is shaped and reshaped in the course of linguistic interaction.

What counts for spoken discourse is equally true for writing. Though written texts form a medium which necessitates certain types of explicit formulation because producer and interpreter usually do not share the same time and space, nor in many cases a joint communicative purpose, they carry along an equal amount of unexpressed information which is assumed to be known. Thus (2), *1996 will be a year of prosperity and peace* may be very explicit about time reference, but even with respect to time it leaves things implicit: for a good interpretation one has to assume that the reader will know what calendar system is used for placement of the year 1996. A large chunk of world knowledge is required, moreover, to even begin interpreting *prosperity* and *peace*. And acceptance of the statement depends crucially on specific ideological frames of reference, as we will demonstrate (see section 8.2.2).

The impossibility of full explicitness, and the need to 'explicate' aspects of general background information to achieve a full understanding of any instance of language use, are so pervasive that a (somewhat confusing) term was invented for the products of fleshing out the meaning of an utterance by means of more explicit representations: **explicature**. For instance, *The Center is closed in January* requires as 'explicatures' a further specification of which 'Center' it is that one is talking about, of whether 'January' is meant to be January of a specific year or of every year, and of whether 'closed' means closed for every living creature or simply for people who would otherwise come in to use the centre for its usual purposes. Confusion can be avoided if we remember clearly that explicatures in this sense are simply representations of implicit forms of meaning.

Conventional means for conveying implicit meaning

Languages provide numerous conventionalized carriers of implicit meaning, tools for linking explicit content to relevant aspects of background information.

A first category of such tools are **presupposition**-carrying expressions and constructions ('presuppositions' being aspects of meaning that must be pre-supposed, understood, taken for granted for an utterance to make sense). 'Referring expressions' such as *Como* in *we went down to Como* (in (1)2.), or *1996* in *1996 will be a year of prosperity and peace* (in (2)), or *Napoleon* and *Waterloo* in *Napoleon was defeated at Waterloo*, all presuppose the existence, at a given place and/or time, of entities in a 'real' world, be it a town, a historically situated and labelled time span, or a person. These are called **existential presuppositions**, which have to be satisfied in order for the sentences in which they occur to be 'meaningful'. Thus *The King of France is talking to Napoleon*, said at this time in history and using the present tense, is devoid of real meaning because the existential presuppositions carried by the referring expressions *The King of France* and *Napoleon* are not satisfied. This example also shows that whether the existential presupposition of a referring expression can be said to be satisfied depends as much on the sentence in which the expression is used as on the expression itself. There is nothing anomalous about *President Clinton is crazy about Napoleon*. This sentence structure requires only Napoleon's 'existence' as a historical figure, not as one of our contemporaries. (Note how the two predicates *is talking to* and *is crazy about* allow for a different anchoring in time.)

Many constructions carry other kinds of presupposition. Let us try some variations on example (2):

(2) a. The year of prosperity and peace has ended.
b. I regret that the year of prosperity and peace has ended.
c. The UN managed to bring about peace.
d. A time of prosperity and peace will return.
e. While the UN was keeping the peace in Bosnia, a war broke out in Zaire.
f. It was the UN that brought about peace in Bosnia.
g. What the UN did was to bring about peace in Bosnia.
h. 1996 will be a year of prosperity and peace, and 1997 will be a **real** disaster.
i. 1996, which was a year of prosperity and peace, will be remembered forever.
j. If 1996 had been a year of prosperity and peace, there would not be so many refugees today.
k. Will 1996 be peaceful or violent?
l. Even 1996 could be called peaceful.
m. If even 1996 could be called peaceful, 1995 was heaven.
n. All of 1996 will be peaceful.

In (2)a. the 'definite description' *The year of prosperity and peace* and the 'change-of-state verb' *end* both presuppose that there has been a stretch of time that can legitimately be described in those terms. ('Definite description' is a term used in logical semantics to talk about any phrase, usually a proper name or a noun phrase with a definite article, that describes a specific, or definite entity rather than a category; all other terms introduced in this paragraph are quite common in the literature and can only be defined by means of examples in the present context.) In (2)b. the 'factive verb' *regret* presupposes the fact that the year of prosperity and peace has indeed ended. In (2)c. the 'implicative verb' *manage* presupposes that the UN tried to bring about peace (and that it was not easy to do so). In (2)d. the 'iterative verb' *return* presupposes that there has been a time of prosperity and peace before. In (2)e. the 'temporal adverb' *while* presupposes that it is true that the UN was keeping the peace in Bosnia. In (2)f. the 'cleft construction' *It was ...* presupposes that someone brought about peace in Bosnia, while the 'pseudo-cleft' *What the UN did ...* in (2)g. presupposes that the UN did something in Bosnia. The contrast introduced in (2)h. by stressing *real*, presupposes that it is a disaster (presumably for arms manufacturers) that 1996 will be a year of prosperity and peace. The non-restrictive relative clause in (2)i. presupposes that 1996 was indeed a year of prosperity and peace. The 'counterfactual' in (2)j. presupposes that 1996 was not a year of prosperity and peace, while the question structure in (2)k. presupposes that 1996 will be either peaceful or violent. The particle *even* in (2)l. and (2)m. presupposes that some other year(s) is/are (a) more likely candidate(s) for being called peaceful. Finally, the 'scalar' notion *all of* in (2)n. presupposes that *parts of* 1996 will be peaceful (as higher values on a scale tend to imply the lower values). Needless to say this list does not exhaust the possibilities.

The main property to note about the foregoing examples is the following: the specified presuppositions hold no matter whether the sentences are true or false. In general, therefore, the main propositions of those sentences can also be negated without affecting the presuppositions. Just try (2)a. with . . . *has not ended*, (2)b. with *I do not regret* . . . , or (2)c. with *The UN did not manage* . . . . Yet presuppositions can be strangely susceptible to small changes in (linguistic or non-linguistic) context. Consider (2)o., (2)p. and (2)q.:

(2) o. I know that 1996 will be a year of prosperity and peace.
p. He does not know that 1996 will be a year of prosperity and peace.
q. I do not know that/whether 1996 will be a year of prosperity and peace.

Although (2)o. and (2)p. are characterized by the same presupposition (that 1996 will be a year of prosperity and peace), that presupposition vanishes from (2)q. This phenomenon is called the **defeasibility** of presuppositions – just another term for context-sensitivity.

One aspect of context-sensitivity or defeasibility that has received a lot of attention is the so-called **projection problem** for presuppositions: in some cases where presupposition-carrying constructions are embedded into a more complex structure, they preserve their presuppositions (i.e. they project them onto the wider structure), whereas in other cases they lose them. Consider (2)r. to (2)w.:

(2) r. When the UN managed to bring about peace, the world changed.
s. Since the UN did not manage to bring about peace, the world will remain a miserable place.
t. If the UN does not manage to bring about peace, the world will remain a miserable place.
u. The UN managed to bring about peace even without trying.
v. The UN announced that it had managed to bring about peace.
w. The UN neglected to announce that it had managed to bring about peace.

The presupposition that the UN tried to bring about peace, observed in relation to the simple sentence (2)c. above, remains untouched in the more complex structures (2)r. and (2)s. In (2)t., however, it may or may not belong to the interpretation, though probably the suggestion is at least that the UN *should* try to bring about peace. In (2)u. the presupposition is plainly cancelled or blocked by its explicit negation in *even without trying*. In (2)v. it is neutralized, either interpretation being possible, as a result of its embedding under *announce*. Finally, in (2)w. it is clearly restored.

Presuppositions are relations between a form of expression and an implicit meaning which can be arrived at by a process of (pragmatic) **inference**. In addition to 'pragmatic' inference, i.e. the process of inferring meaning in a way that cannot be imagined without taking contextual information into account, there are also inference types that are supposed to lead *logically* to relations between forms and implicit meanings. These are usually called **(logical) implications** or **entailments**, or sometimes **conventional implicatures**. (The technical term 'implicature' was introduced by the philosopher of language Paul Grice to cover a variety of non-explicit meanings, such as suggestions, implications and the like; some are 'conventional', i.e. attached conventionally to the linguistic forms; others are 'conversational', as will be explained in the next part of this section.) Logic, however, is also influenced by usage constraints, which is why we have to devote some attention to the phenomenon here. To the extent that systematic distinctions are made, logical implications or entailments are said to be truth-conditional (in the sense that A entails or logically implies B if and only if every situation that makes A true also makes B true) while conventional implicatures are non-truth-conditional inferences that are nevertheless attached by convention to specific forms of expression, such as lexical items. Consider (2)x. to (2)z.:

(2) x. This UN soldier is the local peace-keeper.
  y. The UN managed to bring about peace and forgot to announce it.
  z. The UN managed to bring about peace but forgot to announce it.

In (2)x. ***the*** *local peace-keeper* logically implies or entails that 'this UN soldier' is ***a*** *local peace-keeper*: the former is true if and only if the latter is true. Examples (2)y. and (2)z., however, have the same truth conditions but differ in that *but* in (2)z. conventionally implicates that there is a contrast between the two conjuncts. Though these analyses are acceptable at a decontextualized level, as soon as actual usage is involved the picture may change significantly. Thus there is no way in which *the* in (2)x. can simply be replaced by the indefinite article *a* without really changing the meaning. At a deeper logical level, moreover, the substitutability is also dependent on the scope of *local*: if it means 'in relation to the specific locality where the UN soldier in question is to be found' the substitution does not work (since in that case the soldier in question would normally be the only 'local peace-keeper' and hence not an individual member of a category at all), whereas it does if it means 'in relation to any locality where the UN has soldiers'. As to the difference between *and* and *but* in (2)y. and (2)z., it may disappear as soon as a different intonation is used for (2)y., making the second part into an exclamation thus introducing the expression of surprise and hence contrast. More to the point, *but* is not predetermined to necessarily emphasize (i.e. conventionally implicate) contrast, as should be clear from (2)z'.

(2) z'. There has never been a peace brought about but the UN will forget to announce it.

Here *but* establishes a correlation between the bringing about of peace and the UN forgetting to announce it. Contrast, though typically implicated by the word (also in its non-co-ordinating use – often treated as a different lexical item – meaning 'except' as in *There was nothing there but a pair of socks*), is not a necessary property of the word itself but largely a function of its use.

Strategic avoidance of explicitness

As the final example should make the reader suspect, and as will be demonstrated later in this book (see especially Chapter 5), whatever conventional means are provided for conveying implicit (as well as explicit) meaning, they are always manipulable. In the same way, the impossibility of being fully explicit in language lends itself to strategic exploitation. The best point of comparison for this phenomenon in the non-linguistic world may be gravity. Gravity is a serious restriction on people's manipulation of objects in space, but it can be creatively exploited in the construction of buildings and ultimately it is even a precondition for construction to take place at all. Similarly, a creative exploitation of restrictions on the possibility of explicitness is one of the resources for the generation of meaning by means of language use.

A straightforward case to illustrate this is what has been called 'presuppositional lying'. When asked why you did not show up on time, you may answer *I didn't manage to get away*, even if you did not try. By means of the usual presupposition attached to *manage*, you will give the impression that you tried, thus taking away some of the guilt. But no-one can accuse you of having *said* that you tried to get away, and hence to have lied about it.

No doubt the major contribution to our understanding of this type of process, however, has been Grice's theory of **conversational implicature**. Grice proposed a system of 'conversational logic' based on a number of 'maxims of conversation', i.e. intuitive principles which are supposed to guide conversational interaction in keeping with a general 'co-operative principle' (often referred to in the literature as CP). 'Maxims' differ from 'rules' in that they are seen as generally valid rather than to count only for specified (and specific) cases. The CP says:

> Make your conversational contribution such as is required, at the stage at which it occurs, by the accepted purpose and direction of the talk exchange in which you are engaged. (Grice 1975, p. 45)

The maxims are:

1. *The maxim of quantity*:
   (i) Make your contribution as informative as is required for the current purposes of the exchange.
   (ii) Do not make your contribution more informative than is required.
2. *The maxim of quality*: Try to make your contribution one that is true
   (i) Do not say what you believe to be false.
   (ii) Do not say that for which you lack adequate evidence.
3. *The maxim of relation* (later called *relevance*): Be relevant.
4. *The maxim of manner*: Be perspicuous
   (i) Avoid obscurity of expression.
   (ii) Avoid ambiguity.
   (iii) Be brief.
   (iv) Be orderly.

Assuming that these maxims are generally or 'normally' adhered to in the communicative culture in which they were formulated, they give rise to 'conventional' or 'standard' conversational implicatures (not to be confused with what was called 'conventional implicatures' in the foregoing pages). Thus a regular operation of the maxim of quality on *1996 will be a year of prosperity and peace* in (2) leads to the implicature that the author believes that 1996 will be a year of prosperity and peace and that he has adequate evidence for making this prediction – an observation which should be reminiscent of the felicity conditions on speech acts. Similarly, on the basis of the same maxim of quality, from Debby's question *Anything to see there?* in (1)3. one can infer that Debby does not know (much) about Como, and that she wants to know. Now consider the following possible response, as an alternative to (1)4.

(1)4. a. It's got a nice cathedral, and a lot of silk.

On the basis of the maxim of quantity, one may infer that the cathedral and the silk are the (potentially) most interesting things to mention about Como, and that it does not have treasures that can make it rival Florence or Rome. Note that the same kind of implicature derives from the maxim of relation or relevance, which is why later theorizing (in particular in the tradition initiated by Sperber and Wilson 1986) has tried to reduce much, if not all, of what Grice described to a single principle of relevance. The assumption of adherence to the maxim of manner, moreover, leads one to infer that the information is clear enough, i.e. that there is one particular cathedral which does not require further specification for anyone to find it and that one cannot miss the silk either.

There is, however, more to conversational implicature than these forms of implicit meaning conventionally inferred from forms of expression in combination with assumed standard adherence to conversational maxims. This is where strategic exploitation of implicitness comes in. On many occasions, the maxims will be breached or 'flouted'. But since speakers are expected to be co-operative by using language in accordance with the maxims, any clear breaching or flouting will be interpreted by a co-operative interlocutor as a conscious act signalling special (implicit) meaning. The inferencing based on this leads to conversational implicatures in addition to or different from the 'standard' or 'conventional' ones, i.e. aspects of meaning that go even further beyond what is literally said. Thus when Dan says in (1)4., when commenting on Como in response to Debby's question, *Perhaps not the most interesting of Italian towns, but it's worth the trip*, he is breaching the first submaxim of the maxim of quantity by not giving any real information, as well as the maxim of quality by using a form of expression (*perhaps*) which does not adequately reflect his beliefs and which obviously does not do justice to his own access to evidence (the other participants in the conversation knowing very well that Dan has visited many other Italian towns). But by doing so, he implicitly conveys the meaning, made explicit later in the conversation, that Como is by no means the most interesting of Italian towns. In other words, *it's worth the trip* as long as one does not expect too much.

Before giving further illustrations, let us quickly summarize the types of implicit meaning that we have reviewed so far:

1. *Presupposition*: implicit meaning that must be pre-supposed, understood, taken for granted for an utterance to make sense.

2. *(Logical) implication, entailment, conventional implicature*: implicit meaning that can be logically inferred from a form of expression.
3. *Conventional or standard conversational implicature*: implicit meaning that can be conventionally inferred from forms of expression in combination with assumed standard adherence to conversational maxims.
4. (Non-conventional or occasion-specific) *conversational implicature*: implicit meaning inferred from the obvious flouting of a conversational maxim in combination with assumed adherence to the co-operative principle.

Whereas 1., 2. and 3. bear on conventional means to convey implicit meaning, all of which can also be strategically exploited, 4. fundamentally involves the strategic avoidance of explicitness. Let us give some additional examples of the latter.

Consider a few more possible responses to Debby's question *Anything to see there?* in (1)3.:

(1)4. b. A city.
c. A stone cathedral and a lot of silk produced locally by millions of silk worms.
d. It rivals Florence.
e. There isn't a greater city in the world.
f. Yes.
g. Thousands of people, each with a nose, two eyes, two ears, a mouth, speaking an Italian of sorts, and going about their daily business.
h. If you keep your eyes open.

Since (1)4.b. is certainly not as informative as is required for the current purposes of the exchange, since (1)4.c. contains more details of information than are required, since (1)4.d. can hardly be expected to literally represent what the speaker believes, since the same can be said about (1)4.e., which also cannot be based on full evidence (no-one, presumably, having seen all of the world's cities), since (1)4.f. and (1)4.g. do not seem really relevant answers (just like, for that matter, (1)4.b., (1)4.c. and (1)4.h.), and since (1)4.h. evades the issue and lacks clarity, they all implicate depreciation to various degrees. The processes are slightly different in each case. But there are no doubt two dominant ones: (i) evasion of the relevant issues, which could be further illustrated with (1)4.i.

(1)4. i. On a clear day you get a nice view of the Alps.

and (ii) saying something that is recognizably untrue. In the latter case, as illustrated in (1)4.d. and (1)4.e., the implicated meaning may simply be the opposite of what is said literally. This process is usually called **irony**. Different ways of producing a recognizable untruth, which therefore carry implicatures, are illustrated in (1)4.j. and (1)4.k.:

(1)4. j. Como is a giant silk worm.
k. Como is Italy's Cleveland.

The processes involved here are **metaphorical**. (Note that not all metaphors can be explained in this way. All languages contain numerous conventionalized structures and expressions which may be metaphorical in origin, but which do not require inferencing steps of the kind described here. See 6.2.1 for examples.)

Conversational implicatures are 'cancellable' or 'defeasible', i.e. they can be eliminated or changed by modifying or adding to the utterance, as in (1)4.l.:

(1)4. l. If you keep your eyes open – but then you can find real gems.

They are also 'non-detachable', i.e. they are properties of the meaning of utterances as a whole, and not simply attached to a single form of expression. That is why there is no fundamental difference between (1)4. and (1)4.m. or (1)4.n, in spite of the different forms of expression.

(1)4. m. Como is perhaps not Florence, but it's worth the trip.
n. Como is perhaps not a metropolis, but it's worth the trip.

Moreover, conversational implicatures are 'calculable', so that they can be questioned as in (1)6. and made explicit as in (1)7. Finally, they are 'not fully determinable', so that – in spite of their being calculable – their meaning does not have to be stable across instances of use or does not even have to be the same for different users. This should be especially clear in the metaphorical cases in (1)4.j. and (1)4.k. Como's being *a giant silk worm* may implicate that it has nothing of interest to offer except for silk, or that it has an amazing silk industry, or for interpreters familiar with silk worms it may allude to properties that could not even be imagined by anyone lacking such familiarity. Como's being *Italy's Cleveland*, on the other hand, may implicate that it is a regular but not uninteresting town, or more specifically that it is – like Cleveland, Ohio – heavily industrial, or has a great orchestra.

Grice's theory of conversational implicature is predicated on a model of communication which attaches the highest normative value to demands for rationality and efficiency. As has often been observed in the pragmatic literature, however, social behaviour also incorporates norms which would seem to require breaches of the maxims.

Norms of **politeness**, in particular, often do not allow for fully informative utterances, unmitigated truth or complete clarity (see also 1.2). It is this intuition that was captured by Dan at a pretheoretical level when he made the metapragmatic statement *Just trying to be polite* in (1)8. Similarly, there are types of verbal activity, such as those covered by the label **humour**, which would barely be possible with complete adherence to the maxims (see Illustration 2) – though a stretch of discourse which follows the maxims diligently might itself turn out to be quite humorous for precisely that reason. Politeness and humour both exploit the impossibility of full explicitness strategically, using many of the mechanisms described by Grice, to generate implicated meaning.

Plate 1.2 An attempt at humour in advertising: what about the maxims?

1.1.4 Conversation

Let us turn to a fourth common topic in the literature on pragmatics. There is more to language use, from the perspective of its contribution to attempts at generating meaning, than can be talked about in terms of deixis, speech acts and implicit meaning. In particular, the idea that speech acts would be the basic building blocks in terms of which all of linguistic action could be understood was not accepted for very long by most pragmaticians. They turned, instead, to the study of chunks of **linguistic interaction**, usually **conversations** of various types. A lot of attention has been paid to their structural properties and how they reveal what is actually going on in language use. Let us return to example (1), repeated here for convenience, to illustrate some of the things that happen in conversations.

(1) 1. Debby: Go anywhere today?
2. Dan: Yes, we went down to Como. Up by bus, and back by hydrofoil.
3. Debby: Anything to see there?
4. Dan: Perhaps not the most interesting of Italian towns, but it's worth the trip.
5. Debby: I might do that next Saturday.
6. Jane: What do you mean when you say per**haps** not the most interesting of Italian towns?
7. Jack: He means **cer**tainly not the most interesting . . .
8. Dan: Just trying to be polite . . .

Though there are many institutionalized types of conversations (such as in the classroom, in court, and the like) which impose a structure from the start (such as the teacher addressing students who can themselves take the floor only after having asked or having been asked), and though there are many communities in which similar structural restrictions result from more general social rules (as when age differences dictate who can speak when), it is probably accurate to say about informal exchanges in English of the type presented in (1) that they are **locally managed**. That is, who takes what **turn** in the conversation is decided as the interaction develops. Yet this **turn-taking** is not random. It reveals aspects of social organization, which is why conversation analysis – with its basis in sociology (see Chapter 9) – takes a focal interest in turn-taking phenomena. (See section 7.2.2 for an instance of institutional organization involving the pre-allocation of turns.) There is a system, which is why overlaps, as well as silences between turns, are usually minimal – though we should not forget that the frequency of overlaps and the length of silences may vary greatly as aspects of the communicative habits that predominate within a given community or in a specific type of context. The initiation of a turn, or 'taking the floor', may be either the product of **self-selection** or **other-selection**. In (1)1., for instance, Debby self-selects to introduce a new topic into the conversation. But following the rule 'current speaker selects next', she selects Dan for the next turn. She does so by not just blurting out her question, but by addressing him directly, an activity underscored by posture, gesture and/or gaze. Dan knows when his turn has come because the end of a question is a typical, prosodically marked, **transition relevance place** or **TRP**, the clear end of a **turn constructional unit** or **TCU** which, in this case, coincides with a complete turn. When Debby closes the topic in (1)5. and forfeits her 'right' to make any further speaker selection, this gives Jane the opportunity to self-select in (1)6. Jane uses this opportunity to return to the previous topic. Some of the intricacies of the system are revealed by the fact that Jack, in (1)7., without having been selected and ignoring Jane's selection of Dan as next speaker, can in a way **interrupt** without disrupting the flow of the conversation. This is largely a function of the topical relevance of the volunteered (and imposed) turn (which could also partly **overlap** with (1)6. without causing disturbance of any kind). In the same way Jane, having made the trip to Como with Dan, could have added *It was really fun* after Dan's statement in (1)2., without having been selected by anyone. She could even have taken the floor in (1)2., saying exactly what Dan says, thus cancelling Debby's selection of Dan, even though that might have been felt to be a little rude.

When turns are longer than in example (1), the local management of the turn-taking system also involves the addressee's production of **back channel cues** (ranging from nods to *mhm*'s and *yes*'s). It is their function to signal to the speaker that one is listening and that one does not assume that a TRP has been reached yet. Therefore, they are sometimes also called 'continuers'.

An important aspect of conversational structure is the **sequencing** of turns. This involves conversational **openings** and **closings**, neither of which are illustrated in (1), which simply represents a (coherent) chunk of interaction taken out of a wider conversation. In (1) the sequencing is determined by the occurrence of three **adjacency pairs** (i.e. pairs of turns which are normally expected to follow each other), all of the same type: question–answer. The third question in (1)6. is not followed by an immediately adjacent answer but by Jack's inserted comment in (1)7. This basically cancels the need for a real response and leads to Dan's metapragmatic comment in (1)8., which is a confirmation of Jack's comment rather than a direct response to Jane's question. Yet, the overall structure remains relatively simple. Let us consider, briefly, an alternative piece of conversation which can be imagined to replace (1) entirely.

(3) 1. Debby: Have you been to Como yet?
2. Dan: We went last week.
3. Debby: How do you get there?
4. Dan: We went by bus, and returned by hydrofoil.
5. Debby: Anything to see there?
6. Dan: Depends what you're interested in.
7. Debby: I mean, any historical monuments, and maybe some interesting shopping.
8. Dan: It's got a nice cathedral, and lots of silk.
9. Debby: I'd like to go on Saturday. Do you want to join me?

Though this is just a two-party conversation instead of the four-party exchange in (1), the structure is more complex, even if it looks almost completely like a concatenation of adjacency pairs. Consider, first, turns (3)5. and (3)8., which are the two elements of a regular question–answer pair: they are interrupted by an **insertion sequence** consisting of the request for clarification in (3)6. and the clarification given in (3)7. What the insertion sequence does is to explore the common ground needed for Dan to give a maximally relevant answer to Debby's question. Further, looking at the relationship between the two question–answer pairs in (3)1.–(3)2. and (3)3.–(3).4., the former can be interpreted as a **pre-sequence** to the latter because an assessment of whether Dan has been to Como yet, has direct implications for the likelihood of his being able to give an informative answer to the question in (3)3. In much the same way, (3)1.–(3)2. serves as a pre-sequence to the question asked in (3)5., and the entire exchange from (3)1. to (3)8. is an elaborate pre-sequence preparing the invitation extended in (3)9.: an assessment of whether Como exerts some attraction to Dan is useful to decide whether to invite him to come along for a trip. The overall structure of (3) clearly implies a kind of hierarchical organization, certain acts in the sequence being central while others are subsidiary. It can be represented as in Figure 1.1.

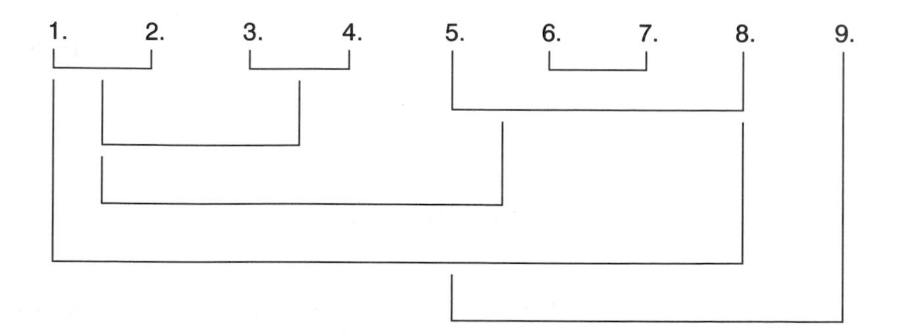

Fig. 1.1 Sequential organization of an exchange

The motivation for pre-sequences, as informally spelled out above, is a phenomenon called **preference organization**. There are preferred and dispreferred responses to different types of utterance (not in the sense of personal preference, but in terms of an observable status, socially agreed upon, that guides both production and interpretation). A request is preferably granted, so that a speaker will have a tendency to first find out, e.g. by means of a preceding question–answer sequence, what the likelihood is of the request being granted. Similarly, a question for information is preferably responded to with an informative statement. Therefore, it makes sense for Debby to enquire first whether Dan has been to Como yet, before asking him how to get there. A negative response on the part of Dan might not have stopped her from asking basically the same question, but probably it would have been phrased differently, as in (4)3.

(4) 1. Debby: Have you been to Como yet?
2. Dan: No, I haven't.
3. Debby: Do you know how to get there?

Note that (4)3. is in fact a potential pre-sequence move itself: if the response is that Dan *knows* how to get to Como, Debby can then ask her real question, *How do you get there?* In practice this almost never happens. In speech act theory, (4)3. would be called an indirect speech act because it does not directly ask for the desired information, but simply whether one of the preconditions for the addressee to be able to give the information is satisfied or not. From such an act the addressee infers, invoking the principles of relevance, that the asker actually wants the information in question. But all of this is so conventionalized that conscious inferencing is no longer needed. Indirect speech acts of this kind, therefore, could be regarded in conversational terms as 'conventionalized pre-sequence–sequence mergers'.

Returning to example (3), once Debby has ascertained that Como has some things that Dan regards as being of interest, one of the factors that could stand in the way of his accepting her invitation to join her for a trip has been eliminated, thus making it easier for her to extend the invitation in (3)9. – a possibility that would have been virtually blocked by an exchange as in (5).

(5) 1. Debby: Is Como an interesting place?
2. Dan: I hate it.

There are of course still other factors that could lead to non-acceptance, such as conflicting plans, which is why pre-invitation sequences often take the shape illustrated in (6).

(6) 1. Debby: Is Como an interesting place?
2. Dan: It's got a nice cathedral, and lots of silk.
3. Debby: Do you have plans on Saturday?
4. Dan: Not really.
5. Debby: I would like to go. Will you join me?

By the same token, the more conventionalized strategies of this kind are so recognizable that they often lead to insertion sequences used by the addressee to protect him- or herself against the expectation of a preferred response, as illustrated in (7).

(7) 1. Debby: Are you doing anything on Saturday?
2. Dan: Why?
3. Debby: I'd like to go to Como.
4. Dan: OK.

Note that the invitation does not even have to be expressed to be understood and accepted.

Conversations rarely consist of model sentences that would be found in grammar books. The examples I have been using (of which only (1) was authentic) are not really typical in that sense. Usually there are significant **pauses** and **hesitations**, as well as **false starts** and **repairs**. Repairs can be either other-repairs (where a speaker corrects what another speaker has said) as in (8)2., or self-repairs as in (9) (where '=' at the end of one line and the beginning of the next indicates that the two are latched onto each other and '. . .' indicates a pause).

(8) 1. Debby: Have you been to Cuomo yet?
2. Dan: You mean Como . . .

(9) Debby: Have you been to Cuomo yet?=
=I mean Como . . .
I always confuse it with that guy in New York.

Except for interesting confusions (such as Como–Cuomo), 'imperfections' are rarely retained in memory. The same is true of most of the 'technical' properties of the organization of conversations. Yet, they usually exert an influence on the way in which meaning is attached to utterances and thus contribute significantly to the dynamics of interaction. That is why conversation analysts will always stress the need for using authentic data. And that is also why recording techniques (audio, and even more so, video) are no doubt an invention that has revolutionized the study of language use as much as the invention of the microscope revolutionized the sciences. Careful transcriptions, which would not be possible without recordings, combined with the possibility of listening to and looking at the oral and visual data over and over again, make it possible to study the actual functioning of language in ways that were not possible before. (For a good introduction to available data-gathering techniques, see Goodwin 1993.)

The principle of authenticity should be taken very seriously in pragmatics. Why then, the careful reader may ask, is that very principle violated in the preceding paragraphs, which do not only contain a (simple) rendition of one authentic exchange, but a number of imagined exchanges as well? The reason is that, in order to fully understand patterns of language use, explanations must be contrastive, to the point where we have to be able to talk about what is possible as well as about what is observed in 'reality'. This claim, however, will not be fully transparent until we have been able to expand on some of the basic principles of a coherent theory of pragmatics in Chapter 2.

Before closing this brief overview of common topics in pragmatics, and beginning to discuss their interconnections with equal brevity, let us just introduce one additional term that will be used regularly in this book, viz. **speech event**. This term has been reserved for any (often oral) type of language use, whether it can be characterized as a conversation or not, viewed from the point of view of its full social (and often institutional) embeddedness (see section 5.2 for a more explicit definition).

1.2 *What the common topics have in common*

The foregoing overview links this book to focal points in a 20–30-year history of studying language use. Once introduced, there are good reasons to stop using these focal points as organizing principles for a book on pragmatics. The main reason is that they represent *different ways of speaking about common phenomena* rather than different phenomena. Thus speech act theory is a somewhat structure-oriented way of handling meaning processes of which a theory of implicatures highlights the processual (inferential) nature. But let us give a few practical examples of the interrelationships, some of which we have already hinted at in passing.

More often than not, speech act rules are specific applications of the more general maxims of conversation. Take, for instance, the second submaxim of the maxim of quantity ('Do not make your contribution more informative than is required') and the maxim of relation ('Be relevant') which are both reflected or 'applied' in the preparatory condition for asserting which says 'It is not obvious to the speaker that the hearer knows the propositional content p of what he/she is saying.' Similarly, the sincerity condition for asserting, 'The speaker believes p,' simply applies the maxim of quality ('Try to make your contribution one that is true').

Further, maxims of conversation are also relied on as steps in the 'illocutionary derivation' which, according to speech act theorists, is needed to arrive at the meaning of indirect speech acts. Thus, to use one of Searle's examples as well as his analysis, if you get an exchange such as (10):

(10) 1. John: Let's go to the movies tonight.
2. Ann: I have to study for an exam.

John must first of all assume that Ann is co-operating in the conversation, so that her remark (10)2. is intended to be relevant. Otherwise he would have to conclude that she is not responding to his proposal since his knowledge of language use, or speech acts, or even more specifically adjacency pairs (which gets us immediately into the domain usually covered by conversation analysis), dictates that valid responses can only be acts of acceptance, rejection, counterproposals, attempts to discuss the proposal and the like. Knowing that (10)2. is not one of the expected response types, but believing that Ann is nevertheless trying to be relevant, John must infer that Ann means more than she says, and presumably that the primary illocutionary point of her utterance is different from the literal one.

If there could still be any doubt about that, indirect speech acts represent a type of implicit meaning and they involve conversational strategies. As to implicit meaning, John's further inferencing makes use of factual background information (in particular the knowledge that both studying for an exam and movie-going take a large amount of time relative to a single evening, so that they are hardly compatible) to arrive at the final conclusion that (10)2. is an implicit rejection of his proposal. (Needless to say the linear ordering of such inferencing steps is not likely to match actual cognitive processes, and some of the steps may not even be necessary; but that discussion would lead us too far at this point.) As to conversational strategies, we already hinted (in section 1.1.4) at the link with preference organization and its consequences. Preference organization not only motivates the use of indirect speech acts of the 'conventionalized pre-sequence–sequence merger' type, but also, as illustrated here, of a type that makes it possible to avoid flatly choosing a dispreferred response type.

Example (10) shows that it is not just the mere *fact of interconnections* between the different traditional topics of pragmatics that should prompt us to stop treating them separately. More fundamentally, we should realize that divergent points of view *have to be combined* to achieve adequate understanding. Thus the classical inferencing model for explaining the indirect speech act in (10)2. only invokes rather essentialist 'knowledge that'. What we also need is reference to more procedural 'knowledge how' of the turn-taking-as-social-interaction type upon which conversation analysis relies.

Indirect speech acts are not the only link between speech act theory and the study of implicit meaning. Thus one of the main early definitions of presuppositions advanced in the literature crucially depends on functions of language which are generally discussed in terms of speech acts:

> Sentences in natural language are used for asking questions, giving commands, making assertions, expressing feelings, etc. [. . .] We may identify the presuppositions of a sentence as those conditions which must be satisfied before the sentence can be used in any of the functions just mentioned. (Fillmore 1971b, p. 380)

To use one of Fillmore's examples, *Please open the door* can be used as a command only if the addressee is in a position to know what door has been meant and only if that door is not open at the time of speaking. Clearly, such presuppositions amount to the satisfaction of some preparatory conditions on requests.

Further interconnections between the different traditional topics of pragmatics include phenomena such as:

- The discourse–deictic character of explicit performatives.
- Discourse deixis and the use of metapragmatic comments in ongoing interaction, such as (1)6., (1)7. and (1)8.
- The use of natural language metapragmatic notions such as 'request', 'invitation', 'greeting', and the like in conversation analysis – for which speech act theory provided an analysis that may still be relevant for explaining certain conversational processes, even if the speech act accounts cannot be taken at face value as descriptions of the necessary and sufficient conditions for universally valid basic building blocks of linguistic interaction, but might have to be reinterpreted as reasonably adequate first approximations of the prototypical core of the meaning of speech act verbs in English, i.e. of lexicalized concepts in terms of which certain aspects of linguistic interaction (a form of social behaviour which cannot be detached from the interpretations associated with it in the minds of those engaged in the behaviour) can be better understood; (see section 6.4.2).

These cursory remarks raise too many questions for an adequate treatment to be possible at this stage. They will be returned to in due course. Before leaving the topic of interconnections between the different common topics of pragmatics, however, two more will be dealt with briefly, since they have developed into entire domains of research in their own right.

The first one has to do with the relationship between what we have called attitudinal deixis and principles underlying conversational interaction, in particular those that often seem to require breaches of the Gricean maxims. The domain in question is the study of **politeness**. Whilst **deference** is reserved for expressions of respect for people of a higher status, 'politeness' has become a cover term in pragmatics for whatever choices are made in language use in relation to the need to preserve people's **face** in general, i.e. their public self-image. A distinction is made between **negative face**, a person's need to have freedom of action, and **positive face**, a person's need to be treated as an equal or insider. Any act that puts face wants at risk is a **face-threatening act** or **FTA**. For instance, an example of an act threatening negative face would be the plain request in (11): it endangers the addressee's freedom of action.

(11) When you're down in Como, buy me a silk tie.

An example of an act threatening positive face would be the plain refusal to respond to a question for information in (12)2.: it denies equal status to the addressee.

(12) 1. Debby: Where did Dan get that new silk tie?
2. Jane: I'm not going to tell you.

Both (11) and (12)2. are real threats to face because they are, as the politeness literature would say, **bald on record**, or completely open and direct, without any attempt to let the addressee preserve some freedom of action or some sense of equality. The assumption is that rules or principles of politeness come in to make acts of this kind less threatening.

Politeness strategies, then, usually involve mitigation and/or indirectness, as in (13), an example of **negative politeness** or an attempt to save the addressee's negative face, or in (14)2., an example of **positive politeness** or an attempt to save the addressee's positive face.

(13) I hate to impose on you, but when you're down in Como, could you buy me a silk tie?

(14) 1. Debby: Where did Dan get that new silk tie?
2. Jane: I know it's stupid, but I promised him not to tell anyone. I did not know **you** would be interested.

In both of these, the utterer still goes **on record**: it is still obvious that (13) is a request and (14)2. a denial of access to information. But the threat to face is reduced to a more tolerable level by use of a different formulation.

Another strategy is to go **off record**, as when (15) would be uttered casually without being addressed to anyone in particular, to achieve the same effect as the one intended in (11) and (13).

(15) I should probably get myself one of those silk ties.

It is up to the addressees to interpret this utterance as a request or not.

It should be clear from these few examples how intricately the issue of politeness is linked up with many of the 'common topics' that have already been reviewed. Before moving on, we should also point out that we cannot allow this treatment of politeness, based on Brown and Levinson (1987), to hide the fact that some acts, instead of being face-threatening, may be actively face-enhancing (see Kerbrat-Orecchioni 1997), and that impoliteness and rudeness may be as functional in communication as 'politeness' (see Kienpointner 1997).

The last inter-topic connection to be dwelled on in this section is the area where principles analogous to the maxims of conversation (especially related to relevance, and often phrased in terms of coherence) meet certain types of strategies in a variety of speech events. The area in question is covered by studies of **argumentation**, in which, for the present purposes, two main trends ought to be distinguished. One trend, which appeals strongly to principles of reasonableness, relevance and coherence in the build-up of arguments to reach specific communicative goals, has a close affinity with the field of 'rhetoric', which can in many ways be seen as a form of 'pragmatics'. A second trend, associated most closely with the French linguist Oswald Ducrot, promotes argumentation to the basic organizational force underlying all linguistic communication. The 'argumentative orientation' of utterances is said to explain a wide range of phenomena, from the use of conjunctions such as *but* in *The weather is beautiful, but I don't have time for a walk*, through the conversationally implicated suggestion that we should go for a walk when I say, under given circumstances, *The weather is beautiful*, all the way to classical rhetorical argumentation patterns. (Another dividing line in the field of argumentation studies, less directly relevant for our present purposes, is that between a prescriptive as opposed to a descriptive approach.)

1.3 *The problem of intentionality*

A first glimpse at what the pragmatics literature has to offer – which is what this chapter really is – would not be complete without a brief discussion of one of its most controversial notions, viz. intentionality and its relation to meaning. Moreover, a position on the controversy is crucial for whatever else a theory of pragmatics can say about language use.

Although meaning used to be seen as a property of words and sentences which could be studied in isolation, pragmatics recognizes a vast domain of meaning which permeates people's life and activities – a recognition which was already common fare in a range of research traditions long before it re-entered linguistics (as will be explained in Chapter 9). Acceptance of a non-structure-bound view of meaning by linguists and philosophers was initiated by Grice's account of 'non-natural meaning'. Grice contrasted 'non-natural meaning' with the 'natural meaning' represented by *mean* in *Those clouds mean rain.* While allowing for the existence of conventional meaning as a property of certain linguistic expressions (even conventional meaning of an implicit kind, as in the case of conventional implicature; see section 1.1.3), Grice focused primarily on those types of non-natural meaning which he saw as dependent on the utterer more than on the structure of words or sentences. In the subsequent research tradition in pragmatics, dominating most of the research on implicit meaning, all of orthodox speech act research, all the way to recent coherent attempts to come to terms with language use (such as Clark 1996), meaning was made fully dependent on **intentions** (even when giving a central status to notions such as 'joint action', as Clark does). This was a direct consequence of Grice's definition of speaker meaning as *the speaker's intention in the making of an utterance to produce an effect in the hearer by means of the hearer's recognition of the intention to produce that effect.* Successful communication, or the successful transfer of meanings, is thus seen as a process by which a state of mutual knowledge of a communicative intention is attained, with the help of (intentionally applied) principles of co-operation.

We should be clear about the conceptual moves involved. By introducing utterer's meaning, meaning was as it were 'removed' from language even if language was still seen as the carrier. This was no doubt one of the major steps in the development of linguistic pragmatics. After all, to apply Morris's definition of pragmatics, linguists and philosophers started to deal with the relationship between signs and their users. But at the same time, to the extent that extra-linguistic reality was allowed to enter the discussion of meaning, the unique locus of meaning was clearly placed in individual cognition – in spite of the regular explicit recognition of society and culture.

One of the clearest expressions of the dependence of meaning on speaker intentions is to be found in the standard version of speech act theory. The original Austinian idea that speaking was a type of action was gradually channelled towards near-complete emphasis on one ingredient of linguistic behaviour: a mental state on the part of one of the actors, interpretation being merely the recovery of this mental state by the other actor(s). That is why systematic attention to 'perlocutions', or the effects of speech acts, is not in evidence. That is also why aspects of social practices, supposedly counterbalancing intention-based theorizing, were merely seen as circumstantial and entered only under the guise of *preparatory* conditions on speech acts.

This is hardly the place to enter into a full technical discussion of the issues involved. It would be unwarranted to downplay the role which intentions *also* play. An important philosophical correlate of intentionality is 'directedness'. Being directed at certain goals is no doubt an aspect of what goes on in language use (see sections 3.2.2 and 6.2.2). But it would be equally unwise to claim that every type of communicated meaning is directly dependent on a definable individual intention on the part of the utterer. Such a claim would be patently false. Just consider the case of a Minister who has to resign after making a stupid remark that was felt to be offensive, even if many people would agree that it was not meant offensively. Or, at a more trivial level, look at the exchange in (16).

(16) 1. Dan: Como is a giant silk worm.
2. Debby: Yukh! What a disgusting idea!

Dan's innocent metaphor may simply be intended to mean that Como produces a large amount of silk. But that does not stop Debby from activating a meaning potential that was not intended at all. And by doing so, (16)1. really *gets* the meaning Debby is reacting to. In other words, (16)1. does not simply *have* a meaning once uttered (which would be the case if meaning were determined by intentions). Different meanings can follow each other in dynamic succession. Given the indeterminacy of meaning in general, which is by no means restricted to metaphor and other carriers of implicit meaning, this is not a trivial observation but one that touches the core of what actually happens in the generation of meaning by means of language use. (Note that this observation contains one of the reasons for opting for 'meaning generation' rather than 'meaning construction' as a cover term to designate the central target of a pragmatic theory; see section 0.4 on page 8). In other words, there is a need for *a pragmatic return to meaning in its full complexity*, allowing for interacting forces of language production and interpretation, and doing full justice to the central role of meaning in human reality, whether cognitive, social or cultural. That is the perspective we take in this book.

This theoretical move, detaching meaning even further from language than Grice already did by fully recognizing the role of crucial phenomena traditionally labelled 'non-linguistic' or captured with terms such as 'context', is not without risk. In particular, it could give rise to endless speculation about meaning. In order for this stance to lead to productive scholarship, therefore, the theoretical move needs to be counterbalanced by a methodological re-attachment of meaning to language in such a way as to make it into as empirical an object of investigation as possible in spite of the intangible nature of many of its constituent forces. That is the basic challenge which this book faces. (The first full illustrations of how this double movement works, are to be found in section 5.4.)

1.4 *Genres of language use*

A few remarks have to be made about language use as the object of pragmatics. Language is not a monolithic entity. Nor is language use a unified phenomenon. There are important distinctions to be drawn between different manifestations of language in use. This idea may have been best captured, at its most general level, by Bakhtin's theory of **speech genres**. According to this theory, every sphere of human activity and hence every sphere of communication (from an intimate tête-à-tête to a battle field) shows essential links with a wide range of utterance types (which may go from simple turns in a conversation to a fat book, some of which are therefore primary or simple while others are secondary or complex), which are relatively stable in terms of thematic content, linguistic style, and compositional structure. These are called speech genres.

Traditionally, pragmatics has mainly focused on four types of units that could be captured by this label: a significant number of speech act types (but robbed largely of their embeddedness in spheres of human activity by focusing on supposed universality), conversations of various kinds (where more attention has been paid to compositional structure than to either linguistic style or thematic content), some non-conversational types of speech events (usually paying due attention to institutional context), and certain kinds of texts (where either content, or linguistic style, or structure has tended to dominate). So far, not a single pragmatic theory has been proposed which combines all of these. Let alone that the range would be expanded to match more closely what Bakhtin may have had in mind. On the contrary, there is a distinct tendency to restrict the topic of investigation. One favoured way of doing so is by claiming a primordial status for, for instance, conversation. Though there is a sense in which conversation is primordial (people were talking before they started writing, and children learn language first through face-to-face interaction), it would be a mistake to let that fact dictate the range of language usage phenomena we include in the scope of pragmatics. It would even be a worse mistake to uphold the myth that, ultimately, all communication can be measured in terms of correspondence with or deviation from parameters operating in conversation. That is why we started this chapter with two very distinct examples, one conversational, the other taken from a published text. Let's have a quick look at the latter again:

(2) 1996 will be a year of prosperity and peace.

Now imagine that, at the end of 1995, you would have said (2) introducing a new topic during a dinner conversation. You would probably not have been taken seriously. Yet, in the context it was taken from, (2) was very serious, and could be published as the first line of an editorial introduction to a self-respecting publication. Ultimately, there is nothing mysterious about this difference. We hope to show that it can be adequately explained. At this stage the point is simply that different genres operate under different restrictions and that, for instance, what happens with certain written genres is not derivative of what happens in an informal conversation.

In the remainder of this book, some terms will be needed to talk about broad categories of types of language use. **Discourse** will be used to designate any spoken or written variety of language use. Unlike in some traditions, **text** will be restricted to written types of discourse. **Conversation** will be used for any form of spoken discourse involving more than one speaker, no matter whether the setting is informal or strictly institutional. Most other terms to be used will refer to concrete instances representing subtypes of any of these, and will be defined as we go along, to the extent that definition is needed.

1.5 *Summary and further reading*

We have reviewed four traditional areas of pragmatic research:

- *Deixis*, the 'anchoring' of language use in a real world by pointing at variables along some of its dimensions, in particular time, space, society and discourse.
- *Speech acts*, the 'things one does with words' at the structural level of the sentence.
- *Implicit meaning*, what can be meant or communicated beyond what is explicitly or literally said, by means of presuppositions, implications, and implicatures.
- *Conversation*, the linguistic interaction between two or more people as co-ordinated and collaborative social action.

It was argued:

- That these traditional areas have more concerns in common than would seem at first sight.
- And that, therefore, keeping them separate by using them as focal points for the organization of a new book on pragmatics would not be a productive decision.

While illustrating interconnections between the four areas mentioned, two additional domains of research were briefly introduced:

1. *Politeness*, the strategies employed by language users to protect their own and their addressees' face.
2. *Argumentation*, the global structuring of discourse to reach specific communicative goals.

In further preparation for a more coherent and systematic approach to pragmatics:

- The *status of meaning* as the product of the interacting forces of language production and interpretation, firmly located in a cognitive, social and cultural world, was clarified.
- Some of the basic terms to talk about instances of language use were (re)introduced: *speech genres*, *discourse*, *text* and *conversation*.

The following readings are recommended. On most of the topics dealt with in this chapter, Levinson (1983) is still the most comprehensive one-volume information source. On deixis: Fillmore (1975a), Irvine (1995), Nunberg (1993) and, from an explicitly interdisciplinary point of view, Watson (1987). On speech acts: Austin (1962), Sbisà (1995a, 1995b), Searle (1969, 1975a, 1975b), Verschueren (1983a, 1983b and the first chapter of 1985a). On implicit meaning of various types: Blakemore (1992), Fillmore (1971a, 1971b), Gazdar (1979), Grice (1975, 1978, 1979, 1981), Horn (1984), Karttunen (1974), Lakoff (1973, 1995a, 1995b), Leech (1983), Östman (1986), Stalnaker (1974), Sperber and Wilson (1986), Wilson and Sperber (1986). On conversation: Atkinson and Heritage (1984), Goodwin (1993), Gumperz (1982), Kerbrat-Orecchioni (1997), Roulet *et al.* (1985), Sacks (1992), Sacks, Schegloff and Jefferson (1974), Searle *et al.* (1992). On politeness: Brown and Levinson (1987), Eelen (1998), Kienpointner (1997). On argumentation: Ducrot (1980, and in English 1996), Eemeren and Grootendorst (1992, 1995) and, from a strongly interactional point of view, Coulter (1990). On the problem of intentionality: DuBois (1987), Duranti (1988), Grice (1957, 1968), Rosaldo (1982), Searle (1983, 1992), Stroud (1992), Verschueren (1995b). On genres of language use or discourse types: Bakhtin (1986), Dittmar (1995),

Gregory and Caroll (1978), Heinemann and Viehweger (1991), Holdcroft (1979).

1.6 *Research topics*

1. In mid-1996, one year before Hong Kong was integrated into the People's Republic of China, a conference was held in Hong Kong to assess linguistic changes that might accompany the political shift. Papers and debates from that conference were published in *Current Issues in Language and Society* (3: 2, 1996; 'One country, two systems, three languages', edited by Sue Wright). What follows is the published transcript of the opening turn in one of the debates:

> **Benjamin T'sou (City University of Hong Kong)**: I think that this idea of cross-border contact implying that there might be increased use of Mandarin is open to question. You mentioned holidays in your paper and you talked about cross-border marriages in your presentation. My impression is that cross-border marriage is usually between partners who speak the same dialect. On the border here it is, of course, Cantonese. I cannot envisage a monolingual mother tongue Cantonese speaker attempting to marry anyone who only spoke Mandarin. The early negotiations of the relationship would be too difficult. So what we are dealing with here is most likely the case where a bilingual Mandarin–Cantonese speaker marries a monolingual Mandarin or Cantonese speaker. I imagine the effect on language shift is not as significant as you suggest – the language capacity was there already. (p. 152)

Plate 1.3 Emergency window exit

Discuss this text in terms of deixis, speech acts, and implicit meaning.

2. Discuss the message in Plate 1.3 in terms of speech acts, and ask yourself what aspects of its meaning speech act theory (in the rudimentary form presented in this chapter) cannot deal with.

3. The message in Plate 1.4 is about as explicit as any utterance can get. What does it leave implicit?

4. Shortly after Israeli commandos had rescued (in the middle of the night between 3 and 4 July 1976) the Jewish passengers of the Air France Flight 139 (from Tel Aviv to Paris), who were kept hostage by

Plate 1.4 Fire instructions

members of the PFLP (Popular Front for the Liberation of Palestine) at the Ugandan airport at Entebbe, the following telephone conversation took place between the Israeli Colonel Baruch Bar-Lev and President Idi Amin Dada of Uganda, who had supposedly collaborated with the hijackers and who, by that time, did not yet know what had happened at the airport:

Bar-Lev: Sir, I want to thank you for your co-operation and I want to thank you very much.
Amin: You know I did not succeed.
Bar-Lev: Thank you very much for your co-operation. What? The co-operation did not succeed? Why?
Amin: Have I done anything at all?
Bar-Lev: I just want to thank you, sir, for the co-operation.
Amin: Have I done anything?
Bar-Lev: I did exactly what you wanted.
Amin: Wh- Wh- What happened?
Bar-Lev: What happened?
Amin: Yes?
Bar-Lev: I don't know.
Amin: Can't you tell me?
Bar-Lev: No. I don't know. I have been requested to thank you for your co-operation.
Amin: Can you tell me about the suggestion you mentioned?
Bar-Lev: I have been requested by a friend with good connections in the government to thank you for your co-operation. I don't know what was meant by it, but I think you do know.
Amin: I don't know because I've only now returned hurriedly from Mauritius.
Bar-Lev: Ah . . .
Amin: . . . In order to solve the problem before the ultimatum expires tomorrow morning.
Bar-Lev: I understand very well, sir . . . Thank you for the co-operation. Perhaps I'll call you again tomorrow morning? Do you want me to call you again tomorrow morning?
Amin: Yes.
Bar-Lev: Very well, thank you sir. Goodbye.
(From: Stevenson, William 1976: *90 minutes at Entebbe*. New York: Bantam Books, pp. 215–16.)

Describe what happens in this conversation.

2

Key notions

The question we are trying to address in this book is a bold and impertinent one. What we want to understand is the functioning of language in its full complexity. Ultimately this amounts to trying to understand what, and how, language contributes to life and survival, at the level of the human race, smaller and larger communities, individuals, and day-to-day situations. But let us formulate some practical-sounding questions that are more amenable to an answer. Try the following. What do people do when using language? Or, what do they do by means of language? Or, what happens to people when using language? Though it is the intention to grasp the complexity, that does not mean we cannot reduce complexity in a step-by-step attempt to formulate answers. As a matter of fact, we will start out with an extremely trivial answer to the question of what people do when using language. From that trivial answer we will deduce some key notions that will help us to get closer to an understanding of what happens in language use. One of these notions, in turn, will provide us with clearly distinguishable angles from which we can look at linguistic behaviour, so that – in combination – they provide a conceptual framework for studying any linguistic phenomenon from a pragmatic perspective (chapters 3 to 6), as well as guidelines for the construction of topic-specific methodologies (chapters 7 and 8).

After having introduced some amply illustrated common topics in pragmatics, this chapter is necessarily theoretical. It forms the very basis for an understanding of why pragmatics is at all interesting, and it lays the groundwork for the remainder (and hence the bulk) of this book. I will do my best, however, to keep it as short as possible.

2.1 *Making choices*

Whatever else can be said about it – and here is the trivial answer to our general question – using language must consist of *the continuous making of linguistic choices*, consciously or unconsciously, for language-internal (i.e. structural) and/or language-external reasons. These choices can be situated at any level of linguistic form: phonetic/ phonological, morphological, syntactic, lexical, semantic. They may range over variety-internal options, or they may involve regionally, socially or functionally distributed types of variation. A theory of language use should, therefore, be able to make sense of this 'making of choices'. A few preliminary remarks are in order, some to clarify what is already in this paragraph, others to prevent further misunderstandings.

First, choices are indeed made *at every possible level of structure*. To begin with, one of roughly 6000 languages has to be chosen, or a mixed form may be opted for, or a new choice can be made with each new word or phrase. Though this observation may also be trivial, the choices in question rarely are. They may have minute effects on interpretation, or grave political consequences. Further, a genre has to be chosen, and sentences have to be constructed for which choices of words and grammatical forms are required. When speaking, intonation patterns are selected and produced, and words are formed from a variable range of phonological and/or phonetic options. This choice-making, of course, does not have a linear ordering comparable to the listing in this paragraph. For instance, an assessment of the appropriate genre may be needed before a language choice can be made, or occasion-specific restrictions on phonetic/phonological choices (e.g. depending on who some of the listeners are) may put limitations on the accessibility of certain genres. And more often than not, choice-making at different levels is simultaneous.

Second, speakers do not only choose forms. They also choose *strategies*. It may be more accurate to rephrase the first point, therefore, by saying – rather than that choices are made *from* every possible level of structure – that choices are made that have every possible level of structure *within their scope*. Choosing a strategy of deference, for instance, may require specific choices to be made on a wide range of structural levels, such as language, style, terms of address, lexicon in general, and so on.

Third, the term 'making choices' may be misleading in the sense that it may invariably suggest a conscious act. The processes we are talking about, however, may show *any degree of consciousness*. Some choices are made very consciously, as when an avowed anti-royalist shouts *Vive la république!* instead of *Vive le roi!* at the oath-taking of the Belgian King (being well aware of some of the risks), or completely automatically as when a native speaker of English adds the sibilant *s* to the verb *bark* in *This dog barks too much* (an act which may become very conscious again for a beginning learner of English). Note that even linguistic features that are normally regarded as merely 'grammatical', such as subject–verb agreement, are included in the scope of the processes referred to as choice-making. This follows directly from the perspective approach sketched in the introduction to this book.

Fourth, choices are made *both in producing and in interpreting* an utterance, and both types of choice-making are of equal importance for the communication flow and the way in which meaning is generated. Remembering the discussion in section 1.3, this observation is probably the main reason for not allowing exclusive emphasis on the utterer's intentionality in the study of language use.

Fifth, a language user has no freedom of choice between choosing and not choosing, except at the level where he or she can decide either to use language or to remain silent (the latter being as meaningful as the former under certain circumstances). Once language is used, the user is *under an obligation to make choices*, no matter whether the range of possibilities can fully satisfy the communicative needs of the moment. That is why scientists, for instance, continuously create new terminologies. But they have the advantage of being able to spend a lot of time pondering the available options, deciding that none of them are satisfactory so that a new option has to be created; and along the way they can explain all of this. Everyday communication would simply stop if regular language users were to be as choosy in their choice-making. We always have to settle for what comes to mind as the closest approximation of what we need – a formulation which illustrates its own point since it carries the risk of drawing too much attention to the conscious levels of linguistic choice-making and the intentionality involved. In other words, there are always serious risks involved in using language.

Sixth, as a rule, *choices are not equivalent*. This has been best illustrated so far with the phenomenon of preference organization as handled in conversation analysis (see section 1.1.4). Technically, an offer can be responded to with either acceptance or refusal. But acceptance is the preferred choice, which is why there is a need to mitigate refusals. Another traditional way of speaking about this kind of phenomenon in linguistics is by distinguishing *marked* from *unmarked* choices. In this terminology, the preferred response to an offer, i.e. acceptance, is unmarked, whereas refusal would be marked, in the same way as in which *How tall is he?* is the unmarked way of asking about a man's size along the vertical dimension, whereas *How short is he?* would be marked, thereby providing a basis for the inference that 'he' is, by mainstream standards, at the short end of the short–tall scale. Note, however, that *unmarkedness* is not to be confused with *neutrality* in a general sense of that word. There was a time when the personal pronoun *he* in the contrast set *he–she* was felt to be unmarked and could thus be used generically to refer to any human being. This does not mean that even then there was anything 'neutral' about the choice. Clearly there was a correlation with patterns of social dominance, which is why, under the influence of ongoing social changes, generic *he* has become unacceptable in many parts of the English-speaking world, thereby acquiring a markedness of its own.

Finally, *choices evoke or carry along their alternatives*. In other words, any choice of a form motivated by its placement along any dimension of meaning not only designates that specific placement but conjures up the entire dimension as well. This is why tense choices in English almost inevitably bring the dimension of time into the representation of an action or event (because of the availablility of grammaticalized reference to past, present and future). In the area of lexical choices, it is easy to demonstrate that communicative effects are often scored as much by *not* choosing an available option as by the actual choice that is being made. Consider an employee who has been receiving obscene messages, knows who is the source, and goes to complain to the manager. If the manager says *His behaviour is no doubt objectionable*, the term *objectionable* is certainly not inaccurate. Still chances are that the employee will – or would like to – react with something like *How about plain unacceptable, if not an outrage!* Such processes are the clearest when choices get explicitly challenged. But they are always at work. At a lower level of conceptual complexity, where relatively simple contrast sets have to be chosen from, the same principle holds. Thus *come* evokes the *come–go* contrast, just as *buy* appeals to the *buy–sell* contrast (and complementarity); neither could even be understood without its fundamental connectedness with the other – which remains intact throughout the choice-making process (though one can of course manipulate it in various ways). This property of linguistic choice-making is one of the reasons why we said, towards the end of section 1.1.4, that in order to understand language use, explanations must be contrastive to the point where we have to be able to talk about what is possible as well as about what is observed.

With these preliminary remarks in mind, we should now take further steps to make sense of the notion of 'making choices', thus alleviating its trivial role in answering the question about what it is that people do when using language.

2.2 *Variability, negotiability and adaptability*

It seems that at least three, hierarchically related key notions are needed to understand the process of 'making choices' as the base-line description of language use. They are variability, negotiability and adaptability. Let us try to define them briefly.

Variability is *the property of language which defines the range of possibilities from which choices can be made*. More than two decades ago, Hymes said that 'in the study of language as a mode of action, variation is a clue and a key' (1974, p. 75). This statement may most readily evoke what is traditionally called 'varieties of language', whether defined geographically, socially or functionally. But given our pragmatic perspective on language use or verbal action, the statement remains true after generalizing the notion of variability to the entire range of variable options (also those that are strictly speaking 'variety'-internal) that must be assumed to be accessible to language users for them to be able to 'make choices'. The sexually harassed employee would not have been upset about the manager's *His behaviour is no doubt objectionable* if she had not had access to a wider range of options for adequately describing 'his behaviour', some of which were more suitable not only to her own emotional response but also to her assessment of what corporate policy should be in relation to the protection of her integrity, and if she had not assumed that the manager had the same access. Any change in this constellation – note that we are *really* talking about variability – could have made the employee adapt her interpretive choices and her subsequent reaction. For instance, knowing that the manager did not have access to the same range of options because of a less developed proficiency in English, she might have been satisfied with the phrasing of the verdict. Similar satisfaction might have resulted from an awareness that corporate policy banned words such as *unacceptable* and *outrage* from the vocabulary of managers, thus putting real limits on available options. The notion of variability must be taken so seriously that the range of possible choices cannot be seen as anything static or stable. It is not fixed once and for all; rather, it is constantly changing. It would be a mistake, moreover, to place this element of 'change' exclusively on a wide diachronic dimension. At any given moment in the course of interaction, a choice may rule out alternatives or create new ones for the current purposes of the exchange – though these effects can always be renegotiated, which brings us to our second key notion.

Negotiability is *the property of language responsible for the fact that choices are not made mechanically or according to strict rules or fixed form–function relationships, but rather on the basis of highly flexible principles and strategies*. Thus there is no rule that tells you when to choose *I'm reasonably satisfied* over *I am not dissatisfied*, representing two distinct logical forms of expression for a comparable state of mind; but there is a (manipulable) principle saying that the form with the double negation, even if it rules out real negation, is further down the negative end of the positive–negative scale than the utterance that avoids negation altogether. There is a long tradition in linguistics to contrast different structures and to relate them to each other on a scale of grammaticality and/or acceptability, marking the clearly ungrammatical or unacceptable cases with an asterisk. Negotiability is so strong, however, that pragmatics does not lend itself to this asterisk approach. Although it makes perfect sense for pragmatics to look at the possible as well as at the actual to learn about the principles of language use, a search for the limits of what is possible, i.e. the impossible (which, if found, would turn the principles and strategies into real rules), is futile. Remember Russell's classical example of an impossible, or meaningless, utterance, *Quadrilaterality drinks procrastination*, which was soon made to refer to post-WWII four-power meetings which failed to produce desirable results at a desirable speed. Even Chomsky's equally classical *Colourless green ideas sleep furiously* could be put to use if need be. Or look at what Meredith Quartermain does in poetry:

Air

horse lips
  breath
hair
on flat-palmed apple

(From *Terms of sale*, Buffalo: Meow Press, 1996)

For all practical intents and purposes, this is a real utterance in English. Even if it is the business of poets to break the rules of language or to expand its potential, that does not make their poetry any less part of the language they are using. Brushing this aside as too exceptional to be relevant would be to put on a blindfold and might prevent us from seeing important aspects of the more mundane functioning of language.

Negotiability also implies *indeterminacy* of various kinds. First of all, there is indeterminacy in the choice-making on the side of the language producer. As pointed out in section 2.1, language users operate under the constraint of having to make choices no matter whether they correspond exactly to their needs or not. Thus the imaginary manager in the sexual harassment case, operating under – equally imaginary – corporate guidelines that ban the use of *unacceptable* or *an outrage* from the language of managers, may feel quite frustrated by having to opt for *objectionable* or a similar term which does not exhaust the meaning he or she may wish to express. Yet something has to be said, even if there is no way of making a good choice. To illustrate a point like this, imagined examples are particularly useful because they enable us to manipulate constraints in such a way that they become very visible. In everyday usage the choices we make are usually taken from such a conventional and habitual set of options that we barely realize that we are constrained by that set at all and that other possibilities could easily be created – which, in turn, would soon begin to impose new restrictions. On the other hand, making choices that do not seem fully appropriate to the current purposes, may ultimately expand the usability and meaning of the chosen forms. This is one of the predicaments of language use comparable to the impossibility of being fully explicit, which can, therefore, also be exploited creatively.

Second, there is also indeterminacy of choice on the side of the interpreter. Remember, in this respect, what was said about the properties of conversational implicature (in section 1.1.3). This observation, however, extends beyond the realm of implicature. Whatever is said can be interpreted in many ways, one of the reasons being (as was pointed out in section 2.1) that choices do not necessarily exclude their alternatives from the world of interpretation.

Third, indeterminacy is also involved because choices, once made, whether on the production or on the interpretation side, can be permanently renegotiated. It is here that we touch a fundamental dynamics of language use which we hope to illustrate in the rest of this book (Chapter 5 being devoted to it completely).

If using language consists of the continuous making of linguistic choices from a wide and unstable range of variable possibilities in a manner which is not rule-governed, but driven by highly flexible principles and strategies, as well as permanently negotiable, it is only natural to ask how it is still possible then for language to be used successfully for purposes of communication. This is where our third key notion, adaptability, comes in – not as an explanation, but as a property which we must assume language to have in order for us to be able to understand that a certain degree of success can be achieved in verbal communication. But before going into this more deeply it should be pointed out that there is no reason to eulogize the powers of language. The properties of language use to which we have drawn attention so far, carry in them a guarantee of communicative difficulties and failure. We should realize that communicative success, except in some purely practical areas (or spheres of human activity, to borrow Bakhtin's term), is always extremely relative and can never be taken for granted.

Adaptability, then, *is the property of language which enables human beings to make negotiable linguistic choices from a variable range of possibilities in such a way as to approach points of satisfaction for communicative needs*. This definition calls for a few caveats immediately. First of all, reference to 'communicative needs' does not mean that the needs served by language use all have to be 'communicative' in the strict sense of the word. Though we take the position that just about all language use is in some sense communicative (even if only one person is involved), we do not want to make this into a point of faith on which everything that follows should depend; we do allow for ways of using language that at least come close to being purely expressive without any communicative intent or effect. Second, the phrase 'communicative needs' may sound as if it is meant to refer to needs that are somehow 'general'. We should stress, therefore, that the 'needs' in question mostly arise in context and can therefore be quite specific. Third, note that 'satisfaction' in the above definition is only 'approached' – which may happen to varying degrees. That term, moreover, should not be interpreted as precluding the possibility – already clearly offered earlier – of serious communication failure nor the incidence of circumstances under which there is a need for non-communication or even miscommunication.

Finally, adaptability *should not be interpreted unidirectionally.* The term itself may be conducive to a simplified vision of language choices being made in accordance with pre-existent circumstances. That, too, is involved. But it is not where the story ends. The other side of the coin is that circumstances also get changed by, or adapted to, the choices that are made. Consider, for instance, systems of politeness which are shaped by and simultaneously shape social relationships. The choice of a system of solidarity politeness (*tu*, first name, etc.) as opposed to a system of deference politeness (*vous*, family name, title, etc.) is typically based on closeness between the interlocutors. But when this closeness is absent, speakers may nevertheless opt for solidarity politeness. By doing so, an appearance of closeness is created to such an extent that it may be impossible to retreat from it without overt hostility. After having spoken to someone on a first-name basis before, a switch to more formal forms of address can only be made for special reasons and will therefore carry extra (implicit) meaning. Typically, either playfulness or antagonism would be involved. In the latter case, the choices might be regarded as very impolite indeed, in spite of the objectively higher degree of politeness that would usually be associated with the linguistic choices involved. This example is at the same time an extra illustration of the negotiability of linguistic choice-making, or the lack of fixed form–function relationships.

The three notions we have introduced in this section are fundamentally inseparable. They do not represent topics of investigation, but merely interrelated properties of the overall object of investigation for linguistic pragmatics, the functionality or meaningful functioning of language. Their hierarchical ranking is but a conceptual tool to come to grips with the complexity of pragmatic phenomena, which will allow us to use the higher-order notion of 'adaptability' as the point of reference in further theory formation and empirical research, keeping in mind that it has no content without both variability and negotiability. Using adaptability as the starting point, we will be able to assign four clear tasks to pragmatic descriptions and explanations (to be discussed at length in chapters 3 to 6). But before introducing those tasks or 'angles of investigation' (see section 2.4 below), we would like to make a few more remarks about the notion of adaptability, explaining its relationship to the seemingly incompatible notion of universality. (In section 9.3 we will return to the notion of adaptability once more, pointing at some of the ways in which it has already figured in language-related sciences, and linking it to parallel concepts in biology and psychology.)

2.3 *Adaptability and universality*

An approach to pragmatics which places adaptability, in the sense described, at the core of what is interesting about language use, is basically incompatible with a kind of universality that would rely on the idea of an innate linguistic competence which is a genetically based, autonomous, component of mental structure, and which would comprise a complete universal grammar so that language acquisition, for instance, would not have to be guided by more general learning strategies. A strong genetic basis can be accepted, but certainly not autonomy, neither in the process of acquisition, nor at the level of adult functioning. Yet the notion of *pragmatic universals* or *universals of linguistic (inter)action* is not self-contradictory. People have the ability to learn new languages and to start functioning more or less effectively in communicative styles different from their habitual one, even if that is an experience fraught with frustration and frequent failure. Hence there must be a universal core of some kind. However, there are at least two different views of universality that we need to distinguish.

First, *an assumption of maximal universality* can be made. According to this view, the researcher's own experience can be treated as maximally representative of the corresponding universal experience. An example from the social and political sciences is, for instance, the tendency to posit a strong belief in 'minimal rationality', where the measure of that rationality is the researcher him/herself. Such an attitude not only characterizes certain syntactic theories which used to ignore the relevance of looking at a wide range of languages to discover the principles of the universal grammar to be described, but also certain trends in pragmatics, such as Searlean speech act theory, the avowed aim of which was to provide universally valid accounts of universal categories of speech acts in spite of an introspective philosophical approach. The dangers of such an approach should be obvious. Though the learning of other languages and communicative styles can only be explained with reference to the existence of a universal core of grammatical and pragmatic competence, the point of learning is always to get mastery of the differences. And at a more fundamental level, even the specific notion of variability which we have proposed above would have to be rejected on an assumption of maximal universality, let alone what we have said about negotiability and adaptability, as well as many of the properties of linguistic choice-making to which we have drawn attention.

Therefore, *an assumption of minimal universality* is a much safer starting point to look at languages and their use. When talking about 'universals of adaptability', or 'pragmatic universals', or 'universals of linguistic (inter)action', this assumption is necessary. That is why very few claims of universality will be found in this book. At most, we will point at supposedly universal tendencies, always trying to remind ourselves of the need for hedging in this area. That is also why, even if this book has theoretical ambitions of some kind, it has been written with a basic distrust of *theories* of pragmatics. There is, of course, a fundamental paradox in empirical research: empirical work is needed to substantiate and validate any theoretical claims; yet theoretically based frameworks are needed as descriptive and heuristic tools even for the most empirical of undertakings. Therefore, we may simply have to describe the ambitions of this book as an attempt to *define* a field of pragmatics. To the extent that theorizing is needed to reach that goal, a 'theoretical framework' will be constructed. But we should not allow ourselves to indulge in strong 'theory building' with universalist aspirations.

While duly exercising caution, an interesting link between universals and pragmatics should be pointed out. To that end, let us briefly review Comrie's (1981, pp. 22–27) overview of types of explanation for universals. In his view, *monogenesis* – the assumption of common ancestry for all known languages – is ruled out because it is not testable and because it cannot explain universals which can only be observed to hold as tendencies across a wide range of languages (without necessarily characterizing all individual languages). *Innateness* is rejected as a somewhat empty explanation because it is not subject to independent verification. Still, '[. . .] it may well be the case that at least some language universals are to be explained ultimately in terms of human genetic predispositions' (p. 24). Other *psychological* explanations show a higher degree of plausibility. It is 'possible that certain language universals can be correlated with other aspects of human cognitive psychology that are amenable to independent testing' (p. 24). The validity of *functional* explanations, which identify certain universal traits of language as strategies to reduce dysfunctional elements or 'to make language more functional, either as a communication system in general, or more particularly relative to the communicative needs of humans' (p. 25) is straightforwardly accepted. An element is said to be dysfunctional when it makes recovery of the meaning from the structure more difficult. From this definition, as well as from the examples adduced by Comrie (e.g. genitives are harder to relativize than subjects; constituents of embedded sentences are harder to relativize than those of main clauses; retention of a pronoun in the position relativized is found only for positions that are harder to relativize) it should be clear that functional explanations are in fact a type of psychological explanation: the crucial problem referred to is cognitive information processing. Comrie links them up with *pragmatic* explanations:

> This kind of functional explanation could, of course, be carried over to any kind of communicative system, and is not necessarily restricted to one used by humans. When one looks at pragmatic explanations, however, there are certain instances where there seems to be a clearer correlation between properties of language structure and properties of language use in human communities. (p. 26)

As an example, the presence of a deictic system for referring to speaker and hearer is mentioned. Since other types of languages could be constructed but don't occur, it is 'hardly accidental that the presence of a deictic system of person reference correlates so highly with the basic use of human language in face-to-face interaction' (p. 26).

From this brief sketch it appears that, to the extent that explanations are possible, universals can be regarded – in our terminology – as aspects of language interadaptable with genetic predispositions, cognitive processes, and communicative needs. One should never rule out the possibility of purely formal universals that have come about more or less accidentally. We should be careful, furthermore, not to attribute inherent dysfunctionality too fast to specific properties of language (since negotiability is such a fundamental trait of actual linguistic functioning). But whenever a universal can be explained, chances are that the explanation will be in terms of adaptability, and in that sense functional or pragmatic in the broad meaning of the terms used in this book. Hence, it may very well be the case that all explainable universals are ultimately pragmatic universals.

2.4 *Four angles of investigation*

As announced (in section 2.2), the notion of adaptability will enable us to assign four clear tasks to pragmatic descriptions and explanations. Each will be dealt with at length in chapters 3 to 6. These four 'tasks' or 'angles of investigation', which do not constitute separable topics of investigation but which should be seen as focal points in one coherent pragmatic approach to language use, are the following.

First, **contextual correlates of adaptability** have to be identified. These potentially include all the ingredients of the communicative context with which linguistic choices have to be interadaptable. The range goes from aspects of the physical surroundings (e.g. distance as an influence on loudness of voice) to social relationships between speakers and hearers and aspects of the interlocutors' state of mind. Including states of mind under the label of context is a deviation from common practice in linguistics. Doing so, however, eliminates the misleading implications of treating context as simply 'out there'. It goes without saying that contextual correlates should not be seen as static extralinguistic realities. First of all, language users select from a wide range of available 'realities', turning them into relevant correlates (see section 3.1). Moreover, once selected, such correlates are themselves subject to variation and negotiation in interaction with aspects of the unfolding speech event in relation to which they can be seen to function.

Second, the processes in question have to be situated with reference to the different **structural objects of adaptability**. Since the making of communicative choices takes place at all possible levels of linguistic structure that involve variability of any kind, pragmatic phenomena can be related to any layer or level of structure, from sound feature and phoneme to discourse and beyond, or to any type of interlevel relationship. Not only 'structures' are involved, but also principles of 'structuring'.

Third, any pragmatic description or explanation must account for the **dynamics of adaptability** as manifested in the phenomenon under investigation, in other words the development of adaptation processes over time. By its very nature, this task cannot be performed without lending full force to the negotiability of choices. It involves an account of the actual functioning of adaptation processes. That is, questions have to be answered about the ways in which communication principles and strategies are used in the making and negotiating of choices of production and interpretation.

Fourth, we have to take into consideration differences in the **salience of the adaptation processes**. Not all choices, whether in production or interpretation, are made equally consciously or purposefully. As said before, some are virtually automatic, others are highly motivated. They involve different ways of processing in the medium of adaptability, the human 'mind in society' (a clumsy term, borrowed from Vygotsky, to avoid the suggestion that either the individual or society would be primary, or to emphasize what could be called the non-dichotomous dual nature of the medium of adaptation). With reference to this issue, the distinction between explicitly communicated meaning and implicit information takes on special relevance. Salience is basically a function of the operation of the reflexive (or, as we call it, 'metapragmatic') awareness involved in language use. Note that we are dealing here with characteristics and mechanisms of processing, not to be confused with the actual 'content' of certain mental states (which we included among the contextual correlates of adaptability).

Together, these four tasks can be seen as *necessary ingredients of an adequate pragmatic perspective on any given linguistic phenomenon.* But these four tasks for pragmatic investigations are not to be situated all on a par with each other. Their contributions are not only complementary, they have different functional loads to carry within the overall framework of the pragmatic perspective. They relate to each other as depicted in Figure 2.1 and as described below.

First, a combination of *contextual correlates* and *structural objects* of adaptability can be used to define the **locus** of adaptation phenomena, i.e. they describe the combination of linguistic and extra-linguistic co-ordinates in the communicative space of a speech event. Note that their interrelationship is of primary importance. Thus, our topic of inquiry may concern children's socialization processes in relation to choices at the code level, or hearer involvement in relation to information structuring in the sentence, etc. Contextual correlates and structural objects are relatively straightforward notions which can often be conveniently used as a starting point for specific descriptive tasks in pragmatics and as parameters which have to be referred to continuously throughout an investigation. Note, however, that they are not stable entities; for instance, once a structural choice has been made in using language, this choice enters into context; also remember the warning about interpreting adaptability as unidirectional. Moreover, the precise way in which they combine can usually not be

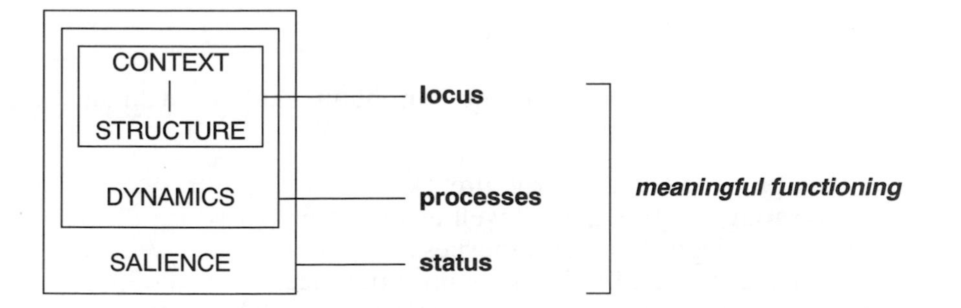

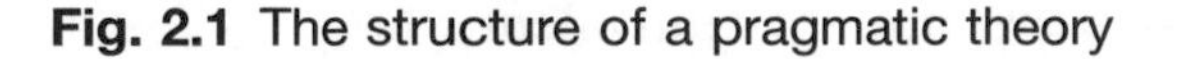
Fig. 2.1 The structure of a pragmatic theory

stated until the investigation is completed; such statements then tend to take the form of explanations.

Accounting for the *dynamics* of adaptability, taking into account the full impact of variability and negotiability, is no doubt the central task of most specific pragmatic investigations, since it is essentially concerned with a definition of the **processes** of adaptation. Dynamics concerns the nature and development over time of the relationship between context and structure. It is a characteristic of the processes involved in their interaction. Or, put differently, processes are the dynamics of context–structure interrelationships. Hence the placement of dynamics in a box surrounding context and structure in Figure 2.1.

Finally, the dynamic interadaptability of context and structure can be more or less salient in the language users' minds. Hence an investigation of the *salience* of adaptation processes sheds light on their **status** in the realm of the consciousness of human beings involved, i.e. in relation to the type of reflexive awareness (which may be actualized to various degrees in different instances of use) which can be supposed to have been the original prerequisite for or immediate corollary of the development of human language in the first place. It is the importance of this aspect that has made the study of language ideologies a prime topic in pragmatics, and that has prompted the development of a metapragmatics concerned with linguistic traces of a speaker's awareness of the processes he or she is involved in.

The superordinate concern which guides the study of pragmatic phenomena as dynamic processes operating on context–structure relationships at various levels of salience, is simply to understand the **meaningful functioning** of language, i.e. as explained before, to trace the dynamic generation of meaning in language use. What we are concerned with, in other words, are indeed what Bruner (1990) calls 'acts of meaning', cognitively mediated, and performed in a social and cultural environment.

2.5 *Summary and further reading*

Language use can be defined as the continuous making of linguistic choices:

- At every possible level of structure.
- Concentrating on strategies as well as on forms.
- With various degrees of consciousness.
- Both in producing and in interpreting utterances.
- Even when the range of available options is not fully suitable.
- From options that are not equivalent.

- In such a way that choices evoke their non-selected alternatives.

Three key notions are needed to make sense of this 'making of choices':

- *Variability*, the property of language which defines the range of possibilities from which choices can be made.
- *Negotiability*, the property of language responsible for the fact that choices are not made mechanically or according to strict form–function relationships, but rather on the basis of highly flexible principles and strategies.
- *Adaptability*, the property of language which enables human beings to make negotiable linguistic choices from a variable range of options in such a way as to approach points of satisfaction for communicative needs.

Adaptability (which does not conflict with acceptance of some universality in language) can then be used as a starting point to define four angles of investigation, to be combined whenever a linguistic phenomenon is approached pragmatically:

- *Contextual correlates of adaptability*, including any ingredient of the communicative context with which linguistic choices are inter-adaptable.
- *Structural objects of adaptability*, including structures at any layer or level of organization as well as principles of structuring.
- *The dynamics of adaptability*, the unfolding of adaptive processes in interaction.
- *The salience of adaptation processes*, the status of those processes in relation to the cognitive apparatus.

The general concern for the study of linguistic pragmatics is to understand *the **meaningful functioning** of language as a **dynamic process** operating on **context–structure** relationships at various levels of **salience***.

For further reading, it is useful to consult the references provided in section 9.3, where precursors and parallels to the idea of pragmatics as a theory of linguistic adaptability are reviewed. However, for a particularly powerful account of the role of variability and negotiability – though the used terminology is different – see Hanks (1995, 1996b); Hanks shows that for successful communicative practice it is not even necessary for people to literally share the same grammar; he also shows (underscoring the idea of interadaptability without using that term) how language emerges from communicative practice as much as it feeds into it.

2.6 *Research topics*

Each of the following definitions of or claims about pragmatics may be usefully contrasted or compared with what I have said so far:

1. 'Here we come to the heart of the definitional problem: the term *pragmatics* covers both context-dependent aspects of language structure and principles of language usage and understanding that have nothing or little to do with linguistic structure. It is difficult to forge a definition that will happily cover both aspects. But this should not be taken to imply that pragmatics is a hodge-podge, concerned with quite disparate and unrelated aspects of language; rather, pragmaticists are specifically interested in the inter-relation of language structure and principles of language usage.' (Levinson 1983: 9)

2. 'I have mentioned that my principal subject in this book is GENERAL PRAGMATICS. By this term I mean to distinguish the study of the general conditions of the communicative use of language, and to exclude more specific 'local' conditions on language use. The latter may be said to belong to a less abstract field of SOCIO-PRAGMATICS, for it is clear that the Cooperative Principle and the Politeness Principle operate variably in different cultures or language communities, in different social situations, among different social classes, etc. [. . .] In other words, socio-pragmatics is the sociological interface of pragmatics. Much of the work which has taken place in conversational analysis has been limited in this sense, and has been closely bound to local conversational data. The term PRAGMALINGUISTICS, on the other hand, can be applied to the study of the more linguistic end of pragmatics – where we consider the particular resources which a given language provides for conveying particular illocutions.' (Leech 1983: 10–11)

3. 'Perhaps we now have a way to distinguish between a theory of satisfaction and a theory of pragmatics. We can say that the former must give an account of the satisfaction conditions of sentences, including the satisfaction conditions that certain sentences have relative to a particular context of use. This requirement means that within a specification of context-relative truth conditions, a theory of satisfaction must mention the speaker's intentions where those intentions play a role in determining the referent of terms that have no semantic referent given by the conventions of the language. Pragmatics will have as its domain speakers' communicative intentions, the uses of language that require such intentions, and the strategies that hearers employ to determine what these intentions and acts are, so that they can understand what the speaker intends to communicate.' (From the introduction to Davis (ed.) 1991: 11)

4. 'Our task is to show how the principle of relevance explains the interaction between these two types of knowledge in the interpretation of utterances.
   The assumption underlying this task and, indeed, the whole discussion so far is that there is a distinction between a hearer's knowledge of her language and her knowledge of the world. In this section I shall argue that it is this distinction that underlies the distinction between *semantics* and *pragmatics*.' (Blakemore 1992: 39)

Part II

Aspects of the meaningful functioning of language

Introduction

The four chapters in this second part of the book literally cover 'aspects' of the meaningful functioning of language. These aspects cannot be seen as separable objects of investigation. Rather, they are different angles from which to approach any linguistic phenomenon in order to fully investigate its pragmatics (see section 2.4). Chapter 3 takes the angle of the contextual correlates in relation to which processes of linguistic adaptation unfold. Chapter 4 deals with elements of structure and structuring which are the true objects of adaptability. Chapter 5 glances at the dynamics of the processes themselves, whereas Chapter 6 gives an account of their status in relation to the cognitive tools and mechanisms available for people to use language adaptively for communicative purposes. Briefly, Chapters 3 to 6 provide the 'nuts and bolts' of pragmatics, the concepts we need to *do pragmatics*. In Chapters 7 and 8 of Part III, then, it will be shown how they can be used in combination to approach specific research topics pragmatically.

3

Context

If adaptability is to be a useful concept to account for what people do when using language, we should be able to ask what it is that language or linguistic choices are interadaptable with. In other words, what are the **correlates of adaptability** that motivate and/or are affected by the choices that are made? After sketching the general picture of what is involved (in section 3.1), ingredients of the communicative context will be reviewed (section 3.2). Aspects of the linguistic context will also be discussed briefly (in section 3.3), though they will return in full force in chapters 4 (dealing with linguistic structure) and 5 (dealing with the dynamic development of choice-making, which cannot ignore previous choices and hence linguistic context). Finally (in section 3.4), it will be argued that, in spite of the apparent limitlessness of the range of potentially relevant contextual objects of adaptability, 'context' is not a vague notion since contexts are themselves generated or even actively constructed (as choices made from the infinite range of possibilities, for specific instances of language use) and this generation process – called 'contextualization' – can be linguistically traced.

3.1 *The general picture*

In 1923, Malinowski coined the term 'context of situation':

> Exactly as in the reality of spoken or written languages, a word without *linguistic context* is a mere figment and stands for nothing by itself, so in the reality of a spoken living tongue, the utterance has no meaning except in the *context of situation*. (Malinowski 1923, p. 307)

While we should not accept the implicit message that written language may not have a 'context of situation', Malinowski's observation can be seen as one of the necessary pillars of any theory of pragmatics. Indeed, language use is always situated against a complex background with which it is related in a variety of ways. Let us try to give, to start

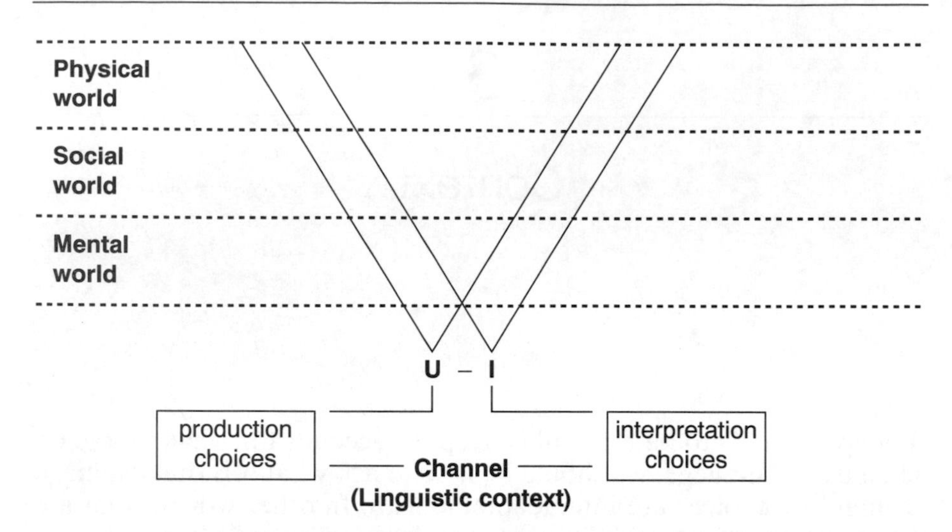

Fig. 3.1 Contextual correlates of adaptability

with, a sketchy summary of what is involved in the form of a visual representation (in Figure 3.1).

The focal points in this representation are the utterer (U) and the interpreter (I). Without them, and the functioning of their minds, there is no language use. For the purposes of a theory of pragmatics, they are functional entities or social 'roles' rather than real-world people, though they usually are that too. Their being functional entities should be clear from three facts. First of all, as happens in most forms of face-to-face interaction, the roles indicated by U and I switch constantly between different real-world people. Second, it is not impossible for an utterer to take on the role of interpreter for his or her own utterance at any stage subsequent to the moment of uttering or, in principle, while monitoring his or her own linguistic behaviour. Third, not only can utterer and interpreter coincide at certain moments, there are also stages in certain types of speech events (e.g. the writing of a novel, solitary practice for an oral performance, or the production of a report that is expected to be filed and forgotten) when there is no interpreter outside the one mentally constructed by the utterer; in those cases, and at that stage, the interpreter role is simply incorporated into the world of the utterer, even if at a later stage a flesh-and-blood language user may take on that role (e.g. the readers of the novel, an actual audience for the performance, or the unexpectedly diligent bureaucrat). Thus the worlds of U and I are not strictly separate; in fact, I can be telescoped into U, but not the other way around, since there always is or has been an utterer.

Utterer and interpreter are presented as focal points because the contextual aspects of the physical, social, and mental worlds (which are not strictly to be separated either – hence the broken lines) do not usually start to play a role in language use until they have somehow been activated by the language users' cognitive processes. (Note again the distinction we maintain – for purposes of presentation – between ingredients of a mental world as contextual correlates and mental or cognitive mechanisms responsible for actual linguistic processing; see section 2.4 and Chapter 6.) Minor exceptions will be pointed out later. The lines in Figure 3.1, converging in U and I, can thus be seen as forming *lines of vision*. Every aspect of context within the lines of vision can function as a correlate of adaptability. The metaphor is useful, because, graphically, it represents the basic fact that U and I (unless they coincide) inhabit different worlds. Of course, there is overlap between those worlds, but even elements of common background from the overlapping areas may look different because the perspective always differs, at least slightly. Common ground, in other words, is almost never really common. The metaphor is also useful because it explains why, in spite of a reasonable degree of stability, the worlds of U and I are changeable at any given moment; a shift in gaze is sufficient.

Figure 3.1 also indicates that the utterer makes production choices, whilst the interpreter makes interpretation choices. The content of these activities will be dealt with in the following chapters. Meanwhile it is necessary to point out that the chosen channel of communication is itself a contextual element. This will be discussed in section 3.3, with other aspects of what can be called the linguistic context. Just as other elements of linguistic context, it is already the product of linguistic choices itself. Before entering that topic, however, we will systematically spell out some of the details pertaining to the non-linguistic ingredients of the communicative event.

3.2 *Ingredients of the communicative context*

In this overview, we start at the bottom of Figure 3.1, with utterer and interpreter. We will then take their point of view to look out into the world of potential correlates of adaptability, starting with aspects of the mental world, going on to the social, and ending up in the physical realm.

3.2.1 Language users: utterer and interpreter

In section 1.1.1, **person deixis** was described as one of the ways in which language is anchored into a context of use. It is a universal feature of language that it provides the means to distinguish between a speaking subject (first person, the deictic centre in face-to-face communication), an addressee (second person), and 'others' (third person). The specific linguistic means that are provided by natural languages to realize this vary greatly. In some languages (e.g. Afrikaans) personal pronouns are the exclusive tools to make the distinctions; other languages combine a pronoun system with a verbal conjugation system, sometimes to be used obligatorily in combination (e.g. English, German), sometimes allowing for variable use (e.g. Spanish or Hungarian, which can drop the pronouns in many contexts). Even within these categories there is considerable variability. Thus Hungarian has one peculiar verbal suffix *-lek* which expresses at the same time first person as subject and second person as object: *szeret-lek* means 'I love you'. There is also variability in the way in which person markers combine pure person deixis with properties such as number (singular–plural, as in English, or singular–dual–plural, as in Classical Greek), gender distinctions (masculine–feminine–neuter, as in English, or masculine–feminine, as in Spanish and French, or completely without gender distinctions in the third-person pronoun system, as in Hungarian), or animacy (sometimes according a high degree of animacy to first and second person in opposition to a less 'animate' third person). But there is much more to be said about the interadaptability between language and aspects of the language users. Let us briefly investigate the roles of utterer and interpreter.

The utterer's many voices

Utterers or speakers should not be treated as if they were the unmistakable source of the meaningful utterances they produce. Language use is not that simple. Imagine a university student in Manchester, Beatrice, who has applied for a three-month stay at the Universidad Autónoma de Madrid in the context of a European student mobility programme. One day she passes by the department secretariat, and the following exchange takes place between her and the department secretary, John.

(1) 1. Beatrice: Can I go?
    2. John: You sure can!

Though the secretary is unmistakably the physical **utterer** of (1)2., it will be equally clear to both the student and the secretary that the latter is not the one who determines the content. In other words, he is not the **source** of the information that is provided. Now consider that on the previous day, two other exchanges took place. The first one is again between Beatrice and the secretary, John.

(2) 1. Beatrice: Do you know yet whether I can go?
 2. John: I'll check with Ann. Can you come back tomorrow?

Subsequently, John talks to Ann, the chairperson of the department.

(3) 1. John: Can Beatrice go?
 2. Ann: She sure can!

Note that John, though no doubt interested in the answer himself, is not the ultimate source of his question in (3)1. Rather, Beatrice is. Note also that Ann, in stating (3)2., is not only a source of the information provided by John in (1)2., but even of the form of expression – a common phenomenon when a message is relayed in this kind of way. It should also be clear from this example, that Ann is not the *ultimate* source of the information. What she says is probably based on a message just received from the section of the university administration in charge of these European (and other international) programmes. That message, in turn, is based on a letter from the European Union's 'capital', Brussels, written by someone authorized to do so by a committee that has taken the decision. In a case like this, it is virtually impossible to ever identify the ultimate source.

There have been many attempts to create a terminology that would not only distinguish between utterer and source, but that would also label and thereby describe all intermediary roles. None have been successful. For one thing, as just illustrated, there is often no way of even identifying a real source. Moreover, any label for an intermediary role puts unwarranted restrictions on the involvement of a speaker at a given moment. Thus, for instance, describing Ann as the 'reporter' in the communicative chain between the Brussels administration and Beatrice would seriously downplay her personal involvement; she is probably the one who has sent in the application after approving it at the department level; she puts genuine enthusiasm (notoriously lacking from bureaucratic messages) into her 'report', thus adding to its meaning; and maybe she even has the power to block the final approval at that stage. Therefore it is probably best to stick to a simple terminology which distinguishes **utterer** (as a general term also covering 'author' – a term which is itself sometimes used in the general sense we give to 'utterer') from **sources**, allowing for further characterizations of sources as 'once removed' (**source^1**), 'twice removed' (**source^2**), . . . 'n times removed' (**source^n**), though we should not let ourselves be misled by the linearity of this order. The utterer and all the possible sources represent the kinds of **voices** involved in any instance of language use. Here we borrow a term from Bakhtin, based on his view that every utterance contains some kind of implicit dialogue. Following Ducrot, one could conceptualize this in terms of the 'polyphony' involved in language use.

The story of the utterer's many voices does not end here. Consider that instead of (1), a less happy exchange took place, as in (4).

(4) 1. Beatrice: Can I go?
2. John: I'm really sorry. Your application was not accepted.
3. Beatrice: So, I'm not good enough.

It is very unlikely that Beatrice, a confident young woman who knows that she is one of the department's top students, would be passing a serious judgment on herself when saying (4)3. In her utterance, however, she invokes what could be called a **virtual utterer** (or **utterer**$^{\mathbf{V}}$). Somewhere along the line, someone could have said *She's not good enough*. But there is no evidence that anyone ever did. Suppose, now, that the conversation on the previous day between the secretary and the chairperson of the department develops as in (5), followed by an exchange between the secretary and the student as in (6).

(5) 1. John: Can Beatrice go?
2. Ann: She's been turned down.
3. John: Why? She's one of our top students this year.
4. Ann: It's just crazy. Another application that wasn't good enough, I guess.

(6) 1. Beatrice: Can I go?
2. John: I'm really sorry. You've been turned down.
3. Beatrice: Why?
4. John: I know it's crazy. You're one of our top students. But they've decided you're not good enough, I guess.

In this chain of communicative events, Ann does in (5)4. what Beatrice did in (4)3. Ann knows very well, of course, that decision-making involves many factors that cannot be reduced to plain judgments about 'how good' someone is. But by conjuring up a virtual utterer whose literal judgment is that *She's not good enough*, Ann indirectly criticizes the decision-making process which should pay more exclusive attention to an applicant's scholarly qualities. John, in turn, re-uses Ann's strategy in (6)4. Considering that Ann is source^{1} of his message, the virtual utterer invoked becomes a **virtual source** 'once removed' (or **source**$^{\mathbf{1-V}}$). The exchange in (6) could continue as follows:

(6) 5. Beatrice: Is that what Ann said?
6. John: Right. She does not think very highly of the Brussels bureaucracy.

This actualizes or makes explicit the underlying pattern of voices.

Virtual utterers play a more wide-ranging role in language use than might be expected. They are implicitly invoked by most utterances that emphasize one end of a contrast. Typical in this respect are many forms of negation. Consider (7) and (8).

(7) I never said that.
(8) I am not a crook.

These sentences may in fact be reactions to *actual* utterers, as when (7) is said in response to a question such as *You mean I am a crook?*, or in the historically attested case of Richard Nixon saying (8) while under attack from people who obviously regarded him as a crook. In those cases, the invoked contrast is a matter of real-life intertextuality, and hence linguistic context (see section 3.3). But in the absence of such immediate triggers, one may still say (7) or (8) in response to a possible claim made by a virtual utterer. In many cases a pre-emptive strategy is involved, a typical example being the so-called 'response-controlling *but*-prefaces' as in (9).

(9) I'm not a racist, but there are just too many foreigners in this school.

This phrasing is meant to take away grounds for a potential accusation based by a virtual utterer on what follows *but*.

There is one more type of case we have to review before closing this section. Especially in written discourse, elaborate patterns of utterances can be found which are embedded into the main utterance. Here, as elsewhere in this book, an utterance is simply defined as a stretch of discourse produced by the same utterer(s), with a relatively clear beginning and end. Hence an utterance may be a turn in a conversation or a 1000-page trilogy. The trilogy is likely to contain numerous embedded utterances which the main utterer (the author) presents as having been produced by an **embedded utterer** (or **utterer^E**). Needless to say that such an embedded utterer may also speak in many voices. This is why Figure 3.2, containing a summary of the categories of voices we have distinguished in the foregoing paragraphs, adds three dots to the label 'utterer^E' to indicate the possible recursiveness of the entire structure.

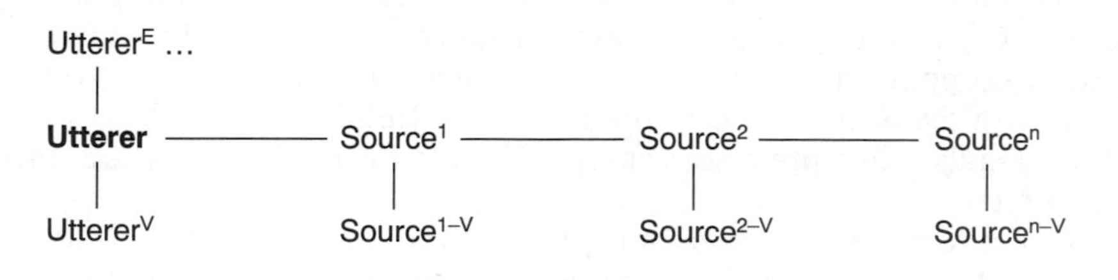

Fig. 3.2 Categories of voices

Though embedded utterers, as said, are especially frequent guests in written discourse, they are not absent from spoken language either. They are present in every form of direct quotation, including stories of the *A said – B said* type (in contrast to other types of reported speech, as well as indirect speech, where an identified source would be involved). A special case, moreover, is that of the **self-embedding utterer**, one who is knowingly producing discourse that is or will be embedded in a wider communicative context. Thus in the world of television, an interviewer and an interviewee are consciously engaged in the uttering and interpreting of linguistic forms which they know or want to be embedded into a wider communicative event with the television network at one end and a mass audience at the other, either simultaneously or consecutively.

The interpreter's many roles

Although utterers have many voices, hearers or – to use the term we prefer – interpreters may play many different roles. We should not forget, first of all, that they are a subcategory of what could be called **presences**, i.e. the totality of persons who are 'present' at or in the vicinity of a speech event or, put differently, in a position that would enable them to become engaged in the event. This not only counts for oral exchanges. For anybody 'present' within earshot from a conversation, 'engagement' becomes conceivable. In the same way, anybody walking through a bookstore or library is a 'presence' and may 'engage' with any of the books at any moment simply by picking one up and starting to read. From the moment 'presences' become 'engaged', whether by listening or by reading, they become **interpreters**. This does not mean they do not play a role until that moment. To the extent that an utterer *knows that* they are around somewhere, even if not actually seen, so that they could become engaged at any given moment, he or she may adapt his or her utterances radically to that possibility. Thus Beatrice, saying (6)5., may lower her voice, knowing that Ann, as the department's chairperson, may walk into the secretariat any time, and John may respond in the same way in (6)6., for the same reason. To give an example from written discourse, Julius Caesar may have adapted his account of a near-defeat to the possible future 'engagement' with his text on the part of a number of 'presences' – important for his grip on influence and power – by introducing it with the claim that his opponents, the Belgians, were the bravest of the Gauls. Thus **presences** can play a role even while they are **non-interpreters**.

Once presences become interpreters, they can play a variety of roles. Let us sketch an interactional context briefly, as visualized in Figure 3.3.

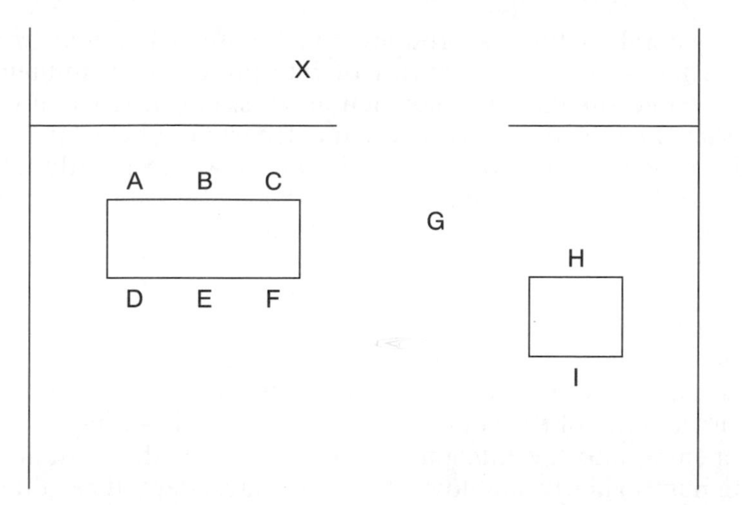

Fig. 3.3 A restaurant scene

The setting is a restaurant. The people around the large table in the corner are all faculty members of the linguistics department, except for D, who is a molecular biologist specializing in malaria, an old friend of A who happens to be in town. C and F are exchanging the latest gossip about the chairperson of the linguistics department. B and E follow the exchange attentively, reacting now and then, but not contributing much, while A and D are engaged in a conversation of their own. In a constellation like this, C and F are each other's direct **addressees**, whereas B and E are **side participants**. All others in this picture may be interpreters while remaining **non-participants**. Two categories of non-participants can be distinguished. First of all, there are those who are close enough to the exchange for C and F to know for sure that they will pick up bits and pieces of the conversation, thus inevitably functioning as interpreters at a certain level. This counts for A and D sitting at the same table, as well as for the waiter G. They can be called **bystanders**. But in addition there are those about whom C and F cannot know for sure that they are acting as interpreters. They form the category of possible **overhearers**. Some of them may be plainly in view, such as H who sits at another table, acting as a **listener-in** since he is pricking up his ears to catch parts of the gossip about the linguistics chairperson, whom he happens to know. Other overhearers may do so more secretly, like the **eavesdropper** X, a linguistics student working in the restaurant kitchen, who remains hidden behind the wall. Clearly, any of the *known presences* mentioned before may act as eavesdroppers; but most of the time they don't, and the category of eavesdroppers is not restricted to them, which is why these categories have to be kept separate.

This general picture is presented in Figure 3.4. None of this is trivial. That is, all the categories of interpreters may influence the utterers' choice-making in fundamental ways. For instance, if C and F know that B has a special liking for the department's chairperson, this would not necessarily stop the gossip, but it would greatly influence the phrasing. Any offensive language would be carefully censored. Similarly, if C or F know that H is a faculty member of the English department who may know the linguistics chairperson, they might want to make sure that, in the case of attempts to listen in, he would not know whom they are talking about. This can be easily realized by selecting a code name on the spot, though even then the details of what is said would have to be monitored in such a way as not to give away the identity of the coded person. Or C and F, sitting close to the door opening into the kitchen, and knowing that this restaurant just off campus regularly employs students, may adapt their utterances continuously to the possibility of being overheard by eavesdroppers, either by lowering their voices, or by seriously obfuscating and/or expurgating content.

Moreover, there are even types of speech events that require particular kinds of presences. For instance, side participants (viz. witnesses) are needed for a promise of marriage to be valid during some kinds of wedding ceremonies. Or consider the way in which someone being harassed in a public place may turn potential overhearers into side participants by raising his or her voice for all to hear (a form of verbal behaviour corresponding to the African American concept of *loud-talking*).

One feature of Figure 3.4 has not yet been explained. It has to do with the top node above 'presence'. Remember Beatrice's question *Can I go?* in (1)1. Although this is a question for information directed at the department secretary, John, it also constitutes an act of asking for permission. But that act is not targeted at John personally. It assumes, however, **presences** at various steps 'removed' (i.e. **presence**$^{\mathbf{1,2,\ldots n}}$) that are or have been involved as real-world interpreters in the long communicative chain that led to acceptance or rejection of her application to go to the Universidad Autónoma de Madrid, who are not *acting* as interpreters at the moment of speaking, but whose 'presence' could be *re-actualized* (e.g. if calling them would be the only way of getting the required information at that moment). As real-world 'people', source$^{1,2,\ldots n}$ and presence$^{1,2,\ldots n}$ may be identical. But functionally they are different.

The category of 'removed' presences, moreover, covers more specific functional types similar to some of the lower nodes in Figure 3.4. In particular, **addressees** at various steps 'removed' (**addressee**$^{\mathbf{1,2,\ldots n}}$) are regular occurrences. For instance, when *sending for* someone, the addressee is not the target of the 'request to come', which is directed

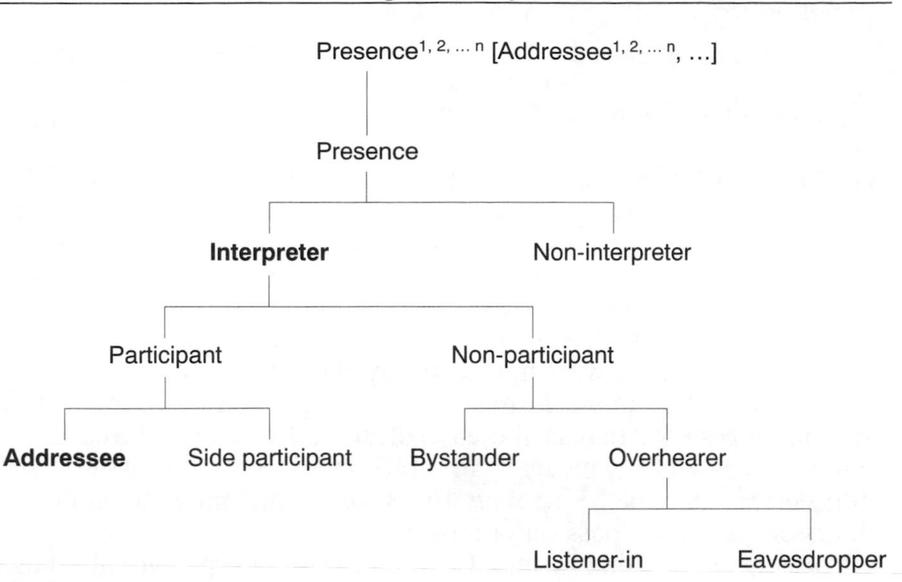

Fig. 3.4 Interpreter roles

at a removed addressee^{1}. The direct addressee is thereby turned into an **intermediary**. A similar process takes place when a company sends a press release to journalists or media (the addressees) for them to act as intermediaries in the envisaged communication with a wider public (addressee$^{1,2,\ldots n}$). Or consider self-embedding utterers of the interviewer–interviewee type in a television programme, aiming their utterances at each other as addressees, but at the same time targeting much wider addressees$^{1,2,\ldots n}$, the television audience. To demonstrate the effect of such an audience structure on linguistic choice-making, we can adduce the following example from Clark and Carlson (1982, p. 339), where (10) is a private conversation and (11) a television interview, both with the same 'content':

(10)	Crothers, to Senator Smyth:	Well, Joe, what do you think of the New Hampshire stink?
	Smyth, to Crothers:	It's a goddam mess. If Bill doesn't watch his ass, Bert may take away all his marbles.
(11)	Crothers, to Smyth:	Senator Smyth, what do you think of Jones's controversial remarks in the New Hampshire election campaign last week?
	Smyth, to Crothers:	They were unfortunate. If Senator Jones does not watch his step, Bert Appleman may get impatient with him and cut off all his campaign funds.

Crothers, to Smyth: You're speaking of Bert Appleman, the Democratic Party National Chairman, aren't you?
Smyth, to Crothers: Yes, I am.

As Clark and Carlson explain, there are at least three ways in which the utterances get adapted to the new audience structure in (11): (i) all private references such as the Christian names *Joe*, *Bill*, and *Bert*, and expressions such as *the New Hampshire stink* and *all his marbles* are made explicit enough for a wider public to be able to understand them; (ii) Crothers makes a request for clarification to 'identify' Bert Appleman, though he does not need any clarification for himself; (iii) the style becomes more formal, and expletives are dropped. This example also shows that in the case of an addressee$^{1,2\ldots n}$, the direct addressee is not always an intermediary. Addressee and addressee$^{1,2,\ldots n}$ may be spoken to at the same time, without the addressee having to 'pass on' a message.

Processes of adapting forms of expression to interpreter roles have been discussed extensively by conversation analysts. The label they use is **recipient design**: utterances are designed specifically for an intended audience, to ensure continued attention as well as the desirable level of understanding.

When utterer becomes interpreter

When explaining Figure 3.1, it was said that the interpreter I can be telescoped into the utterer U. Such is the case when there is no interpreter outside of the one mentally constructed by the utterer, so that the interpreter role is fully incorporated into the world of the utterer, even if that role is later taken on – as is normally the expectation – by real language users. Let us speak, in such a case, of a **virtual interpreter** (or **interpreter**^{V}). Note that this case is really distinct from the presences that are at various steps 'removed' from the utterance, where the utterer *knows that* others *are or have been* involved as real interpreters even though they do not fulfil that role at the moment of speaking. A virtual interpreter, on the other hand, is really *only imagined* at the moment of producing the utterance. Thus when writing this book, I am mentally constructing an audience for which I assume that what I say will be both relevant and accessible; I may even think of individuals I know for modelling that audience; but there is no guarantee at the stage of writing that there will ever be a real audience, nor that the audience will look even remotely like the one I had in mind. When writing is backed by a contract with a publisher, the risks diminish, though they do not disappear. But the process I am describing is even more manifest when writing a novel, or a scientific treatise, for which no publisher may even be found.

Similarly, an actor practising a role alone imagines an audience and tries to shape the performance in such a way as to make it accessible and revealing to the type of audience he or she has in mind. Or, when writing a report of any kind, even when one knows that it will only be put away, the linguistic choices get adapted to the criteria that are assumed to be expected by a constructed reader to be met. While such examples are sometimes adduced to show that language use is not necessarily communication, they also demonstrate how fundamentally communicative language can be even when no actual communication is taking place (yet). One can even go as far as to side with Bakhtin in defining a 'superaddressee' (definitely a type of virtual interpreter) to whom utterances are directed: a mental model of something or someone able to perfectly understand what one is saying (whether a person, a god, truth itself, or history). In other words, there always seems to be 'directedness' in language use.

The influence of numbers

The nature of linguistic utterances is influenced not only by the types of utterers and interpreters involved, but also simply by *how many* there are. It makes a significant difference whether there is one utterer holding the floor for a considerable length of time (monologue, novel), two or more utterers taking turns (conversation, debate, correspondence, etc.), or two or more utterers engaged simultaneously in the same act (as in a joint recitation, i.e. the kind of act which requires a previously determined form of the utterance). Similarly, it makes a difference whether just one person is addressed (in a private conversation, or in a private letter), whether there are more interpreters (some of which may be addressed directly while others fulfil other roles, as in most conversations), or whether a group of people is addressed as a collectivity (as in a lecture context, a political meeting, a radio broadcast). The latter kind of event, with one utterer and a collective addressee, is not necessarily to be found everywhere; apparently there are pre-literate societies to which it is completely foreign (see Gnerre 1987); in most cases it requires a strong institutional backing.

3.2.2 The mental world

Verbal interaction is no doubt communication from mind to mind – though we should never forget that minds are 'minds in society' (more about which will be said in Chapter 6). That is why Figure 3.1 has at its base the utterer's and interpreter's 'perspective' on a mental, social and physical 'reality'. Aspects of physical, social, and mental reality get 'activated' by the utterer and the interpreter in their respective choice-making practices, and that is how they become part of language use as elements with which the making of choices is interadaptable. We start the overview of those objects of adaptability with the mental world. Needless to say such an 'overview' can only be suggestive, never complete.

Let us begin with an example again. Consider a meeting of the board of governors of the international leather-manufacturing company Croc & Co. The chairperson of the board, Al, has come under attack from Topcroc, one of the company's most efficient and productive branches, for refusing to divert some of the production from smaller branches that are less modern and less favourably situated to meet demands at short notice. Trying to force the issue, Topcroc managers have incited some of their direct customers to threaten a complete stop of their orders unless Topcroc's capacity is expanded to guarantee a faster supply. Not only has Al's good judgment been called into doubt, he is also said to have been inspired by anti-Topcroc sentiments. One of Al's friends on the board, Mike, says (12).

(12) Al, I think you should seriously consider resigning.

The interpretation work in relation to the state of mind behind Mike's decision to utter (12), set in motion by this utterance, is of gigantic proportions. Any aspect of interpretation, moreover, may point at properties of Mike's mental world that triggered the choices he made. Aspects of his **personality** will be hypothesized about. Knowing that he is one of Al's friends, is Mike a trustworthy friend? Does he lack the courage to face a storm? Or is he, maybe, the calculating type trying to create a situation in which his own influence could increase? **Emotions** may be brought in. Is Mike actually afraid that things will get out of hand? Is he, maybe, inspired by his sympathy for Al, and does he fear the possible consequences of Al's having to face more antagonism? Further, what are the **beliefs** involved? Does Mike truly believe that what he proposes is the best possible course of action? Best for whom? What does he think is going to happen if Al does not resign? Or does he think Al really made a mistake that is grave enough to ask him to resign? What **desires** or **wishes** are involved? Does Mike *want* Al to resign? How strong is this wish? Is it a wish that has anything personal to it, or is it purely circumstantial? Are there any specific **motivations** or **intentions**? Is it the intention to save Al? To save the company? Or simply to achieve personal gain (e.g. by being able to succeed Al as Chair of the board)?

The terms we are using are not very discrete, but neither are the hypothesized mental states they refer to. Yet they play an important role. As it stands, (12) is very ambiguous along most of the mental dimensions enumerated. Insight into the situation could normally disambiguate a lot. But also alternative linguistic choices could be made, interadapted with mental states in such a way as to preclude some of the above speculations. Consider the following.

(13) We don't want any more trouble. Al, I think you ought to resign.
(14) Al, as a friend, I really think you should consider resigning, in your own best interest.
(15) The company will suffer greatly if you don't resign while you can still do so gracefully.
(16) You've really messed up. So, I think you should resign.
(17) Al, I really want you to consider resigning.
(18) This may be the time to pass the chair on to someone else.

The adaptedness to specific mental states may be stronger or less vague and ambiguous in these reformulations. Note, however, that this does not give an interpreter less room for legitimate speculation. Just as the utterance needs to interadapt with the utterer's mental world, the choices made are always adapted, whether tentatively or successfully, to the utterer's assessment of what the mental world of the interpreter(s) looks like. Thus judgments of the interpreter's personality traits, emotional involvement, patterns of beliefs, wishes and desires, motivations and intentions, may all enter the picture. Obviously, it is completely impossible to take all these factors into account in such a way that communicative problems and conflicts can be completely avoided. Choices have to be made. Choices even have to be made with respect to *which* interpreter's assumed mental states the utterance should be most tuned in to. 'Trouble' being bad for the smooth functioning of any enterprise, utterance (13), for instance, clearly takes the company perspective that Mike can assume to be shared by most members of the board. Hence saying (13), overriding personal considerations related to Al as an individual and as a friend, may be expected to be received favourably. The same holds for (15), whereas (14) is overtly tuned in to the personal relationship between Mike and Al, with due consideration for the latter's personal position. Of course, (14) may simply be a clever way of combining two goals, not only related to two types of interpreters, but with the potential to score better on all fronts: Mike positions himself as a loyal friend, which may make it easier to convince Al; at the same time, by combining this show of loyalty with a proposal that is clearly inspired by the company perspective, the sensitivities of all other interpreters (who definitely want to think of themselves as valuing friendship and loyalty as well as company interests) are maximally taken into account. From this point of view, (16), (17) and (18) are all riskier, though they may be better adjusted to specific known or suspected mental states of some of the interpreters.

Note that on the interpreter side it is not only properties of the direct participants that count, with Al as addressee and all other board members as side participants for (13)–(17), and with possibly all board members as direct addressees for (18). The form which Mike gives his utterances may as much be inspired by what he expects the reactions to be on the part of any known presence$^{1, 2, \ldots n}$, such as absent board members and important stockholders to whom whatever he says in the meeting is likely to be reported by others.

Mental states have always been central to certain endeavours in linguistic pragmatics. Beliefs, for instance, are at the core of the 'background assumptions' that verbal behaviour is anchored into and that are implicitly communicated. Similarly, a variety of mental states has been relied upon for the definition of speech act types, as ingredients of felicity conditions. The foregoing discussion, however, will have shown that attributions of mental states can rarely be as discrete as would seem to be suggested in speech act theory. It would be hard to decide what dominates in (12), Mike's voicing of a belief, i.e. an honest assessment of a situation, or the expression of a wish, i.e. an attempt to make Al follow a certain course of action. In (14) this is further complicated by the addition of what would appear to be the true expression of heartfelt concern. It seems, then, that any systematic attempt to take mental states into account will have to leave all abstractions behind and has to *allow for a variety of interacting mental phenomena to move in and out of focus in a mental space that is perpetually in motion.* Simple theorizing is ruled out. Moreover, a pragmatic perspective that searches its way through the reality of language use (which includes its possibilities), guided by the notion of adaptability, cannot ignore the interplay between linguistic choices and the mental states of interpreters – a phenomenon that has rarely been approached at all in pragmatics. Though it may seem to be a self-evident truth that the latter do not exert any influence except through their mental processing by the utterer, even that is an oversimplification. As will be demonstrated later (especially in Chapter 5), interpretations – and hence also the interpreters' mental states – really create meaning as much as utterances and their utterers do.

It will be clear from these brief remarks that the mental world activated in language use contains **cognitive** and **emotive** elements. While the former provide a bridge between the mental and the social in the form of **conceptualizations** in terms of which social interaction is interpreted, the latter provide a bridge in the form of phenomena usually studied under labels such as **affect** and **involvement**, the attitudinal prerequisites for engaging in, sustaining and 'colouring' interaction.

3.2.3 The social world

Person deixis is not restricted to an identification of utterers and interpreters (see 3.2.1). Also 'others' (the third person) are focused on, a process which often involves foregrounding of properties (such as sex) which position people in a social world. Even where the identification of utterer and interpreter is concerned, the aspects of social deixis that we labelled **attitudinal deixis** get involved, affecting forms of address, (in many languages) pronoun choices, and the like. Elements of social structure, moreover, not only affect deictic choices but also matters of style and content.

There is no principled limit to the range of social factors that linguistic choices are interadaptable with. Most of them have to do with properties of **social settings** or **institutions**. Sometimes the very fact of linguistic choice-making has to be institutionally sanctioned: only a judge can pass a sentence, and it does not make sense to (literally) read someone's rights unless he or she is a suspect; in such cases (extendable to more informal constraints imposed by the social setting) we can speak of *ratified utterers* and *ratified interpreters*. (See also the remarks on the pre-allocation of turns in section 1.1.4, and its exemplification in 7.2.2.) Within these settings and institutions many linguistic choices depend on relationships of *dependence* and *authority*, or *power* and *solidarity*, not only between utterer and interpreter but also between utterer and/or interpreter and any third party which either figures in the topic of the discourse or is otherwise involved. In addition, social settings and institutions impose many types of *principles* and *rules* on the ways in which certain types of linguistic acts can be performed, or who has the right to perform them. They even determine the 'performability' of certain acts under specified circumstances. Institutionally defined power on the part of the utterer, for instance, enables someone to order, command, permit, while institutional power on the part of the addressee may make an utterer ask and beg. Acknowledged superior knowledge (also a form of authority) enables an utterer to advise and counsel; reversal of the knowledge-based authority relationship makes an utterer ask questions.

Some of these processes can easily be illustrated with reference to the examples in the previous section. It is unlikely that Mike would utter any of the sentences (12) to (18) if he were a newly introduced member of the Board. In order to suggest that Al should resign as chairperson, he has to be well-established, a person with considerable influence and authority himself, and maybe even a likely candidate for succession (though the latter should not be so 'natural' that a direct conflict of interest could be invoked to discredit his suggestion). Also, the making of the suggestion for Al to resign, whether by Mike or anyone else, presupposes an institutional context in which standard practices can be called upon to legitimate such a proposal: earlier events of a similar kind may be used to justify the expectation that Al should resign; or there may even be established rules dictating such a course of action. Such contexts of legitimation are alluded to at least in (13), (15), (16) and, more implicitly, in (18). In a broader perspective, the suggestion may even fit into a world of business practices in a free market model, where any object or person standing in the way of profits or carrying the risk of diminished returns is removed as standard. Going back to the lower-level choices involved, all of the utterances, except (18), suggest, through forms of address and the ways in which the content is phrased, a high degree of familiarity between Mike and Al. And a relationship of friendship or closeness is explicitly invoked in (14).

Phenomena of the utmost importance in the relationship between linguistic choices and the social world are the *setting-*, *institution-*, or *community-specific communicative norms* that have to be observed. All of (12) to (17) have a strongly 'Western' ring to them; in a different cultural context, different norms might be at work even in comparable institutional contexts, requiring forms of expression closer to (18) or even more indirect and formal.

Culture, with its invocation of norms and values, has indeed been a favourite social-world correlate to linguistic choices in the pragmatic literature. It is also one of the most (potentially) misleading notions, being a prime example of a concept in terms of which social interaction is interpreted pre-theoretically. Its use in linguistic analysis has a tendency to unduly reify or even mythologize cultures as real-world 'entities' that can be handled as natural organisms with clearly identifiable properties. A truly pragmatic approach to linguistic behaviour does not place social variability at the level of idealized groups, but along a range of intersecting dimensions contributing to interlocutors' *social identities*. 'Cultural' dimensions include the contrast between oral and literate societies, rural versus urban patterns of life, or a mainstream versus a subcultural environment. Other social dimensions of variability with which linguistic choice-making is interadaptable include social class, ethnicity and race, nationality, linguistic group, religion, age, level of education, profession, kinship, gender, sexual preference, and so on. The linguistic significance of all of these variables has been studied at length, though often only in view of correlations between groups and repertoires, rather than in terms of processes of use.

The adaptability of language to the social world is truly pervasive. We are all familiar with institutional speech events which require fixed phrasings, sometimes even in a language other than the one in current use in the society and even in the event in question: e.g. the defence of a doctoral thesis at any Dutch university (conducted in Dutch) ends when a person walks in, invested with the power to do so, saying *Hora est!* (Latin for 'the hour has come'); this phrase cannot really be replaced by *Let's call it a day.* In a variety of attested cases, a completely different 'code' of a language has to be chosen in the course of certain specific types of activities or when addressing a specific category of people. Speakers of some languages of Papua New Guinea, for instance, may switch from an everyday version of their language to a 'hunting language' when hunting (Pawley n.d.). Kinship relations may dictate similar switches, as in the case of the 'language of respect' in Tongan (Churchward 1953), or the 'mother-in-law' variety of Dyirbal (Dixon 1972), to be spoken in the presence of certain taboo relatives. Less extreme cases of the same type, involving milder forms of adaptability, are to be found in all societies in which people grow up with a local dialect, which they may keep using in day-to-day interaction in their own region and/or family, but are expected to turn to a standardized version in some areas of public life (starting with the educational context).

For some languages, the concept of 'social relationships' may have to be expanded – in order to explain certain linguistic choices – to relationships not only between people but also between people and animals, people and plants, and even people and things, to the extent that certain animals, plants and things are 'interacted with' as an essential part of people's daily activities. It is on this basis that one can explain the sailor's choice of *she* as the pronoun to refer to a ship in English, a language which normally makes all lifeless things grammatically neuter. A more exotic case in point is provided by Rapanui which, as most other Polynesian languages, has two sets of possessive pronouns and possessive adjectives. Two different possessive forms are used for the following two sets of nouns, for both of which English provides *my* (Fuentes 1960: 602):

- A-series (*taaku*):
  my son, my husband, my wife, my sheep, my potatoes, my fish, . . .
- O-series (*tooku*):
  my father, my master, my car, my horse, my house, my clothes, . . .

The A-series not only includes husband, wife, children, all descendents, people of inferior rank but also food, edibles, tools, trees, plants, domestic animals (except for the horse), etc. The O-series includes all ancestors, parents, people of a higher rank, the horse, boats, cars, all means of transportation, clothing, houses and furniture. At first sight these categories seem rather random. However, Fuentes (1960) tries to explain them in the following way. The basic distinction is that the A-series is used for objects and persons which depend on the speaker, whereas the O-series includes objects and persons on which the speaker depends (or which are superior to the speaker). This dichotomy may be easy enough to understand when it comes to distinguishing 'son' from 'father' or 'master'. It also explains clearly enough why domestic animals belong to the A-series. But why not the horse? The logic behind this choice seems to be that, within the network of 'relationships' characterizing Rapanui life, people are (or were) viewed as dependent on the horse (like any other means of transportation) to get somewhere (or at least to get there in a reasonably short period of time without too much effort). The final test confirming this explanation may be that a horse that has never been used by its owner, according to Fuentes' observations, belongs to the A-series. Similarly, people are dependent on clothes and houses to keep warm and healthy. But what about food? Vegetables are cultivated and would die if it were not for the care people take of them. And (though this may be a weak point in the chain of reasoning) it is considered to be totally up to humans to leave fish in the sea or to take them out. Others (e.g. Krupa 1982) have interpreted the distinction as one between alienable (dominant) and inalienable (subordinate) possession. Even if we do not accept all the details of the account – allowing, as we always should when language is concerned, for inconsistencies, whether real or apparent – it is almost inevitable to see the point that the linguistic choices in question could be hardly explained without referring to the way in which speakers of Rapanui view themselves in relation to each other and to other 'entities' with which they interact in the course of their daily activities. As Krupa puts it, 'it is the relationship between the possessor and the possessed that is characterized by *o* and *a*, not the possessed item itself' (1982: 113). Similarly, Biggs reports on Maori particles, placed at the beginning of a phrase, which express the same distinction: 'Possession of anything towards which the possessor is dominant, active or superior, is expressed by *a*; possession of things in respect to which the possessor is subordinate, passive or inferior, is expressed by *o*' (1969: 43).

This reference to phenomena that are not directly accessible to the language competence of most readers of this book only serves as a reminder that we should not let our thinking about language use, and its relation to the social world, be determined by expected patterns. At the same time, the example may serve as a transition to the next section. One final remark before making that transition: any immediately preceding linguistic context is also part of the social world in which an utterance is situated. But this phenomenon will be dealt with separately in section 3.3.

3.2.4 The physical world

Temporal deixis and spatial deixis are the most studied, and most visible, ways of anchoring language choices into a physical world. Both phenomena have exerted a strong fascination on linguists, from long before 'pragmatics' became a common notion. Therefore, there is an extensive and interesting literature to rely on, so that the following overview can be kept quite rudimentary.

Temporal reference

Let us start with a few examples that – though simple – show that 'time' is *a relative notion* rather than an absolute value in relation to language, and that it interferes with a lot of other considerations. Just look at *greetings*. They do not only offer us the trivial observation that *Good morning* is only appropriate in the morning and *Good evening* in the evening (an observation which becomes somewhat less trivial when we try to determine the variable time spaces covered by 'morning', 'evening', and their equivalents in different languages). But, in addition to their being related to 'stretches of time', greetings tend to be related to time relative to certain events. *Good morning*, for instance, would normally be used only when meeting someone for the first time in the morning; uttering the same formula again when meeting the same person once more later that same 'morning', would lead – at least – to suspicions of absent-mindedness. *Good evening* can be used when meeting or parting in the evening, whereas *Good night* can only be used when parting at a time (typically 'bed-time') when there is not a sufficiently significant part of the 'evening' left for the speaker to be able to say *Good evening*. *Hello* and *Good-bye* can both be said at any time of the day or the night, but the former only when meeting, the latter only when parting – a division of labour which is less than self-evident for some learners of English as a foreign language.

That there is nothing trivial about these facts – though the consequences are rarely grave – becomes especially clear when we observe to what extent they change from language to language. Thus the Dutch leave-taking formula *Tot straks!* literally means 'till later'. This 'later', however, is necessarily within the same day. This temporal meaning (which is more strict than is the case, for instance, with its direct Spanish equivalent *Hasta luego*) has consequences even for the types of communication in which the formula can be used. Thus a letter, usually not expected to be delivered on the day of writing, nor followed up with another letter on the same day, cannot end in *Tot straks!* Some learners of Dutch have been known to make that mistake, which ceases to be a mistake in a fast exchange of e-mail messages.

Still in the area of greetings, some languages have found ways of making it easy for themselves along the dimension of time. Thus, the well-known Hawaiian greeting *Aloha* can be used at any time of day or night, whether meeting or parting (which follows from its very general basic meaning of 'love', 'affection', 'to express affection'). Another example is spoken Hungarian which has managed to drop the time indications from *Jó napot kívánok* (I wish [you] a good day), *Jó reggelt kívánok* (I wish [you] a good morning), etc. while sometimes preserving the accusative suffix attached to the noun indicating the relevant stretch of time as in *'t kívánok* which, as a result, can be used at any time.

When talking about temporal reference, it is useful to make a distinction between **event time**, **time of utterance** and **reference time** (in relation to a clear deictic centre, other than the time of utterance). A simple example of event time is the phrase *in 1963* in (19).

(19) JFK visited Bellagio in 1963.

Time of utterance serves as the deictic centre in (20) to (22).

(20) Yesterday I defended my PhD thesis.
(21) I'm planning a party now.
(22) I'll start looking for a job tomorrow.

Utterances may also place events in relation to a deictic centre other than the time of utterance. Often relations to such a reference time are indicated with temporal adverbs, such as *when*, *after*, *before*, and the like.

Like most aspects of the linguistic generation of meaning, temporal reference is usually characterized by a significant degree of *indeterminacy.* Consider examples (23) to (25).

(23) Just a sec.
(24) Today it is not easy to find a job.
(25) JFK visited Bellagio in 1963. He was not alone that day.

Clearly, *sec* in (23) does not literally refer to a 'second'. Depending on who the utterer is and what the circumstances are, any interpreter will form context-specific expectations on how much longer he or she will have to wait for the speaker to be 'available'. Nor does *today* in (24) refer to the day of speaking only, but to a wider (and again variable) time span surrounding the present moment. More interesting still is (25), with its logically impossible coreference between *in 1963* and *that day*, where *that day* can only be interpreted as 'at the unspecified day in 1963 when JFK visited Bellagio', leaving 365 possibilities for further specification (minus 40 for those whose world knowledge – or encyclopedia – tells them that President Kennedy was murdered on 22 November of the same year).

To the extent that **temporal order** is matched by a linear order in linguistic choices (as in some types of narrative), we are confronted with one aspect of the *iconicity* of language, i.e. the property of non-arbitrary similarity between form and meaning. Consider, for instance, (26).

(26) JFK visited Bellagio in 1963. He was murdered later that year.

Often, the order of simply conjoined phrases is, for that reason, irreversible, as in (27).

(27) JFK went to Bellagio and spent one night at the Villa Serbelloni.

Such forms of expression, however, often combine temporal order with meaning relations of different kinds, such as causality (which, with enough fantasy, could be read into a string such as (26)). And, more often than not, narrative forms do not strictly correspond to temporal order, even while explicitly indicating such order as in (28).

(28) JFK visited Bellagio in 1963. He spent one night at the Villa Serbelloni, where his room is now referred to as the 'Kennedy room'. Four years earlier, in 1959, this property had been bequeathed by the late Ella Walker, Principessa della Torre e Tasso, to the Rockefeller Foundation. He was murdered later that year.

This example also shows how thoroughly event time, time of utterance, and reference time can be intertwined in an utterer's perspective on the temporal dimension of 'reality'.

Note, finally, that a simple 'point of view operation' or 'perspective manipulation' makes it possible to handle a delayed *time of receipt* as the time of utterance. Just think of writing a letter to someone who is leaving on vacation and whom you know will not get your letter until their return. You have a choice between

(29) I hope you'll have a nice holiday

and

(30) I hope you had a nice holiday

where (29) takes the perspective of the time of writing whilst (30) is oriented towards the anticipated time of reading.

Spatial reference

In many ways, spatial concepts are central to human thinking, as they form the basis of standard metaphors in numerous areas of experience: *before the end of the year* (time), *close friends* (social relations), *high voice* (sounds), *high society* (status), *high amount* (quantity), *ups and downs* (moods, etc.), *the rising tide of pluralism*, *a narrow mind*, *go downhill*, etc. Hence, the relevance of space as a contextual correlate of adaptability stretches beyond mere spatial reference.

For the linguistic encoding of space and spatial relations, a language such as English uses prepositions (*in*, *on*, *under*, *behind*, *between*, *in front of*, . . .), verbs (*come–go*, *bring–take*), adverbs (*here*, *there*), pronouns (*this*, *that*), and place names (*London*, and in a wider sense of 'place', the name of a store such as *Harrods*). Other languages may combine any of these linguistic resources with others, such as elaborate morphological systems. A case in point is Hungarian, which does not only provide nominal suffixes for common case forms such as accusative or dative, but a wide range of basically spatial ones (themselves usable in metaphorical ways) as well: inessive (*-ban*/*-ben*, 'in'), illative(*-ba*/*-be*, 'into'), elative (*-ból*/*-bòl*, 'out of'), sublative (*-ra*/*-re*, 'onto'), superessive (*-n*/*-on*/*-en*/*-ön*, 'on'), delative (*-ról*/*-ròl*, 'off'), allative (*-hoz*/*-hez*/*-höz*, 'towards'), adessive (*-nál*/*-nél*, 'at'), ablative (*-tól*/*-tòl*, 'away from'), terminative (*-ig*, '[up] to').

Just as there is reasonably precise reference to event time, it appears that there are indicators of **absolute spatial relations**. Examples would be dimensions such as *North–South*, *East–West*. But a few caveats have to be formulated immediately. First, such points of orientation make sense only on a planet rotating in a fixed direction around a fixed axis. (Note that not only spatial relations, but probably about all aspects of the physical world, depend on this particular property of the planet we are on: the division of time in hours, days, seasons and years, the gravity-related positioning of our bodies and hence bodily postures, etc.) Second, the representation of these points of orientation is highly conventionalized in domains of human activity such as map-making. Third, a consequence of this conventionalization is – somewhat paradoxically – that in some areas of activity there is less of a need for precision in referring to such spatial co-ordinates. For instance, sections of a highway that go east or west may still indicate north as its direction if it can be demonstrated, on the map, that the end point of the highway in question (in the direction we are going in) is to the north of its starting point. Fourth, some absolute systems based on fixed points in a landscape, may rotate. For instance, if island dwellers take a central mountain top as their main point of orientation, directions will be indicated differently depending on where one is on the island.

A different type of 'absolute' system is dependent on **intrinsic orientations**. Thus the head and the tail of an animal, or the front and the back of a car, related to a typical direction of movement, determine the default values of *in front of* and *behind* in relation to animals and cars. Similarly, many houses, with their main entrance towards the street, have an intrinsic orientation of the same kind.

However, spatial reference is usually *relative to a perspective*, which can be either **utterer space** or **reference space** (the latter defined as having a deictic centre distinct from the perspective of the utterer). Thus spatial concepts such as *left* and *right*, *here* and *there*, or the phrase *10 o'clock* used to indicate direction, typically require a perspective determined by the spatial orientation of the utterer. But anything outside the utterer can be made into the deictic centre. The sentence *The silk store is near the cathedral*, for instance, exemplifies such use of relative reference space, locating *the silk store* (traditionally labelled **figure** in the context of spatial relations) in a specific relation to *the cathedral* (the **ground**, i.e. the entity used as deictic centre for spatial placement of the figure).

Often, utterers make their perspective coincide with the intrinsic orientations of objects talked about. Thus *to the left of the car* will usually mean 'left from the perspective of a driver or passenger facing forward in a car viewed from the point of view of its typical direction of movement'. The utterer, however, is able to overrule aspects of intrinsic orientation. For instance, the phrase *in front of the car* may simply mean 'between the utterer and the car'; or, when facing the (intrinsic) left-hand side of a car, the phrase *to the left of the car* may mean 'located on that side of the car usually seen as its (intrinsic) front'. Note that such perspective manipulations are subject to more restrictions when the car in question is moving. Similarly, utterers may make their own perspective coincide with that of an interpreter, as usually happens when giving directions over the telephone. Or the utterer perspective may be altogether abandoned in favour of an interpreter's, as when *left* and *right* are adapted to facilitate comprehension.

Even simple sentences may prove problematic as tools for communication if the relativity of spatial perspectives is not taken into account. Once, when making a stopover at the Frankfurt airport to meet a colleague, I was trying to find my way to the terminal where we had agreed to meet. Confronted with a security check that looked too much like one of the stages passengers have to pass through before getting to their aircraft, I thought I'd better ask before continuing in the same direction. The following exchange took place:

(31) JV: I want to get **out**, not **in**.
Official: OK, it's this way.

Reassured, I continued through the checkpoint only to find that I had entered one of the boarding areas, as I had feared. Clearly, while my *out* and *in* had been oriented to the airport building, the official's *out* and *in* were oriented to Frankfurt, or even Germany.

Many of the examples given so far have already indicated that spatial reference is usually linked up with conceptions of **motion** through space. Needless to say that motion may also become the focus, either directly as in *to pass through*, or with reference to a **source** (*from*, *to leave*) or a **goal** (*to*, *to arrive*).

Utterer and interpreter in the physical world

The relativity of temporal and spatial reference is primarily a function of the positioning of language users in the 'world'. A lot of linguistic choice-making is dependent on properties of this positioning beyond the few lines sketched above in 'pure' temporal and spatial terms. Consider the way in which the *loudness* of one's voice tends to get adapted to location. Not only is loudness a function of distance between utterer and interpreter – a phenomenon that can still be accounted for in relatively pure spatial terms. But we go beyond simple spatial dimensions of positioning when we observe that in some American daycare centres one of the first things children are taught is the difference between their *inside voice* and their *outside voice*. In this example, elements of (spatial) location interact with social norms and activity types.

In many cases, the interlocutors' position in the physical world is important in determining certain linguistic choices and their meanings. It is this basic fact that makes videotaped materials so useful for the analysis of conversations and other types of speech events. Many types of verbal behaviour are strongly associated with particular **bodily postures**. A military officer lying on his back, sunbathing, will hardly feel comfortable bellowing drill commands to a group of privates. On the other hand, a patient's being stretched out on a sofa is supposed to be favourable to the process of therapeutic discourse, as well as – at least in one therapeutic paradigm – the therapist's positioning behind the patient. **Gestures** tend to accompany spoken language to varying degrees and in varying ways, from the violent gesticulations that may add little to the meaning of an utterance but may indicate a great deal about emotional states and involvement, through the thoughtful scratching of one's cheek or chin (for instance to signal sustained interest), to fully conventionalized movements that may accompany or even stand in for speech (such as the thumbs-up gesture meaning 'OK'). Similarly, **gaze** is a significant accompaniment of oral interaction; note, for instance, the ways in which utterers can direct their gaze away from an addressee, while an addressee (barring cultural or contextual restrictions) usually has to keep looking at the utterer to signal that he or she is listening. Even aspects of **physical appearance** (including clothing) may greatly influence the effectiveness of one's speech. This is generally understood by those whose professional success depends on public appearances or on persuasiveness in private. This is also why policy on Alcatraz, the notorious prison in the San Francisco Bay, dictated that inmates should be confronted with each other without clothes as often as possible. As tour guides will explain, it is hard to play the bigshot when you're naked, even if your name is Al Capone. More trivially, though not necessarily with fewer consequences, the way in which one speaks is influenced by **physical conditions** such as exhaustion, illness or drunkenness. And there is a vast literature on the way in which a basically **biological property** such as **sex** is related to choices in uttering and interpreting.

'Material' conditions of speech

This is not where the physical world ceases to exert its influence on the use of language. In the pragmatic literature, however, insufficient attention has been paid to purely 'material' conditions of speech which induce or prevent certain types of choices. Consider (32) and (33).

(32) What shall we have for dinner?
(33) Are you printing?

Sentence (32) is the kind of sentence uttered in a material context where utterer and interpreter have some control over what they will have for dinner; for instance, they have to decide what food to prepare at home, what kind of restaurant to go to, or what dishes to select from a menu. Though its literal meaning simply inquires about a state of affairs in the future, this form of expression is unlikely to occur under conditions where dinner choices are beyond the control and responsibility of the interlocutors (who are, for instance, students in a boarding school or guests in the hands of some prestigious foundation). Sentence (33) used to be uttered dozens of times in our poorly equipped office where up to eight people could be dependent on one and the same printer simultaneously, having to plug and unplug all the time. In that context, it was an expression of courtesy, indicating that one needed the printer but did not want to block someone else's access – though that was the only way. When we acquired a new printer, with an automatic switching device, the utterance disappeared from our linguistic repertoire, having lost all its meaning by a simple change in material circumstances.

Many kinds of linguistic change depend on such phenomena. Consider, at a somewhat trivial level, the growing size of American newspaper headlines in the late nineteenth century, as explained by Schudson:

> Riding an omnibus or street railway was a novel experience. For the first time in human history, people other than the very wealthy could, as part of their daily life, ride in vehicles they were not responsible for driving. Their eyes and their hands were free; they could read on the bus. George Juergens has suggested that the *World's* change to a sensational style and layout was adapted to the needs of commuters: reading on the bus was difficult with the small print and large-sized pages of most papers. So the *World* reduced the size of the page, increased the size of headlines and the use of pictures, and developed the 'lead' paragraph, in which all of the most vital information of a story would be concentrated. From the 1840s, the 'lead' had been pushed by the high cost of telegraphic transmission of news; now it was pulled by the abbreviated moments in which newspapers were being read. It is likely, then, that the growing use of illustration and large headlines in newspapers was as much an adaptation to the new habits of the middle class as to the new character of the immigrant working class. (1978: 103)

Similarly, some instances of markedness in language are directly related to material aspects of the physical world. This is most visible in the event of changes in markedness. Thus Witkowski and Brown (1983) report the following instance of lexical change in Tenejapa Tzeltal, a Mayan language spoken in the Mexican state of Chiapas:

	UNMARKED	MARKED
Phase 1 (pre-conquest)	*čih* 'deer'	Ø
Phase 2 (early post-conquest)	*čih* 'deer'	*tunim čih* 'sheep' (lit. 'cotton deer')
Phase 3 (contemporary)	*čih* 'sheep'	*te 'tikil čih* 'deer' (lit. 'wild sheep')

This markedness reversal is explained by nothing more mysterious than that there were no sheep in pre-conquest Mexico whereas now they are certainly a more dominant presence than deer.

Though the connectedness of language with material circumstances is most visible when changes take place, these examples show that it is always there, usually leading to conventionalizations (fully lexicalized in the Tzeltal case, purely *ad hoc* in (33)), but always subject to adaptability.

3.3 *Linguistic channel and linguistic context*

The final contextual objects of adaptability to pass the review are themselves part of the communicated form. They pertain to the linguistic channel chosen for communicating and to aspects of linguistic choice-making itself, i.e. the linguistic context.

3.3.1 Linguistic channel

For verbal communication (in contrast to the use of sign language), only one linguistic channel is biologically given: **speech sounds**, or vibrations of the atmosphere produced with air from the lungs and by means of speech organs shared by the users of all human languages, i.e. the vocal cords and the vocal tract with a pharynx, glottis, uvula, tongue, soft and hard palate, alveoli, teeth, lips, and nasal cavity. Those sounds, furthermore, are always produced against the background of **non-verbal channels** of communication: gesture (the basic ingredient of sign language), gaze, and the like (see section 3.2.4).

All other linguistic channels are somehow 'artificial'. Yet, there is no simple opposition between **spoken** and **written** language. Often, **oral** and **literate** usage are said to differ in that the former is situated in context, whereas the latter would be de-contextualized. Everything we have said about context so far should point to the conclusion that there is no such thing as de-contextualized language use. What could be maintained is that the way in which context functions in relation to some types of oral discourse (e.g. face-to-face conversation) is different from the way it functions in relation to types of language use employing different channels. But no generalizations can be made on either side, because channels themselves are too varied along discursive, situational and social dimensions of anchoring. Remember, in this respect, what was said before about genres of language use (see section 1.4). Thus face-to-face conversation follows different patterns from the ones characterizing conversations for which the telephone is used as a channel. On the side of written channels, handwriting and printing are guided by different constraints, and the linguistic choices for a book are not those for a letter (even though, for instance, the letter and novel genres can be mixed). Furthermore, there is the borderline category of radio and television broadcasting, the content of which is often pre-scripted (in much the same way as other texts written-to-be-spoken, such as plays), providing a kind of 'secondary orality' (with the possibility of being played over and again in different situations – a significant difference indeed in comparison with the fleeting occurrence of day-to-day oral language use). Or consider electronic mail, that strange written channel associated with expectations of near-conversational speed of exchange. Or interactive multimedia communication.

When considering linguistic channels, we should also keep in mind that basically the same speech event is often destined to pass through several channels consecutively. Just think of a typical political speech, written down at first (often by an aide), spoken by a politician, recorded by means of audio- and/or video technology, and later reported on (often in written form again).

3.3.2 Linguistic context

As was pointed out in relation to discourse deixis (section 1.1.1), discourse itself forms a dimension into which linguistic choices are contextually anchored, for instance by referring back to earlier discourse, by being self-referential, or by projecting towards a future linguistic context. The study of such phenomena often goes under the label of cohesion. Other features of linguistic context to be discussed are intertextuality and sequencing.

Contextual cohesion

The label **cohesion** is generally used to designate *the overt marking of relations within a discourse or text* (which is then often called the **co-text** of the discourse or text fragment under consideration). One aspect of cohesion was already discussed in relation to temporal ordering (see section 3.2.4). A wide range of other phenomena are involved, which are illustrated briefly with the first paragraph of Norman Fairclough's introduction to Sarangi and Slembrouck (1996: ix):

(34) (a) There are two powerful interlocking tendencies affecting contemporary public discourse in Britain and other similar societies. (b) The first is a tendency to what we might call the 'marketisation' of discourse – the extension of the discursive practices of commodity markets to, for instance, professional and public service domains. (c) An example is the proliferation in these domains of forms of advertising discourse. (d) The second is the 'conversationalisation' of public discourse, the appropriation and simulation in public discourse of features of conversational discourse. (e) These changes in discursive practices are part of wider processes of social change affecting late modern societies – the incorporation of vast new areas of social life into markets, and the colonisation of ordinary life by economic and bureaucratic systems. (f) Social change in advanced capitalist societies is increasingly centred upon cultural change, and cultural change often takes a pre-eminently discursive form. (g) Consequently, analysts of discourse are in a position to make a substantive contribution to understanding the fundamental processes

> of social restructuring which dominate contemporary life, by investigating tendencies such as the marketisation and conversationalisation of public discourse. (h) This book takes a significant step in that direction in its analysis of the discursive aspect of major current changes in the ways in which bureaucracy works in modern societies.

Markers of cohesion in a brief text like this include:

- **Conjunctions** such as *Britain and other similar societies* in (a), *economic and bureaucratic systems* in (e), or *marketisation and conversationalisation* in (g).
- **Anaphora**, or terms referring to the same entity as some other term prior in the discourse, thus establishing forms of **coreference**, as with the relative pronoun *which* in (g) and (h), the demonstratives in *these domains* in (c), *these changes* in (e) and *that direction* in (h), the possessive *its* in (h).
- A demonstrative used for **(anticipatory) self-reference** as in *this book* in (h).
- Placement side by side, or **juxtaposition**, as in *the 'marketisation' of discourse – the extension of [. . .]* in (b).
- **Exemplification** by means of *for instance* in (b), *an example is* in (c), or *such as* in (g).
- The **explanation** following the dash in (b), the comma in (d) and the dash in (e).
- Other types of **logical relations** such as the 'conclusion' indicated by *consequently* in (g).
- The omission of words, or **ellipsis**, as in *the first [powerful tendency]* in (b) and *the second* in (d), or the omitted intermediate conclusion from (f) ('Thus social change takes a pre-eminently discursive form'), which is needed to justify *consequently* in (g).
- The **numerals** *two* in (a), *the first* in (b), and *the second* in (d).
- **Highlighting** by means of the quotation marks surrounding *'marketisation'* in (b) and *'conversationalisation'* in (d), or by means of the explicit labelling practice in *what we might call* in (b).
- **Contrasting** as accomplished by means of *the first* in (b) as opposed to *the second* in (d), or by means of the conjoined elements in *the incorporation of vast new areas of social life into markets, and the colonisation of ordinary life by [. . .]* in (e), or by means of lexical qualifications as in *social change* versus *cultural change* in (f).
- **Comparison** as by means of *similar* in (a).
- Forms of **repetition** (often incorporating elements of **contrast** and **comparison** or various types of **semantic relations** such as meaning equivalence or synonymy, meaning opposition or antinomy, meaning inclusion or hyponymy – not all fully represented in this fragment) such as *public discourse* in (a), twice in (d), and again in (g), or just *discourse* in (b) and (g), with further specifications as in

forms of advertising discourse in (c) or *conversational discourse* in (d), and linked to lexically related notions such as *discursive practices* in (b) and (e) and *discursive* in (f) and (h), this short fragment containing many additional patterns of repetition, whether contrastive or not, surrounding concepts such as *tendency*, *change*, *process*, *market*, *social*, *cultural*, and the like.
- Forms of **substitution** such as *Britain and other similar societies* in (a), *late modern societies* in (e), *advanced capitalist societies* in (f), and *modern societies* in (h).
- Putting closely together (here by means of a conjunction) what is conceptually close for the purposes of the current discourse in phrases such as *professional and public service domains* in (b) or *appropriation and simulation* in (d); this is called **structural iconicity** (where 'iconicity' is a general term to describe non-arbitrary aspects of language form, in this case the non-arbitrariness or meaningfulness of structurally conjoining linguistic choices).

Intertextuality

The same example demonstrates the intertextual dimension of linguistic context. There is no way of interpreting (34) unless one is aware of at least three intertextual dimensions.

First, it is the initial paragraph of an instance of an established genre, the 'foreword', which derives its discursive status, and hence part of its meaning, from its intertextual connectedness with the body of a longer text, typically produced in the form of a book. There is no sign of this in the text itself until (h). Yet there is no ambiguity for the interpreter, since the text is materially presented in the first pages of a book (before the regular numbering starts) and is explicitly labelled *Foreword*. Usually, the author of a 'foreword' (as opposed to a 'preface' or 'introduction') is not the author of the anticipated longer text. This has significant functional consequences. Though anticipatory in nature, a foreword is clearly written after reading the full book (usually after its having been accepted for publication) and with the unmistakable purpose of commending its consumption to potential readers (whose interest, at that stage, has already been sufficiently roused for them to acquire a copy of the book) and providing it with a frame of interpretation. This has significant consequences for the linguistic choices that are made. Though much of the typical content, placing the topic and the approach of the book in a wider perspective, could also have been written by the authors themselves, there is usually a clear aspect of evaluation which the authors of the book could not have introduced in the same way. This is even the case for the choice of *significant* in *This book takes a significant step in that direction* (h), and it becomes progressively clearer in the rest of the foreword, where its author makes third-person references to *Sarangi and Slembrouck,* or *they*, or *the authors*, literally praising properties of their work as *a strength of the book*, or their *careful and detailed way* of analysing examples, ending with an unambiguous *This book is to be welcomed as a valuable addition to the growing literature of critical discourse analysis.*

Second, as this last quotation says, the foreword as well as the book are to be situated intertextually in the context of a *growing literature of critical discourse analysis*. In a very real sense, much of what (34) says cannot possibly be understood without a certain degree of knowledge about that literature and the research tradition of which it is the product (and which was judged important enough to warrant a place for it among the established pragmatics-related traditions in the *Handbook of pragmatics*). Going even further, the embeddedness of critical discourse analysis in a much wider range of 'critical' approaches in the social sciences needs to be grasped. The term 'critical' itself requires for its interpretation an awareness of ideas – largely Marxist in origin – about the ideology-sustaining character of the 'traditional' social sciences. This intellectual lineage, in which Fairclough (1989) occupies a specific position, also explains much about the way in which *market*, *appropriation*, *colonisation*, *system*, *capitalist societies* and other concepts are used in (34).

The third intertextual dimension of (34) is its being *about* discourse of a specific type, here characterized as *public discourse*, more precisely the language of bureaucracies. This dimension, however, is not restricted to the seemingly unproblematic fact that bureaucratic language serves as an 'object' out there, about which the authors of the book (and, by extension, the author of the foreword) are trying to convey some scientific knowledge, presenting as many 'samples' as possible in the process. A fundamental aspect is that the authors, as well as their readers, are involved, directly or indirectly, in the communicative processes under investigation as true participants. In addition, all reports on linguistic research being basically *metalinguistic* forms of language use, they usually appeal to such participant knowledge on the part of the readers. Thus in (34), line (c) works as an example because readers can be reasonably assumed to be regularly confronted with advertising and to have some experience with professional and public service domains, so that they can grasp the idea that, indeed, there is a tendency for professions and public services to engage in verbal activities that can be characterized as advertising, whereas advertising is typically associated with purely commercial domains. Further, (d) appeals to experience with conversations to convey an idea about changes in public discourse.

Before leaving this topic, it should be pointed out that we do not extend the meaning of 'intertextuality', as often happens, to the domain of 'voices' or 'polyphony', though there is an area of overlap, as in examples (7) and (8) in section 3.2.1. At the same time, our notion of intertextuality is wider than a common alternative usage in which it comprises only quotations, allusions, and other concrete references to a specific pre-text. (Also see the end of section 5.4.4 for further remarks on intertextuality.)

Sequencing

A universal property of linguistic utterances is the linear ordering of their constituent parts. The sequencing of those parts, therefore, is always a meaningful aspect of linguistic context. This phenomenon has been most extensively studied in conversation analysis, as was cursorily illustrated in section 1.1.4. Sequential properties of linguistic context, however, are equally important in other types of language use. A few hints to that effect can be culled from the foregoing remarks on the intertextual connectedness of example (34). Consider, for instance, the positioning of the 'foreword' in relation to its functional status. Clearly, a metacomment by a scholar other than the author(s) of the main body of a text could also be placed at the end of that text, in which case we would get an 'epilogue'. Such a piece of writing would serve less of a commendatory function (though the aspect of praise might still be expected), nor could it be restricted to a mere framing of the core text. In terms of content, it could presuppose at least partial knowledge of the analyses offered by the authors of the book, with immediate consequences for *what* could be said by way of metacomment, and *how*, and resulting in the expectation that some substance would be *added*. In other words, the linguistic choice-making would have to be thoroughly adapted at various levels of structure and content.

Chapters 4 and 5 of this book will essentially deal, respectively, with *ingredients of* and *operations on* linguistic context.

3.4 *The generation of context*

One of the gravest impediments to the development of a principled theory of pragmatics, avoiding random restrictions on the range of features from the situatedness of language that are allowed into pragmatic analyses, has been an understandable type of vertigo. The apparent unboundedness of context could indeed have a dizzying effect. This is why the Gricean option (see section 1.3) to define meaning – after introducing a clearly pragmatic perspective – entirely in terms of the individual utterer's intentionality, was so easily adopted as a standard for many years. It gave a false impression of manageability. However, the fear of an uncontrollable, ever-widening, extra-linguistic background is based on the misguided view of context as purely a reality 'out there'. In fact, ***contexts** are **generated** in language use*, and thereby restricted in various ways. Though in principle every possible ingredient of a speech event can show up as a contextually relevant element to be taken into account, *not all those ingredients are relevantly mobilized on every occasion.* In other words, out of a virtually infinite range of possibilities, contexts are created by the dynamics of interaction between utterers and interpreters in relation to what is (or is thought to be) 'out there'. As a result, there are boundaries to relevant context, even if they are not stable and permanently negotiable. The challenge is to discover those in specific instances of language use, rather than to impose them on the basis of a pre-conceived theoretical model. At least three phenomena are involved that have to be taken into account: the 'lines of vision' which determine a language user's positioning *vis-à-vis* a surrounding 'world' (see section 3.4.1); the many ways in which contexts can be mentally manipulated (3.4.2); and active processes of contextualization (3.4.3).

Before briefly reviewing those phenomena, two preliminary warnings have to be formulated. First, *some context may be relevant without being 'mobilized'.* Just consider loud noise distracting the utterer and impeding clear reception by the interpreter. Second, *viewing context as generated in language use does not imply radical constructivism.* Radical constructivists would maintain that context is always and (nearly) completely constructed or created by the language user. Such a position, denying the existence of any independent 'reality' (or at least a reality that could be 'known'), cannot explain the interpretability of (35):

(35) Oh, look!

This utterance was made on a gray day when suddenly some sunlight broke through the clouds. No supporting gestures were needed. Nor had the weather been a topic of conversation. The physical environment itself, with its grayness and the sudden contrast of light, provided a sufficient and 'objective' contextual trigger for both uttering and interpreting to make unambiguous communication possible without explicitness. Similarly, there are contextual elements 'out there' – this time of an historical nature – to make (36) 'objectively' funny:

(36) Roederer [was] selling a large consignment of Cristal to South America in 1919. Since this was Champagne which had originally been intended for the Tsar of Russia who, for one reason or another had been unable to pay for the wine of which his court was the sole purchaser [. . .].

This is taken from a guide to the white wines of France, a text which is not trying to make historical jokes. The phrase *for one reason or another* ignores historical context which does not have to be 'constructed' (no matter how disputable some types of historical knowledge may be): Tsar Nicholas II lost his buying power with the February Revolution (March 1917 on our calendar), and he was killed in July 1918; so there was no Tsar to sell wine to in 1919.

3.4.1 Lines of vision

Remember Figure 3.1 in section 3.1. It was suggested that the lines converging in U (for utterer) and I (for interpreter) form 'lines of vision' demarcating the (fuzzy) boundaries of the range of ingredients of the mental, social and physical worlds that can function as contextual objects of adaptability. The inadequacy of this visual representation (more of which will be said in Chapter 6) should be clear by now: similar lines should extend into the world of linguistic context. The figure remains useful, however, to symbolize the 'positioning' of language users which imposes restrictions on the type and amount of 'world' that can be activated. Those restrictions determine the site and the building materials for the context-generation process, both on the utterer's and the interpreter's side. For instance, familiarity with a range of societies is necessary for someone to be able to identify Great Britain as an instance of a society type and thus to talk about *Britain and other similar societies* in (34)(a). It could be precisely the degree of familiarity and the range of societies with which an utterer can be assumed to be familiar that would be questioned by an interpreter who would have doubts about the utterer's claims. Similarly, judgments about where the lines of vision are influence interpretation processes in a court of law or in attempts at historical understanding: the answers to questions as to whether someone could have known something at a given moment are often decisive.

3.4.2 The manipulation of contexts

Language users have a remarkable ability to manipulate contexts by moving in and out of what is commonly referred to as **mental spaces** (cf. Fauconnier 1985). Just consider (37), which is a sentence from the editors' introduction to Bakhtin (1986):

(37) He [Bakhtin] is a figure very much still in the process of becoming who he will be.

This one sentence moves through *time* from present to future, through a *social world* from the historical reality of a person who died 11 years earlier (in 1975) – thus also implying reference to the past – to a timeless scholarly figure whose life continues, and through a *mental and linguistic context* from the realm of bounded scholarly production to less limited potential for interpretation. It is only by intertwining all of these perspectives that (37) can be said and understood.

An equally interesting example is (38), representing the way in which a Berkeley street artist by the name of Swami X used to introduce himself:

(38) I'm the one defined by the *Who's Who* as *What's That?*

In this sentence, the perspectives of the utterer, an outside authority, and the audience, are carefully mixed to obtain the humorous effect.

The manipulation of contexts does not always work in this carefully designed way. Sometimes different mental spaces are mixed inadvertently, as in (39), taken from an old anthropology textbook:

(39) Many of the simpler peoples see no causal connection between conception and childbirth.

Here the anthropologist's frame of interpretation is superimposed on that of the people whose beliefs are being described. For an adequate description of those beliefs, the concept of *conception* could not normally be used in a way that ascribes it as a concept to the people in question, because it implies an understanding of the causal connection they are said not to understand. Hence, (39) only makes sense when *conception* is interpreted as a euphemism for *sexual intercourse*.

3.4.3 Contextualization

In isolation, just about all utterances are highly indeterminate because of the multiplicity of contextual constellations they can fit into. Far from introducing vagueness, allowing context into linguistic analysis is therefore a prerequisite for precision. As said before, however, we should avoid the mistake of reifying or petrifying context. Context contributes to clarity by being subject to negotiation, uptake or rejection, acceptance of uptake or renegotiation, and so on. This process, called **contextualization**, is one of the most important – if not *the* most important – ingredients in the verbal generation of meaning. In other words, contextual interpretations are actively *signalled* and/or *used*, and it is this fact that makes them most *useful* in linguistic analysis, because it is what makes them *traceable*. The signalling can take place at the moment of uttering or, as will be illustrated at length in Chapter 5, interpretations that are used and agreed upon in later interaction may rule out ambiguity in earlier bits of discourse. Consider the many meanings that can be attached to example (12), and what happens to them when (12) becomes part of the following longer exchange (as (40)2. below):

(40) 1. Dave: What should we do now?
2. Mike: Al, I think you should seriously consider resigning.
3. Dave: What good will that do?
4. Mike: It would be a signal that Topcroc is taken seriously. In its reaction, the board can further fuel that perception, even while rejecting the resignation.

(40)4. can be said to contextualize (40)2. retroactively in a way that eliminates a certain kind of ambiguity. At the same time, (40)4. may be contextualizing itself – eliminating further ambiguity – by means of, for instance, a jocular tone and/or special emphasis on *rejecting*.

Gumperz invented the term **contextualization cue** to designate linguistic signals, many of them prosodic (but also including back channel cues, as defined in section 1.1.4, code switching, as described in 4.1, and the like), for the situated understanding of socio-cultural aspects of meaning. The notion can easily be generalized to *any linguistic trace of a contextualization process*. Such traces are potentially to be found at any of the levels of linguistic structure that will pass the review in Chapter 4. (For a further explicit and illustrated treatment of this issue, see section 5.4.2; all later analyses should provide further illustration.)

3.5 *Summary and further reading*

Asking ourselves what it is that language is interadaptable with, we can answer that any ingredient of a communicative event is a potential contextual correlate of adaptability. These potential correlates are 'activated' by being brought within the 'lines of vision' of an utterer (U) and/or interpreter (I). It is particularly important to remember:

- That U and I incorporate multiple functional roles (called 'voices' in the case of U).
- That contextual correlates may be found in the mental, social (or cultural), and physical worlds, and that they also include properties of the linguistic channel that is used and the linguistic context in which the event takes place.
- That context is the product of a generation process involving both what is 'out there' and its mobilization (and sometimes manipulation) by the language users.

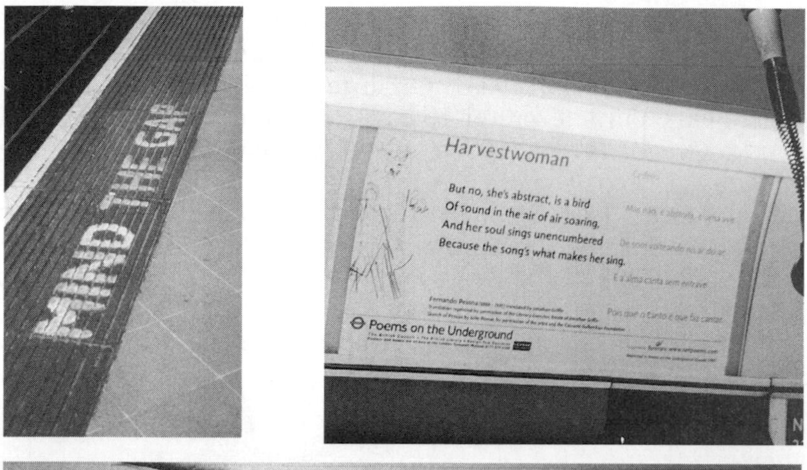

What I love most about you is a space,
A slender, glistening absence that makes my heart fonder,
Buttressed by uncompromising teeth to either side,
Quite regular, quite white, following the usual conventions,
(Until one reaches the left canine,
Which veers off independently; even in dentition you are sound but idiosyncratic)
That small gap in the implacable, otherwise impenetrable, wall of your smile,
Is the making of you.

Mind the Gap
by Elizabeth Speller
Award Winner Theramed Poetry Competition in Association with the Poetry Society
Theramed 2-in-1 toothpaste and anti bacterial mouthwash.

Plate 3.1 The London Underground

For a further elucidation of what is involved in 'context', see Auer (1995), Auer and Di Luzio (eds.) (1992), Duranti and Goodwin (eds) (1992), and Malinowski (1923). On utterer's voices: Bakhtin (1981), Ducrot (1996). On interpreter roles: Clark and Carlson (1982), Eco (1979), McGregor (1986a, 1986b, 1990). On participant roles in general: Hanks (1996a), Irvine (1996). On mental states: Bruner (1990). On social context (settings, institutions, etc.): Fasold (1984), Sarangi and Slembrouck (1996). On time: Comrie (1985), Moeschler (1996). On space: Hanks (1990), Levinson (1992a). On linguistic channel: Halliday (1989), Slembrouck (1995), Tannen (ed.) (1982). On linguistic context: Halliday and Hasan (1976). On the generation of contexts: Fauconnier (1985). On contextualization cues: Gumperz (1982).

3.6 *Research topic*

Any urban environment is a network of dense semiotic fields. Plate 3.1 contains some snapshots from one such field, the London Underground. Describe the messages it contains in terms of their contextual parameters.

4

Structure

Pragmatics, focusing on processes of language use, does not need its own basic unit of analysis, since linguistic choice-making operates on all levels of structure that show variability of any kind. To investigate aspects of the meaningful functioning of language, therefore, the processes in question have to be situated with reference to specific **structural objects of adaptability**, including 'structures' in the strict sense (at various layers or levels of organization) as well as principles of 'structuring'.

The layered structures, it should be noted, cannot simply be seen as a linearly ordered set with increasing complexity. This misguided assumption haunted pragmatics during various episodes of its history. Thus, at one point, there was the idea that entire texts could be analysed analogously to sentences, at a higher level of complexity. Later, when speech acts had been proclaimed as basic units of pragmatic analysis, higher-order structures were often approached as 'macro-speech acts', whether or not that term was used. Instead of just listing hierarchically related layers, an account of linguistic structure in relation to the making of linguistic choices requires a discussion of the following five topics.

First, there are some overarching levels of choice-making: *languages, codes, and styles* (see section 4.1). Second, there are basic *utterance-building ingredients* that are potentially to be found in any utterance and at various levels of structure (see section 4.2). Third, we have to review the functioning of different structural types of *utterances and utterance clusters*, where the term **utterance** is reserved for any stretch of language, no matter how long or short and no matter how many voices it may contain, with a clear beginning and end, produced by the same person(s) (see section 4.3). Fourth, attention has to be paid to *utterance-building principles* which guide the production and interpretation of utterances and utterance clusters (see section 4.4). Finally, the way in which actual choice-making involves all the above needs to be scrutinized, without losing sight of the fact that choices in one area are often co-adaptable with those in another (see section 4.5).

4.1 *Languages, codes and styles*

A decision to use language already involves a choice from a set of options, including all sign systems. As was pointed out in Chapter 3, moreover, there is usually a high degree of interaction between linguistic choices and accompanying forms of non-verbal behaviour, from physical appearance and bodily posture to the production of paralinguistic sounds, laughter, gestures and gaze. Similarly, when the written channel is used, linguistic choices may be underscored with pictorial representations of various kinds. Consigning all else to the province of context, let us stick to language choices for now, i.e. the domain that has traditionally been covered by the term 'variability'.

Once natural language has been opted for, a particular **language** has to be chosen from a stock of roughly 4000–6000 (depending on how one counts). However trivial this may seem, the choice will at least be based on the utterer's language proficiency and assumptions about what the interpreters understand. Thus, when writing a grant application for an American foundation, more often than not it is useful to do so in English. Similarly, speaking at a large international scientific conference is usually done in a narrow range of languages of international communication, again with English at the top. The consequences of this are not quite trivial: they may result, as has often been claimed, in patterns of intellectual dominance and hegemony. Many other contextual objects of adaptability influencing language choice in a consequential way transcend (judgments of) ability and practicability, and are situated in profoundly social dimensions of the world from the start.

Consider, for instance, *bilingual* or *multilingual societies*, a category to which almost all societies belong in one way or another (and to which all of them belong if we take dialectal variation seriously), though they have often been approached as marked or exceptional. In theory there should be two types: societies where different groups speak different languages, and societies where most members speak more than one language. In practice, these are always mixed, even if there are approximations such as Belgium (with its frozen language border separating linguistically different communities, and with only a few pockets of French–Dutch bilinguals) at one end, and Luxembourg (which prides itself on French–German–Letzburgisch trilingualism for most of its native citizens) at the other. The making of choices, at the level of face-to-face communication as well as at the level of institutions, is often a source of *conflict* because it is guided by *political forces*, *ideological forces* and *language attitudes*, usually in ways that make it impossible to keep these three separate. Take the Dutch–French language border in Belgium, making it impossible, for instance, to get subsidized education in Dutch south of that border or in French north of it, or determining whether road signs direct you to Luik or Liège, depending on where you are rather than where you are going. This is the product of a political struggle. Similarly, political forces are activated to achieve standardization, or to develop the language planning that led to trilingualism in Luxembourg or to the language choices in the Tanzanian education system (with little or no schooling in the vernacular languages, primary education mostly in Kiswahili, and all higher forms of education in English). More often than not, political choices are inspired by ideological rather than just practical considerations. The Belgian language border reflects a belief in the normality of territorially based homogeneity. The dominance of Modern Standard Arabic (closely related to the Classical Arabic of the Koran) among the élites throughout the Arab world is partly explained by its practical usefulness in an otherwise diversified linguistic landscape, but it is also related to the politically endorsed conviction that Arabic is one and indivisible, having been given by Allah. The argument of 'having been given by Allah' reveals its own ideological underpinnings, the standard language not being identical to the language of the Koran, and the argument being applied politically to most everything else that one wants to defend forcefully. Permeating all of this, either as source or as consequence, language choices are influenced by language attitudes, i.e. the sentiments inspired by particular languages because of their socio-cultural role as markers of identity (whether at the level of social class, majority–minority relationships, ethnicity, nationality, and the like). The making of language choices, however, does not always have to be situated in a context of conflict. Often a (near-)complete *consensus* can be achieved, as when a community of Zairian expatriates in Antwerp, consisting of speakers of Lingala, Kiswahili and various other African languages, converges without problems around the use of Lingala (see Meeuwis 1997).

Needless to say multilingual settings are extremely adaptable. Any **language contact** situation can lead to patterns of *convergence* (the mutual adoption of linguistic features between different languages, basically a product of *accommodation* to each other's communicative needs, whether conscious or not), *divergence* (the strengthening of differences when, for instance, negative language attitudes block accommodation), language *maintenance* (the preservation of a language or linguistic feature in spite of pressure from another language), language *interference* (the insertion of linguistic features from one language into another), language *shift* (a change in balance between different languages in use in the same society), language *spread* (the geographical widening of the use of a specific language), language *dominance* (where one language is favoured over others), the *minoritization* of a language (the opposite of dominance), and sometimes even language *death* (or, indeed, *revival*). In all of these, various types of language *change* are involved. From a pragmatic point of view, therefore, any analytical attempt to impose stability on a system is by definition suspect. One such attempt was the introduction of the notion of *diglossia*, intended to describe 'relatively stable language situations' in which there is a clear functional distribution between a 'high' variety and a 'low' variety of a language (or sometimes a 'high' language and a 'low' language). Taking Arabic as an example, it should be clear that there is no real stability in the division of labour between the common Modern Standard Arabic and the local varieties of Arabic, even if it has persisted for a long time. For one thing, there is a serious discrepancy between norms and actual usage; for instance, whereas Modern Standard Arabic is generally regarded as the norm for university teaching, it is not always used. Moreover, even the norms are a constant source of dispute and language-related social tension, partly guided by political and religious forces; for instance, many educators contend that access to education in the local variants is an absolute prerequisite for the social advancement of large segments of the population.

Diglossia, however, often involving only variants of the same language, takes us to the notion of 'code', the second – but not completely separable – overarching level of choice-making. We define a **code** as any distinguishable variant of a language, involving systematic sets of choices, whether linked to a specific geographical area, a social class, an assignment of functions, or a specific context of use. The range of codes for any given language spoken in a sizeable community is virtually infinite: there is often a *standard dialect*, as well as *regional dialects* and *sociolects* (some representing 'elaborated' codes that can be used in a wide range of contexts, others showing a more 'restricted' code confining their use to face-to-face conversation within narrow circles), and even *idiolects* (characterizing the usage of an individual); there are sometimes group-specific languages, either for the initiated few, such as *argots* or *slangs* (comparable to the situation-specific versions of a language referred to in section 3.2.3), or for larger segments of a population, such as *women's language* as opposed to *men's language*; there are domain-specific or activity-specific *jargons* or *registers* (closely related to, but not completely covering, what we have called *genres* of language use in section 1.4), ranging from literary language to legalese, journalese, bureaucratese, political language, scientific language, medical language, the language of advertising, the language of aviation, etc.; finally, there are also context-specific adaptations of a language, for instance where it serves as a lingua franca for communication between non-native speakers, or when a native speaker simplifies it to *foreigner talk* in order to be understood by a non-native speaker with a poor command of the language.

Once chosen, a language or a code does not have to be held on to at all cost. In fact, **code switching**, a cover term for language or code alternations, is an extremely common occurrence and a favoured strategy, especially in oral discourse. It may serve many different functions. In (1), for instance, which is the translation of a Moroccan Arabic joke, code switching is a way of circumventing a social taboo.

(1) Two flies are copulating in front of a boy and his mother.
Child: Do you know what these two flies are doing?
Mother: No.
Child: Ils font l'amour. [French for 'They are making love']
Mother: OK, OK.
Child: You know, if I'd said this in Arabic, you would have left the room immediately.

Because languages and codes are associated with places, groups, activities or functions, switching is one of the resources for speakers and addressees to interactionally generate the meaning of their social world, to negotiate mutual investment in the linguistic marketplace. It can be used to show affect and solidarity, or to mark and maintain power relationships. Thus when Jesse Jackson, in one of his campaign speeches in 1984, makes a switch from standard American English to Black English by saying:

(2) Well, I done a li'l observin' now

followed by a long, metaphorical, crescendo episode of a type common in African American public rhetoric, he signals identification with his predominantly black audience (see Verschueren 1989a; the example is studied more closely in section 8.2.1). But when a German beggar, after holding a conversation with a Turkish–German passer-by in standard German, suddenly turns to 'foreigner talk' to say:

(3) Türkishmann du? ['Turkish man you?']

he restores a threatened power relationship by putting the immigrant 'in his place' (see Hinnenkamp 1991).

In the context of interethnic or intercultural communication, codes that are restricted to or typical of the verbal behaviour of ethnically or socio-culturally identified groups in specific settings are often called **communicative styles**. Thus in example (2), Jesse Jackson can be said to switch from a general American to an African American communicative style, a move which may cause interpretation difficulties for white Americans who happen to witness the event. Since properties of such codes or communicative styles are highly subject to habit formation (often carrying meanings that are hard to question consciously, as with certain aspects of prosody), they may indeed cause communicative problems. At the same time, their adaptability should be heeded, remembering that an intercultural encounter may change aspects of code or style in unexpected ways, whereas an expectation of problems may drastically heighten the tolerance for otherwise unintelligible utterances, thereby strengthening the participants' capacity to interpret.

Although communicative styles, which may characterize different variants of the same language, are in fact codes, the term 'style' can be used to refer to a third overarching level of linguistic choice-making in addition to language and code. We reserve **style** to describe variability along dimensions of *formality* and *informality*, from casual or colloquial speech to highly formal uses. All languages are amenable to variable stylistic use, and so are most codes, though some codes (such as argot or slang) are usually to be found at the informal end of the scale, whereas others (such as legalese) are typically formal.

Language, code and style were said to be overarching levels of choice-making, because the differences between languages, between codes, and between styles are made up of *systematic sets of choices* from utterance-building ingredients (see section 4.2), from types of utterances and utterance clusters (see section 4.3), and from utterance-building principles (discussed in section 4.4), the relevance of the latter two being somewhat higher for codes and for styles than for languages.

4.2 *Utterance-building ingredients*

In theory, this section should contain a full description of all properties of 'grammars' (in the widest sense as complete descriptions of languages as formal systems) which language users have at their disposal as resources for making linguistic choices. In practice, that would be an impossible task. Remember, however, the brief hints that were given earlier (in section 0.2 on pages 2–6) on the relevance of pragmatics for the study of different levels of linguistic structure. It is at all those different levels, traditionally covered by different components of a theory of linguistics, that utterance-building ingredients are to be situated: from sound, via morphemes and words, to clauses, sentences and propositions. Let us briefly review a few phenomena here, most of which have received a good deal of attention in the pragmatic literature.

4.2.1 Sound structure

At the level of sound structure, the most commonly studied features have been aspects of **prosody**, especially **intonation**, because of their prominent functioning as contextualization cues. Clearly, often it is intonation that turns syntactic structures into statements or questions. And in spite of a certain degree of correspondence across languages in this domain (e.g. with a high and/or rising contour to mark questions and a low and/or falling contour to mark statements, and with similarities in ways of signalling affect, intention or emotion), there are significant differences as well. It is because of such differences that an Asian woman saying *Gravy!* with a falling intonation when she wants to know whether a person she is serving wants gravy on his or her meat or not, is perfectly polite within her own communicative style, but may be perceived as rude and unfriendly by a British person (see Gumperz 1982). In any conversation, or in conversational story-telling, intonation is a major clue to the interpretation of what is said. Similarly, **pausing** systems and the '**chunking**' of the stream of uttered sounds are some of the major indicators of how content is organized in spoken discourse. The same goes for patterns of **hesitation**, **stress**, **speed**, **rhythm**, and the like, which are often responsible for much of the rhetorical build-up of spoken discourse. Even aspects of **voice quality** that are harder to describe constantly provide clues to the interpretation of utterances. Consider the following comment by Hedrick Smith (1976: 234) on what is said by the leader of a band which has just played the Lara's theme from *Doctor Zhivago* (strictly prohibited at the time) at the Berlin restaurant in Moscow, after being asked to play it again:

(4) 'No, you must have been mistaken. We didn't play it and so you didn't hear it!' The reply was spoken in *that frozen Soviet voice that is less a denial of the actual truth than a rejection of an inconvenient one.* (Italics added)

However intangible, such judgments are always made.

Not only these obvious usage aspects of sound structure are pragmatically important. Sometimes the types of codes distinguished in the previous section are to a large extent definable in terms of systematic alternations in the **phoneme system** of a language. In addition to the dialectal variations we are all familiar with (but which function in a more complicated way than is often assumed, involving for instance a good deal of code switching), there are cases where, as reported by

Everett (1985) on Pirahã, a Brazilian language of the Mura family, phonemic adaptations take place on the basis of contextual circumstances such as the presence or absence of foreigners.

Finally, it is often sound features, such as stress, that disambiguate syntactic structures in discourse, as in *John has plans to* ***leave*** (i.e. 'intends to leave') versus *John has* ***plans*** *to leave* (i.e. 'has blueprints to deliver').

4.2.2 Morphemes and words

At the level of morphemes and words, we should remember earlier remarks on **derivation**, **inflection** and **compounding** (in section 0.2 on pages 3–4), the functioning of **anaphora** (see sections 1.1.1 and 3.3.2), as well as the fact that a large portion of the literature on presuppositions hinges on observations related to the implicit meaning carried along by the choice of certain words, including **nouns**, particular **verbs**, many **particles**, and **scalar notions** (see the examples under (2) in section 1.1.3).

More generally, **lexical meaning** provides an unlimited resource for the generation of meaning in language use. The very structuring of the lexicon of natural languages is suited to that end. Both the word-internal semantic structure and the overall semantic structure of the vocabulary are partial reflections of patterns observable in the world while answering the need for cognitive economy. Just as it is impossible for a language user to say explicitly everything one means, it is impossible for a natural language to provide labels for all distinguishable aspects of 'reality'. The consequence for *word-internal semantic structures* has been the organization of word meaning around relatively clear **prototypes**, leaving room for fuzziness on the edges. Thus a prototypical *bird* has feathers, can fly, has a beak and lays eggs. All these properties are combined in eagles and robins, which are therefore prototypical examples. The fact that neither penguins nor ostriches can fly makes them less typical examples of birds, though there is enough **family resemblance** (to use Wittgenstein's term) left for inclusion in the category and conceptualization with reference to the prototype. What makes the creation of prototypes possible is the existence of 'natural discontinuities' in the world, or 'feature clusters' which make it predictable, for instance, that when we see a flying animal (barring insects), it will most probably have feathers and a beak and it will lay eggs, with a few exceptions (and keeping in mind that not all the features in the cluster have the same power of prediction or 'cue validity' – think of the laying of eggs, which birds share with reptiles and fish). By capitalizing on this structuring of reality, human cognition can cope with the multitude of distinguishable entities in a relatively economical fashion. At the same time, these properties of lexical meaning make words usable in multiple ways, thus necessitating the negotiation of meaning in interaction, and allowing for a wide range of strategies of use. The processes producing relatively stable cores of meaning are not restricted to nouns. Consider the speech act verb *to congratulate*. A prototypical congratulation is (i) an expression of the utterer's being pleased, and (ii) about the interpreter's success in doing or obtaining something important. That is why (5), a headline from the *International Herald Tribune*, is felt to deviate from expected usage.

(5) Begin [then Israeli Prime Minister] congratulates Sadat [then Egyptian President] on *their* Nobel [the Nobel Peace Prize which they jointly received].

Clearly, (ii) is being tampered with. Similarly, (i) may be absent from many formal acts of congratulating, which can nevertheless still be described by means of the verb *to congratulate*. (Compare this to what happens with *to thank* in the conversation quoted as research topic 4. in section 1.6.) The more abstract a concept becomes, as in the case of *prosperity*, *peace*, or *democracy*, the harder it will become to precisely define the semantic core and the more room there will be for negotiation and manipulation. Yet even those terms tend to be used *as if* there were a clear prototypical meaning. The rhetorical consequences of this will become clear later (see section 8.2.2).

As to the overall *semantic structure of the vocabulary*, it has long been noted that it is hierarchically structured and that not all levels of the hierarchy are equally salient. It is again an interaction between the structure of the world and the demand for cognitive economy that creates a set of **basic level terms**, i.e. those that would be most readily used to identify an object. Thus, if you present an apple to someone and ask *What's this?* the answer is more likely to be *an apple* than either *fruit* or *a Golden Delicious*, unless the communicative needs of the moment dictate the choice of the superordinate term (e.g. in a classroom context where the topic is the difference between fruits and vegetables) or of the subordinate terms (e.g. in a fruit store). Because of the experiential basis of this aspect of conceptual structuring, the basic level terms are not necessarily the same for all speakers of the same language. Thus, a life-long city-dweller is not unlikely to have *bird* as a basic level term rather than *sparrow* and *robin*, which are obvious choices in an environment with many kinds of birds. Differences may even be more subtle: inhabitants of some pigeon-infested European cities may be expected to have *pigeon* as a basic level term for pigeons and *bird* for all other birds, so that cognitive structure and biological hierarchy cease to coincide.

Given a pragmatic perspective on lexical meaning, allowing for variability and negotiability both in relation to word-internal semantic structures and in relation to the semantic relationships between words in the vocabulary, it usually makes little sense to engage in word *classifications*, which tend to be based on a false sense of stability. Rather, to determine lexical meaning, the functioning of words along a range of relevant *semantic dimensions* should be systematically scrutinized. (An example of this approach, as well as further justification, is to be found in Verschueren 1985a.)

Note how the composition of the lexicon of a natural language can be said to 'generate' a semantic pattern organizing whatever serves as context and whatever may have to be singled out for specific reference in language use. Just as the generation of context in actual language use (see section 3.4), this is a process involving interaction between mind and outside reality. This counts for lexical items belonging to all three types of signs distinguished by Charles Sanders Peirce, from the most concrete *icons* (resembling what they refer to, as in the case of onomatopoeia) over *indices* (merely 'pointing to', as when an expletive serves as an indicator of a state of mind) to the most abstract and arbitrary *symbols* (associated with a referent by convention, as is the case with most words).

4.2.3 Clauses and sentences

There is barely a **syntactic construction** type that has not received attention from a pragmatic point of view. As a matter of fact, though much of the inspiration was found in the work of philosophers, pragmatics was brought into linguistics by syntacticians seeking to solve problems by allowing both meaning and context to enter description and explanation (see Chapter 9). Some remarks on the pragmatics of syntactic choices were made before (in sections 0.2 on page 4 and 1.1.3). Remember also that one of the most-used pragmatic notions, the *speech act* (see section 1.1.2) is essentially a sentence-level action concept. This is why, for instance, in attempts at classifying speech acts, attention was paid to syntactic correlates (such as interrogative sentences for questions, imperatives for directives, and the like). The fact that speech act theory was said not to be a complete pragmatic theory because it focused exclusively on sentence-level structures, or that one-to-one correspondences between speech acts and sentence types were said to be illusions, should not distract from the attention that needs to be paid to aspects of form. Without the notion of **sentence types**, for instance, it would be hard to discuss the kind of implicitness inherent in what has commonly been called indirect speech acts, no matter whether this terminology is still used or not.

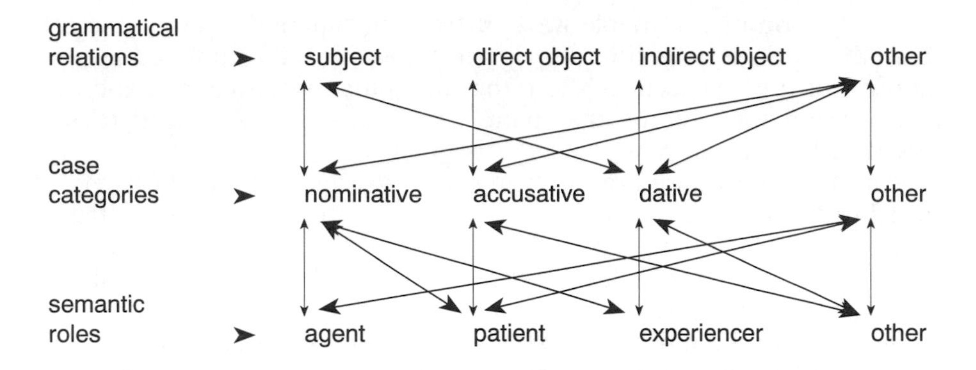

Fig. 4.1 Grammatical relations, case categories, semantic roles (from Rudzka-Ostyn 1995)

A fruitful focus of attention at the clause level is the domain of functional relations between nominal contituents: **grammatical relations**, **case categories** and **semantic roles**. As is shown in Figure 4.1, these three types of relations interact in complex and interesting ways, with case categories serving as interface between semantic roles and syntactic functions.

These distinctions cover a range of grammatical tools which language users have at their disposal to conceptualize events in different ways, i.e. the options from which choices are made to generate meaning at the clause level. Just consider the difference between (6) and (7).

(6) We don't manage to sell those shirts.
(7) Those shirts don't sell.

Sentence (7), in contrast to (6), puts the patient of *sell*, i.e. *those shirts*, in subject position, thus diverting the attention from the agent we, and ascribing the lack of success in attempts to sell the shirts to an inherent property, say 'sellability', of those shirts. Though equivalents of *to sell* in other languages may not offer the same specific possibilities, and though, more generally, different languages offer different 'standard' perspectives on comparable states of affairs (as in *I am cold* or *I am sad* versus Russian forms which would literally mean 'It is cold to me' or 'It is sad to me'), similar strategies of meaning generation are to be found in all languages. Nor does this have to be restricted to aspects of propositional content. For Polish, for instance, some uses of the dative forms of personal pronouns have been described which signal mainly affect, involvement and solidarity (see Rudzka-Ostyn 1995). Some would even go as far as to ascribe different world views or socio-cultural value systems to speakers of different languages depending on their variable ways of framing functional relations. But here there is a serious risk of forgetting the caveats formulated before about 'culture' (in section 3.2.3), the manipulability involved, and the basic pragmatic premiss that there are few – if any – fixed form–function relationships.

Another interesting area with important pragmatic ramifications is **word order**. Even in languages with so-called 'free word order', there is usually an ordering of constituents (subject, verb, object) (SVO) that is more common or less marked than the other possibilities. Thus word order is never really 'free', only the constraints may be different (ranging from the more 'grammatical' to the more 'pragmatic'). What determines deviations from a basic word order in most languages is usually the need to foreground or emphasize a constituent – often with further implications of meaning. Thus the basic SVO order in English, as in (8), can be changed to the object, subject, verb (OSV) order in (9).

(8) You won't get more money.
(9) More **money** you won't get (– only more **work**).

Sentence (9) would normally require a heavy emphasis on *money*, which implies a contrast that can be made explicit, as with *only more work*. In certain contexts, the 'deviations' may also become standard, as when newspaper quotations routinely (though not necessarily) replace the English SVO basic word order with an object, verb, subject (OVS) word order as in (10) or an object, subject, verb (OSV) word order as in (11):

(10) 'It's provocative,' said Dr Regina Ziegler, an epidemiologist at the National Cancer Institute. (*International Herald Tribune*, Friday, 2 May 1997)
(11) Swastikas and other fascist symbols were scrawled on tombstones in a Jewish cemetary southwest of Zagreb, a human rights group reported Thursday. (Idem)

This ordering is motivated by the fact that the content of what is quoted (with or without quotation marks) is the more salient part of the sentence, even if it is not too substantial, as in (10). The choice between OVS and OSV seems to be determined by processibility: the subject precedes the verb, unless the subject requires too much further information for the object and the verb to be close enough together for easy interpretation. Constraints on cognitive processing are never far away, also in the explanation of some universal tendencies in word order. As Comrie says,

> [. . .] the tendency for subjects to precede objects [. . .] may be explainable in terms of the correlation between subject and agent, the correla-

> tion between object and patient, and the tendency for agents to be more salient perceptually than patients. (1981: 88)

(See Figure 4.1 for the correlations involved.)

Whatever **rules of 'grammar'** are basic to the construction of clauses and sentences in a given language, we should remember that from a pragmatic point of view they merely reflect structural habits which can be broken in a variety of ways, though rarely as drastically as in the poem we quoted in the discussion of negotiability (in section 2.2). What lends the rules their relative stability is the fact that straying too far from the habitual path renders interpretation too difficult for a reasonable degree of communicative success to be expected.

4.2.4 Propositions

Propositions structurally coincide with clauses or sentences. Yet they deserve a separate treatment here because the term itself invokes a different perspective, one that goes beyond formal structure to probe into the 'formatting' of meaning, and because its various aspects have been the frequent subject of pragmatic investigations.

The basic constituents of a 'pure' proposition are in grammatical terms **subject** and **predicate** and in semantic terms **reference** and **predication**. In other words, something is 'predicated' about a person, thing, process, event or action pointed at by means of a 'referring expression'. The point has been made repeatedly that referring, or establishing reference, is already an action, often accomplished interactively. A great deal of energy is spent in verbal interaction, even if unwittingly, in making sure or trying to negotiate what it is that one is talking about. One reason is that the same form can have many different referents, whilst the same referent may be pointed at by means of different forms; note that this observation goes far beyond the realm of strict homonymy and synonymy. Another is the difference in 'lines of vision' between utterer and interpreter. At a more fundamental level, some referents may simply be very difficult to identify, or it may be useful to promote one type of identification over another. This is not only the case with abstract notions, such as *democracy*, which may require an entire conversation to reach the point where the term can simply be used in a mutually comprehensible way. Even the identity of concrete objects is negotiable, and this negotiability may be the prerequisite for any further interaction to take place. Imagine that you receive a telephone call from an unknown person who introduces himself as a representative of FilterX, the world's leading manufacturer of air cleansing devices.

After finding out that you have children who may suffer from minor allergies so that you are interested in clean air, he asks (12):

(12) Would you be interested in a demonstration of our air cleansing devices in your home?

If you accept this offer, it may turn out that the *air cleansing device* is what you would normally refer to as a *vacuum cleaner.* The FilterX representative knows very well that he would probably not get his offer for a demonstration accepted if he had proposed to show you a vacuum cleaner. Once in your home, much of the demonstration may still concentrate on the air cleansing capabilities of the device, presenting its use as a vacuum cleaner as rather marginal (while maintaining that you could not get a better vacuum cleaner either). And whether you end up buying the machine will be largely a function of how successful the representative is in making you think about it in the terms he proposes. Sherzer (1987) reports on bargaining practices in a Bhojpuri-speaking community in northern India, where both the social status of the buyer and the price to be paid for milk products are negotiated by means of the choice of labels to refer to the products in question (where a label for a high-quality product may be used for a lower-quality product to get a higher price, and vice versa). A comparison with the vacuum cleaner is not far away. In other cases reference may be accomplished by means of expressions that are entirely uninterpretable unless one already knows who or what is being referred to. Consider (13):

(13) The *you know who* will be gone for the weekend. Enough time for us to get *the thing* finished.

The 'syntactic amalgam' in the first sentence, putting the complete clause structure *you know who* in a nominal constituent slot, is designed for vagueness, as when it is necessary to hide someone's identity from a bystander or overhearer. Though equally vague, *the thing* is a more common form of expression, which has come to assume the function of anaphora, pointing back to a referent the identity of which has already been established in the preceding discourse.

What about predication? 'Predicating' something about a person, thing, process, event or action, can be done in various ways. Just consider (14) to (16):

(14) What a poor man!
(15) That man is poor.
(16) That man lives in poverty.

The reference remains constant, and the content of the predication in each of these sentences (whether it takes the shape of an adjective, with or without copula, or a full verb phrase) is very similar. Usage conditions, however, vary greatly.

Various kinds of meaning ingredients contribute to the 'modification' or 'colouring' of the proposition or reference-and-predication structure. As a general cover term, we may use **modality** (called **modalization** in systemic functional grammar, and not to be confused with grammatical **mood**, which is a morphosyntactic property of verb forms – such as indicative, subjunctive, and imperative – on a par with tense, aspect and voice). Modality is an inherently pragmatic phenomenon. It involves the many ways in which attitudes can be expressed towards the 'pure' reference-and-predication content of an utterance, signalling factuality, degrees of certainty or doubt, vagueness, possibility, necessity, and even permission and obligation. This may be accomplished by means of verbal moods (only to a limited degree in present-day English, though the subjunctive used to fulfil a certain range of these functions), modal auxiliaries (such as *can*, *could*, *may*, *might*, *shall*, *should*, *will*, *would*, *must*, *ought to*, and *have to*), adjectives (such as *probable* in *It is probable that . . .*), adverbs (such as *really*, *certainly*, *possibly*, *probably*, *inevitably*, and the like), and the so-called 'sentence adverbs' (such as *frankly*, *seriously*, *obviously*, when used to introduce a sentence as in *Frankly, I don't give a damn!*). A special kind of modality, called **evidentiality**, marks the source of information, for instance in terms of objectivity or subjectivity (which some languages signal in the morphology of verbs, others lexically – as in *I guess . . .* – or by prosodic means).

Some linguists include **negation** in the scope of modality. Whether this is justified or not, 'negating' is clearly an operation that affects propositions. But since it does so in ways that cannot be captured in strictly logical positive–negative terms, it is an interesting phenomenon in its own right from a pragmatic point of view. Let us look at just a few aspects of the negation problem. First, a negation could often be replaced by a semantically near-equivalent positive form, but the choice is rarely neutral. Thus consider (17) and (18):

(17) Jack's behaviour is not acceptable.
(18) Jack's behaviour is atrocious.

Both sentences appeal to the same set of norms in terms of which Jack's behaviour is being evaluated. But though *atrocious*, when talking about behaviour, is one of the many possible opposites of *acceptable*, the negation *not acceptable* is at most a semantic approximation, and by no means a usage equivalent of *atrocious*. The intricate relationship between such seemingly opposite terms, where the negation of one should in theory be equal to the other in its positive form, becomes even clearer when we try the other way around: *not atrocious* is not at all equivalent to *acceptable*.

A second interesting fact is the potential 'scope ambiguity' of negation. When a German leader is reported to have said (19):

(19) We Germans will not let ourselves be divided

different interpretations (which, in the original spoken form, could be underscored prosodically) are possible depending on the context: (i) there are attempts to divide the Germans, but 'we Germans' *will not let ourselves be divided*, with the entire predication within the scope of negation; (ii) Germans being perfectly capable of dividing themselves on their own initiative, will *not let* themselves be divided by others; (iii) there may be others who will let themselves be divided, but *not we Germans*. Given our knowledge of recent history, we can rank these possibilities according to their degree of likelihood as (i)–(iii)–(ii).

Third, there are different ways of handling negation in discourse, which are sometimes language-specific. Consider a regular question–answer pair as in (20):

(20) Q: Did Czechoslovakia not split up a couple of years ago?
A: Yes.

Depending on the negation system one uses the answer *Yes* may either express agreement with the predication within the scope of *not*, namely that Czechoslovakia did indeed split up a couple of years ago, or it may accept the negation *not*, thus contradicting any suggestion that Czechoslovakia split up a couple of years ago. Meeuwis (1994) has documented a case in which different negation styles lead to misunderstandings between Flemish instructors and Korean engineers in the context of a training programme in a multinational company.

4.2.5 Suprasentential units

No doubt, linguistic units of a higher order than sentences can still be identified as utterance-building ingredients. For instance, a long monograph contains chapters, sections and paragraphs. But these have few, if any, structural properties that do not follow from principles of organizing content, a subject which we will address later (in section 4.4), and some aspects of which have already been addressed in the discussion of linguistic context (see section 3.3.2).

4.3 *Utterances and utterance clusters*

As said in the introduction to this chapter, we reserve the term **utterance** for any stretch of language, no matter how long or short and no matter how many voices it may contain, with a clear beginning and end, produced by the same person(s). Examples range from one-word sentences, over speech acts constituting a turn in a conversation, to multi-volume novels. **Utterance clusters** are organized conglomerates of utterances. A typical example would be a conversation, or written correspondence. As was anticipated in the discussion of the utterer's many voices (section 3.2.1), many of the more complex utterances may contain various kinds or layers of **embedded utterances** (or **utterance**^{E}), as when quotations are used in newspaper reports, or even **embedded utterance clusters** (or **utterance cluster**^{E}), as when a novel contains conversations between some of the characters.

The most widely studied, pragmatically defined, utterance types are no doubt those commonly labelled **speech acts**, which are structurally situated at the sentence level, so that often they occur as utterance constituents rather than complete utterances. This level varies itself from one-word structures as in (21) to (24), to complex syntactic constructions with various layers of embedding as in (25).

(21) Ouch!
(22) God!
(23) Sit!
(24) Yes.
(25) This subvocal tracking of the course of sexually climactic experience is a display available to both sexes, but said to be increasingly fashionable for females – amongst whom, of course, the sound tracing can be strategically employed to delineate an ideal development in the marked absence of anything like the real thing.

The one-word speech acts are often exclamations with only an expressive content, such as the expression of pain in (21), and the expression of anything varying from pleasant surprise to utter revulsion in (22). But they may also be orders, as in (23). Or, as in (24), they may constitute complete answers to a question, thus representing a propositional content and a speech act structure which is potentially as complex as the one in (25). Sentence (25), which is Goffman's (1981: 106) description of *the sexual moan*, could be presented as one 'statement', though the part before the dash already contains two separable ones, embedding a 'definition' in the reference part of the first, and though the part following the dash has the status of a 'comment' on the second.

Because of the difficulties involved in applying speech act concepts to more complex structures such as (25), which is by no means the most complex one could think of, there has been a tendency to approach speech act theory as a dead body rather than to use its insights. Most of its achievements, however, can be salvaged if we are prepared to reject both its basic goals and its methodological stance. The ambition of orthodox speech act theory was to provide universally valid descriptions for universal categories of linguistic action. From that point of view, any essential link between those categories and the English verbs used to label them was rejected. This position failed to take into account one important aspect of linguistic behaviour (to which a lot of attention will be paid in Chapter 6), namely that it shares with all other forms of social behaviour the property that it is always interpreted by the people involved in it, that there is no way of understanding social behaviour without insight into those interpretations as well, and that for such interpretations people have habitual concepts available, many of which happen to be lexicalized in language-specific ways. Examples of such lexicalizations, verbs like *to ask*, *to order*, *to promise*, serve as labels for the types of acts analysed in speech act theory, which makes it hard to deny the connection. If we reinterpret speech act analyses (as presented in section 1.1.2) as analyses of lexicalized verbal action categories, we also have to reject the methodological approach in terms of necessary and sufficient conditions. Bearing in mind what we have said about the conceptual structuring of lexical meaning (in section 4.2), we may conclude that Searlean speech act analyses are reasonably accurate approximations of the prototypical instances of verbal behaviour describable by means of the English verbs used as labels.

Rather than destroy the content of speech act theory, such a seemingly destructive salvaging operation can actually protect it. Many attempts have been made to criticize Searle-type analyses in terms of their own methodology by refining the proposals for necessary and sufficient conditions, but only arriving at formulations against which again counterexamples can be found, thus leading to infinite regress and leaving very little content at the end of the road. The same process has haunted attempts to improve Searle's classification of illocutionary acts. The relevance of the class of 'expressives', for instance, can be denied on the basis of Searle's own classification principles and parameters. If expressives are defined as those speech acts whose function is to express a psychological state, this class should logically include all assertives (expressing a belief), all directives (conveying a wish), and all commissives (expressing an intention). After accepting the verb-dependent nature of the traditional speech act categories, comparing the availability of verbs across languages may confirm the significance of a separate class of expressives, even though the latter would have to be redefined as that class of speech acts whose function is to express an emotion that an utterer expects an interpreter to attach particular importance to. Evidence for this was found, for instance, in a contrastive study of the lexicalization versus non-lexicalization patterns of expressions of emotion (Verschueren 1985a, chapter 6). Consider, for instance, the difference between (26) and (27), and between (28) and (29).

(26) I am sorry that you could not come over last night.
(27) I am sorry that I could not come over last night.
(28) I like this plan.
(29) I like your plan.

Although (26) and (27) both express a very similar feeling of 'regret', the lexicalization pattern of the conceptual domain of linguistic behaviour in English (and many other languages) provides a specialized term for the description of the act performed in (27) as an expression of a psychological state, namely *to apologize*, while no such term is available for the act in (26). And though also (28) and (29) express the same state of 'liking' a specific plan, (29) counts as a *compliment*, whereas (28) would normally be described as a plain statement unless 'the plan' can be interpreted as 'your plan'. The difference really seems to lie in the kind and degree of interpreter involvement. In (27), for instance, the addressee is presumably the inviting party who could be offended by the utterer's not having come, so that an expression of regret is called for to 'excuse' the utterer by implying that his or her actions did not match his or her wishes.

When putting speech act theory in this perspective, the vast literature on speech acts provides us with extensive resources of information on utterance types at the sentence level, including acts of affirming, announcing, claiming, estimating, guessing, insisting, stating, swearing, telling, warning, ordering, permitting, promising, threatening, advising, instructing, inviting, prescribing, proposing, requesting, asking, begging, suggesting, apologizing, forgiving, greeting, praising, thanking, wishing, blessing, naming, and the like. Any list of this kind, however, contains numerous concepts (e.g. announcing, instructing, prescribing, proposing) which may also be realized in verbal action types which are structurally situated at the suprasentential level. This means that the reinterpretation of speech act theory we have proposed also forces us to abandon – as we have done in this book from the start – the idea of any structurally basic unit of analysis for pragmatics.

At the suprasentential level, a wide range of **discourse types** have been studied. They include types of **monologic discourse** (often containing embedded dialogue, always being 'dialogic' in the sense explained before in section 3.2.1, often manifested as written **text**, but regularly delivered orally or showing the kinds of mixed channel status hinted at in section 3.3.1) such as advertisements, comic strips, directions for use, essays, jokes, various kinds of legal texts (contracts, treaties, testaments), letters, literary texts (poems, fables, novels, short stories, plays), lectures, sermons, political speeches, many kinds of narrative, obituaries, political documents (e.g. an election manifesto), newspaper reports, medical reports, scientific reports, and so on. They also include types of **dialogic discourse** (often **conversational**, always constituting utterance clusters, and often recurring at an embedded level both in monologic and other dialogic discourse types) such as adult–child and child–child conversations, conversations between native speakers and non-native speakers or simply between different non-native speakers of the chosen language, classroom conversation, conversational narrative, courtroom proceedings, counselling, service encounters, dinner conversations, discussions, debates (in parliament, on television), negotiations, emergency calls, fortune telling, job interviews, medical history-taking and other doctor–patient interactions, cross-examinations, formal meetings, sales encounters, cocktail conversations, talk shows, telephone conversations, therapeutic discourse, e-mail exchanges, letter writing, human–machine interaction, and so on.

Given this enormous range of utterance and utterance cluster types, it goes without saying that examples in the remainder of this book will have to be restricted to a limited choice of samples, which we hope will be sufficiently representative to introduce the basic theoretical apparatus and methodological tools. It should be clear, furthermore, that the labels used to designate these types (whether sentence-level speech acts or suprasentential monologic or dialogic utterances or utterance clusters) do not really describe *structures*. They describe *uses of language* which we will not be able to define further until we start looking at them as processes in the next chapter (see especially section 5.2).

4.4 *Utterance-building principles*

As briefly stated before (at the end of section 4.2), structuring at the suprasentential level is mostly a matter of organizing content. This does not mean that content organization is not a driving force at the sentence level, but only that more purely 'formal' criteria are more clearly operative at the lower levels of structure. This phenomenon follows from human processing capabilities which already diminish the role of grammatical rules within the boundaries of a sentence when it becomes structurally more complex, not only because it becomes more difficult to keep track of grammatical correspondences in more complex structures but also because meaning itself soon takes over as a principle of organization. Just consider (30):

(30) Perhaps the biggest gain in the new therapies is that, unlike chemotherapy drugs, their side effects are few and mild.

Most readers of the newspaper article from which this sentence was taken will find it entirely unproblematic. Yet, a strictly grammatical processing of this sentence would require us to hypothesize about specific patterns of ellipsis: we would have to assume that *unlike chemotherapy drugs* stands for *unlike is the case with chemotherapy drugs*. Otherwise, (30) would lead to the conclusion that while 'the side effects of the new therapies are few and mild', 'chemotherapy drugs are not few and mild', rather than that 'the side effects of chemotherapy drugs are not few and mild'. The grammatical detour, however, is unlikely to be made either in production or in interpretation. In a case like this, which is typical rather than exceptional, both uttering and interpreting are guided by meaning that is built up in the discourse (the text in question being presented as a report on new developments in the treatment of cancer made possible by advances in biotechnology), while relying on information that is contextually given (in particular, some assumed general knowledge about applications of chemotherapy and its unpleasant side effects). Comparable examples of a more conventionalized kind are provided, for instance, by the so-called *dangling participles*, as in (31).

(31) Thinking about the problem of co-reference, the sudden ringing of the phone startled me.

Here the implicit subject of the non-finite clause does not correspond with the explicit subject of the main clause. Following the 'regular' rules of English grammar, the implicit subject should have been made explicit. Yet the desired interpretation of this sentence is not going to be blocked by the fact that it was not.

Remembering that the generation of meaning is what language use is all about, it can be hardly surprising that the main utterance-building principles (extending further into the building of utterance clusters), guiding the production and interpretation of utterances (and utterance clusters), should be related to the organization of content. A formal manifestation of this was already discussed under the label of **cohesion** (see section 3.3.2). At the level of meaning itself, the conglomerate of organizational principles involved could be captured with the term **coherence**, or, if allowed to transcend theory-specific idiosyncrasies of the label, **relevance** (see sections 1.1.3 and 1.2). Though the need for coherence or relevance derives from what utterers and interpreters set out to do at the discourse level, some of the 'work' is clearly reflected at the clause or sentence level in what is commonly called its **information structure** and/or **thematic structure** (depending on theory-internal options; the Hallidayan framework, for instance, handles a strict distinction between the two). That is why, for purposes of presentation, we will distinguish between principles of sentential utterance building as opposed to suprasentential utterance building.

4.4.1 Sentential utterance building

Returning to one of our earlier examples, let us now look at the complete opening paragraph of the editorial introduction to *The world in 1996*.

(32) (a) 1996 will be a year of prosperity and peace. (b) The world will move another notch away from the conventional wisdoms of the previous generation. (c) The American presidential campaign, which runs from the snows of the New Hampshire primary until November 5th, will be the setting for the political ideas that will hold sway for the rest of the century: less tax, less government interference, a drastically reduced welfare state. (d) These are themes that will be taken up on the hustings in Spain, Russia, India and Australia. (e) (In 1996 over a billion people will go to an election booth, proof that democracy is energetically kicking dictatorship from the ring.) (f) Watch out for the European Union's inter-governmental conference, which starts in Italy in the spring, as the last place where the old nostrums of political interference and subsidy have credence.

As was pointed out in the very first chapter of this book (see section 1.1.3), all utterances carry along a world of background information or supposed common knowledge, whether by means of presupposition, implication, or implicature. Barring simple expressives such as *Hi!* or *Ouch!*, it is probably the case that all sentence-level utterances and all sentences used in the construction of longer utterances lift some element(s) out of the background to use them as the **given information** (sometimes also called **old information**) about which something is then said that can be regarded or treated as **new information**. More often than not, this is done by means of a referring expression (with an associated existential presupposition), such as *1996* in (a), *the world* in (b), *the American presidential campaign* in (c). Sometimes an anaphoric pronoun suffices, such as *these* in (d). Whereas these examples show that given information often coincides with the grammatical subject and with the reference slot in the propositional structure, (e) demonstrates that this is not always the case, since the entire sentence is presented as new information about a time period, *in 1996*, which is given. Nor does the given information have to be expressed explicitly. In (f), for instance, the implicit addressees of the exhortation, i.e. the readers, are 'given'. Similarly, consider (33), as a possible alternative to (b):

(33) It is the American presidential campaign that will set the political agenda.

In this sentence, the implicature that there will be some event in particular that will set the political agenda serves as given information. In exceptional cases, the ability of implicit information to represent given information makes it possible for the same sentence constituent to contain both given and new information simultaneously. Consider the following exchange.

(34) Q: What was the leading actress' name in 'The year of living dangerously'?
A: The leading **act**or's name was Mel Gibson.

In the answer, both *the leading **act**or's name* (with stress on 'actor') and *Mel Gibson* are new information, since the question was not about an actor, but about the leading actress. But at the same time, the information presupposed by *the leading **act**or's name*, viz. that someone's name has been asked for or is otherwise available for comment, is given. Constituents of the same sentence structure may also switch givenness and newness, as in (35) and (36).

(35) Mel **Gib**son's the actor.
(36) Mel Gibson's the **act**or.

In (35), responding to the suggestion that someone else was the actor, *Mel **Gib**son* is new information. In (36), possibly a reply to the suggestion that Mel Gibson was the director, *Mel Gibson* is given information.

It is important to realize that 'givenness' is not a monolithic notion. It is no doubt useful to distinguish between truly **given information**, as when *1996* in (32)a. and *in 1996* in (32)e. can be expected to be fully active in the interpreter's consciousness because of their being part of the introduction to a publication called *The world in 1996*, and **accessible information**, as when *the American presidential campaign* in (32)c. has not been mentioned earlier in the discourse but can easily be brought (back) to consciousness, the activation process being further supported by means of the relative clause *which runs from the snows of the New Hampshire primary until November 5th*. Moreover, both 'true' givenness and accessibility are gradable notions. Thus the givenness of *in 1996* in (32)e. is even stronger than that of *1996* in (32)a., because it has been reinforced by the presence of the latter.

At the more structural end of sentential content organization, a distinction is commonly made between the functional constituents called **theme** (or **topic**) and **rheme** (or **comment**, or **focus**). In languages with a strongly 'grammatical' word order, themes are typically to be found at the beginning of the sentence, so that they often coincide with the categories of given information, syntactic subject, and propositional reference, as in the case of *1996* in (a), *the world* in (b), *the American presidential campaign* in (c), and *these* in (d) in example (32). It still coincides with given information in (e), i.e. in *1996*. In such a case in English, where a circumstantial adjunct occupies the theme position, the theme is often described as 'marked'. But in (f) the theme is *watch out (for)*, which does not correspond to any of the other categories mentioned. The rheme, in all cases mentioned, is whatever follows the theme. As should be clear from (e) and (f), the theme–rheme structuring should not be equated with given–new. The need to keep these separate is further underscored by examples (35) and (36), where *Mel Gibson* is the theme and *'s the actor* the rheme irrespective of the given–new articulation. And in (34) the double given–new structure of the first constituent of the response is not matched by any ambiguity or duality in its thematic status: *the leading actor's name* is the theme, followed by *was Mel Gibson* as rheme.

Themes may also undergo extra **highlighting** or **foregrounding**, as in (37) and (38), which might occur instead of (33).

(37) As to the political agenda, it will be set by the American presidential campaign.
(38) As to the political agenda, it will be the American presidential campaign that will set it.

In both (37) and (38), *(as to) the political agenda* is the theme. In (37) this highly foregrounded theme is anaphorically repeated by *it*, so that it fully coincides with the given information. The structure seems analogous to the one in (39).

(39) Mel Gibson, he's a great actor.

As a further illustration, however, of how erratically the different types of concepts interrelate, consider (39) with special stress on both *Mel* ***Gibson*** and ***he***, which preserves the same theme but which has only the implicated claim that someone is a great actor as given information. In (38), then, there are two elements that function as given information, i.e. *the political agenda* and the assumption, implicated by the structure following the comma, that there will be some event in particular that will set the political agenda.

Finally, themes can also receive a special kind of emphasis by being placed in end position, as in (40).

(40) He's a great actor, Mel Gibson.

In a case like this, *Mel Gibson* would usually be called the **antitopic** (or sometimes **afterthought**).

It is the constant interplay between these different principles of content organization or information structuring, guided by a general need for coherence, that determines the sentence-level contribution to the generation of meaning. Note, by the way, that this is such a complex area that terminology is far from consistent. Usage in this section does not necessarily correspond to a generally accepted orthodoxy.

4.4.2 Suprasentential utterance building

It will be clear from the foregoing examples that, even though the structuring principles discussed so far are operative at the sentence level, it is not possible to discuss them without drawing on information derived from the connectedness of sentences with other sentences in a wider discourse (unless they constitute one-sentence utterances). Some other principles, again coherence-driven, are operative directly at the suprasentential level.

A first element in utterance building at the suprasentential or discourse level is the establishment of one or more **discourse topics**. In (32), for instance, the overall discourse topic is the set of 'predictions' that, from the point of view of the editor of *The world in 1996*, can be reasonably made about the year 1996. The author, however, immediately presents his focus on two specific topics: prosperity and peace in 1996. In spite of the opening sentence (a), the dominance of these two specific discourse topics is not entirely clear from the paragraph quoted in (32) which, investigated in isolation, might look like an enumeration of relatively disconnected statements. Let us therefore also look at the two paragraphs that follow.

(41) (g) For this folly, Europe will be rewarded with a slow rate of economic growth in 1996, although Britain, at last, is surprisingly well placed. (h) The United States will enter its sixth year of growth, the longest period of uninterrupted expansion since the war. (i) It is towards Asia, however, that the world's wealth and influence will ratchet one more turn in 1996. (j) Year after year, East Asia achieves a growth rate about three times that of the West. (k) Most of the 90m extra people in the world in 1996 will be Asian. (l) They will be born poorer than the average reader of this article. (m) They will die

richer. (n) The tilt of the world towards the East is scarcely beginning.

(o) The world will be a peaceful place in 1996. (p) Europe's civil wars will finally be over. (q) A Middle East settlement will fall into place, despite attempts by bombers and bigots to disrupt it. (r) A nuclear test ban treaty will be signed. (s) Armies, except in China and Africa, will be standing down.

(32) and (41) together reveal the topicality of the *prosperity* and *peace* in (a). As it turns out, one section of the text, spanning two paragraphs from (b) to (n), deals with prosperity, whereas the third paragraph, (o) to (s), deals with peace. At this textual level we find the necessary clues for interpreting the coherence of the first paragraph, enumerating what the author regards as some of the prerequisites of prosperity, in particular the rejection of the previous generation's belief in the beneficial nature of government interference.

Not all discourse topics are functionally equal. In (32) and (41), *prosperity* and *peace* could be called **central discourse topics**, which are themselves hierarchically subordinate to the overarching topic *1996*. Usually, these are in an asymmetrical relationship with more **peripheral discourse topics**. Examples of the latter would be the side remark in (e), as well as the comments on the shifting economic balance in (i) to (n). What follows the quoted sections of the text are two paragraphs containing a list of further peripheral discourse topics, including the Olympics in Atlanta, the aging world population, and the pace of electronic change. Finally, the text returns to the overarching topic:

(42) [Two paragraphs omitted.]
(t) These are some of the trends and ideas you will find in *The World in 1996*, which will appear in 80 countries and in 12 languages. (u) This is our tenth year of publication: put all our mistaken predictions together and we could probably produce another edition. (v) But along the way much has been right and, I hope, most of it interesting.

Here even the central discourse topics recede into the background and we are given, as it were, a definition of the genre of language use of which the text is an example.

The way in which discourse topics are introduced and developed is often referred to as **discourse progression**. The process nature of this will be more transparent after we have been able to discuss more aspects of dynamics and negotiability (in Chapter 5). At this stage, however, we can already point out that the progressive organization of discourse leads to a **rhetorical structure** built up around *selections from an open-ended set of identifiable* ***relations*** *between functionally* *significant* **utterance constituents** *at various layers of structural organization or (when utterance clusters are concerned) between* **utterances**. Thus the two central discourse topics are **juxtaposed**. The text span (b) to (n) **justifies** the prediction about prosperity, while (p) to (s) **exemplifies** peace. In the justification for the prediction of prosperity, (b) **introduces** and at the same time **summarizes** the main **argument** in terms of movement *away from the conventional wisdoms of the previous generation*, (c) **explains** what that means by means of an **enumeration** (*less tax, less government interference, a drastically reduced welfare state*), whilst adducing a first piece of **evidence** for the realization of the basic ingredients of that explanation, the *American presidential campaign* and its trend-setting power, (d) provides further **evidence** to underscore the general validity of the prediction, (e) brings in a peripheral topic, the rising tide of *democracy*, which may nevertheless serve as further **background**, (f) brings in the European Union as an apparent **exception** to the general trend, using this in (g) to strengthen the argument again by pointing out the **consequences** of exceptional behaviour at the level of prosperity, and by bringing to the foreground the **counterexception** of Great Britain (drawing on presupposed knowledge about the specific position of Great Britain in the European Union after many years of Thatcherism), and (h) **closes** the argument with the final **proof**, namely the observable beneficial consequences of following the recipe in the United States.

While introducing the peripheral topic of the global distribution of wealth, (i) to (n) **elaborates** on the theme of prosperity. The prediction that the balance will shift more towards Asia is **introduced** in (i), reasons for this expectation are **explained** in (j), and (k) to (m) provide a further **elaboration** in terms of the **consequences** of the shift for the Asian population by first sketching **circumstances** in (k) and then introducing a **contrast** between their present and future predicaments in (l) and (m), whereas (n) **intensifies** the prediction.

The second central topic, finally, is **restated** in (o) before being **exemplified** in (p) to (s). The examples are simply **enumerated**, though grouped into two types, **specific** in (p) and (q), as opposed to **general** in (r) and (s). Within each of the two types one of the examples is qualified by means of a **concession**, following *despite* in (q), and *except in China and Africa* in (s). The general picture for (32) and (41) could be represented as in Figure 4.2.

Any representation of this kind can be no more than an approximation. The set of relations activated by and structuring any given piece of discourse or text, is truly open-ended. Even in the example we have used it would probably not be difficult to detect other types of relevant and structure-driving relations beyond the ones we mentioned, such as **cause** (volitional or non-volitional), **result**, **purpose**, **motivation**, **interpretation**, and the like. A theory which would posit a

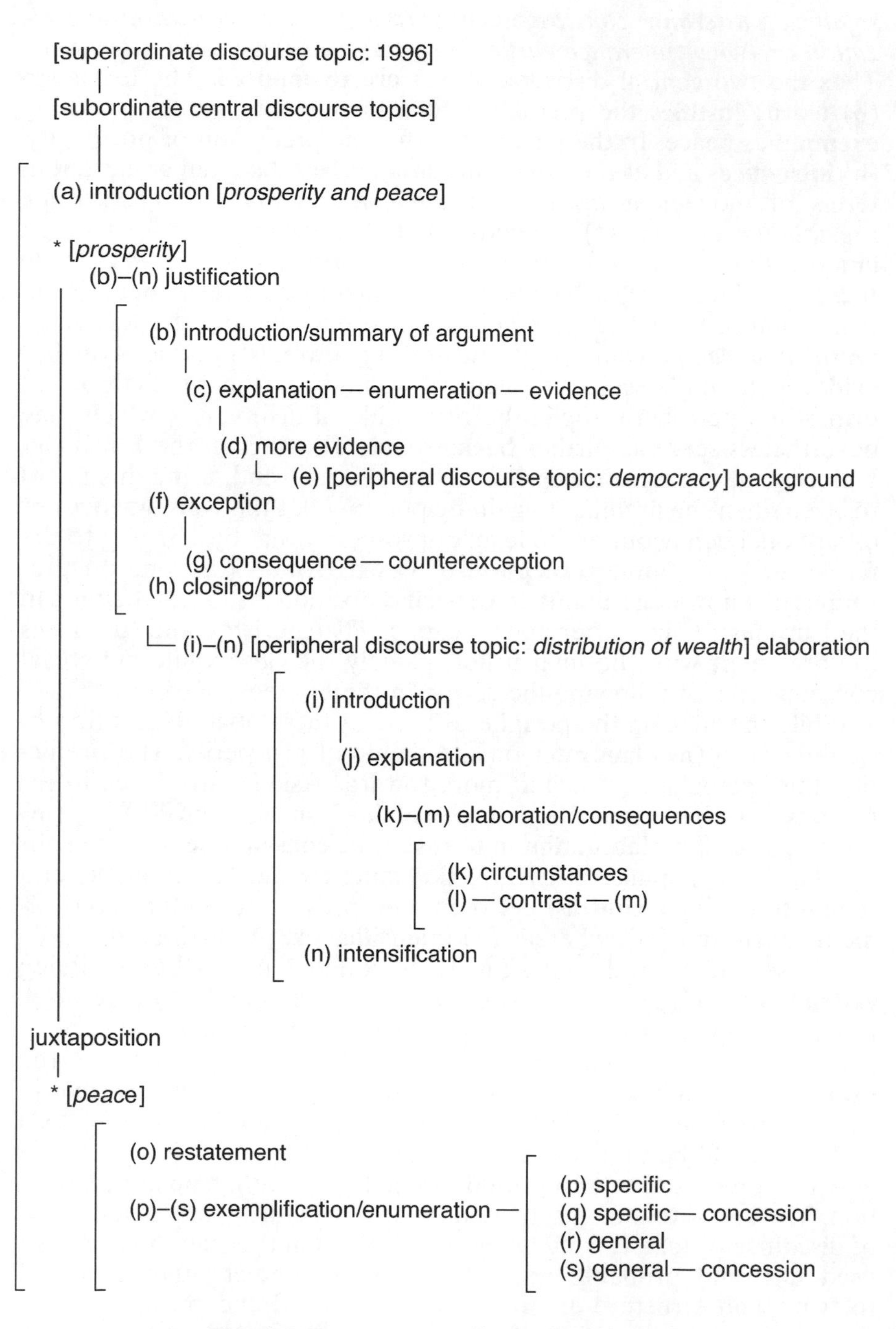

Fig. 4.2 Example of a rhetorical structure

finite set should be immediately suspect. At the same time, however, any investigation at this level should be guided by a concern with the highest possible systematicity and precision in the search for those relation types that are most relevant to the research question.

4.4.3 Building utterance clusters

All principles guiding the organization of utterances at the discourse or suprasentential level are also involved in the building of utterance clusters: discourse topics are chosen and developed progressively, yielding a rhetorical structure consisting of identifiable relations between the utterances of which the cluster is composed.

In conversation, to take the most frequently studied type of utterance cluster as an example, all these aspects are continuously negotiated. Discourse topics in conversation are largely determined by those who take or get the floor. Discourse progression is governed by (adaptable) rules of turn-taking, by expectations guided by common adjacency pairs and interactional preferences, and as it moves along hesitations, false starts and repairs. The end result is an organized (or self-organizing) **sequence** of conversational **moves** and **exchanges**, which does not necessarily follow a linear ordering, but which abides by general principles of coherence and relevance (see section 1.1.4.).

4.5 *Integrated choice-making*

The making of linguistic choices necessarily involves all the above: the selection of a language, code, and style and choices from a range of utterance-building ingredients to construct utterances or utterance clusters of specific types in accordance with general utterance-building principles. Moreover, choices at all these levels are highly interadaptable or interdependent. Earlier in this book (in section 1.4) we made the remark that the opening line of (32), *1996 will be a year of prosperity and peace*, would probably not have been taken seriously if used to introduce a new discourse topic during an informal dinner conversation. In terms of what has been discussed in this chapter, we must observe at least the following about this sentence:

1. It is written in English.
2. A standard variety of English is used.
3. The style is formal.
4. Lexical choices are made with a strong positive connotation but a vague semantic content.

5. A declarative sentence type is chosen, taking the form of a subject with a copula (in the future tense form) and a nominal predicate.
6. The proposition predicates a future state of affairs about a temporal reference.
7. Occurring at the beginning of a wider utterance, this sentence serves as an utterance constituent belonging to a speech act type that could be called 'predicting'.
8. The wider utterance is a monologic text of the type 'editorial', intertextually defined with reference to a series of 'reports' which, unlike ordinary reports, looks ahead rather than back in time.
9. In terms of information structure, *1996* is both given information and the theme, whereas the rest of the sentence is both new information and the rheme.
10. The given information of the sentence represents the superordinate discourse topic (the year *1996*, looked at in global perspective), whereas the new information introduces two subordinate, but central, discourse topics (*prosperity* and *peace*).

All these choices interrelate in more ways than a cursory presentation can reveal. Just consider a few connections, without going deeper into their rationale. Clearly, there is a connection between the formality of the style (see 3.) and the nature of the monologic discourse type (see 8.); between the use of writing (see 8.) and the use of a standard variety of the chosen language (see 2.); between the sentence type (see 5.), the propositional structure (see 6.), and the speech act type (see 7.), and the information structure (see 9.); between the overall purpose of the discourse (see 8.) and the speech act type (see 7.); between the choice of discourse topics (see 10.) and the lexical choices (see 4.); between the global ambitions of the author (see 8. and 10.) and the choice of English as a medium of communication – even if the point is made that the publication is distributed in 12 languages (see (42)). In other words, *every choice is itself a constellation of interadaptable choices*.

4.6 *Summary and further reading*

In this chapter, structural objects of adaptability have been reviewed. Summarizing, language use involves the making of choices:

- At the *overarching structural levels* of languages, codes (distinguishable variants of a language, involving sets of choices which are geographically, socially, functionally or situationally based), and

Dear Virgin Trains Traveller

Thank you for travelling with Virgin Trains.

As I'm sure you're well aware, our trains are far from perfect right now. We're a few months into running our two franchises - the former InterCity West Coast and CrossCountry networks - and have been facing the daily challenge of undoing the 30 years of neglect, demoralisation and structural decline we inherited.

We didn't go into this with our eyes closed. We knew that we were inheriting ineffective air conditioning/heating shabby interiors, disgraceful-looking lavatories and even, on occasion, malfunctioning engines - all the result of antiquated rolling stock and many years of underinvestment. We knew that co-ordination between stations was poor and that, at times, the way disabled passengers were dealt with was less than ideal. We also knew that staffing levels on the telephones were inadequate.

The good news is that we also knew that we could change all this. We believed that within a year of taking over we could sort out many of the short-term problems and begin to build the foundations for the revolutionary plans we have for Virgin Trains. We are now about four months into this process.

In the short term, all 100 of our existing trains are being refurbished at a cost of £1 million each including replacing defective air conditioning/heating. And (although not very comforting if you're sitting reading this on a delayed train) despite the same locomotives that British Rail used and the massive works that are going on to upgrade the lines, punctuality and performance have been improved, cancellations reduced, and we are nearly up to full staff on the Virgin TrainLine (0345 222 333).

In the longer term, we have committed to invest £750 million in new rolling stock and with Railtrack, up to £2 billion on infrastructure improvements to cope with the new tilting trains on the West Coast line that will come into service from 2001. These will dramatically reduce the time of your journey. We also have a range of initiatives designed to give people on-board our trains the products and service they want with a promise of quality and value for money.

When we took over our franchises, we did inherit something we're proud of - a great team of motivated people with good ideas who want to change the railway for the better.

In the meantime, thank you for putting up with Virgin Trains while we fix the problems.

Kind regards.

Richard Branson

Plate 4.1 'Hot Line' word of welcome

styles (variants of a language or code along dimensions of formality and informality).

- From the entire range of *utterance-building ingredients* (from sound structure, morphemes and words, clauses and sentences, to propositional structures and suprasentential units of various kinds).
- From the entire range of *utterance and utterance cluster types*.
- In accordance with *utterance-building principles* at the level of sentential and suprasentential utterance building as well as at the level of utterance clusters (guided mainly by strategies to establish and maintain coherence).

Choice-making at different levels of structure and based on varying principles is always interdependent and interadaptable.

On languages, codes and styles: Auer (ed.) (1998), Bourdieu (1991), Coupland (1995), Eastman (1995), Fasold (1984), Gal (1979), Giles and St. Clair (eds) (1979), Gumperz (1982), Heller (1995), Meeuwis and Östman (1995), Woolard (1989). On utterance-building ingredients, approached from a pragmatic point of view: Bolinger (1986), Comrie (1981), Fretheim and Gundel (1996), Hoye (1997), Palmer (1986), Rosch (1977), Rudzka-Ostyn (1995), Verschueren (1980). On utterance and utterance cluster building principles: Bloor and Bloor (1995), Chafe (1994), Clark and Haviland (1977), Halliday (1985), Lambrecht (1981). Mann and Thompson (eds) (1992), Prince (1981), Sgall (1995a, 1995b).

4.7 *Research topic*

Describe the structuring of the text in Plate 4.1, taken from the inside front cover of *HotLine: The complimentary magazine for Virgin Train passengers* (Autumn/Winter 1997).

5

Dynamics

The chapters on *contextual correlates* of adaptability (Chapter 3) and *structural objects* of adaptability (Chapter 4) have provided us with the basic tools needed to describe the **locus** of any instance or aspect of the meaningful functioning of language in terms of its *extralinguistic* and *linguistic co-ordinates* (a distinction which does not completely match the one between contextual correlates and structural objects, as should be clear from the notion of linguistic context). As already observed (in section 2.4), however, accounting for the *dynamics* of adaptability, or studying actual **processes** of (inter)adaptation, taking into account the full power of variability and negotiability, is the central task of specific pragmatic investigations. How this can be done, making use of the context- and structure-related tools, will be explored in this chapter.

Conceptually, this is the central chapter of the book. From a different perspective, the realm of structural objects is studied in detail by the traditional components of a linguistic theory. Similarly, the contextual correlates also form the subject of research for sociolinguistics, anthropological linguistics, psycholinguistics, and the like. What pragmatics adds is the specifically dynamic perspective on the interadaptability of context and structure in actual language use.

Central to the processes of (inter)adaptation in language use or to the meaningful functioning of language is **the dynamic generation of meaning** (see the Introduction, section 0.4 on page 8). This happens in the course of *activities* and *events*, which provide 'frames of meaning' (to be discussed in section 5.2) and with the help of *strategies* (see section 5.3). After briefly introducing these two aspects, the dynamics of (interactive) meaning generation will be demonstrated by means of some examples (in section 5.4). But first a few more words will be devoted to the concept of dynamics itself, 'locating' it in relation to both contextual correlates and structural objects of adaptability; especially, but not only, the temporal and social dimensions of communication will be shown to be relevant (see section 5.1).

5.1 *'Locating' the dynamics of communication*

Needless to say whatever happens to or with language, i.e. the dynamics of its use, can be located in relation to any aspect of context and structure reviewed in the foregoing chapters. To make sense of the notion of dynamics as such, however, it may be useful to point out a few particularly salient factors, starting out with the raw material of dynamics, i.e. the temporal dimension of language use.

5.1.1 The temporal dimension

If there is one indisputable linguistic universal, it is the bare fact that language use takes place over time. Although space is a powerful contextual correlate of adaptability (speech being incomprehensible at a large distance, spatial distance being influenced by aspects of social relationships relevant for the nature of the communication in question, etc.; see section 3.2.4), and though spatial relations underlie significant chunks of linguistically reflected conceptualization, **time** – as a contextual correlate of adaptability – clearly imposes more universal constraints on verbal interaction. What space is for lexical and grammatical meaning (a set of observable relations which can be metaphorically transformed and extended to build a wide range of concepts), time may be for linguistic action: time or the temporal dimension provides the raw material for communicative dynamics.

The constraints imposed by this raw material are immediately apparent when we consider processing by the medium of adaptation, mind in society (to be discussed further in Chapter 6). At the micro-level, the interlocutors' 'memory' imposes considerable time-related processing constraints; and communicative processing itself involves (again time-related) 'planning'; see sections 6.2.2 and 6.2.3. At a macro-level, earlier stages of development of languages and linguistic conventions are no longer readily accessible to the language user; conversely, communicative success *vis-à-vis* future generations cannot be taken for granted, not even with the channel of writing, and not even at the more trivial levels where few obstacles would be met in interaction with contemporaries.

Also at the micro-level, but now considering co-adaptation processes between contextual correlates of adaptability and linguistic choices, it is possible to distinguish *stages of adaptation* in linguistic interaction. Three types can easily be distinguished (but more configurations are possible): (i) linguistic choices may be made *after* certain circumstances 'in the world' (as seen by the utterer U and the interpreter I) have appeared; (ii) linguistic choices may *create* certain circumstances; (iii) choices may remain ineffective until or become ineffective when certain *later* conditions come into play.

The contrast between (i) and (ii) is characteristic, for instance, of the difference between the traditional classes of *presupposition* and *conversational implicature*. In the case of typical presuppositions, both the utterer and the interpreter are supposed to be aware of the piece of information involved (say, that I did not come to your party last night) before the utterance is made to which the presupposition is attached (say, *I'm sorry I didn't come to your party last night*). In the case of – again typical – conversational implicatures, on the other hand, a piece of information (say, that the garage around the corner has petrol for sale and is probably open) which was already part of U's knowledge of the world before the utterance *There's a garage round the corner* (in response to *I'm out of petrol*), is intended to become part of I's world of beliefs or assumptions by virtue of his or her understanding of the utterance, thus effectively entering the realm of common knowledge in a way that is structurally the same as a presupposition, but at a later stage in the interaction process. There are other types of assumptions (or, for that matter, other states of mind) that relate to the temporal dimension in comparable ways. For instance, an occasion-specific sincerity condition (e.g. U's belief that the earth is round when saying *The earth is round*, or U's intention to come when promising *I'll come*) is an assumption or state of mind that is expected to belong to U's mental world before the utterance, and which enters I's assumptions as a result of successful communication. (See, e.g., Verschueren 1978a, 1981a.)

Examples of (iii) are, for instance, phenomena of the following kind (extensively discussed by Kurzon 1986): *I hereby bequeath all my possessions to my wife* (in a will) will only become effective after U's death; *I . . . take thee . . . to be my wedded wife, . . .* (in a Catholic wedding ceremony) can be declared void at a later time if the marriage is not consummated; a law appropriately enacted (e.g. in the US) may be declared unconstitutional by a court years later.

Note that such examples are misleadingly static in an attempt to cope with dynamic processes. What we describe as 'typical' presuppositions or conversational implicatures may well be abstractions which correspond to very little in actual language use. Below (in section 5.4) we hope to demonstrate that this is indeed possible, given the extreme dynamics of the meaning generation processes that can be traced. Yet, even as abstractions they may be relevant to the extent that they may not only live in the mind of the researcher but also the user's (a statement which should be perfectly understandable after reading Chapter 6).

Returning to the macro-level once more, it should be clear that processes of language change, and hence the perpetual dynamics underlying variability itself, are to be set against the background of temporal progression. It is in this domain that the distinction between macro and micro also loses part of its meaning (as was convincingly shown by Meeuwis 1991). Thus lexical borrowing, to take just one example, may start with an individual case of code switching (see section 4.1) which then gets repeated, copied and generalized, leading to a complete adoption of the 'foreign' item into the language and ultimately to incorporation in such a way that the foreign origin is no longer transparent for the speakers of the language in question.

Similarly, various stages of language acquisition may be approached as progressive adaptations at the micro-level of individual day-to-day interaction to a more or less 'established' adult norm at the macro-level of a wider community or society. At the same time, the unidirectionality of adaptation processes which shines through this formulation should be warned against: there is no doubt that the 'established' norm changes under pressure from successive generations of learners.

5.1.2 Dynamics and context

Time is not the only contextual correlate of adaptability of particular importance to 'locating' the notion of dynamics. Martín Rojo (1994), for instance, proposes that the dynamics of conversational interaction can be explained on the basis of the conflicting tendencies towards the preservation of privacy and the formation of alliances. This would be an explanation completely in terms of *social relationships*. Since communication takes place between human beings, this may indeed be one of the most promising angles to look at this process *as a process*. Thus the conflicting demands for privacy and alliance determine, amongst other things, the establishment and crossing of borders between group identities, the pace at which 'information' is exchanged, the types of information that are exchanged or held back, the status accorded to different types of 'presences' in a speech event, the interplay between positive and negative face and between power and solidarity.

A less direct correlation may be found with two other forces underlying discourse dynamics, viz. involvement versus detachment – less direct because these may depend on highly *personal characteristics* not determined by the social relationship, or on products of socialization barely accessible to the language user's consciousness. In addition, there are the utterer–interpreter's *personal states of mind*. Wishes (e.g. one interlocutor's wish that the other would do something) can be shown to 'develop' throughout an interaction. As was already hinted at (in section 5.1.1), some of the most dynamic ingredients of a speech event are knowledge and belief, which are in constant flux. Even meaning intentions can be retroactively shaped or reshaped in the course of negiotiating meaning.

Different linguistic *channels*, the oral versus the written, relate quite differently to the temporal dimension of communication and show, therefore, different types of dynamics. The effects are to be found especially at the level of discourse organization: constraints on coherence and cohesion, digression, etc. This, of course, leads us directly into the structural aspects of dynamics.

5.1.3 Dynamics and structure

We should keep in mind that *language* itself has a basic time-related property: *linearity.* It is because of the linearity of language that sequencing is so important for communication, or the timing of backchannel cues in conversation, the switching between codes, the entire turn-taking system, repairs, etc. At the level of sentence structure, linearity determines the constraints on word order, in conjunction with the limitations on memory and planning. At the sentential as well as the suprasentential levels, aspects of information structure (such as the ordering of given and new information) and the progressive interplay between implicit and explicit meaning (about which more will be said in section 5.3 below) are some of the most essential ingredients of communicative dynamics.

Though linearity is a powerful constraint, it does not fully determine the shape of the dynamics of language use. Utterer and interpreter can move back and forth along the basically linear dimension at any stage in the process of meaning generation. This property of the meaningful functioning of language, which may be mobilized within any stretch of discourse, surfaces at the level of the wider linguistic context in the form of intertextuality.

5.2 *Activities, events and frames of meaning*

The generation of meaning does not take place in a vacuum. That is why Bakhtin (1986) proposed the notion of a **speech genre** (see also section 1.4) as a relatively stable utterance type associated with a sphere of human activity. That is also why Wittgenstein (1958) thought it useful to introduce the notion of a **language game** to draw the attention to the embeddedness of speech in human activities or forms of life. Both concepts designate a variable range of utterances – from the most simple (such as a shout of anger), via speech acts, to the most complex (such as a long narration) – which derive a significant part of their meaning from their recognizable status within a context of action. Both Bakhtin and Wittgenstein emphasize a reasonable degree of stability and conventionalization (which makes speech genres and language games recognizable and interpretable) while focusing on infinite variability and change. Thus *I'll do it* may be recognized as an instance of a genre or game connected with the sphere of activity involved in the making of commitments between people, with a sufficient degree of comparability (describable, e.g. in terms similar to the speech act account of promising) across a range of occasions of use. Yet those occasions of use, outside of which the genre or game does not even exist, create serious variability between individual instances; just compare *I'll do it* as an act of volunteering one's services and the same utterance made by someone giving in to a threat, both of which may count as 'promises'. These two aspects, stability (mainly the product of interpretation processes) and variability (a property of the 'reality' in question), are constantly interacting in the dynamic generation of meaning.

The question may arise why – except for a brief introduction in section 1.4 – we did not discuss speech genres or language games before, for instance in relation to context (since obviously this is about contextual connections; see Chapter 3), or in relation to structure (where the speech genre or the language game, or both, could have been introduced on a par with speech acts, as frequently studied utterance types; see section 4.3). The reason is that the Bakhtinian and Wittgensteinian notions touch the core of what language use is all about, so that only an approach in terms of processes, drawing on both context and structure, makes sense. How should we conceptualize this?

Remembering the general discussion of contextual correlates of adaptability, but turning our attention to the actual processes of language use, we see that values from the contextual dimensions described in Chapter 3 may combine in an infinite variety of ways. Any combination of ingredients from any set of contextual dimensions may define a **(speech) activity** or **(speech) event**. Sometimes these terms are used to emphasize different aspects of language use, where 'speech event' refers simply to sequentially organized stretches of speech (an analytical domain), whilst 'speech activity' refers to the meaningful form of behaviour which an interpreter has to envision in order to construct an interpretation. In this book, I will not handle a systematic distinction, though my choice between these two alternating terms may sometimes depend on whether I want to emphasize the creative involvement of the participants in constructing the activity or the preset conventionalized nature of the event, while remaining aware that both aspects always play a role. Standard examples of activities or events are classroom teaching, police interrogations, job interviews, dinner conversations, wedding ceremonies, storytelling, service encounters, poetry readings, Amnesty International letter-writing sessions, business meetings, and the like. Each of these can be described in terms of: constellations of utterers (with specific voices) and interpreters (with specific roles); beliefs, intentions, emotions, and other aspects of the mental world; social parameters; properties of a physical world; aspects of linguistic channel and linguistic context.

Giving examples of a 'type' of speech activity or speech event, complete with a description of what we regard as the 'typical' pattern of parameter values which the type represents, is always risky. The reason is that such a description attributes stable properties to an unstable reality, which may nevertheless be relevant for certain aspects of interpretation. This ambivalence is precisely the same as in the case of speech genres or language games (see the 'promising' example above). To take just one example, a typical pattern for *job interviews* could be said to contain the following kinds of ingredients:

- The interlocutors are typically one interviewee (applying for a job) and one or more interviewers. When the interviewee is the utterer, he or she is usually the direct source of what is said, but in attempts to anticipate questions and objections, an utterer^V may be invoked on various occasions. As to the interviewer(s), they may either be the direct source(s) of the questions and comments, or they may speak on behalf of source^n, i.e. their direct superior or the more impersonal body of the employing company or institution, in which case an initiated interviewee will take into account a potential addressee^n. (The superscripts were explained in section 3.2.1.)
- The interviewee comes to the interview with the intention to present him- or herself in such a way as to maximize chances of convincing the interviewer(s) and/or the addressee^n that he or she is the right person for the job. A variable degree of hope is involved and, more often than not, some uncertainty. The interviewer's goal is to elicit the information needed to take a hiring decision. Both parties are equally involved in the interaction, but from clearly different points of view.
- The social context is a completely asymmetrical one, with an amount of power (depending on their precise position of authority within the company or institution) on the part of the interviewer(s), and a lack of control on the part of the interviewee. The precise constellation depends a lot on the institutional parameters involved but also on personal matters which may interfere (such as possible personal connections between interviewee and interviewer(s)). In an interethnic context, aspects of cultural background (to be han-

dled with the utmost care in the analysis; see section 3.2.3) may enter the picture as well.

- Different types of temporal reference are involved depending on the topical segment of the interview: there is usually some 'history-taking', an exploration of skills and attitudes, and an anticipation of tasks to be performed.
- The positioning of the interlocutors in physical space is typically face-to-face, with interviewee and interviewer(s) on different sides of an object such as a desk or table. The interviewee's physical appearance, gestures and gaze are carefully monitored.
- 'Material' conditions of speech are of the utmost importance for job interviews. For one thing, they crystallize economic relationships. Furthermore, economic circumstances such as the abundance versus scarcity of jobs and job candidates not only determine the outcome of an interview but also the way in which it is conducted.
- The linguistic channel for job interviews is usually spoken language. In terms of linguistic context, they are intertextually connected with other forms of discourse: a preceding job announcement, an interview report, and a later letter or phone call notifying the job applicant of acceptance or rejection.

What is presented here as 'typical' may not be 'representative' of the collection of real-world job interviews. Just think of the local plumber hiring a hand. Thus, labelling an instance of language use as a specific type of speech activity can be done safely only on condition that the true range of variability and negotiability is allowed into the empirical description, in conjunction with abstractions such as the above account whenever they can be shown to contribute to certain aspects of interpretation.

Note that the *uses of language* that were listed (in section 4.3) as types of monologic discourse (e.g. advertisements, directions for use, jokes, letters, political speeches, etc.) or dialogic discourse (e.g. conversational narrative, adult–child conversations, counselling, debates, talk shows, and the like) fit comfortably under the description of speech activity types or speech event types. Hence, as was pointed out (also in section 4.3), they do not really designate structures but complex contextual–structural categories, i.e. activities or events.

Such activity or event types are always *'meaningful'* in the sense that, like any other form of social action, they are interpreted by the actors involved – which is where abstractions may come in that do not fully fit the (other) empirical 'facts'. *Those 'interpreted'* ***activities*** *or* ***events***, products of complex processes of socialization, *provide* ***frames of meaning*** *for the* ***speech genres*** *or* ***language games*** *of which they consist.* It is because of the interpretation frame provided by the activity or event type of the job interview, which requires skills of presenting oneself in the best possible light, that a job applicant can seal his or her own fate by making honesty the dominant guideline of his or her answers to the interviewer's questions. Consider the exchange in (1), adapted from Gumperz *et al.* (1979):

(1) Interviewer: Why did you apply for a job at this particular college?
Interviewee: I have already made 50 applications. This is my third interview. I just need a job.

Analysing this in terms of a simple adjacency pair consisting, in speech act terms, of a question for information followed by a sequence of three statements – however accurate this may be at a certain level of structure and content – would be missing the point if we are interested in what is really happening. The interviewer's question represents an activity- or event-specific genre or game. Within the context of the activity or event, this is a formulaic question probing for how much the interviewee knows about the place. It is an invitation to display the relationship between the candidate's biography and the possible new job, or to show how the candidate thinks he or she would fit in. It may also be a way of fishing for compliments. The interviewer may want to hear something about the college that exerts a special attraction on the applicant, which might lead to the conclusion that the latter would develop a significant degree of devotion to the new employer. By not responding to the question in that capacity, the interviewee, however honest, displays a lack of interest in the eyes of the interviewer and ruins his or her chances of getting hired. The point is not that the interviewer would be fooled by a potentially hypocritical response as in (2).

(2) I can't imagine a better place to work. It's got a great reputation, and it's a friendly place in a beautiful environment.

This response would simply have been within the borders drawn by the frame of interpretation that gives meaning to job interviews (within a particular, maybe culture-specific, setting). If nothing else, it would have been a display of social skills and it would have assured the interviewer that the job candidate disposed of the tools to help underscore the image of the college, both directly and indirectly. This frame is challenged in (1), where the answer brings in the frame of meaning associated with a different sphere of activity, the social struggle and problems involved in finding employment. Curiously enough, job interviews are always embedded in that wider sphere, but the type of explicit reference to it, as exemplified in (2), is shunned. The gravest mistake a pragmatic analysis could make is to ignore the embeddedness of 'what is really happening' in such frames of interpretation – both the ones that are expected and the ones that are impermissible in the context of use.

5.3 *Strategies of meaning generation*

As repeated over and again, none of the above is absolutely stable. That is the essence of negotiability and adaptability. In a context of job scarcity, no doubt new genres or games emerge which allow reference to aspects of social struggle, thus modifying the overt interpretation frame of the activity of a job interview, but without really challenging or breaking it. The interviewer, for instance, is privileged to refer to the abundance of applicants, both as a strategy to alleviate later rejection and to strengthen the later bond upon hiring (thereby reinforcing the asymmetrical relationship while putting on an air of near-total lack of control on the hiring side). This is only one way, however, in which **strategies** are involved in the dynamic generation of meaning.

There are many strategies that are highly conventionalized. But everything conventional is liable to further strategic use or exploitation. That is why there are hardly any fixed form–function relationships in language when regarded from a pragmatic perspective. In general, ***strategies*** *of language use are ways of exploiting the interplay between explicitness and implicitness in the generation of meaning*, at the level of sentential and suprasentential utterances as well as the level of utterance clusters, and whether it is done consciously or not. Manifestations of this – some more conventionalized than others – are to be found in the range of phenomena discussed (in section 1.1.3) as instances of the strategic avoidance of explicitness: conversational implicature, some instances of irony, metaphor, politeness and humour.

The relevant phenomena are not restricted to the members of this list. They range from the use of referential expressions, over grammatical choices, all the way to principles of suprasentential utterance building. Restricting the discussion to these three examples, consider, first of all, a definite expression such as *My ex*, used standardly as a combination of subject, given information and theme, and carrying the existential presupposition that there is such a person to whom I used to be married but from whom I was divorced. The surface function of this referential expression is to anchor information in a common ground. Yet, such presupposition-carrying constructions can, and often are, strategically used to convey new information in a context where the utterer knows perfectly well that the 'common ground' is not at all common since the interpreter does not share the presupposed knowledge. Thus an utterance may start with *My ex* . . .

simply to bring up the subject of the utterer's having been married, which may be relevant to an addressee (say, a potential new partner) who does not know anything yet about the utterer's marital history.

As to an example of grammatical choices, question tags are said to lower the assertiveness of statements and, in that capacity, their frequency of occurrence in women's speech is often cited as proof of female submissiveness. There is no doubt that *I can stay in your house, can't I?* is less assertive than *I can stay in your house*, the latter being rather rude unless it can be interpreted as an offer. But at the same time, such tags can be used strategically to turn the content of an assertion into a presupposition, thus making it more difficult to disagree with, and hence strengthening its argumentative or persuasive power. By 'presupposing' that I can stay in your house, I put you in a position where, in order to refuse, you have to pass two moral checkpoints rather than just one: you have to deny me a form of hospitality, but you also have to contradict my declared expectations.

At the level of suprasentential utterance-building principles, the way in which discourse topics are introduced and handled to build up a rhetorical structure is highly strategic all the way, even though some patterns are more 'neutral' than others. The processes involved include topic avoidance as well as topical highlighting, argumentation, uses of directness versus indirectness, and the like.

It should be stressed that strategies are always involved in any type of communication, and that they do not necessarily imply attempts to deceive, manipulate, express (non)solidarity, establish one-upmanship, and the like. Often, though, the most regular types of language use carry seeds of such less noble goals and designs – although we should not let the term 'design' trick us into imputing full consciousness to all choice-making (see Chapter 6).

5.4 *The dynamics of interactive meaning generation*

In this section, we will review four brief examples of language use from real life, of the kind anyone can become involved in, to illustrate the dynamics of the processes that they incorporate. The first two, as well as the fourth, are examples of true interaction, however simple. In the third there is no real exchange. Yet the analysis will show that what happens cannot be accounted for unless we assume interaction of some kind. I hope to demonstrate, then, *that meaning generation is always dynamic and interactive.*

Concluding section 1.3, I said that the theoretical movement which pragmatics makes in detaching meaning from linguistic form beyond the point of invoking intentionality (the Gricean point of reference), has to be counterbalanced by a methodological re-attachment of meaning to empirically observable facts of language. The following sections are meant to illustrate that double movement.

5.4.1 The Budapest opera

The following exchange took place in the Budapest opera house when Hungary was still behind the Iron Curtain. I went there with my wife, came in almost late, so that everyone had ceased talking, and sat down next to a middle-aged couple. During the intermission we began to talk, in Dutch. The woman, who was sitting next to me, turned to me and this exchange followed:

(3) 1. Woman: [gesticulating] Pause . . . pause.
[pointing at watch] How long?
2. JV: [slowly articulating] Ten minutes.
[holding both hands up, fingers stretched] Ten.

My neighbour seemed satisfied, turned to her husband and started talking to him in English, with an unmistakably native Texas twang, which prompted me to intervene, saying something like *Oh, you're American!*, followed by a somewhat normal conversation in idiomatic English.

The activity type represented in (3) is purely information-centred, consisting of two adjacent utterances belonging to a fact-finding and a fact-giving genre. Though it may look like everything of interest could be said about this in terms of the general speech act categories of a question for information followed by a response, the nature of the genres involved is strongly determined by the specificity of the activity type and its particular institutional embedding. The context of organized and highly institutionalized musical performances is such that large numbers of people, strangers to each other, can be spatially confined closely together, without any expectation of interaction amongst them beyond a friendly smile (if anything at all), so that if they interact at all, barring the occasional exception, conversations are restricted either to brief exchanges of information or to equally cursory comments on the performance. In other words, options are limited, both structurally and content-wise.

Being total strangers to each other in this kind of context, people nevertheless form hypotheses about each other, which help to guide the process of communication dynamically, both in aspects of its production and interpretation. Upon hearing – and seeing – (3)1., I assumed that my neighbour was either Hungarian (a low-probability option, since in that case she would probably have had better ways of getting the information she wanted than to ask a foreigner in broken

English) or else another foreigner (but not a native speaker of English – the articulatory effort was such that traces of what later turned out to be a quite recognizable accent were hidden). I naïvely assumed, therefore, that the linguistic-cum-gestural choices she made reflected her level of proficiency in English, which made me choose, as a code for my response, foreigner talk – a standard strategy for coping with such circumstances, even if one is not a native speaker of the used language oneself.

For all practical purposes, the exchange was a successful piece of communication, concluded to everyone's satisfaction: my neighbour got her answer and I had been able to help. Being turned into a bystander when she addressed her husband, and hearing the perfectly idiomatic Texas English she had at her disposal, I was then forced to revise my hypotheses. From one moment to the next, her entire identity changed from a general, but definitely non-English-speaking, foreigner (if not a Hungarian, the less likely option), to a native speaker of English with a recognizable place of origin (if not of residence). Now I could also hypothesize that she had probably diagnosed us as speakers of this unintelligible language, Hungarian, and that, having been frustrated by earlier attempts to make herself understood in idiomatic English, she had opted for expressions of a somewhat simpler nature. This interpretation suddenly changed the status of her utterance, after the fact, and after an exchange had already been successfully concluded on the basis of a different interpretation. What had been perceived as broken English, now came to assume the status of foreigner talk, while obviously leaving all linguistic choices of (3)1. intact.

This anecdote, as so many others, shows that – given the right circumstances – probably well-educated people are even prepared to mutilate their own language to accomplish the tasks that belong to the frame of meaning of the activity at hand. Clearly, this is adaptability of some sort.

5.4.2 The Berkeley coffee shop

Let us now look at another extremely brief encounter, a slightly more elaborate exchange this time, which illustrates the dynamics of communication more clearly than a first glimpse might suggest. The sphere of human activity in which the example is situated is the world of establishments for eating and drinking, where the types of genres or games to which utterances belong are strongly defined by the well-understood roles of the interactants, one side expecting service, the other side providing it (and using whatever strategies are needed to be perceived as providing good service). The example is the following (where, as in earlier examples, bold-face marks emphasis):

(4) [Situation: coffee shop in Berkeley, California, in 1981]

1. Customer [just coming in] to waitress:	Is this non-smoking?
2. Waitress:	You can **use** it as non-smoking.
3. Customer [sitting down]:	Thanks.

There is no way of making sense of this conversation without taking into account historical time and place and the dynamics of group relations at a macro-level. By the time the exchange took place, non-smokers had created a strong group identity for themselves in opposition to smokers, and they had been successful in defining their rights and in enforcing them in some areas of social life. As one of the results, most coffee shops and restaurants in the geographical area in question had created non-smoking sections. By asking *Is this non-smoking?*, the customer (a woman in this example) identifies herself as belonging to the group of non-smokers and declares her intention to make use of the established privilege not to be bothered by smokers. Though it would be possible for a smoker to ask the same question with the intention to find out what section he or she had to avoid, this would clearly be a marked choice (in contrast to *Is this smoking?*, which is what one would expect the smoker to ask), which is why the waitress responds on the basis of the assumption that the customer's self-identification as a non-smoker is signalled by her question. One can also assume that more than 15 years later, when smoking sections have become marked in California, if not banned, as opposed to non-smoking sections (which were still felt to be an innovative improvement, and hence the marked case, in 1981), non-smokers would assume a place to be mainly non-smoking, so that the question would lose much of its relevance (while *Is this smoking?* might be a more crucial question to ask). This is a case of markedness reversal based on 'material' conditions produced by social change (analogous to the case of markedness reversal reviewed in section 3.2.4 as a product of changes in the physical world). It provides a further illustration of why local and historical context are crucial to a pragmatic approach to meaning.

Returning to the actual example, although *Is this non-smoking?* is basically a question asking for information (with the implications sketched regarding group identity and awareness of group rights), it is not responded to as a question. The illocutionary dynamics of the exchange consists in the following process: *the customer's original question is transformed into a request by the waitress's response which leads to the customer's thanking for the granting of a request which was not really made to begin with.* The following phenomena are characteristic of the process sketched in these rudimentary terms.

With reference to the social interaction context, we observe a high degree of co-operativeness on the part of the waitress (where 'co-operation' is to be interpreted as a general property of human interaction which is as likely to be absent as it is likely to be present, rather than in terms of the more restricted Gricean conversational co-operation seen as a default value). She could simply have answered negatively as in (5), a response which is now given implicitly.

(5) No, it isn't.

But this response, which would have given the question the treatment it deserved in its capacity as a question, would probably have been perceived by the customer as rude (which turns it into a strategically unsuitable option), since, without further modification, it would not have been tuned in to non-smokers' rights implicitly claimed in the question that was obviously asked to check out the facts which would determine where she was going to sit down. A somewhat higher degree of co-operativeness would have yielded a combination of the negative response with an apology on behalf of the owners for not yet having institutionalized non-smokers' rights, as in (6) or (7) – the latter being the more apologetic of the two.

(6) I'm sorry; we don't have a non-smoking section yet.
(7) I'm sorry; we have not yet decided where to put the non-smoking section.

But the waitress goes further. She does not only accept the customer's self-identification as a non-smoker, and she does not only signal recognition of the legitimacy of non-smokers' rights (which is also implicit in (6) and (7)), but she demonstrates her willingness to take action immediately to correct earlier neglect.

Skipping all the intermediary steps, the waitress transforms the customer's question about the location of the non-smoking section immediately into a request for the protection of non-smokers' rights. This transformation is achieved by a (mild) *violation of linguistic norms* at the *word level* underscored by *prosodic means*. The 'violation' consists in a slightly aberrant use of the verb *to use*, in fact a form of semantic overextension. 'Using x as y' normally involves 'action' of some sort, whereas in this example non-action is involved. Literally, *You can **use** it as non-smoking* gives the addressee the permission not to smoke at the table where she wants to sit down. (Compare with *You can use this knife for not cutting.*) Obviously, the utterance was neither intended nor interpreted in that way; since there is no obligation to smoke even in a smoking section, giving permission not to smoke does not make sense. The aberrant usage of the verb *to use* is underscored by the emphasis placed on 'use' in the utterance. It is this aspect of the prosody of the turn which makes the sentence carry the implicit information that the coffee shop does not yet have an established distinction between a smoking and a non-smoking section (which is the response to the question asked by the customer in the first turn). No doubt, some degree of irony or even mild sarcasm may have been involved, but without undercutting the co-operativeness.

A potential objection to this analysis could be that the participial adjective *non-smoking* is not equivalent to 'not smoke-ing'. Structurally it is not, since the one cannot replace the other: a *non-smoking section* is not to be defined as a section that does not smoke. But the activity sense inherent in the verbal construction is not eliminated at all. It is embedded in the adjectival state sense which can be paraphrased as 'designated for customers who do not smoke (at least while on these premises)'; moreover, since a *non-smoking customer* means 'one who does not smoke', the embedding is simply necessitated by the nature of 'section' (just like the nature of a 'district' necessitates the transfer of the property 'not wearing a top' to (some) girls in a *topless district*). The activity sense, moreover, is highlighted by the (stressed) combination with 'use'.

The example clearly demonstrates the strategic uses of presupposition. Presupposition serves as a shortcut, a time-saving device; but at the same time it signals the degree of co-operativeness (i.e. the waitress skips over the statement of the problem related to the customer's question and immediately proposes a solution), while it may also avert criticism (which could easily be voiced against a simple explicit statement of the fact that the coffee shop does not yet have an institutionalized non-smoking section).

The end result of the exchange signalled by *Thanks* is the customer's acceptance of the waitress's utterance as a commitment to keep smokers away from the customer. The section in which the customer is sitting down has thus been declared to function as a non-smoking section for all immediate practical intents and purposes. *Thanks*, the customer's expression of gratitude for the granting of the request that was not made originally, also signals that the customer has the expectation that the waitress will keep smokers at a distance.

This dynamic piece of interaction clearly generates meanings that are not directly related to speakers' intentions (see section 1.3). As in every form of human behaviour, there is of course intentionality involved (in particular the customer's intention to secure smokeless space around her, and the waitress's intention to accommodate the customer's wishes), but there is no direct link between the customer's original illocutionary intention and the illocutionary meaning which her own utterance takes on as a result of the social dynamics generated by the waitress's response, and which she then gratefully accepts as a fully appropriate reinterpretation.

The example is distinctly different from the question structures with actual or potential directive meaning (as studied by Ervin-Tripp 1976 and Merritt 1976, and as accounted for in the chapter on conversation in Levinson 1983), many of which assume the status of pre-requests in conversational structure. The inferential steps needed to go from *Do you have coffee to go?* to the response *Cream and sugar?* (namely an implicit *Yes we do. Would you like some?* followed by *Yes, please*) do not have to go beyond the assumption of requestive intentions conventionally expressed in the customer's original question. In other words, in such examples the question *is* a request at the time of utterance while the utterance itself takes a shape that makes it possible for the request to be cancelled if a specified contextual condition (the coffee shop having coffee) is not satisfied. A straightforward account in terms of intentional meaning is in this case combined with aspects of conversational dynamics. On the other hand, *Is this non-smoking?* is *not* a request to *designate* a non-smoking section, unless one assumes that the customer is fully aware of the fact that the answer is *No* and that the implied pre-condition that a non-smoking section has already been designated is not satisfied. Thus, in every case where that assumption is not valid, the request granted by the waitress is not part of the intentional meaning; it is an element of meaning effectively 'generated' by the waitress's response and 'endorsed' by the customer's reaction. This is also why an analysis in terms of indirect speech acts cannot be given.

The example also differs, e.g. from those adduced in Weiser's (1974) early attack on speech act theory for being too static in its approach to be able to cope with the dynamics of conversation. Weiser writes about cases of deliberate ambiguity in which the illocutionary status of an utterance does not get determined until a later stage in the interaction, but in which the different possibilities are calculated in advance by the speaker and are therefore directly linked to intentions. An example would be someone's saying *I found the most beautiful flowers on my doorstep!*, addressed to someone who may or may not have been the one who put them there – an utterance which will assume the meaning of a mere statement versus an indirect act of thanking depending on whether the addressee had anything to do with the flowers. Similarly, Stroud's (1992) attempt to extend the criticism on intention-based views of meaning and communication to the analysis of code switching concentrates mostly on (intentional) forms of ambiguity, so that he does not really move away from the analyses (as those by Gal 1979 or Gumperz 1982) which he regards as too meaning-and-intention oriented, even though he places due emphasis on the dynamics of collective meaning generation and negotiation.

Briefly, (4) shows that communicative dynamics, even in the briefest of encounters, creates meaning on the basis of processes to which individual intentions are not more fundamental than other ingredients of the speech event. Maybe a strict meaning–intention link was posited to keep the task of meaning description manageable after the discovery that there was more to meaning than could be found in the linguistic form (see the problem raised in section 0.5). Placing meaning into the custody of context must indeed have seemed a risky business at one time. Recent approaches to context and contextualization (see Chapter 3), however, have shown that this is exactly the prerequisite for an empirical methodology in the study of the meaningful functioning of language. Context is indeed not manageable as long as it is seen as purely extralinguistic. But what happens in linguistic interaction is the gradual build-up of a discourse-specific context, the calibration between reality 'out there' and the communicative needs of the moment, which leaves clear linguistic traces (see section 3.4 for an earlier introduction of this issue). Careful scrutiny of those traces, as we hope to have shown with the above example, enables us to provide an account for real 'acts of meaning'. Note that this account of context should by no means be misinterpreted as a recommendation to pay attention only to details on a micro-level of discourse organization. On the contrary, linguistic details at the micro-level have to be seen as anchoring points which provide heuristic support for a viable empirical methodology. For their interpretation, however, and even for the formulation of research questions, macro-level contextual phenomena should be taken into account. Just consider the reference we had to make to a certain type of group dynamics to put the non-smoking example into an interpretable social frame of action.

5.4.3 From Brussels to Frankfurt

The dynamics of language use in communication is such that it does not even require a conversational exchange to see change in the meanings emerging around an utterance. Take, for instance, sentence (8), which was uttered by a German Lufthansa pilot after apologizing for a delayed departure from Brussels due to heavy fog at the destination airport of Frankfurt, and after announcing that his flight had just been cleared:

(8) Once we are in the air, we'll fly as fast as possible.

Though the utterance was made in the most serious manner imaginable, it caused quite some giggles among the passengers. The pilot's intention was clearly to assure the passengers that he would do everything possible either to make up for some of the lost time or to make sure that the destination would be reached before weather conditions could change again. This intention-based part of the meaning was fully transparent. But somehow the utterance conjured up, e.g., the somewhat funny image of an airliner pilot racing through the air, much like the Mercedes and BMWs on German freeways (once virtually without speed limits). This type of image (representing only one of the possible specific triggers of the amused reaction), however unintended, was clearly part of the meaning of (8) for at least some of the giggling passengers. But how did it 'emerge'? Very simply by the fact that the utterance passed from one (primarily mental, though also physical) activity context – with its own frame of interpretation – to the next. At the production end, in the cockpit, speed is something which the pilot has to deal with all the time (with both technical and regulatory limits defining the range of what is *possible*), whilst the concept of speed in the air has virtually no experiential basis for an airline passenger (thus allowing for a different reading of *as fast as possible*). This is why (8) could be uttered in total seriousness with a fully transparent intended meaning while clashing, however mildly, with a conceptual framework at the receiving end, thus producing unintended additional meaning with a humorous effect.

The interesting question here is: What exactly is it that makes additional meaning (beyond what was intended) emerge in the interaction between the utterance and the context of interpretation? Usually there is nothing mysterious about this. A classical linguistic substitution test could already help. If the pilot had chosen different forms of expression, such as *Once we are in the air, we'll try to make up for some of the lost time* or *Once we are in the air, we'll try to get to our destination as fast as possible*, chances are that there would not have been amused reactions at all even though there are the same implications of speeding. This suggests that the potential for the image which emerges without having been intended, was already there in the utterance, more specifically in the way in which *to fly* was used in combination with a human agent and the explicit (though potentially ambiguous) description of the manner of flying. But even though the potential was there, it could only be actualized in the recontextualization process at the interpretation end. The conclusion could be that the German pilot was a clumsy user of English. But then such clumsiness would have to be defined as the inability to avoid forms of expression which, in interaction with the context and the related patterns of expectation of the audience, allows for the emergence of unintended meanings. Given this definition, it should also be clear that clumsiness is probably the norm in communication, rather than the deviation, except in highly standardized forms of exchange (such as the language of air traffic control, though Cushing 1994 demonstrates convincingly that even there 'errors' are legion).

It could also be argued that the passengers' giggles recast or reframe the utterance in the way described by Goffman (1976), as when *Do you have the time?* receives responses such as *No, but I still have the Newsweek* or *Yes, do you have the inclination?* Indeed, such responses consciously construct a meaning for the original question which was clearly not intended. But there are two important differences. First, such reframings result from the intentional meaning of the interlocutor's verbal response. In the case of (8), there is no such response, and even the non-verbal response (the giggles) results from the additional non-intended meaning rather than to produce it (except, maybe, for a possible group of slower passengers for whom the unintended meaning potential is not activated until they hear others giggle). Second, to the extent that reframing is involved in the reactions to (8), it is not a matter of one activity-related frame substituting another. Rather, the shared activity frame of pilot–passenger communications under circumstances of a flight's being delayed, calling for a brief message to take away possible worries, is fully preserved in the interpretation. But the linguistic forms of expression with which this frame is evoked, in interaction with specific contextual constraints on interpretation, allow for an associative link with a non-matching additional frame to emerge.

5.4.4 From Bellagio to Linate

The final example in this chapter is intended to show that the dynamics of interactive meaning generation does not necessarily end when an exchange has been completed, even if 'successfully'. A typical case in point is the activity type of giving and receiving road instructions. One day I had to drive from the Bellagio Study and Conference Center to the Linate airport of Milan (the one serving domestic and European flights, as opposed to the large international airport, Malpense). The Center's secretary had asked their regular driver how to give me the best instructions, since he was more familiar with (regularly changing) road conditions. She had jotted down a few notes on a piece of paper which she then used to refresh her own memory while giving me the necessary directions. I tried to follow her explanation, trying to interpret it with reference to a map. It should already be clear, then, that the communicative set-up, though nothing out of the ordinary, was relatively complex. Figure 5.1 is an attempt to represent it visually.

The exchange itself went as follows:

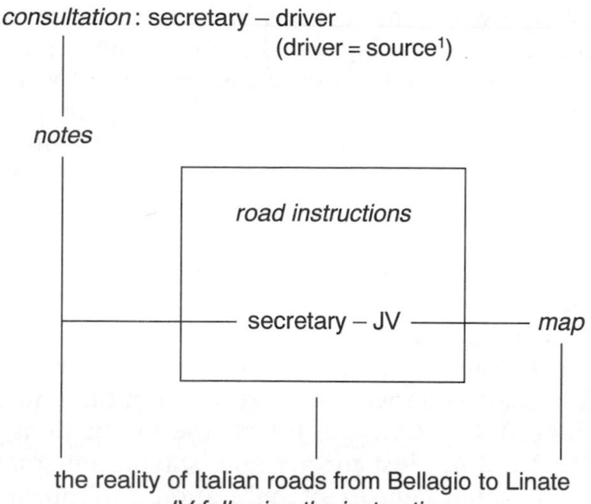

Fig. 5.1 Road instructions

(9)

1.	Secretary:	From here you go to Lecco.
2.	JV:	Hmh.
3.	Secretary:	Don't go into Lecco, but follow the SS36 to Milano . . . superstrada.
4.	JV:	[looking at the map] How do I find it?
5.	Secretary:	[after some searching on the map, and pointing] After the second tunnel to the right. First it's a small road, but then you see signs.
6.	JV:	OK, sounds easy enough.
7.	Secretary:	Y'know, it's Valmadrera, Cincello Balsamo, Milano.
8.	JV:	[searching the map, which is not detailed enough] I'll find it.
9.	Secretary:	Go on the Tangenziale Est.
10.	JV:	[pointing on the map at a freeway north of Milan] This one?
11.	Secretary:	Yes. You look for Forlanini . . . that is the name of the place where the airport is.
12.	JV:	Right.
13.	Secretary:	The exit for the airport is on your left.

In addition to the usual aspects of context to be taken into account, intertextuality plays a particularly important role in this example. The interconnections between the consultation of the driver (figuring as source[1]), the secretary's notes, the actual exchange during which road instructions are given, the map which is used as a point of reference but which is itself no more than a representation of the reality of Italian roads, embody a variety of interpretive steps, culminating in my attempt to follow the instructions in such a way as to accomplish the task of driving from Bellagio to Linate within a reasonable time span allowing me to get there in time for the plane I wanted to catch. I want to illustrate the processes of meaning generation involved by concentrating on the interpretation processes I went through from the moment I started to drive. In particular, I will demonstrate how, though (9) was no doubt a (successfully) completed exchange by that time, the negotiation of meaning did not stop until I had reached Milan, and some elements are a mystery until today.

The easy part was to follow instruction (9)1., partly because I had followed the road from Bellagio to Lecco before, and partly because once you have followed the initial signs, you have no choice but to follow the right road; otherwise you get lost in mountains, or else you end up in a lake. When trying to follow the instructions in (9)3. and (9)5., however, I did get lost for a while, staying on small roads and straying through small centres of habitation for much longer than could obviously be necessary. Eventually, I did see signs saying 'Milano', and was kept uncertain for a few minutes as to whether I would end up on the 'superstrada' SS36 or not, but ultimately I did. Anyway, even though my mission was successful so far, it was clear by then that I was not performing a task which simply consisted in the matching of actions to directions. Rather, I was really generating interpretations as I went along. What had gone wrong in the link between (9)3. to (9)5. – ironically, but without irony, reacted to with *sounds easy enough* in (9)6. – and the reality of driving, is something I will not be able to decide unless I get a chance of doing the whole thing over again. Now there are only questions and (marginally) hypotheses. Was (9)5. simply too ambiguous or imprecise? Did I have to turn right immediately after the second tunnel or maybe at the first major intersection? Had I miscounted tunnels? Had I missed a turn-off? Had I simply missed road signs? Had some error or misunderstanding crept into the flow from the consultation with source[1] to the secretary's notes and to her direct communication of instructions to me? Or had I missed elements of the instruction? A brief mental exploration of some of these possibilities, however, did not lead to a true renegotiation of meaning, for lack of fresh input.

It was time now to concentrate on things to come. Confronted with (9)7., and probably prompted by the experience of difficulties with (9)3. to (9)5., I was wondering for a while what the precise status of this statement was – a question that did not even come up in the course of direct interaction with the secretary before I left. Did it belong to a purely descriptive genre, pointing out the different places I would pass? Or was it instructive in the sense that I would have to keep Valmadrera and Cincello Balsamo in mind to make sure that I stayed on the right track? Just following the road, I learned that the first interpretation was the correct one. Thus the pragmatic status of the utterance did not become clear until long after the exchange.

If anything seemed clear and unambiguous, it was (9)9. So I kept looking for signs that would say *Tangenziale Est*. Keeping in mind that I could overlook such a sign even if there was one, I tried to focus on anything that could point me to *Linate* or, because of the instruction in (9)11., *Forlanini*. None of them appeared or, alternatively, I looked past all of them. The only signs I saw said *Malpense* and *Aeroporti*. The plural 'Aeroporti' made me hesitate, but since it pointed in the same direction as the fully specified 'Malpense', which is quite far away from Milan and in the opposite direction of Linate from where I was at that moment, I kept going. Soon it became clear that there was an intertextual mismatch between instructions and road signs: I was headed straight towards the centre of Milan, high time to decide that I had missed the Tangenziale Est entrance and to make a U-turn. On my way out again, it was impossible to miss clear signs for both the Tangenziale Est and Linate. Once on the Tangenziale Est, *Linate* was indicated unambiguously all the way. Not until just before I reached the airport did I see a sign to *Forlanini*. At that moment it became clear that (9)9. and (9)11. had to be interpreted sequentially, and that the *Yes* in (9)11. was not followed by further clarification – a hypothesis I had worked with while looking for the entrance to the Tangenziale Est – but by a new instruction: first get onto that freeway, then you will know you are close to the airport as soon as you see signs for Forlanini. This interpretive choice-making was not finished a minute too soon, because I barely had the time to move safely over to the left to get onto the tricky little exit to the airport. While avoiding a collision, (9)13. was assuming the status of a serious warning.

As with all the other examples, there is nothing exceptional about this one. The generation of meaning is simply a dynamic process – the very core of what people do when using language. It is interactive, furthermore, even if no interaction is visible; and it preserves that status long after an actual exchange of words has ceased. As with road directions, most conversations are mentally conducted over and over, even if less-than-consciously, to build up the multiple meanings with which all further discourse is imbued. We hope to have also demonstrated that interpretations truly give meaning to utterances. In a real sense, once spoken, an utterance is no longer in the control of the utterer: it begins to lead a life of its own in the mental worlds of others (a phenomenon which was already anticipated in section 3.2.2).

There are still further lessons to be drawn from this exercise. First, not everything that happens in and with conversation, but is nevertheless essential to an understanding of how it works, is recordable. Non-recorded data like (9) above (written down from memory immediately after the exchange, which gives them a status comparable to 'field notes') may be extremely relevant: the way I remembered the conversation was probably more instrumental to its meaningful functioning than what 'really' happened. But that only counts if you are interested in language as a form of behaviour and action. And this still leaves us with the unsolved methodological problem of the 'accuracy' of non-recorded data – which is not a trivial matter.

Second, the exercise deals with processes that form the essence of all intertextuality (see section 3.3.2). Processes similar to the ones described link the consultation, the notes, the map and the actual exchange in Figure 5.1. To account for those links, furthermore, one would have to take seriously the difference in language (Italian versus English) in which the preceding activity types must have taken place. This might also reveal some language-related significant features of what happens in (9). Extending the analysis in the opposite direction, comparable processes take place inside a conversation, though there is less of a time lag and more opportunity for checking and correcting. One may indeed look at turns in a conversation as 'texts', and at what happens in moving through the turns as the dynamic generation of intertextual links.

5.5 *Summary and further reading*

The central task of a pragmatic analysis is to account for the dynamics of meaning generation. This dynamics can be 'located' in relation to:

- The temporal dimension of language use (providing its raw material).
- Other contextual dimensions, such as social relationships.
- Structural properties of discourse.

It involves:

- The infinitely variable range of *speech genres* or *language games* which form the substance of 'interpreted' *speech activities* or *speech events* which provide frames of meaning for the negotiation of interpretations.
- The use of *strategies* of language use which exploit the interplay between explicitness and implicitness in the generation of meaning.

Four brief examples were given to illustrate how the dynamic generation of meaning can be described without compromising on the range of phenomena to be allowed into the analysis, while keeping the account empirical.

On the dynamics of language use in general: Kurzon (1986), Markovà and Foppa (eds) (1990), Martín Rojo (1994), Verschueren

Plate 5.1 Beermats

(1981). About the collaborative nature of meaning generation in conversational exchanges: Schegloff (1990). About activities, events and frames of meaning: Bakhtin (1981), Briggs and Bauman (1992), Goffman (1974), Gumperz (1982 and 1996), Hanks (1995), Hymes (1962), Levinson (1992b), Winch (1958), Wittgenstein (1958). An interesting extensive account of a speech event, in this case a type of political speech-making, is to be found in Duranti (1994).

5.6 *Research topics*

1. To learn more about the dynamics of meaning generation, it is a useful exercise to take any random pragmatic analysis (say, an article from *Journal of Pragmatics*) and to ask yourself systematically to what extent the author succeeds in capturing real-life processes rather than to present a somewhat abstracted static picture.

2. Record a piece of ordinary conversation in a setting of your choice. Make a simple transcription (following your own intuitions, or consulting, e.g., Gumperz and Berenz 1993) and describe the dynamics of meaning generation that it involves.

3. Beermats with an advertising text may seem like pretty static objects. Describe the dynamics involved in the three samples in Plate 5.1.

6

Salience

In this chapter we have to define the fourth angle of investigation which we need, in combination with the three dealt with in Chapters 3 to 5, in order to approach aspects of language use coherently from a pragmatic perspective. Put simply, if the discussion of contextual correlates and structural objects tells us what is interadaptable with what, and if the study of dynamics shows the processes involved, we are still left with the question of *how the processing actually works*. All *(dynamic) aspects of language use*, which can be situated in terms of *structurally identifiable choices* and *contextual properties and influences*, require processing in a **medium of adaptability**, i.e. a medium through which people can use language in a variable, negotiable and adaptable fashion. The general cover term we use to designate the **status** of processes of meaning generation in relation to the medium of adaptability, i.e. their status as determined by characteristics and mechanisms of processing, is **salience** (originally inspired by Errington's 1988 use of this term, but adapted to our needs). It hints at the fact that not everything that happens in linguistic behaviour occupies the same place in consciousness – while realizing that consciousness always plays a role.

This chapter is organized as follows. First we characterize the medium of adaptability, which we have already labelled *'mind in society'* before (section 6.1). Then (in section 6.2) we will pick out some of the mental phenomena that are most visibly at work in the meaningful functioning of language, i.e. *perception and representation*, *planning,* and *memory.* Later (in section 6.3), various *manners of processing* or *degrees of salience* will be focused on; the role of different levels of consciousness will be investigated. Finally (in section 6.4), we will concentrate on one specific aspect of salience: the metapragmatic awareness that is involved in any form of language use.

6.1 *Mind in society*

With Vygotsky, from whose work on developmental psychology the clumsy term 'mind in society' is borrowed, I am strongly convinced that *any serious pragmatic theory must reject a strict opposition between society and cognition.* A succinct survey – by no means complete – of cognitive or cognition-related notions that we have already used in this book should suffice to illustrate this point.

- Even a traditional pragmatic phenomenon such as deixis cannot be understood without assuming that a cognitive apparatus is at work, identifying points of reference in trying to cope with an outside 'reality' (to a significant extent 'social' in the sense of 'socially defined', which already implies a multitude of mental operations the product of which is shared by a sufficiently large group of people to become one of the bases for interaction).
- Phenomena of indirectness and implicit meaning would have no function in communication, unless inferencing processes (i.e. mental operations) can be relied upon to activate them, in a manner that is sufficiently based on socially shared norms (sometimes institutional in nature) to be negotiable.
- Preference organization in conversation is not just a 'fact' of verbal behaviour; it is largely based on experientially and socially produced patterns of expectation, which are further linked to the kinds of affective desiderata which also guide the need for deference and politeness (thus reinforcing the connection which is now generally agreed to exist between emotion and cognition).
- Intentionality is obviously cognition-based. The argument against sole emphasis on individual intentionality was largely inspired by the observation that guides this chapter, namely that cognitive phenomena derive much of their meaning and operational power from the organizational level of society.
- Making linguistic choices, our rock-bottom identification of the topic of pragmatic research, is of course a mental operation, though necessarily situated in a context. Similarly, it does not make sense to talk about variability, negotiability and adaptability – the concepts that give meaning to the making of choices – without assuming cognitive processes that can flexibly handle socially sanctioned principles and strategies.
- An entire mental world (with beliefs, emotions, desires and intentions), inseparable from the social and the physical, is within the range of contextual correlates of adaptability.
- Utterer voices and interpreter roles are mentally constructed and socially sanctioned.
- Societies themselves, especially when culturally defined, as well as institutions corrrespond to and impose categorizations.
- The existence of languages, codes and styles depends more on perceptions of difference and coherence than on their 'objective'

properties, and those perceptions are significantly guided by established social norms.

- Lexical meaning is structured, both in terms of word-internal semantic structure and in terms of semantic relationships between words, on the basis of cognitive principles that interact with extra-linguistic 'reality'.
- Grammar does not lead an independent life. On the one hand it is manifested only in the socially 'agreed upon' structure of utterances, i.e. a structure that does not overtly violate expectations held by most members of a speech community. On the other hand, it is full of phenomena guided by cognitive constraints.
- The structuring of utterances and utterance clusters (beyond what is given by 'grammar' in the strict sense of the word) is strongly inspired by what the interlocutors assume that the other's mental representation of the world looks like.
- Speech activity types and speech event types are behaviourally, and hence socially, based. Yet, their importance is to be found in the frames of meaning they provide for speech genres and language games. The frames themselves are merely products of the cognitive or conceptual organization of experience (as the subtitle of Goffman 1974 suggests). Or, to quote Vygotsky, the emergence of speech activities, i.e. the convergence of speech and practical activity, is 'the most significant moment in the course of intellectual development, which gives birth to the purely human forms of practical and abstract intelligence' (1978: 24).

Briefly, whatever social correlates there are to language, they are always cognitively processed to have any influence at all on linguistic behaviour. What is more, those social factors do not exist without being interpreted, i.e. cognitively processed (sometimes cognitively produced). Conversely, abstract cognition, without any social embedding, does not exist. In other words, the medium of adaptability shows a *non-dichotomous dual nature*. Its duality is captured by the rough glosses *mind* and *society*. The rephrasing *mind **in** society* draws attention to the non-dichotomy.

In addition to the phenomena mentioned above, both the duality and non-dichotomy of the medium of adaptability are clearly in evidence in **language acquisition**, the interactive – and hence social – activation and acquisition of the cognitive skills needed to use language for the generation of meaning. The same goes for language-related **socialization** and **enculturation**, the incorporation of behavioural norms and expectations – linguistic as well as non-linguistic – prevalent in a community (where a 'community', as said before, is itself always the product of complex forms of interaction between social practices and categorization processes).

6.2 *Perception and representation, planning, memory*

The mental 'work' that is most visibly involved in the use of language can be discussed under three labels: *perception and representation* (section 6.2.1), *planning* (in 6.2.2), and *memory* (section 6.2.3). Before devoting a few words to each of these topics, it should be pointed out that the processes in question (including perception and representation) operate both, and often simultaneously, on the (often non-linguistic) 'object' of verbal communication and on language and language use itself. The implications will be clear from the following cursory account.

6.2.1 Perception and representation

The 'lines of vision' metaphor, which we used to describe the way in which elements of the mental, social, and physical worlds are activated in language use as contextual correlates of adaptability (see section 3.1), incorporates much about what we will have to say about the role of perception and representation. In order to have anything at all to talk about, we have to **perceive** (i.e., become conscious of, whether through visual perception or otherwise) certain 'realities'. However, we also have to make sense of perceptions; in other words, we have to **represent** what we perceive in a way that makes it interpretable and usable for communicative purposes.

These two mental activities are inseparable. Just consider the way in which language itself is perceived. Speech sounds are not just heard as the continuous stream of air which is their physical substance, or in terms of their acoustic or articulatory properties, but primarily in terms of the way in which the linguistic knowledge of language users represents the perceived auditory stimuli in relation to a functional system of contrasts, which allows them to identify phonetic segments (see section 0.1 on page 1, where this is presented as the basis for the distinction between phonetics and phonology), morphemes, words, and ultimately sentences and beyond. Representational mechanisms interfere with 'pure' perception to such an extent that, as experiments have shown, chunks of sound cut out from a stretch of speech (even when corresponding precisely to a word, for instance) are often unrecognizable in isolation, though perfectly understood in context. But just as patterns of representation may aid perception, they may also produce misperceptions.

Similar things happen in relation to the non-verbal reality that enters communicative content. One of the basic representational processes interacting with perception, to which we have already devoted some attention in earlier remarks on lexical meaning (see section 4.2.2), is the process of **categorization**, which produces semantic contents organized around prototypes and lexical fields structured around a cognitively basic level – none of them alsolutely fixed once and for all, nor necessarily identical for all users of the same language, nor for the same users at different moments and under different circumstances. Once established, however, categories do not lead an innocent life. Not only can they vary and change, but to the extent that they show some stability, they guide perceptual input as well as communicative output, i.e. most of what is involved in generating meaning. As to the *perceptual input*, when scanning an environment, the habitual categories we have available will strongly influence what we see or what we find interesting (or interesting enough to say something about). This counts for the social and mental environment as much as for the physical environment. Thus it will be hard (literally, in the sense that it takes extra communicative effort) to comment on a shade of red corresponding to the colour of a certain kind of bird, unless we have a matching lexicalized concept; yet we should remember that comment is never impossible, and that new conceptual tools may be created as the need arises. Similarly, describing a mixture between anger and sadness would be easier if we had a term available that incorporates the meaning of both *anger* and *sadness*. Or talking about a political spectrum would be different if we did not habitually apply the notions *left* and *right*. In fact, partly because of the varying availability of habitual conceptual tools, people differ greatly in degrees of refinement in perceiving (and speaking of) what they feel or think, in levels of sophistication in viewing (and talking about) what goes on in the social and political world, as much as in the precision with which they observe (and comment on) their physical surroundings.

Turning more directly to the *communicative output*, and using the last sentence of the previous paragraph as an example of the issue at hand, the evaluative phrasing ('refinement', 'sophistication', 'precision') implies the assumption of a hierarchy among categorization systems. It is because of the ready availability of these three concepts to us, which may at the same time betray an underlying normative inclination (more or less scientific in the case of 'precision', intellectual and political in the case of 'sophistication', and intellectual and ethical in the case of 'refinement'), that we are tempted to rank categorization systems. Yet, writing for an audience with which I presumably share a distrust of absolute characterizations, especially when they are evaluative, and having ready access to the concept of 'evaluation', I am prompted to make the foregoing metacomment to relativize my own more radical statement. What happens at this abstract level is all the more visible with more tangible phenomena (remember the examples from section 4.2.2).

Among categorization devices, **metaphorization** is one of the more influential. This process consists in expanding the applicability of a term, used in a certain domain of experience (often relatively concrete), for use in a different domain. We have already pointed at the way in which spatial reference forms the basis for standard metaphors in numerous areas of experience (see section 3.2.4). This goes from relatively transparent forms of meaning transfer as in *over the top* or *the end of the tunnel*, to less overtly motivated ones such as the political usage of *left* and *right*. Other favourite examples are to be found in the many ways in which body parts show up in domains such as natural phenomena unrelated to the human body (*sea arm*, *the foot of the mountain*, *the mouth of a river*), a variety of artifacts (*the arm of a chair*, *the nose of a plane*, *the hands of a watch*), and even social ranking (*the head of the department*). The point is that these are usually not random choices, but that they form part of sometimes elaborate systems which are conducive to (though themselves probably produced by) specific ways of looking at certain aspects of reality. Thus *time* tends to be treated as a commodity, as is clear from expressions such as *saving time*, *wasting time*, *spending time*, *running out of time*, and *giving someone a few minutes of your time*. Similarly, *attacking*, *defending*, and *undermining an argument* put argumentation in a framework of verbal warfare. There is, by now, a large literature on these phenomena.

A few representational devices on a par with categorization (but often involved in or involving categorization, sometimes of the metaphorization type) deserve special mention, namely processes of **association**, **abstraction**, **generalization**, and **reification**. A process of association – the conceptual linking of otherwise distant notions – is involved in the construction and interpretation of concepts such as *landscape architecture* or *installation art*. Describing a football player's seemingly erratic movements as *tactics* requires abstraction, i.e. the transformation of what is physically observable into a higher dimension of conceptualization. Generalization (i.e. the mental act of attaching general validity to specific facts), in combination with abstraction, is the name of the game when events in America in 1776, in France in 1789, in Russia in 1917, and in Iran in 1978–9 are all called *revolutions*. And reification – or the making of something abstract into a thing – is accomplished when *culture* (or *language*) is given its plural form *cultures* (or *languages*).

To illustrate that these processes are not just characteristic of meaning generation at the lexical level, that they are visibly at work in natural discourse, and that they are not restricted to spontaneous everyday usage, let us briefly look at (1).

(1) (a) Archaeologists who don't excavate? (b) Surely that is heresy. (c) Yet surveys are a well-established archaeological practice. (d) American anthropologists working in the Southwest and in Meso-America refined the technique in the 1960s and 1970s. (e) Later, British archaeologists picked up the New World habit, wedded it to French modernist theories on the history of 'ordinary' life and brought it to bear on Old World problems. [*The Sciences*, May/June 1997: 12]

This text reflects a representation of a perceived reality of scientific practice, which makes use of all the mental tools that we have mentioned so far. First of all, a category of scholars called *archaeologists* is identified, with prototype properties of which one (the fact that he or she *excavates*) is challenged in (1)a. This challenge itself is immediately reflexively conceptualized in terms of a category that establishes an associative link between the worlds of academia and religion: *heresy* in (1)b. Two groups of 'archaeologists', *American anthropologists* in (1)d. (obviously referring to a subcategory of 'American anthropologists', viz. those engaged in archaeological work) and *British archaeologists* in (1)e., are handled as general categories instead of identifying the specific scholars involved. The topic, a specific archaeological method, moves through representational space from the relatively concrete form *surveys* to the more abstractly categorizing *a well-established archaeological practice* in (1)c., back to the more concrete *the technique* (tangible enough to be *refined*) in (1)d. and on to the more general and abstract *the New World habit* in (1)e., which is nevertheless sufficiently reified to be *picked up* and *wedded to French modernist theories*. The range of metaphorizations stretches from really dead metaphors such as *bring to bear on* in (1)e., over fully conventionalized ones such as *established practice* in (1)c. and *pick up the habit* in (1)e., to fully creative ones such as *wedding a habit to a theory* in (1)e. In addition to the processes already named, example (1) shows to what extent representation is dependent on the establishment of **contrasts**: excavation versus surveys; American versus British archaeologists; New World versus Old World; habits vversus theories. What we see, briefly, is the manifestation of an ongoing struggle over the perception and representation of an episode of academic life. The example shows that in actual discourse, even when direct interaction is not so clearly involved, representation surfaces as a negotiable on-line activity.

In other words, all language use activates mappings of semantic space. The communicative output, as in (1), involves acts of **referring** (discussed before in section 4.2.4) and a great deal of **highlighting**. So far, highlighting has only come up in the sense of drawing special attention to (see section 3.3.2) or thematic foregrounding (see 4.4.1).

Such processes are not to be ignored in this context. Yet there is a more fundamental way in which a process that can be called 'highlighting' contributes to the nature of representation, and hence also perception. The process in question is involved in all categorizations and identifications. To borrow Goodwin's (1994) comparison, particularly appropriate in relation to example (1), it is enough for one archaeologist to draw a line around a patch of dirt that is slightly different in colour or texture or both, to make other archaeologists see this as the remains of a wooden pole. Similarly, the way in which a text fragment such as (1) carves up the landscape of archaeology could easily make us forget a wide range of questions pertaining to the 'perceptual field' in question: What about American archaeologists who did not consider themselves anthropologists, if there were any? What about those who were not working in the Southwest and Meso-America? Was there a complete consensus about surveys as an archaeological practice? If not, what were the points of dispute? What about European archaeologists outside of Britain? Or consider the effect of describing the same historical event as *the reunification of Germany* instead of *the unification of the two Germanies*. Briefly, even the simplest acts of referring, because of the highlighting they imply, go far beyond 'copying' what is 'out there'.

It should be clear, then, that an uncompromising pragmatic look at the way in which language functions, taking seriously 'mind in society' as medium of adaptability, demands adherence to some kind of **linguistic relativity principle**. There is indeed a connection between habits of speaking and habits of thinking, even if one cannot possibly maintain that the one fully determines the other. In comparison with the version attributed to Sapir and Whorf (but with roots in German romanticism, the work of Wilhelm von Humboldt, and Saussurean structuralism), a pragmatically inspired linguistic relativity principle does not focus exclusively on the role of grammar and lexical categories as internalized by individual members of a society, but also on the way in which these are put to work in actual contexts of use, at a micro-level of interaction (see Chapter 7) as well as on a societal macro-level (see Chapter 8). Their being 'put to work' – and here a truly pragmatic principle of linguistic relativity contrasts sharply with later deterministic versions of what came to be called the 'Sapir–Whorf hypothesis' – means that their role is itself relative, because variable, negotiable and adaptable. But that makes the entire phenomenon all the more interesting. By thus placing relativity within the scope of a relativistic attitude, any potential conflict between relativity and the existence of a degree of universality in language and language use – a conflict that follows directly from some utterly particularistic views of linguistic relativity – is eliminated (see also section 2.3).

6.2.2 Planning

A second type of mental activities involved in language use could be put under the general label of **planning**. The term can be used to cover any influence of any type of 'looking ahead' on aspects of linguistic behaviour. A multitude of phenomena are involved.

First of all, though there seems to be a temporal relation between planning activities and verbal output (turning planning into an important contributing factor in the dynamics of language use; see section 5.1.1), 'planning' is by no means restricted to mental operations that are carried out *in advance*. Consider the road instructions discussed in the previous chapter (section 5.4.4). In that particular case, the conversation was preceded by a careful planning stage: I had informed the secretary that I would have to find my way to Linate; she had promised to ask their regular driver for instructions; she had indeed asked the driver, and during that conversation she had taken notes that could guide her instructions to me. But just imagine having to give *impromptu* road instructions. In such a situation, planning and the execution of plans develop hand in hand, virtually simultaneously. It still makes sense, however, to talk about 'planning'. The reason is that the extemporaneous search for the proper strategies to enable the addressee to find his or her way on the basis of the verbal output makes use of **scripts**, i.e. mental representations (in the sense touched upon in section 6.2.1) of activity or event types (as discussed in 5.2). In the road instruction example, the script surrounding the task of finding one's way through the road system and helping someone to accomplish that task contains points of departure and arrival, types of roads, turns to the left and to the right, traffic signals, indicators along the road, place names, and the like. In most forms of spontaneous interaction, planning is of this kind (resulting in false starts, pauses, hesitations, and the need for repair; see section 1.1.4), though the scripts to be followed are not always equally clear.

Second, to the extent that planning is involved in the behaviour of the utterer, it is **intention**- or **goal**-related, though not always with the same degree of consciousness. But just as meaning in general cannot be reduced to intentionality (see section 1.3), planning is not only involved in intention-related utterer behaviour. Also interpretation involves planning. In particular, processes of interpretation are partly guided by expectations and the anticipation of speech plans based on a knowledge of scripts. When reading (1) for instance, I expect a further explanation of the 'archaeological survey technique', as well as a substantiation of the 'Old World problems' to which it is being applied, with an indication of how the two relate and what results have been or are expected to be reached. My approval or disapproval of the article from which it was taken will be partly a function of the extent to which these scripted expectations are met. In the course of face-to-face interaction, similar processes allow for the possibility of continuous feedback, leading to adjustments to the planning on the (other) utterer's side (in the case of an information-giving activity). In the case of most ordinary conversations, the result is a complex criss-crossing of the different interlocutors' production and interpretation planning and adjustment processes.

6.2.3 Memory

In a sense, **memory**, though also interfering with planning (witness a phrase such as *Before I forget, . . .*), is its reverse: the concept is used to point at the influence of any type of 'looking back on', or retrospective representation of, the course of linguistic behaviour. So far the topic of memory has come up only in passing, and only as a processing constraint. Of course, memory is primarily a resource rather than a constraint, however limited it may be. Language use is not possible without the constant tapping of memory, which either takes the form of **recognition** (the spontaneous mobilization of memory that is needed to understand ongoing discourse) or of **recall** (an active effort to bring something back from memory). Day-to-day interaction will rely predominantly on recognition, aided by the availability of categorization schemes (see section 6.2.1) and of scripts (see 6.2.2) – which are themselves products of (at least partial) recognition based on memory). But whatever is told about the past, whether a non-linguistic event or an earlier act of communication, requires active recall.

For most language users, only short-term memory is able to retain the actual form of utterances. Typically, only a few short turns in a conversation can be remembered literally at any given moment. Longer-term memory focuses more on content, interspersed with sporadic bits of verbatim memory. This way of using memory in the course of verbal interaction is activated even within the boundaries of conducting a longer conversation or reading a text longer than a few paragraphs. This means that *memory is interpretive* (not only, of course, in relation to linguistic behaviour, but in relation to any extra-linguistic state of affairs as well). Such an observation has great methodological consequences for the study of spoken interaction. On the one hand, minute details of what goes on in spoken interaction can only be studied with the help of recordings (which is why recording equipment has revolutionized the study of conversation). On the other hand, however, what is on tape (whether audio or video) can never be enough: what happens in conversational interaction is not only informed by a wider context, it also hinges on retrospective (as well as anticipatory – remember section 6.2.2) representations which are detached from actual (recordable) forms of expression, being largely interpretive and content-oriented once the limits of verbatim memory have been exceeded. Unfortunately, this final point is often forgotten by conversation analysts. For an example of the relevance of non-recorded (and non-recordable) data, consisting of interpretations rather than what could possibly be remembered with the amount of detail to be found on a tape (without downplaying the methodological importance of recording as well whenever possible), go back to section 5.4.4.

Before moving on, let me express the hope that the foregoing exposition (from the beginning of section 6.2 onwards) has shown that the seat of cognition is indeed a 'mind in society'. None of the processes described, though obviously taking place in individual minds, have any sense at all without a social dimension. Representations (and the planning and memory partly based on them and partly producing them) have to be interpersonally 'established' (though never statically) for them to function at all in language use. Also, planning and memory are at least partly guided by what happens to be socially important.

6.3 *Degrees of salience*

Section 6.2 reviewed a few of the *types of processes* taking place in the medium of adaptability, the human 'mind in society', and contributing to the overarching operation of linguistic choice-making which pragmatics tries to account for. All of these, i.e. the making of choices in general as well as the contributing mental processes, are subject to different *manners of processing*. In particular, they can all take place with different *degrees of salience*. Their operation may be completely conscious or not conscious at all, with every shade in between. Clearly, there is a relation between salience and individual 'knowledge', as the discussion below – formulating (too) much in individual terms – will clarify. But at the same time we should not forget that there is such a thing as *social salience*: social norms establish patterns of markedness; what is more 'marked' (e.g. refusing an offer, as opposed to accepting it – remember 'preference organization' in section 1.1.4) will be more clearly 'noticed', hence more conscious or salient.

When discussing degrees of salience, we really need to distinguish between **the actual making of linguistic choices** and what we now refer to as **the 'contributing mental processes'**. As to the latter, some elements in a categorization pattern (such as protoypical examples and basic level terms) are cognitively more salient than others. Similarly, advance planning can be expected to show a higher degree of salience or consciousness than planning on the spot. And active recall obviously requires more conscious operations than spontaneous recognition. Though there is a relationship between these and the degrees of consciousness with which actual choices are made, there is no automatic correspondence. For instance, the more salient a term is in a categorization scheme, the more easily or automatically it will be retrieved. In fact, ease of processing has been used by cognitive psychologists as a prime indicator of conceptual basicness or cognitive salience. In the same way, the more carefully an exchange has been planned in advance (i.e. the better it has been 'practised'), the less conscious processing effort it will require to say the right thing at the right time.

As to the actual making of linguistic choices, much – though by no means all – of what is involved can be assumed to take place at a subliminal level. Let us briefly comment, to illustrate this, on the coffee shop example (discussed at length in section 5.4.2) again:

(2) [Situation: coffee shop in Berkeley, California, in 1981]

1. Customer [just coming in] to waitress:	Is this non-smoking?
2. Waitress:	You can **use** it as non-smoking.
3. Customer [sitting down]:	Thanks.

With the earlier analysis in the background, we can make the following assumptions regarding the salience of the processes of meaning generation that take place in this exchange:

- The customer can be assumed to be consciously looking for the information she needs, namely whether a given area is non-smoking or not; the actual 'looking for' the non-smoking section may become a routine action comparable to the way in which an experienced driver shifts gears, but if the routine search was not successful so that a question needs to be asked, the level of consciousness rises drastically (just as when the same driver enters an unfamiliar car).
- She must also be conscious of the inevitable self-identification (in terms of socially defined categories) which is implicit in her question, but there is no compelling reason to believe that she is conscious of the fact that asking the question may be taken as an attempt to actively enforce the rights of the group she belongs to, though this kind of intentional strategy could be involved (i) if the customer knew that the coffeeshop did not yet have an established non-smoking section and/or (ii) if she belonged to a group of anti-smoking activists roaming the coffeeshops to put subtle pressure on them to establish non-smoking sections; in the case of (i) or (ii) the possibility of interpreting her question as a mere routine would be cancelled; in the case of (ii) conscious planning would be involved.
- The waitress is consciously trying to accommodate the customer's needs as well as she can, but in her eagerness to co-operate she

takes some shortcuts which lead to – possibly subconscious or at least unintended (except in case irony or sarcasm is involved) – violations of linguistic norms, however mild they may be.
- Once the waitress's turn is over, however, most of the implications have become sufficiently salient to form the basis of further interaction.

This example is by no means exceptional. It is also typical in the sense that it is impossible to get definitive answers to all the questions that can be asked about the precise status, in terms of salience, of the meaning-making processes involved. It is important to remember that, though degrees of salience really matter (even in the sense that they often become the subject of explicit dispute), for linguistic analysis they *only* matter to the extent that they are needed to explain what happens in the discourse (in its widest sense), and that, if they can be used convincingly for explanatory purposes, in most cases we *will* be able to answer the questions that arise. Thus our interpretation of (2)1. would change seriously if (2)3. were not *Thanks!* but rather *That's not good enough!* Little speculation would be needed about the place which the search for a non-smoking section and the rights of non-smokers occupies in the conscious awareness of the customer.

Just as the salience of actual linguistic choices is related to that of the contributing mental processes, but not in a one-to-one fashion, it is also related to the distinction between **explicit and implicit meaning** (see section 1.1.3). Again, the relationship is not mechanical or invariable. Typically one would expect aspects of implicit meaning to be more backgrounded. But the reality of language use is not that straightforward. First, as pointed out before (in section 5.3), the interplay between explicitness and implicitness can be exploited strategically – which is the main reason why the study of language use, the domain of pragmatics, cannot be satisfactorily defined in terms of implicitness alone. Thus, when a presupposition or implicature clashes with an interpreter's assumptions or expectations, it may suddenly assume a higher degree of salience than whatever is being said explicitly. Returning to a classical example, one may indeed expect the explicit reassurance in *Tomorrow, I will be faithful to you* to fade away in the shadow of the implicit message that the propositional content of the promise may contrast with past conduct and does not necessarily count for points in the future beyond (or even until) *tomorrow.*

Second, a differential positioning of utterer and interpreter in relation to what is explicit and what is implicit may be involved, and may be consciously taken into account by the utterer. This is what happens in information-packed sentences such as (3).

(3) British voters turned out in heavy numbers under warm, sunny skies Thursday in what pollsters, pundits and politicians alike predicted

> right up to the end would most likely prove a watershed election for the Labour Party, ending 18 years of Conservative rule and handing the keys to No. 10 Downing Street to Tony Blair. (*International Herald Tribune*, 2 May 1997)

Faced with the task of addressing an audience, not all the members of which can be assumed to be equally well-informed, the author opts for forms of expression which embed numerous presuppositions (e.g. that there was an *election* in Great Britain, that Britain had been ruled by *Conservatives* in the previous *18 years*, that the election would determine the next Prime minister, whose residence is *No. 10 Downing Street*, that *Tony Blair* was the *Labour Party* candidate, etc.) at a shallow level (where they are easy to extract) that allow informed readers to simply use them as anchoring points (for the information that many people went to vote and that everyone had predicted a clear victory for Labour), while enabling less informed readers to reconstruct a general state of affairs. On the author's side, the choices are relatively conscious, though the style in question and its adaptedness to a mixed audience also get routinized. At the receiving end, processing, and the related degrees of salience, will be different for the different categories or readers.

Third, widely shared patterns of assumptions which tend to escape conscious questioning and, hence, explicit formulation often permeate people's discourse. They may show up mainly in the form of carriers of implicit meaning which subtly interact with explicit content, though sometimes they resist fully explicit formulation, and both utterer and interpreter are only subliminally engaged in the corresponding choice-making. This topic, which touches the area of societal ideologies, will be dealt with at length in Chapter 8.

Salience cannot be measured. Moreover, it is not necessary to determine degrees of salience for all processes in every instance of language use. There is, however, a need to take salience into account whenever its traces can be shown to reveal its relevance for an understanding of meaning generation in the data under investigation. In the following section, the focus is on one specific topic related to the salience of actual choice-making: the area of metapragmatic awareness. This topic derives its special position in a theory of pragmatics from the fact that (i) it leaves many observable traces, and, more importantly, (ii) it touches the core of what salience is all about, the utterer's and the interpreter's reflexive awareness of the choices made when using language.

One more remark needs to be made, however, to round off the more general discussion. The requirement to take into account aspects of processing in a pragmatic approach to language implies that a reinterpretation of Figure 3.1 (in section 3.1) is needed. First, the 'lines of vision' postulated for utterer and interpreter not only encompass mental, social and physical phenomena which the interlocutors are consciously aware of. Whatever can be activated for communicative purposes, even at the deepest subconscious level, is to be situated within those (porous) 'lines'. Second, aspects of the mental and social world outside the 'lines of vision' also enter language use, not as contextual correlates of adaptability, but as properties of the 'mind in society' itself, the processing mechanisms characterizing the medium of adaptability.

6.4 *Metapragmatic awareness*

Let us briefly look at examples (1), (2) and (3) again. Sentence (1)b. comments on (1)a. by describing it as *heresy*, an evaluative characterization with reference to a world of expectations concerning archaeology. Furthermore, by means of *surely*, it qualifies its own assertive status along a dimension of certainty or evidentiality. In (2)2., the waitress's prosodic choices, with heavy emphasis on *use*, betray some reflexive awareness of the fact that her response goes beyond the pattern of the expected (and hence awareness of the customer's default expectations), in an effort – whether consciously chosen or routine-like – to be cooperative. Example (3), finally, shows keen awareness of the assertive status (*predicted right up to the end*), communicative lineage (*pollsters, pundits and politicians alike* – a phrasing which further reflects some conscious ironic distancing), and epistemic value (*would most likely prove*) of the predicted outcome of the elections. What do these observations have in common?

Defining language use as the making of linguistic choices, taking into account the mediating role of both the utterer's and the interpreter's minds, and attributing a prominent role to consciousness, implies that *language users know more or less what they are doing when using language*, even if certain choices are virtually automatic in comparison with others that may be highly motivated. This 'knowledge' truly manifests itself in all the choices that are made. Additionally, however, it is manifested in the language user's **reflexive awareness** of those choices, as choices from a range of options, and hence with a specific conceptual or communicative status: while *all* linguistic choice-making implies *some* degree of consciousness, *some choices openly reflect upon themselves* (as does *surely* in (1)b. or the accentuation pattern in (2)2.) *or upon other choices* (as does *heresy* in (1)b. as well as the description in (3)). Reflexive awareness may be so central that it could be regarded as one of the original evolutionary prerequisites for the development of language. It is so central, furthermore, that *all verbal communication is self-referential* to a certain degree. In other words, *there is no language use without a constant calibration between pragmatic and metapragmatic functioning*. The systematic study of the metalevel, where indicators of reflexive awareness are to be found in the actual choice-making that constitutes language use, is the proper domain of what is usually called **metapragmatics** (other usages of this term being somewhat confusing; for Mey, for instance, metapragmatics 'studies the conditions under which pragmatic, i.e. users', rules are supposed to hold' (1993: 277) – a topic which is plainly 'pragmatics' in the sense in which we employ it in this book).

Metapragmatic awareness, just like all other mental processes and phenomena involved in language use, may show different degrees of salience. Some of its indicators betray a very conscious choice (as illustrated with *heresy* in (1)b.), whereas others are not so easily accessible (such as the emphasis on *use* in (2)2.). Thus the topic is highly complex because of two fuzzy definitional boundaries: first, it is not so easy to distinguish reflexive awareness from other aspects of the operation of consciousness in language use (and a strict distinction might not even make sense); second, not all reflexive awareness is equally salient and accessible (to the point where one may wonder, without being certain, whether the concept still applies). Moreover, while reflexive awareness does not necessarily imply a high degree of conscious choice-making or salience, choices that are highly conscious do not necessarily imply a serious form of metapragmatic awareness either. Consider (4) and (5).

(4) At the end of the year, 31 new cancer drugs will be in the final phase of clinical trials.
(5) Around the end of the year, more than 30 new cancer drugs could be in the final phase of clinical trials.

There is no reason to assume that there is a significant difference in the salience of the linguistic choice-making underlying these two sentences. It may even be the case that (4) is the product of a very conscious effort to give precise information, i.e. to get a perfect match between the message and the anticipated state of affairs. Yet, (5) may be higher on a scale of metapragmatic awareness: it contains more elements that betray the utterer's awareness of the status of the utterance as a prediction, with all the uncertainty this implies in relation to the precise moment at which a state of affairs is expected to materialize (hence *around* versus *at*), details of that state of affairs (*more than 30* versus *31*), and the degree of certainty itself (*could be* versus *will be*).

This complexity is reflected in an insufficiently coherent treatment of the corresponding phenomena in the pragmatic literature. Many concepts have been proposed to deal with the issue, which has always intuitively been felt to be important. But all proposals so far have selected, or focused primarily on, subsets from the range of indicators, thus losing sight of the wider perspective which places them at the very core of what happens when people use language.

6.4.1 Indicators of metapragmatic awareness

Let us briefly present an overview of some of the phenomena, to be situated at various structural levels of adaptability, that have attracted the attention of linguists and that are candidates for inclusion under the label of 'indicators of metapragmatic awareness'. But first we should point to some of the concepts that have been or are in current use and that pertain to the issue of reflexivity in language. First, there is the category of what Jakobson (1971) – followed in this usage by Silverstein (1976) – called **shifters**. 'Shifters' are indexical symbols such as personal pronouns and other deictic expressions (see sections 1.1.1, 3.2.3, 3.2.4), aspect (see 4.2.4), tense (see 1.1.1, 3.2.4), mood (see 4.2.4), modality and evidentials (see also section 4.2.4), which necessarily 'shift' in relation to changes in the context of use, and which require reflexive awareness of the process of matching structural to contextual properties, except when a default or unmarked choice is made from the structural system of available options. Second, a wide range of indicators of metapragmatic awareness passes under the variable and often overlapping labels **discourse markers**, **pragmatic markers**, **discourse particles** or **pragmatic particles**. More often than not, these notions are used to deal with lexical indications – often sentence adverbs (see section 4.2.4) or markers of cohesion and coherence (see sections 3.3.2 and 4.4) – of how an utterance fits in with surrounding discourse (*anyway*, *however*, *actually*, *to the contrary*, and the like), or of the epistemic and/or illocutionary status of the propositional content (as is the case with *surely*, *undoubtedly*, *frankly*, *I guess*, etc.), or of interpreter-oriented involvement (as with *you know*). Third, the functioning of **contextualization cues** (see sections 3.4.3 and 4.2.1), whether in the form of prosodic markers, code switching, or back channel cues, though 'rarely consciously noted and almost never talked about directly' (Gumperz 1982, p. 131), betrays an awareness of 'co-occurrence expectations between content and surface style' (Gumperz 1982, p. 131) in the sense that they are identifiable as bases of contextualizing interpretations.

A more systematic and integrated look at these phenomena would be highly desirable. In the context of this book, we can barely begin to scratch the surface. We will, therefore, simply exemplify or draw attention to a number of metapragmatic indicators situated with reference to aspects of linguistic context (see section 3.3.2) and the structural objects of adaptability we have distinguished in Chapter 4. For a serious analysis, we would have to make use of whatever we have learned so far in chapters 3 to 6; one case study, with reference to a specific problem concerning the reflexivity of language, will be presented in Chapter 7 (section 7.1.2).

In the light of this chapter, it will be clear that much of what was said about languages, codes and styles (in section 4.1) pertains to choices showing a certain degree of metapragmatic awareness. In particular, the examples we gave of code switching may qualify (though this should not be taken to imply that necessarily all types of code switching serve as indicators of metapragmatic awareness). One more example may be useful.

(6) (From Gumperz 1982, p. 30)
[Following a graduate seminar, a black student approaches the white instructor, who is about to leave the room accompanied by several other black and white students.]

1. Black student: Could I talk to you for a minute? I'm gonna apply for a fellowship and I was wondering if I could get a recommendation?
2. Instructor: OK. Come along to the office and tell me what you want to do.
3. Black student [turning his head slightly to the other students, while they are all leaving the room]: *Ahma git me a gig!* [Rough gloss: 'I'm going to get myself some support']

In this example, (6)3. shows a double form of reflexivity. On the one hand, the code switch is symbolic in the sense that it represents a choice that explicitly signals solidarity with the group, in this case the Black students, whose code is being adopted. Probably, the white members of the group would not even understand the utterance. The Black student, after having openly demonstrated his dependence on a white instructor for a recommendation, reasserts his Black identity and his belonging to the Black community. On the other hand, (6)3. is also an explicit metacomment on the preceding discourse.

As far as utterance-building ingredients are concerned, sound structure is a rich resource for contextualization cues which, at a low level of salience, indicate various degrees of metapragmatic awareness (see section 4.2.1). Thus the British interpreter of an Asian woman's saying *Gravy!* with a falling intonation when she wants to know whether a person she is serving wants gravy or not, will be able to tell you that he or she would not have found her impolite if she had said *Gravy?* with a rising intonation, which is the usual English way of asking or offering. (See Gumperz 1982.)

At the word level, we find some of the most explicit indicators of metapragmatic awareness. In particular, all natural languages contain a wide range of verbs and verb-like expressions to describe forms of language use. Let us simply call the members of this lexical field, as has been done in the pragmatic literature, **verba dicendi**, 'verbs of speaking'. Or, keeping in mind (i) that language use is more than what can literally be called 'speaking', not only in the sense that there is not only non-spoken discourse but also in the sense that interpretation is also a form of linguistic action, and (ii) that not only verbs but also verb-like expressions are involved, we may venture the term **linguistic action verb(ial)s**. Henceforth, the two terms will be used interchangeably. Some of the lexical items in question belong to the set of speech act verbs (*to promise*, *to state*, *to threaten*, *to ask*, *to order*, etc.; see section 1.1.2), some of which can be used in explicit performative formulae (*to promise*, *to order*, etc.; see also section 1.1.2); others describe aspects of verbal behaviour different from illocutionary force (*to argue*, *to persuade*, *to continue*); and in addition to the verbs there are indeed large numbers of verb-like expressions (*to give carte blanche*, *to lay down the law*, *to angle for*, *to pose a question*, *to worm out of*, *to request the pleasure of someone's company*, *to lay claim to*). Their relevance will be discussed below in section 6.4.2. Later we will return to the problem of performativity in Chapter 7 (section 7.1.2).

In relation to the *verba dicendi*, we should point at a phenomenon which (predominantly French) linguists have named **delocutivity**: the reflexivity of some *verba dicendi* already appears from their being derived from 'locutions'. Thus Latin *salutare*, 'to greet', is derived from the greeting *salve* or (plural) *salvete*. Similarly, the English locution *OK* has given rise to the delocutive verb *to okay*.

In addition to such verbs, as well as the nouns and nominal expressions related to them, at the lexical level we find many of the discourse markers, pragmatic markers, discourse particles or pragmatic particles discussed in the literature. Here are some examples.

(7) a. *Admittedly*, John's a lousy driver.
    b. *Regrettably/Unfortunately*, John's a lousy driver.
    c. *Frankly/Honestly/Truthfully*, John's a lousy driver.
(8) a. *Probably/Possibly*, humanity is planning its own extinction.
    b. *Certainly/Undoubtedly*, humans are a danger to themselves.
(9) *Reportedly/Allegedly*, the royal family is in for more scandals.
(10) I've always had *like* – lots of nightmares.
(11) He's *just* – he's *just* crazy, the captain.

The **sentence adverbs** in (7) to (9) all specify the status of the ensuing propositional content: (7) does so in terms of attitudinal markers, (8) in terms of epistemic properties, and (9) by indicating a (vague) source of information (a phenomenon referred to with the term 'evidentiality'). Both (10) and (11) indicate, by means of *like* and *just*, reflection on the wording process.

Some choices at the word level serve as overt markers of supra-sentential connections to surrounding elements of the linguistic context (see section 3.3.2):

(12) It was already late. *So*, we went home.
(13) a. It was already late. *But* we stayed.
b. It was already late. *However*, we did not have the courage to leave.
(14) We were the first to leave. *After all*, it was already late.
(15) We should have left. *Instead*, we stayed all night.
(16) 1. Do you want to leave already?
2. *Well*, it will be dark soon.
(17) *Incidentally/By the way*, John's a lousy driver.

Certain word groups serve as illocutionary force indicating devices in a way that reflects upon earlier discussion of or reference to the topic at hand, as in (18) and (19). A similar reflection is implied in (20) and (21); in these two examples, the italicized word groups do not define the illocutionary force, they only add emphasis. Finally, (22) qualifies the propositional content in much the same way as the sentence adverbs in (7).

(18) *How about* staying for the night?
(19) *Why not* stay for the night?
(20) *For Pete's sake*, why don't you stay?
(21) *By all means*, stay!
(22) *As a friend*, I have to warn you that you should be more flexible.

Further, metapragmatic awareness is indicated by a wide variety of clause types, as in the following examples:

(23) a. This Dr Hammer is nuts, *you know.*
b. *You know*, this Dr. Hammer is nuts.
(24) This Dr Hammer is nuts, *I guess*.
(25) *I mean*, he must be crazy.
(26) *I believe that* hot weather damages the brain.
(27) *I think* she's a good piano player.
(28) He did not get any pilot training, *you see?*
(29) He didn't get any pilot training, *did he?*
(30) He was trained as a pilot, *wasn't he?*
(31) *It's just that* I don't like him.
(32) *You'd better* stay overnight.
(33) *(You) know what,* Debby's getting married.
(34) *Read my lips*, no more taxes!
(35) *In case you didn't know*, Debby's getting married.
(36) I'm a good runner, *even if I say so myself.*

(37) *Rumour has it that* more dark clouds are gathering above the White House.
(38) *Speaking for myself*, your proposal is right on target.
(39) *It can be convincingly argued that* linguistics is a branch of psychology.
(40) *Forgive me, but* I cannot possibly accept.
(41) *I'm not greedy, but* I refuse to work without pay.

Sentences (23) to (28) all contain mental state verbs, explicitly describing the relationship between a propositional content and its relationship to mental states or processes. This is most clearly the case in (24) to (27), with *I* as subject, the first person being the only one about whose mental states an utterer can say something authoritatively. The relationship is much weaker in (23) and (28), with a second-person subject. In (23)b., *you know* functions in basically the same way as *well* in (16). Both *you know* in (23)a. and *you see?* in (28) appeal to the addressee in a way comparable to the **question tags** in (29) and (30). All the italicized clauses in (31) to (39) provide reflexive contextualizations for the messages within their scope. The **response-controlling 'but'-prefaces** in (40) and (41) anticipate, and react to, possible interpretations of what the utterer is about to say.

Direct modifications of propositional content, without the detour of commenting on its status in attitudinal, epistemic or evidential terms, but equally indicative of metapragmatic awareness, are carried by the **hedges** in (42) and (43).

(42) He's *sort of/kind of* crazy.
(43) *In a sense*, universities are just factories.

Words, as well as full sentences with a complete propositional content, may enter a process of metapragmatic distancing which has been commonly discussed under the label of **mention (versus use)**. Consider (44), (45) and (46).

(44) Spell *shibboleth* for me.
(45) 1. He was a bit shaken.
2. *A bit shaken?* Absolutely terrified he was.
(46) [The phone rings. Eve answers, then turns to Sophie, sitting in the same room.]
1. Eve: It's Jack.
2. Sophie: *I'm not here*

In (44), *shibboleth* is 'mentioned' rather than used: the word itself is referred to as a word in the English language; more specifically, its orthography is at stake; since its meaning is completely irrelevant in the context of this sentence, it cannot possibly be 'used' in any normal sense of that word. In (45)2. the meaning of *a bit shaken*, far from being irrelevant, is focused on; but while the phrase is really 'used' in (45)1., in (45)2. the fact of its having been chosen to describe a particular state of affairs is at stake: it is 'mentioned' as inappropriate. It is hard to imagine, finally, that *I'm not here* is simply 'used' in (46)2., as it is patently false in the context, whereas the same sentence would be a perfectly acceptable and literally interpretable part of a message on an answering machine. *I'm not here* can be said to be 'mentioned' rather than used because it mainly functions as a device to offer the addressee, Eve, the form of expression she can use, with minor deictic adaptations, to formulate a message – involving a language game of pretence – for Jack: *Sophie's not here.*

In longer pieces of discourse, and often at an intertextual level, explicit comments are to be found on the status of surrounding linguistic context or related utterances and utterance clusters. Just consider (47) and (48).

(47) *As was argued above/As will be shown later*, linguistics is a branch of psychology.
(48) These are some of the trends and ideas you will find in *The World in 1996*, which will appear in 80 countries and in 12 languages. This is our tenth year of publication: put all our mistaken predictions together and we could probably produce another edition. But along the way much has been right and, I hope, most of it interesting.

Example (47) situates a sentence in relation to other parts of the same overall utterance. Example (48), which we have encountered before (see section 4.4.2), links the preceding linguistic context to a description of the status of the immediately adjacent cluster of utterances (the articles in the publication in question) in relation to an intertextual assessment of a series to which the cluster belongs. This kind of metapragmatic phenomenon is directly related to the wide range of data yielded by practices of **direct quotation** and **reported speech**, in which linguistic action verb(ial)s are called upon to frame the communicative status of earlier language use. Sometimes, as with direct quotations and reported speech in regular news reporting, such framing is rather unimaginative, as in (49) and (50). On other occasions, when more interpretive freedom is taken, descriptions can be quite vivid, as in (51).

(49) 'If the Soviets would identify the U-2 as the plane they shot down, we would quit looking for it,' Mr. Bonney *said*.
(50) The report *noted* that there was no further word from the pilot.
(51) Mr Khrushchev *made his account a story of high drama and low skullduggery interspersed with bitingly sarcastic remarks* about Washington's *contention* that the pilot was on a regular weather reconnaissance mission and had probably gotten lost during a blackout due to the failure of his oxygen equipment.

We will have occasion to return to these examples in Chapter 8.

All these devices can be said to **entextualize** discourse, i.e. to provide discourse with a textual status, an interpretive frame of reference, by means of metapragmatic contextualization. (This use of 'entextualization' extends the term's common reference to the transformation of discourse into a text-artefact – as when an anthropologist writes down an orally communicated story – to an inevitable aspect of all language use; also, it ignores the distinction sometimes drawn between entextualization as a matter of production and contextualization as an interpretive recasting; see Silverstein and Urban (eds) 1996.) Extreme examples of this process are to be found in linguistic activity types which literally require a *manufacturing* of texts. A case in point (discussed at length by Jacobs 1997) is the production of press releases, written in such a way that they show all the properties of regular newspaper reports, complete with direct quotations (no doubt, usually invented) of utterances produced by officials of the issuing body or company. These forms of language use require a complete shift in point of view, away from the utterer in the direction of the direct addressee (press agencies or journalists), so that the latter can simply use the preformulated text in their communication with their own audience. One might go as far as to regard truly preformulating press releases as instances of 'mention' instead of 'use', comparable to the example in (46)2.

6.4.2 Metapragmatics and the nature of linguistic action

In the introduction to this section on metapragmatic awareness, we said that all verbal communication is self-referential to a certain degree, that all language use involves a constant interplay between pragmatic and metapragmatic functioning, and that reflexive awareness is at the very core of what happens when people use language. The examples in section 6.4.1 should have shown that metapragmatic awareness is indeed pervasive, to the extent that linguistic traces can be found basically at all levels of linguistic structure. A further analysis, only bits and pieces of which could be hinted at, would have shown that this awareness pertains to just about any aspect or dimension of language use, from any contextual parameter, over minute details of structure and elements of semantic content, to global principles of meaning generation. The reason is to be found in the nature of linguistic action.

Concepts, practices and language ideologies

Linguistic behaviour shares with other types of social behaviour, as Winch demonstrated convincingly as early as 1958, the property that it is always 'meaningful' in the sense that it is interpreted by the actors engaged in it (see also the discussion of activities and events in section 5.2, anticipated by remarks on speech act theory in section 4.3). In other words, in social life, *conceptualizations* and *practices* are inseparable. Consequently, there is no way of understanding forms of social behaviour without gaining insight into the way in which the social actors themselves habitually conceptualize what it is they are doing. Preconceived theoretical frameworks just do not suffice. If a sociologist leaves for India, armed with the concepts 'class' and 'mobility', to study the caste system, he may come back satisfied that caste can be defined as 'class without mobility'. But this will not allow him or her to understand the social structure and dynamics of caste-related properties and processes in Indian society, which would also require insight into principles of hierarchical ranking in relation to religious criteria of purity of which the hierarchy itself, the strict separation, and the division of labour are overt manifestations. There is no reason to believe that anything different would have to be said about scientific approaches to forms of linguistic action.

One way of penetrating 'folk concepts' of verbal behaviour which are ingredients in the meaningful functioning of language would be to look at metapragmatic terms in natural languages. Needless to say the superficial level of lexicalization is not a sufficient basis for wide-ranging conclusions on language-specific ways of conceptualizing and experiencing language use. But once supported by ethnographic data of actual language use, they may provide significant insights. Thus the absence of a clear (lexicalized) notion of promising in Ilongot, a Philippine language, becomes significant when anthropological research reveals that an activity of committing oneself verbally to a future course of action is not a salient form of behaviour at all in Ilongot-speaking communities (see Rosaldo 1982). Similarly, the observation that many Polynesian languages have as their most basic linguistic action verbs terms which combine the meaning of 'saying' with the most general sense or a wide range of senses of 'doing' (cf. Maori *mea* 'to do, deal with, cause, make, say, intend, wish, think'; Kapingamarangi *hai* 'to make, do' versus *hai bolo* 'to say that', where *bolo* is a conjunction equivalent to 'according to, that'; Rennellese *hai* 'to have, own, do, get, act as, say'; etc.), may lead to sensible hypotheses about the centrality of 'action' in Polynesian conceptualizations of 'speech' (in contrast, for instance, to the intention-oriented view taken for granted in speech act theory), if supported by ethnographic research revealing that in some Polynesian societies the effects of verbal acts are considered more important than an utterer's intentions (see Duranti 1988). Or, to take an example closer to home, consider Reddy's (1979) discovery of a 'conduit metaphor' in ways of speaking about language use in English, viewing language as a container to store, transfer, and extract meaning, as in (52), (53) and (54).

(52) a. Try to *pack* more *thoughts into* fewer *words*.
b. The speech *was filled with emotion*.
c. *Insert* those *ideas* elsewhere *in the paragraph*.
(53) a. Try to *get* your *thoughts across*.
b. None of her *feelings came through to me*.
c. Just *give me an idea* of what you mean.
(54) a. Did you *find* any good *ideas in the book*?
b. Can you *extract* a coherent *view from that essay*?
c. That *remark* is completely *impenetrable*.

Such observations become highly relevant when we see that this metaphorically encoded view of language regularly matches the foundations of theories of communication and language use, at the expense of alternative views. Just consider the following two definitions of communication.

> Simply expressed, the communication process begins when a *message* is conceived by a *sender*. It is then ENCODED – translated into a signal or sequence of signals – and *transmitted* via a particular MEDIUM or CHANNEL to a *receiver* who then decodes it and interprets the message, returning a signal in some way that the message has or has not been understood. (Watson and Hill 1997: 41)

> [. . .] communication may be defined as an activity in which *symbolic content* is not merely *transmitted* from one source to another, but *exchanged* between human agents, who interact within a shared situational and/or discursive *context*. (Price 1996: 5)

The linear presentation in the first definition matches the conduit metaphor completely. The second one adds an element of bidirectionality, emphasizing also the context, but without really challenging the nature of the process as such: 'exchange' is simply a two-way transmission. The phrasing shows that even this minor shift of perspective causes problems of formulation, in particular the logically problematic ellipsis in '*transmitted* from one source to another [source].' With the verb *transmit* one would normally expect 'from a source to a target', but this would have been hardly compatible with the bidirectional perspective. Though the highlighted ingredients of the speech event are similar to those we have focused on in this book, much of what we have said about language use (for instance in terms of its dynamics, interpretive choice-making and negotiability) escapes from the conduit metaphor and these definitions alike.

The relationship between conceptualizations and practices of linguistic action, in spite of the surface reflection of some of its properties in patterns of lexicalization, is to be situated at the more subliminal level of metapragmatic awareness. It forms the basis of **language ideologies**, i.e. habitual ways of thinking and speaking about language and language use which are rarely challenged within a given community. Their not being challenged, however, does not mean that they correspond to actual practice. If they did, there would be no reason for criticizing textbook definitions of communication. This means that the reference to exotic data in earlier paragraphs mainly serves the purpose of making a point, rather than to establish absolute contrasts – a remark which should be reminiscent of the warning that linguistic relativity should itself be approached as relative (see the end of section 6.2.1). Even so, the connection between concepts and practices should never be ignored, and I will show later (especially in section 8.2.1) how language ideologies may influence communicative practice.

Self-monitoring

At the most salient end of the metapragmatic awareness scale, we find true **self-monitoring**. Language users always monitor the ways in which they produce or interpret utterances, being aware of the constant need to negotiate meaning and of the obstacles that stand in the way of such negotiation. Hesitations and repairs (see section 1.1.4) are only some of the most visible manifestations of this process. It should be clear from what we have said about salience so far, however, that utterers and interpreters can never monitor every level of choice-making at the same time and with the same intensity. This observation will lead to important methodological recommendations later (in section 8.2.3), especially in relation to the study of discourse as a manifestation of ideology.

6.5 *Summary and further reading*

In this chapter we have addressed the issue of the mental 'work' that goes into processes of meaning generation in language use. This work takes place in a medium of adaptability, 'mind in society.' Three types of mental processes that contribute to the making of linguistic choices were identified and discussed:

- *Perception* and *representation*, involving processes of categorization, as well as association, abstraction, generalization and reification, all of which contribute to the mapping of semantic space.
- *Planning*, an intention- and goal-related activity guided by scripts and involved in interpreting as well as uttering.
- *Memory*, interacting with categorization schemes and scripts, and manifested in processes of recognition and recall.

These types of processes take place with different *degrees of salience* or different degrees of consciousness which provide them with a different *status vis-à-vis* the medium of adaptability. Of special importance in this respect is the domain of *metapragmatic awareness*, the reflexive awareness of the linguistic choice-making process.

On the medium of adaptability, the human cognitive apparatus, in relation to language: Chafe (1996), Coulson (1995), Edwards (1997), Nuyts (1992), Vygotsky (1978). On perception and representation: Gumperz and Levinson (eds) (1996), Lakoff and Johnson (1980), Lucy (1992a, 1992b), Miller and Johnson-Laird (1976), Ungerer and Schmid (1996). On planning: Linde and Labov (1975), Schank and Abelson (1977). On memory: Chafe (ed.) (1980), Schank (1982). On (indicators of) metapragmatic awareness: Abraham (ed.) (1991), Benveniste (1966), Foolen (1996), Fraser (1996), Jakobson (1971), Janssen and van der Wurff (eds) (1996), Kiefer and Verschueren (eds) (1988), Lucy (ed.) (1993), Östman (1981), Schiffrin (1988), Silverstein (1976, 1993), Silverstein and Urban (eds) (1996), Verschueren (1995c). On metapragmatics and the nature of linguistic action: Reddy (1979), Verschueren (1985a), Winch (1958). On metapragmatic universals (tentatively formulated on the basis of comparative lexical research): Verschueren (1989b).

6.6 *Research topic*

Below you find an excerpt from a report on the US State Department noon briefing, 26 March 1998, as distributed by the United States Information Service. Describe its metapragmatic functioning

> TRANSCRIPT: STATE DEPARTMENT NOON BRIEFING, MARCH 26, 1998
> (Kosovo, Israel, Iran)
>
> Spokesman James Rubin briefed.
>
> KOSOVO – Ambassador Robert Gelbard has met with President Milutinovic in Belgrade and with Kosovar Albanian leader Rugova and a student group in Pristinia, Rubin said. In these discussions, said Rubin, Gelbard has emphasized the importance of dialogue between the two sides and has made it clear to the Serbs that international pressure on them will continue 'unless and until they get the message and begin to focus on dialogue rather than crackdowns as a means of resolving this problem.'
>
> Gelbard reported that Kosovo was calm, but said that the special police are digging in rather than leaving, a situation Rubin characterized as 'ominous'. He warned that the international community will 'proceed to even harsher measures if the Serbian authorities don't get the message'.

In response to a question regarding an alleged pending Russian arms deal with Belgrade, Rubin said the Russian Foreign Minister Yevegny Primakov has told Secretary of State Albright Russia will implement the Contact Group decision to impose an arms embargo against the 'Federal Republic of Yugoslavia' ('FRY'). He also reported constructive negotiations on the drafting of a UN resolution, targeted to go into effect March 31, which will implement the embargo.

Rubin said the Contact Group recommends that the embargo be unconditional and unlimited, and that it be lifted only when Belgrade complies with Contact Group requirements.

'We have no reason to believe that Russia doesn't understand that an arms embargo is an arms embargo,' said Rubin, 'and that means that there will be no transfers of military equipment (to the 'FRY') if that embargo is enacted.'

Part III

Topics and trends

Introduction

Part II was literally an attempt to introduce 'aspects of the meaningful functioning of language'. Each of its four chapters was meant to highlight one of four necessary angles from which language has to be approached in any serious linguistics of language use. These angles are interdependent and can be separated only for heuristic purposes. Our working hypothesis is that a pragmatic perspective on any linguistic phenomenon, property, structure or process requires its investigation in terms of its contextual and structural locus (Chapters 3 and 4), the dynamic processes of language use (Chapter 5), and their status in relation to a human 'mind in society' (Chapter 6). That means that we could now take any phenomenon, any example from the foregoing chapters and re-scrutinize them in terms of such a framework, whereas our earlier reference to them was meant to be illustrative only of some highlighted 'aspect'. Space limitations, however, will not allow us to do so systematically. All we will be able to offer in Part III is an application of the framework to some selected sample topics (in Chapters 7 and 8), showing how the 'theory' can be handled in the practice of answering linguistic research questions, followed by a very rough panoramic view (in Chapter 9) of where pragmatics comes from and what goes by that name today (to the extent that the latter was not dealt with in Chapter 1).

For the topical division of labour between Chapters 7 and 8 we distinguish between *micro-processes*, taking place in the day-to-day context of communication between individuals or small groups of individuals, and *macro-processes* transcending (though still reflected in) those day-to-day contexts. A further distinction could have been made between processes at the level of adult usage, developmental processes, synchronic and diachronic processes. Within the confines of this book, however, there is space only to deal with issues that are basically synchronic and at the level of adult usage; but we should keep in mind that developmental and diachronic processes can also be singled out for pragmatic investigation.

7

Micropragmatic issues

In this chapter, we use the label 'micropragmatic issues' to cover two distinct types of topics. First, there are systemic properties of language which the linguistics of language resources (see section 0.1) cannot say too much about since actual usage patterns have to be invoked for description and explanation, or considerations come into play that inevitably constitute a pragmatic perspective. We will restrict our discussion to two examples, the case of particle ordering in a particle-rich language such as Dutch (section 7.1.1), and the problem of (explicit) performativity which has haunted (and inspired) pragmatics from the beginning (in section 7.1.2). Second, instances of actual verbal behaviour, at the micro-level of small-scale (or face-to-face) interaction will be discussed, one in an informal setting (section 7.2.1), the other in a typical institutional and professional context (in section 7.2.2).

7.1 *Language resources in need of a pragmatic perspective*

Implicit in this book's thesis that pragmatics is really a perspective rather than a component of a linguistic theory, is the conviction that virtually all linguistic phenomena can be investigated pragmatically. At the cutting edge between the linguistics of language resources and the linguistics of language use, however, there are some language resources that cannot sensibly be dealt with at all unless a pragmatic perspective is taken. We will restrict ourselves to just two clear examples.

7.1.1 The ordering of particles

Word order is a typical syntactic topic, but with recognizable and generally recognized pragmatic implications. Change the order of subject and verb in an English sentence such as *This house is too big*, and you do not only transform a declarative sentence type into an interrogative one, but in most cases you will be replacing a simple statement by the question *Is this house too big?* Or perform a somewhat more drastic syntactic operation producing *This house, it's too big* or *It's too big, this house*, and you will end up with utterances with markedly different information structures and conditions of use. But what about linguistic elements for which syntax fails to specify ordering rules? A case in point is to be found in the realm of **particles**. Without going into finer distinctions, particles are (usually) monosyllabic and uninflectable forms, morphologically intermediate between full words and affixes. They do not contribute directly to an easily identifiable propositional content, but they perform a wide range of functions, from modifying an illocutionary force, or indicating the beginning, continuation and end of a turn in conversation, to signalling a coherence break or the background or foreground status of a piece of discourse. In particle-rich languages, they may occur in clusters. And when they do, their order is not random. Just consider the Dutch sentence (1), with eight particles intervening between two fully lexical items, *ga* (imperative form of *gaan* 'to go') and *zitten* (infinitive, 'to sit'), which together mean *Sit down*.

(1)	Ga	dan	toch	ook	nog	maar	eens	even	wat	zitten
	[Go	then	yet	also	still	but	once	a while	a little	sit]
		1	2	3	4	5	6	7	8	

Though many combinations of the particles in (1) are possible, the cluster containing numerous extremely common smaller-scale groupings (only three of which are indicated above: 1–2, 3–4 and 6–7–8), once they are all in place they allow for little or no permutation. A thorough understanding of the pragmatics of a structure like this is needed to even begin asking why.

In terms of context, (1) is uttered by a university professor at the end of the following exchange with a student coming into his office when he is about to leave after a conversation with another student who is still in the room.

(2) 1. Student: Zou ik u even kunnen spreken?
(Could I talk to you for a minute?)
2. Professor: 'k Wou net vertrekken. Kun je morgen terugkomen?
(I was just about to leave. Can you come back tomorrow?)
3. Student: 't Gaat over de paper, en die moet morgen af zijn.
(It's about the paper, which is due tomorrow.)
3. Professor: Ga dan toch ook nog maar eens even wat zitten.
(Roughly: OK, do sit down then.)

The exchange itself would be worthy of extensive comment, but we will restrict the discussion to aspects that are directly relevant to the formulation of (2)4., i.e. (1). The participation framework involves two utterers–interpreters in face-to-face interaction, functioning as sources of what they are saying (except in *[. . .] en die moet morgen af zijn* in (2)3., where a source[1] is invoked which, incidentally, coincides with the addressee: it is the professor who issued the demand that the paper should be finished tomorrow), and treating each other as direct addressees, but in the presence of a bystander, whose role is acknowledged by means of *ook* in (1). On the part of the utterer, (1) expresses a state of mind: there is at least a certain degree of irritation at being obliged to stay longer (the objectionable nature of which is pointed at by means of *dan toch*, where *toch* invokes a contrast with a more desirable state of affairs, and the 'lateness' being indicated by means of *nog*), possibly combined with a sense of criticism, suggesting that the student should have come earlier. At any rate, the particle cluster *eens even wat* indicates the professor's intention to keep the conversation as short as possible. The social context is an institutional one, with a clear hierarchy (and the resulting markers of attitudinal deixis, in particular *u* in (2)1. and *je* in (2)2., corresponding to *vous* and *tu* forms, respectively), which allows the utterer in (1) to express irritation, to show control over the time limitations imposed on the following speech activity, and to issue a directive to sit down. Temporal and spatial parameters, as already described above, are simple, but necessary for a proper understanding of what goes on.

Clearly, (1) requires reference to the linguistic context of the preceding exchange. It could not really be uttered in isolation. The objectionability carried by *dan toch* refers back to the actual objection voiced in (2)2. Similarly, giving in to the request in spite of the objection becomes comprehensible in the light of the student's argument in (2)3., which itself hinges on an intertextual link with the professor's own earlier directives.

All other particles having been given a function in the contextual anchoring of (1), *maar* is left dangling in the middle. Though its functioning is obscured by the surrounding particles, it is probably not too different from the role it would play by itself. Whilst the other particles, in addition to their contextualization roles, also contribute directly to a modification of the propositional content (*dan toch* clearly modifying the imperative form *ga*, and *eens even wat* modifying the 'sitting' resulting from the directive, whereas *ook nog* can either modify the directive or the sitting or both), the particle *maar* co-determines the illocutionary force. Adding *maar* to *Ga zitten!* ('Sit down!') to form *Ga maar zitten!* normally turns a command into a permission (roughly: 'OK, sit down!').

Permission (to sit down for a talk), in the context of the activity type of educational consultation, seems to be indeed the genre to which (1) belongs as a dynamic, negotiated, part of the opening sequence of such an activity. As already indicated briefly, the particle cluster makes a significant contribution to the meaningful framing of an interactional episode.

In terms of salience, not all choices in (1) are made with equal awareness. In particular, there is little doubt that the actual ordering of particles escapes the utterer's conscious choice-making as much as it escapes the syntactician. Still the most promising place to start looking for an explanation of what appears to be a relatively fixed order, is the medium of adaptability, the workings of 'mind in society'. Let us break the ordering question up into two separate questions. First, why do the strings *dan toch*, *ook nog*, and *eens even wat* occupy their respective positions? Second, how can we explain their internal structuring?

The answer to the first question is the easiest. There is a general tendency, deriving from human information processing capabilities, for linguistic items that belong together conceptually to also occur in close proximity in linguistic structure (except when there is unmistakable morphological marking of connectedness). Therefore, the placement of *dan toch* immediately following *ga*, of *eens even wat* immediately preceding *zitten*, and *ook nog* in the middle, can be explained on the basis of their respective contributions to the propositional content (*dan toch* clearly modifying the permission aspect embodied in *ga*, especially the implied reluctance, while *eens even wat* qualifies the nature of the sitting itself, especially its duration, and *ook nog* belongs equally to both aspects, linking the utterance up with the preceding discourse). An equally satisfactory hypothesis cannot be formulated for the second question. The internal structure of the three identifiable substrings of the cluster may be simply a matter of collocation, though for *dan toch* and *eens even wat* we can observe an increasing degree of vagueness in the direction away from the propositional element which they modify: *dan* often has a temporal usage referring to a specific moment in time, and in its particle sense it still refers relatively concretely to 'in that case', whereas *toch* is more vaguely concessive; similarly, though in reverse order, *wat* refers to a concrete, albeit unspecified, quantity, whereas *even* indicates relative duration and *eens* very vaguely points at 'some point in time'.

Using the vocabulary of a general pragmatic theory, then, we can go a long way in attempts at describing and, with much reservation as long as more systematic investigations have not been undertaken, explaining elusive linguistic phenomena.

7.1.2 The problem of performativity

In this section we will try to demonstrate how, taking into account the basic ingredients of a pragmatic theory, one of the longest-standing pragmatic 'problems' may find an easy solution. The problem in question is the following: How can we explain that some speech act verbs, but not others, can be used in explicit performative formulae (see section 1.1.2). Austin (1962) is generally credited with the 'discovery' of a class of utterances, variably called **explicit performatives** or simply **performatives**, containing a verb that names the speech act type which the utterance is used to perform. However, performative utterances were debated by linguists about a century ago. Thus Škrabec (1903, p. 555) identifies a *Praesens effectivum*, 'which not only names the action, but which even performs it at the same time by uttering the verb in question'. Let us first look at the phenomenon, then look at how the 'problem' has been formulated, and finally propose a solution.

The canonical form of an 'explicit performative', as introduced by Austin (1962), is as follows:

(3) I (hereby) $V^{[\text{simple present, indicative, active}]}$ . . .

Typical examples are:

(4) I (hereby) *abdicate*
(5) I *apologize* for stepping on your toes
(6) I *promise* to come on Wednesday
(7) I *order* you to leave the room

Note that the simple present verb form, in these examples, should refer to the moment of speaking, and not – as it does in other cases – to a general or habitual truth.

This canonical form is subject to a certain range of cross-linguistic variation, depending on specific characteristics of individual languages. Thus Hungarian not only offers us the completely analogous:

(8) Kér-em a segít-ség-ed-et
[Ask-I the help(V)-Nominalizer-your-Accusative]
(I ask your help/I ask you to help me)

but also:

(9) Kér-lek, segít-s
[Ask-I(Subject)you(Object), help-Imperative]

The latter form of expression is possible only because of the existence of a verbal suffix which combines the first-person singular as subject with the second-person singular as object (see also section 3.2.1).

There may be no reason at all to regard (9) as less 'canonical' than (8) for Hungarian. However, most languages also have forms of expression which are functionally quite close to examples such as (4) to (7), though they differ from the schema in (3) along one or more significant parameters. The following examples represent some of the types discussed in the literature. A first type of non-central cases of performatives, which we may label 'semi-performatives' for the sake of convenience, makes use of different forms of the verb. A present continuous tense is used in (10), a first-person plural form in (11), a third-person singular form in (12), and the passive in (13) to (15):

(10) I *am asking* you to do this for me Henry, I *am asking* you to do it for me and Cynthia and the children. (Searle 1989)
(11) *We pledge* our lives, our fortunes and our sacred honour. (Searle 1989)
(12) *Le porteur déclare* être majeur. (Cornulier 1980)
(The holder [of this ticket] declares that he/she is over 18 years old.)
(13) *Passengers are* hereby *advised* that all flights to Phoenix have been cancelled. (Searle 1989)
(14) *Passengers are warned* not to lean out of the window.
(15) *You are dismissed.*

Of these examples, (10) is the most disputable case of a performative: it does not even contain the content of the request referred to with 'asking', which indicates that the act is a description of the request after it has been made by other (linguistic) means, rather than the making of a request itself. This does not mean that the present continuous cannot carry a performative meaning; but if it does, at least repetition of a foregoing act seems to be involved. Thus (16):

(16) I'm ordering you to get out!

is likely to occur after the 'primary' performative *Get out!* has failed to yield the desired result. A second class of non-central cases of performatives contains verbal modifiers of various kinds:

(17) I'*d guess* there were 20 of them.
(18) I *would say* that this is completely wrong. (McCawley 1977)
(19) I *would estimate/reply/etc.* that . . . (McCawley 1977)
(20) I *will offer* you the following alternative: . . . (McCawley 1977)
(21) I *will (simply) answer* you that . . . (McCawley 1977)
(22) I'*d like to ask* you to change your plans.
(23) I'*d like to announce* the engagement of . . . (McCawley 1977)

(24) *Let me ask* you what bothers you. (McCawley 1977)
(25) *Let me conclude/respond/etc.* that . . . (McCawley 1977)
(26) *Let us say* that these are semi-explicit performatives. (Cornulier 1980)
(27) *Allow me to call* you a bastard. (Cornulier 1980)

Though such verbal modifiers already add to the semantic and pragmatic complexity of the performatives, there is a third set of non-central cases which, for lack of a better description, contains a variety of 'complex constructions':

(28) That's a squirrel, *shall we say.* (Cornulier 1980)
(29) *This is to thank* you for . . . (Cornulier 1980)
(30) *This is to inform* you that . . . (Cornulier 1980)
(31) *(This is) just to say* hello [e.g. on a postcard]. (Cornulier 1980)
(32) I *am writing/calling to tell* you that . . . (Cornulier 1980)
(33) If I *dare speak* here, it is to *express* my profoundest gratitude . . . (Cornulier 1980)

Finally, even constructions with nouns rather than verbs have been proposed as (semi-) performatives:

(34) I'll come and see you next week, and that's *a promise.* (Searle 1989)
(35) *My question is*, what do you mean by . . . (Cornulier 1980)
(36) *You will find* in this letter *my best wishes* for the New Year. (Cornulier 1980)

The least objectionable of these may be the most complex one, example (36), which *is* itself a New Year's wish, though literally it refers to a wish to be found elsewhere in the letter (where it may not be found at all). To examples (34) and (35) the same comments apply as to (10): in both cases it can be argued that the nouns describe, rather than perform, acts which precede (as in (34)) or follow (as in (35)).

The original, pre-Austinian formulation of 'the problem of performativity' was a logico-grammatical one, an attempt to match grammatical behaviour with functional and logical properties. Thus Škrabec (1903) and Koschmieder (1935) are puzzled by the fact that in Slavic languages mainly imperfective verbs are used for what we now call performative usage, though the momentaneous nature of the acts would logically dictate using perfective forms.

A completely different definition of the problem of performativity is offered by Searle (1989). For Searle, the basic problem to be explained is that I can promise to come and see you by saying *I promise to come and see you*, whereas one cannot fry an egg by saying *I fry an egg*. In more philosophical terms: how do we explain the existence of a class of sentences the meaning of which is such that we can use them to perform the act named by the main verb, simply by uttering the sentence (which literally says that we are performing the act in question)? How do we explain the existence of a class of verbs which lends itself to such usages? How do we explain that many other verbs which look semantically similar, cannot be used in the same way (so that, e.g., I cannot boast by saying *I boast that* ... or insinuate by saying *I insinuate that* ...)? Is there anything in the meaning of the verbs that makes the difference?

In our own terms: are the observed facts merely determined by convention? Or are there any deeper pragmatic constraints involved? Skipping the details of Searle's account (for a discussion of which we refer to Verschueren 1995d), what needs explaining is clearly *the behaviour of a specific type of linguistic action verbs (LAVs) which allows for a maximization of reflexivity in language.* Thus the problem of performativity becomes *the problem of how to define complete self-reference in LAVs.* A general and coherent descriptive model for the analysis of metapragmatic terms should help us to solve it. Such a model is relatively easy to formulate against the background of the theory of pragmatics sketched in this book, taking into account its implications for the study of lexical meaning (see section 4.2.2) and the position it leads to in relation to indicators of metapragmatic awareness (see section 6.4).

A non-circular description of the meaning of LAVs (where 'meaning' is construed in the pragmatic sense of their contribution to the generation of meaning in language use) should specify the prototypical conditions under which a verb V can be used in a description D (which is itself also a linguistic action) of a linguistic action A. Those conditions (C) can be formulated as conditions on or properties of the act to be described (A-conditions; simply abbreviated as C) and sometimes in terms of conditions on or properties of the describing act (D-conditions; abbreviated Cd). Since both A and D involve all the ingredients of a complete speech event, conditions or properties may be attached to utterers (Ua and Ud) and interpreters (Ia and Id), their mental worlds of beliefs, desires, intentions, as well as aspects of the physical and social worlds, in particular social relationships. What needs to be explained is a choice in D at the lexical level, more specifically a verb V (a LAV) describing A as a form of verbal behaviour, in relation to the relevant ingredients of both A and D. A schematic presentation is to be found in Figure 7.1.

Though the descriptions of all LAVs require D-conditions, most of these bear on beliefs or assumptions held by the utterer of D (i.e. Ud) which simply reflect conditions on or properties of A. For instance, if the choice of *to promise* in a description of A is typically governed by the condition that Ua intends to carry out the action specified in the

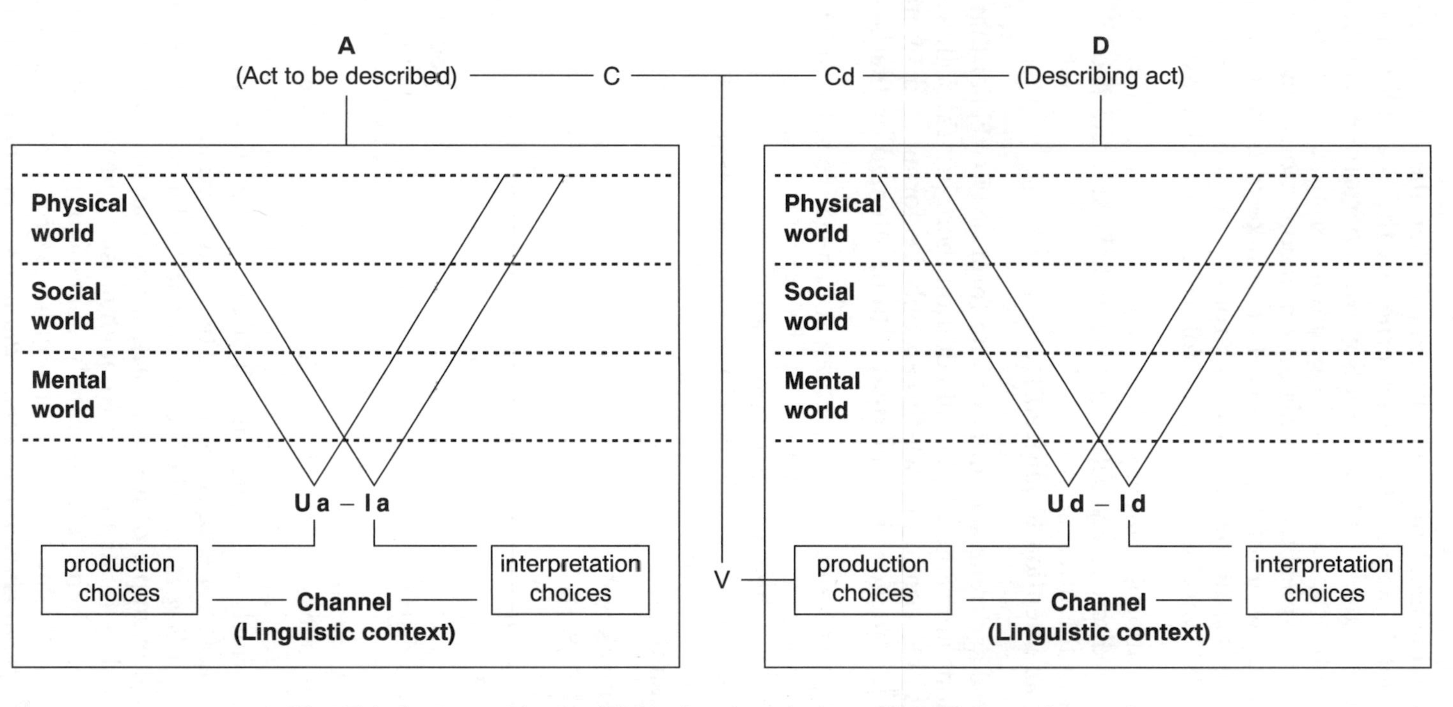

Fig. 7.1 A pragmatic model for the description of linguistic action verbs

propositional content of his/her utterance, then the use of *to promise* in description D is also typically governed by the D-condition that Ud must believe that Ua had this intention when performing act A. But in addition to such 'reflections' of A-conditions, some LAVs also require for their prototypical use the satisfaction of conditions which can only be formulated with reference to D. Let us take *to lie* as an example. Appropriate use of the verb (in its prototypical sense; see Coleman and Kay 1981) involves at least the following A-conditions:

- the propositional content of A deviates somehow from the 'truth'
- there is a discrepancy between Ua's beliefs and the propositional content of the utterance
- Ua has an intention to mislead Ia.

All of these are 'reflected' in D (in the form of Ud's belief that these A-conditions are satisfied), but in addition there are the following D-conditions (i.e. conditions which can only be formulated by making explicit reference to something that is to be situated on the D-side):

- Ud's negative value judgment about A (a negative value judgment is always associated with the use of the verb *to lie*, as emerges from the fact that whenever there are attenuating circumstances in Ud's mind, use of the verb will be avoided as much as possible).
- Ud's judgment about the truth value of the proposition in A (which creates an interpretive distance in a sense to be explained below).

Our hypothesis is the following: complete self-reference in speech act verbs (one type of LAVs) requires the possibility of making A and D coincide maximally. In other words, *speech act verbs which do* ***not*** *require D-conditions (beyond those of the 'reflexive' type) for an adequate description of their meanings, can in principle be used performatively.* As soon as explicit D-conditions are required, there is a **conceptual distance** between A and D which makes it impossible to interpret (i.e. to process cognitively) an utterance in which V would occur self-referentially.

The simplest cases in which complete coincidence between A and D is possible are those in which all Cs are defined by the institutional context in which A belongs: it is not accidental that Austin's most typical examples of explicit performatives involved acts such as *christening* and *adjourning*. The next category, which includes Searle's prototypical example of a speech act, a *promise*, involves acts which are governed by relatively clear (though mostly culture-specific) social norms so that their status is usually unambiguous (or at least lends itself to being treated as unambiguous). *Asking*, *ordering*, *declaring*, *warning*, *announcing*, *apologizing*, *thanking*, and many others also do not require distance between A and D. In other words, the corresponding verbs in English are able to function as maximally reflexive indicators (with a high degree of salience) of metapragmatic awareness.

For speech act verbs that can *not* be used performatively, however, various types of conceptual distance blocking fully reflexive use can be shown to be required. Let us present a brief overview of the most-cited examples (which we list in four groups, which are not meant to represent a taxonomy, since different aspects of the analysis can be at work in the same verbs).

To hint, *insinuate*, *intimate*, *allude to* all require an **interpretive distance** between A and D. The reason is that the 'mode of delivery' in A, as described by the verb, is implicitness; hence the meaning that is hinted at, insinuated, intimated or alluded to is fundamentally 'constructed' by Ud. The D-condition involved is Ud's interpretive intervention which leads him/her to believe that more is meant in A than is actually said. This is not to deny that interpretation is in other cases an active process as well. But this process is completely foregrounded by describing A as an instance of hinting or insinuating, so that such a description is not possible without pulling A and D apart. Therefore, A and D cannot coincide, and the corresponding verbs cannot be used performatively.

To lie, *allege*, *perjure*, *kid*, *boast or brag* also require an **interpretive distance**, but of a slightly more specific kind. The reason is that acts of lying, perjuring, and the like, have a 'status' which is (at least temporarily) not meant to be recognized by Ia; hence, in order to be describable with reference to that status, an interpretive intervention on the part of Ud is needed which creates an inevitable conceptual distance between A and D. The more specific D-condition (as already mentioned above in connection with *to lie*) is the following: Ud's judgment concerning the truth value of the proposition in A.

To threaten, *grumble about* (as opposed to *protest*), *swear or curse*, *whitewash* (as opposed to *excuse*), *slander* (as opposed to *accuse*), but also *to lie* and *to boast or brag*, all require an **evaluative distance** between A and D. Reason: as was already anticipated in relation to *to lie*, the social acceptability of the described acts is low, so that negative value judgments on the part of Ud are associated with the very choice of the LAVs listed. D-condition: Ud's negative value judgment. This D-condition makes it impossible for a speaker to describe his or her own act as an instance of threatening, slandering, lying or boasting, without passing a value judgment on it and thereby undercutting the act while it is performed. This is the classic case of what Vendler (1976) called 'illocutionary suicide' in an article which already contained many of the ingredients needed for the type of explanation I am trying to formulate for the phenomenon of performativity. That this is exactly what is happening can best be clarified with reference to forms of usage in which the negative value judgment is cancelled. Consider (37) and (38):

(37) I boast myself a patriot
(38) I promise I'll kill you

Sentence (37) was taken from a British dictionary; since patriotism is usually evaluated positively, the content of the sentence cancels any negative associations the verb *to boast* normally has. Therefore, the D-condition is overruled, and *to boast* can be used performatively. (The fact that this sentence was found in a dictionary, does not necessarily make it acceptable for all speakers of English. In fact, a self-reflective use of *to boast* is no doubt extremely exceptional – which underscores the general point we have made about this verb.) Similarly *to promise* in (38) does not carry the negative connotations which *to threaten* is burdened with, so that if *to promise* is used as a euphemism one can perfectly threaten performatively.

Finally, *to convince*, *annoy*, *persuade*, *amuse* even require a **temporal distance** between A and D. Reason: the communicative effect of A must already have taken place before A can be described as having convinced, annoyed, persuaded, amused someone. D-condition: Ud's assessment of the communicative effect of A. It goes without saying that A and D cannot coincide if they must be consecutive.

Briefly, our hypothesis concerning the conditions under which a linguistic action verb has performative potential, i.e. the conditions under which it can be used fully self-referentially or as a maximally reflexive indicator of metapragmatic awareness, seems to be completely confirmed by the examples found in the speech act literature to illustrate the 'problem' of performativity. If the explanations adduced so far are sufficiently convincing to justify our hypothesis in connection with the examples we find in the speech act literature, however, we are still stuck with the problem of performativity as formulated by Škrabec (1903) and Koschmieder (1935). How can our descriptive framework help us to explain the predominance of imperfective forms in explicit performative usage? If we replace the earlier logico-grammatical formulation of the problem with a straightforward approach in terms of the descriptive framework we have sketched, then the explanation is relatively transparent. The choice between alternative 'aspects' (in this case perfective versus imperfective) is something that necessarily takes place on the D-side of our model: Ud has to make a choice on the basis of his or her judgment concerning the temporal/aspectual status of the act performed. This inevitable interpretive intervention creates a conceptual difference between A and D. But Ud's role is focused on more explicitly when the perfective is used, since the perfective is the *marked* case (see section 2.1) in the contrast between perfective and imperfective verbs in Slavic languages. Therefore it is predictable that the perfective would be used less – if at all – in a performative utterance since it draws the attention more strongly to an interpretive distance between A and D.

Contrary to some claims (as in Searle 1989) that the performative occurrence of certain speech act verbs is more or less accidental and has nothing to do with the meaning of those verbs, we believe that we have demonstrated how a coherent model for the description of the meaning of speech act verbs (or LAVs, or even metapragmatic terms in general) makes it predictable, on semantic and conceptual grounds (as these are understood within the context of a combined cognitive, social and cultural – i.e. pragmatic – perspective on language), whether a verb is suitable for performative use or not. Facts of nature have nothing to do with this. The phenomenon can entirely be formulated in terms of the processibility, as coinciding acts and descriptions, of utterances containing verbs that are meant to make those utterances self-referential. What is *not* predictable, however, is whether a given verb *will* in fact be used performatively in a given language. At the level of factual occurrence, there are mostly language-specific conventions at work. Thus nothing can block the use of English *to ask* (e.g. in its requesting sense) in an explicit performative formula. But it is a fact of English usage that this is rarely done, whereas the corresponding Hungarian *kér* (as in example (8)) is used in most everyday requests. Similarly, there is a great deal of variation between languages as to whether the canonical form of the performative (examples (3) to (9)) will be used with a specific verb, or whether preference will be given to some non-central performative expression type or semi-performative formula (as in examples (10) to (36)). Though the basic pragmatic principle seems quite clear, susceptibility for performative use may itself be a gradable phenomenon (as was already suggested in our formulation of an explanation for aspect choice in Slavic languages, and as should be clear from the observation that there may be a fuzzy boundary between D-conditions that are 'reflexive' and those that are not). This gradability, in turn, may not be unrelated to the preference for a specific form of expression. But a much more detailed pragmatic investigation is called for to make those issues tangible. In particular, actual patterns of usage, involving the full power of negotiability, will have to be scrutinized. We will be able to refer to one empirical study relevant to the issue in the next chapter (section 8.2.1).

7.2 *The pragmatics of small-scale interaction*

Just like language resources, also instances of language use can, in principle, be looked at from a non-pragmatic point of view. In fact, this usually needs to be done to investigate structural properties of the used resources themselves. Thus a large text corpus may be screened to study the distribution of genitive constructions across sentence types, or to investigate the relative frequency of lexical items such as *plane*, *airplane* and *aeroplane*. Similarly, all instances of language use show 'objective', formal properties that may be investigated in their own right (ranging from quantifiable phenomena such as the average length of a sentence to the patterning of connectors in a text). The most interesting questions about instances of language use, however, will invariably require a pragmatic perspective. One consequence is that the data never 'speak for themselves'. In their capacity as forms of behaviour that generate meaning, they cannot be detached from a complex reality of human functioning. In the remainder of this chapter we will illustrate this further, first with a very simple and informal exchange, then with an institutionally embedded type of discourse.

7.2.1 An informal exchange

Let us have a look at (39).

(39) 1. Daughter: Do you know what time it is?
2. Dad: Yes. Don't **you**?
3. Daughter: Yes?
4. Dad: So, why do you call?
5. Daughter: **Da**-ad!

As should be clear by now, the central task for a pragmatic investigation of this stretch of discourse is to trace the way in which meaning is interactively generated, both in terms of the dynamics involved (as described in Chapter 5) and in terms of the salience of the processes that make up this dynamics (see Chapter 6). Unless one would allow mere speculation, there is no way of doing so, however, without defining its locus, both in extralinguistic and in linguistic terms (see chapters 3 and 4, respectively).

As to its contextual co-ordinates, (39) is a fragment of a conversation between a 13-year-old girl and her father. They are talking over the phone. The daughter is at home and calls her parents at a nearby restaurant where they went for dinner with a couple of friends. The time is about eleven at night, although the parents had promised to be back around ten. This brief information about the channel of communication, the general activity context, and the social relationship between the two utterers–interpreters implies that fragment (39) is intertextually linked with several wider circles of communication. To begin with, a telephone conversation usually begins with a mutual signalling that contact has been established, often combined with explicit indications of mutual recognition. It is also unlikely that the conversation would abruptly come to an end after (39)5. The main body of the conversation is probably still to follow, e.g. in the form of the daughter's eliciting a new commitment from the father as to the parents' speedy return home. The conversation itself is functionally linked to two types of preceding discourse. First of all, unless the father is equipped with a portable telephone, two other conversations must have preceded, the sole purpose of which was to establish the contact for the conversation to be at all possible: one between the girl and the restaurant owner (or waiter) who picks up the phone, and one between the restaurant owner (or waiter) and the parents at the table. It would be a grave error to think that this intertextual link is negligible and irrelevant. What the girl says to the owner may very well influence the way in which her call is announced to the parents, which – in turn – may set the tone for the conversation of which (39) is a part. Second, the content of the conversation is intimately linked to whatever was said between daughter and parents before the latter went off to the restaurant (whether immediately before, or on some earlier occasion).

In structural terms, (39) is a cluster of utterances, the style of which is quite informal. The individual utterances themselves are structurally very simple, all but one containing a single short sentence, and two of them consisting of one word only. Utterances (39)1. to (39)4. all end in the rising intonation characteristic of interrogative structures in English. This may be one of the properties to be explained because a more regular expectation would be to find question–answer adjacency pairs.

Coming to the crucial question, what happens with 'meaning' in (39)? The frame of meaning in terms of which the processes of negotiation have to be interpreted is given by the activity or event type defined in terms of the above ingredients: an informal telephone conversation between close relatives in which the caller is somehow 'checking up' on the person called. In this context, the daughter's utterance (39)1. is hardly to be interpreted as a question about the time (whether seen as 'literal' because of the conventionality of the form, or as 'indirect' because it is literally a question about the addressee's knowledge rather than directly about the time). Drawing on shared knowledge about an earlier commitment (or at least a predictive statement) on the part of the parents in relation to the timing of their return home, the daughter's question takes on the quality of a reproach (the mildness or seriousness of which can only be deduced from aspects of prosody). This interpretation, which can be assumed to be fully accessible to the father, is playfully rejected in (39)2., which recasts the genre of the daughter's utterance as a question (again, whether 'literal' or 'indirect'), adding a sentence which questions (and thereby expresses surprise about) one of the implications usually carried along by questions, namely that the questioner does not know the answer. Taken by surprise, the daughter responds *Yes* to the dad's yes–no question in (39)3., but indicating – by means of the rising intonation contour – that she's puzzled and expects something else to follow. Since this does not challenge his refusal to react 'appropriately' to the initial question (i.e. taking into account its implicit meaning), the father can continue his own game strategy by asking (39)4., which, at the surface, is an attempt to elicit an explicit statement about a hidden purpose which he still pretends not to understand. The daughter suddenly realizes what is happening and utters an irritated vocative in (39)5.

Very little of what actually goes on in this exchange is made explicit. Still it is clear that the implicit meaning of (39)1. is saliently present for both U and I, and that the father consciously plays on the distinction between the implicit and the explicit. The daughter is at first 'tricked' by the father's game, but she catches up fast and voices her irritation (inspired at least partly by her sudden awareness that her dad was making fun of her).

An isolated fragment such as (39) always raises more questions than one can answer without further investigation. The purpose of presenting it nonetheless was twofold. First, it was the intention to demonstrate very briefly how a coherent account can be formulated in terms of the four tasks to be performed in the course of a pragmatic analysis. Second, we want to use this example to further illustrate the kinds of questions that can be relevantly addressed from a pragmatic point of view. Let us just list a few.

- What is the status of this fragment in relation to the rest of the conversation? For one thing, how can we regard it as a separable unit or episode, opened with the question in (39)1. and closed with the exclamation in (39)5.?
- How does this conversation link up with the preceding discourse? What is, for instance, the influence of the phrasing used by the restaurant owner (which will itself vary in relation to the ties between owner and customers) on the genre or approach adopted by the father?
- What is the role of personality factors?
- What is the correlation, precisely, between the style that is used on the one hand, and the channel of communication and the type of social relationship on the other?

- How can we be sure of the uptake of implicit meaning? Or, for that matter, of explicit meaning as well.
- What systematicity characterizes the contextualizing function of prosodic markers?
- How do we explain that it seems easier to ignore aspects of implicit meaning than to challenge them?
- How do we characterize the type of co-operation to be found in an exchange such as (39)? Or, where do the conflictual elements come in that are as much part of everyday interaction as co-operation?

Once we have interesting questions of this kind, the problem is *what would count as evidence* in the search for answers. It should be clear that the nature of the data to be gathered and the methodologies to be adopted can only be decided as a function of the specific question to be addressed. The only general rule is that comparisons across instances of naturally occurring speech (selected along dimensions of variation pertinent to the question at hand) is always a good starting point. To address the final question we formulated, for instance, it is useful to contrast (39) with cases such as (40) (where vertically aligned square brackets indicate overlapping speech).

(40) (From Schiffrin 1994, p. 434)
1. Debby: Yeh it's [the middle
2. Irene: [That's right.
3. Henry: It's the **middle class** . . .
4. Irene: It's the middle class [that gives their kids everything.
5. Debby: [Yeh.

In contrast to the strategic non-co-operation we find in (39), example (40) offers us a case of perfect spontaneous conversational co-operation: three people collaboratively formulating a shared opinion. Yet the conflictual elements underlying (39) are quite subdued, whereas in the conversation from which (40) is taken explicit disagreements surface throughout and regularly participants are fighting to get the floor.

In addition to naturally occurring data, experimentally obtained data may be useful for certain types of questions. To study the uptake of implicit meaning, for instance, the first rule remains to trace what actually happens with the aspects of meaning in question, what is actually done with them, in the course of real-life interaction. Yet, experiments may be conceived to supplement the findings. Controlling all the relevant variables, however, is hardly ever possible in the area of pragmatics (a factor which renders the use of interviews and questionnaires utterly unreliable). Introspection may come in, as was argued before, whenever it is relevant to ask what might have occurred instead of what is actually observed, or why an available option does not get chosen. In other words, nothing is excluded in principle, though there is a clear preference ranking for the types of available evidence.

In addition to the types of questions listed above, research may of course concentrate on processes characteristic of specific groups of speakers. Thus, acquisitional phenomena may be focused on, as may cases of communicative deficiency. Needless to say within the scope of this textbook, where we already have to gloss over most details of topic-specific methodologies, we cannot penetrate those areas of research seriously.

7.2.2 An institutional event

The definition we provided (in the introduction to Part III) for the distinction between microprocesses and macroprocesses, the former taking place in the day-to-day context of communication between individuals or small groups of individuals and the latter transcending (though still reflected in) those day-to-day contexts, already implied that the distinction is an artificial one. Even a telephone conversation between a father and his daughter is embedded in a much wider context which involves socially defined activities and normative products of socialization processes. Our second example of small-scale interaction, showing how meaning can be generated in the institutional context of courtroom proceedings, will show this even more forcefully.

The example is Goodwin's (1994) analysis of the Rodney King trials in Los Angeles. When stopped for a traffic violation on 3 March 1991, King, an African American, was violently beaten by a group of four police officers. When a tape of this event, recorded by an amateur video photographer, was released, public outrage led to the policemen being put on trial for the excessive use of force.

Courtroom proceedings, like any other communicative event, can only be properly understood in terms of the frame of meaning imposed by the activity type, which is in this case predominantly institutional. We say 'predominantly institutional' because the event, which is in principle self-contained and should follow only the relatively strict rules of interaction imposed by the institutions established to administer justice, is embedded in a much wider context of communication. For one thing, there might not have been a trial without the public outrage generated by showings of and comments on the video tape. As a result, from the start the trial was part of a general public and political debate, with real involvement on the part of many people (which became tragically clear when the verdict that found the police officers innocent in the first trial triggered the Los Angeles uprising – without which there might not have been a second federal trial a year later where two of the four officers were convicted of violating King's civil rights). Furthermore, the event was highly mediatized throughout. It would be a grave mistake to ignore the possible, or even probable, influence of this surrounding layer of communication and social strife. Clearly, whatever is said during the trial will be adapted to various degrees, as to both content and style, to a range of addressees$^{1, 2, \ldots n}$, in particular journalists, media audiences and political lobbies.

To the extent that the event can be seen as self-contained, it still represents a highly complex activity type. The following comments bear on the specific type of jury trial that is common in the United States. Structurally, the trial consists of a constellation of different types of utterances and utterance clusters: a variety of monologic utterances (the judge giving instructions, the jury summation) and dialogic utterance clusters (witness interrogations), all intertextually linked (as in interrogation sequences, the jury summation summing up what has preceded, etc.). Contextually, participant roles are well-defined (the accused, the judge, the prosecutor, defence attorneys, jurors, witnesses, expert witnesses). Those institutional roles are defined in terms of the pre-allocation of turns or turn types (or types of verbal genres) to be used by each of them: judges give instructions, attorneys ask questions (of an institutionally permissible kind) and object to each other's questions, witnesses answer them, jurors mostly listen (acting as side participants throughout most of the proceedings, as direct addressees mainly during the summations, and as collective utterers at the very end). The dynamics of the overall interaction is determined by those structures and roles, of which the different participants are quite conscious, in combination with a clear task to be performed: deciding on the guilt or innocence of the accused. The resulting process takes the shape of a contest between prosecution and defence, where it is the task of the prosecution to prove guilt, and it is enough for the defence if they can cast reasonable doubt on the guilt of the accused. Given the competitive nature of the event, participants also know that the main concern of neither prosecution nor defence is necessarily the search for 'truth', but rather the pursuit of strategies to win. In this process, language is the most powerful tool to construct the desired meanings.

In the first Rodney King trial, the prosecution apparently started from the assumption that they had a solid case, with hard and unmistakable evidence in the form of the video tape. As Goodwin (1994) shows, however, it was enough for the defence to impose what he calls a 'professional vision' on what could be seen on the tape to create a frame of interpretation that would at least lead to 'reasonable doubt'. To that end the defence brought in expert witnesses, whose first task it was to decompose what looked like a massive beating, and to label and categorize the fragments, as in (41) (where numbers between brackets indicate pauses in seconds).

(41) (From Goodwin 1994: 617)
Expert: There were,
ten distinct (1.0) uses of force.
...
In each of those, uses of force
there was an escalation and a de-escalation, (0.8)
an assessment period, (1.5)
and then an escalation and de-escalation again. (0.7)
And another assessment period.

The categorization is very consciously introduced to provide what is visible with a new meaning. In a context where professional practice allows the use of force when necessary, especially the term *assessment* frames the event as involving rational and completely responsible behaviour on the part of the police officers. In the same vein, in a different fragment *kicks* are defined as *tools* for police work, on the same level as a *side handle baton*, a categorization strategy which eliminates the associative link between kicks and anger or malice. The impression that the police officers were just doing their job is further reinforced by depersonalizing their actions. Consider (42) (where equation marks at the end of one line and the beginning of the next indicate that fragments are latched on to each other, i.e. follow each other without any pause; and where a hyphen at the end of a word indicates hesitation).

(42) (From Goodwin 1994: 617)
1. Defence: Four oh five, oh one.
We see a blow being delivered.=
=Is that correct.
2. Expert: That's correct.
The- force has been again escalated (0.3)
to the level it had been previously, (0.4)
and the de-escalation has ceased.

Choosing the completely passivized *We see a blow being delivered* in (42)1. instead of the obvious alternative 'We see officer X beating Rodney King', or saying *the de-escalation has ceased* instead of 'they've started hitting again', is a standard strategy to take the attention away from the agent. In other words, the officers are not personally to be held responsible for the unpleasant course of action; they are simply doing, quite responsibly, what any other police officer has been taught to do under comparable circumstances. To make this interpretation fully acceptable, the defence has to demonstrate that there are good reasons to be found in Rodney King's behaviour for the policemen's assessments that lead to the use of force. To that end, the defence brings in Sergeant Duke from the Los Angeles Police Department, presented as an expert on the use of force. In fragment (43) (where a colon indicates vowel lengthening), the prosecutor challenges his testimony, noting that King seems to be moving into a position ready for handcuffing.

(43) (From Goodwin 1994: 619)

1. Prosecutor:	So uh would you, again consider this to be: a nonaggressive, movement by Mr. King?
2. Sgt. Duke:	At this moment no I wouldn't. (1.1)
3. Prosecutor:	It is aggressive.
4. Sgt. Duke:	Yes, it's starting to be. (0.9) This foot, is laying flat. (0.8) There's starting to be a **bend**, in uh (0.6) this leg (0.4) in his butt. (0.4) The buttocks area has started to rise, (0.7) which would put us, at the beginning of our **spec**trum again.

In other words, what the prosecutor interpreted as co-operative is recast by Sergeant Duke as aggressive. The use of vague descriptions such as *starting to* (twice) and *started to* in (43)4. shows how much the framing depends on imposing the desired interpretation. Therefore, the prosecutor can still challenge the ability of the expert witness to penetrate the assessment processes that the policemen are said to be engaged in.

(44) (From Goodwin 1994: 625)

1. Prosecutor:	Can you read their mind uh, (1.4) Sergeant Duke. (1.3)
2. Sgt. Duke:	I can, (0.4) form an opinion based on my training, and having trained people, what I can perceive that their perceptions are. (0.6)
3. Prosecutor:	Well what's Mr. King's perceptions at this time? (0.6)
4. Sgt. Duke:	I've never been a suspect. I don't know.

Thus Sergeant Duke claims the right to speak as a professional expert with insight into the mental processes taking place in the minds of the police officers. The resulting picture is by definition discursively constructed. Though it may not convince jurors of the validity of the defence attorney's judgment that 'Rodney King alone was in control of the situation' while lying on the ground, face down and surrounded by four armed men, it was clearly enough to inspire 'reasonable doubt'.

The extent to which the outcome of institutional events of this kind is the product of verbal processes of meaning generation (in this case even active construction) is also clear from the second trial. On that occasion, the prosecutor no longer relied on uninterpreted visual evidence, but offered an alternative framing: a new motive was introduced (teaching someone who had been disrespectful a lesson), King's body movements were explained as natural jerking of the muscles in response to the beating, and different features of the tape were highlighted (such as the physical posture of the two officers who were not hitting, just standing around and watching rather than ready to control a dangerous criminal). Thus the same evidence can be given completely different meanings. The power of language, indeed.

7.3 *Summary and further reading*

In this chapter a few selected examples were given to illustrate how a theory of pragmatics, as defined in this book, can be used to provide a pragmatic analysis for small-scale linguistic phenomena and for instances of language use at the micro-level of face-to-face interaction. First it was shown how pragmatics can explain seemingly arbitrary facts of language such as the ordering of particles and the performative capacities of certain speech act verbs. Then two examples of linguistic interaction, one in an informal setting, the other institutional, were commented upon.

For further reading on particles, see: Abraham (ed.) (1991), Foolen (1996). On performativity: Récanati (1981), Searle (1989), Verschueren (1995d). On face-to-face conversation: Atkinson and Heritage (eds) (1984), Kerbrat-Orecchioni (1990/92/94), Sacks (1992), Schiffrin (1994). On institutional discourse: Atkinson and Drew (1979), Walter (1988), Drew and Heritage (eds) (1992), Goodwin (1994), Sarangi and Slembrouck (1996), Gunnarsson *et al.* (eds) (1997).

7.4 *Research topic*

The research topic presented in section 6.6 contained an excerpt from a report on the US State Department noon briefing, 26 March 1998, as distributed by the United States Information Service (USIS). The excerpt presented there was written as a regular report, even though the general heading of the USIS message said 'Transcript . . .'. The same USIS message, indeed, also contained the official verbatim transcript of the briefing in question. The portion corresponding to the 'report' in section 6.6 is printed below. Study the interactional generation of meaning in this transcribed version.

US DEPARTMENT OF STATE
DAILY PRESS BRIEFING

DPB # 37

THURSDAY, MARCH 26, 1998 12:40 PM
(ON THE RECORD UNLESS OTHERWISE NOTED)

Mr RUBIN: Welcome to the State Department briefing. It's good to see that at least some of you who traveled with the Secretary managed to make it here today – at least some of you did.

We have a statement on Laos, on the freedom of worship issue, that will be posted after the briefing. Which of the two AP reporters should get the first question is up to them.

Q: Well, can I pick up on a little something left over from yesterday? There was some question whether Gelbard would be able to go on to Belgrade. Do you have any further information?

Mr. RUBIN: Yes. I spoke to Ambassador Gelbard about an hour ago. He was, at the last minute, provided flight clearance. He met with Mr Milutinovic in Belgrade. He also met with Ibrahim Rugova in Pristina and a group of student leaders there. He is emphasizing the importance of dialogue and that on the Serb side, that they comply with the four conditions the Contact Group laid out; that they understand that the message coming out of Bonn was a message that pressure is going to continue on Serbia-Montenegro unless and until they get the message and begin to focus on dialogue rather than crackdowns as a means of resolving this problem.

The situation in Kosovo, as far as Ambassador Gelbard was concerned, is calm. However, we do believe that the special police are digging in; that there is no indication that they're leaving; and that their activities are therefore ominous. What we're facing if they don't get the message the Contact Group tried to send to them is a situation where the violence will increase and where the Contact Group and the international community will proceed to even harsher measures if the Serbian authorities don't get the message.

Q: Is it your understanding that the Russian agreement to the arms embargo will block this alleged Russian arms deal with Belgrade, which has been written about?

Mr RUBIN: Well, Secretary Albright did receive assurances from Foreign Minister Primakov, as indicated by the Contact Group statement. Foreign Minister Primakov told the Secretary that they are going to go forward and implement the decisions to impose an arms embargo.

A deadline of March 31 was set – an objective, rather – to pass the resolution. The discussions are now ongoing in New York, and our diplomats there report that the discussions are taking place constructively. We have every reason to think that an arms embargo will be put in place in time. And if not, that would be troubling.

But assuming that it does go ahead, normally an arms embargo would prohibit the transfer of military equipment from the time the arms embargo went into effect. There was some suggestion that perhaps this arms embargo should be of a limited time frame. That was rejected by the Contact Group; so it is going to be an unconditional, unlimited arms embargo that will only be lifted when Belgrade complies with the requirements of the Contact Group. Every arms embargo resolution that I've ever seen – and I haven't actually looked at this text – would, from the time of enactment, prohibit the transfer of weaponry.

As far as what we do and don't know about what may be going on, all I can say is that we are aware of the possibility of military to military co-operation between Russia and Belgrade. That is a matter that would, in our view, if it involved military equipment, be prohibited by an arms embargo resolution. That's precisely the reason why this resolution will be important.

Q: Was this particular deal or issue discussed in Bonn with the Russians by you?

Mr RUBIN: Well, I'm not in a position to describe every aspect of the discussions between the two ministers; other than to say that we have no reason to believe that Russia doesn't understand that an arms embargo is an arms embargo – and that means that there will be no transfers of military equipment if that embargo is enacted.

Q: If this is so clear what are the discussions in New York about?

Mr RUBIN: Well, as I've indicated to many of you on many occasions, when you write the sentence 'arms embargo' in your stories, then it's over. You said they will impose an arms embargo. But when the diplomats who have to actually conduct the work, prepare a resolution – and for those of you who have worked in New York or read the elaborate texts that are resolutions – they are very carefully drafted documents that require a lot of careful preparation prior to enacting a resolution that would impose such a severe sanction.

So they are now working on the text of a resolution and that takes a number of days; and it is a perfectly normal procedure for that work to take some time so that when and if it's passed and imposed and can't be lifted until Serbia complies, that all the i's are dotted and the t's are crossed before the resolution is passed, not afterwards.

8

Macropragmatic issues

This chapter concerns issues with implications that inevitably go beyond the here-and-now of small-scale linguistic interaction. As was pointed out (at the beginning of section 7.2.2), the distinction with Chapter 7 is an artificial one since all forms of communication, however strictly confined to a face-to-face context, are embedded in a wider social realm, the influence of which can always be traced. Conversely, macro-processes transcending small-scale interaction cannot be studied without investigating details at the micro-level; this is not only of methodological, but also of theoretical relevance. If we want the distinction to make sense, it should be interpreted as one of scale. Some of the variables that come into play will have different values depending on where the phenomenon to be studied is situated on that scale. At the macro-level, for instance, the relevant parameter of 'time' will be more likely to be 'historical time' than either 'time of utterance' or 'available time'. Similarly, though social norms are always relevant, they will play a different role in informal personal interaction (as in section 7.2.1) than in an institutional context which is to be situated further towards the macro-end of the scale (as in section 7.2.2). Also, personality traits and mental states will fade as relevant factors to be taken into account the further we move towards questions transcending direct interpersonal interaction. Questions of methodology will have to be adapted accordingly (as we will try to demonstrate in section 8.2.3).

First we will dwell briefly on what we call a pragmatic perspective on language resources at the macro-level (section 8.1). Then we will review a few instances of pragmatic investigations that are clearly situated close to the macro-pole of the micro–macro scale. These will include problems of intercultural and international communication (in section 8.2.1), the discourse-based study of ideology (in 8.2.2), and the pragmatics of wide societal debates (in 8.2.3).

8.1 *A pragmatic perspective on language resources at the macro-level*

In Chapter 7 we gave two very different examples of a pragmatic perspective on (i.e. a usage-oriented approach to) certain language resources. There was a need to do so because what we have called language resources, certainly at the micro-level, are easily amenable to a formalist, structural approach. At the macro-level, however, a pragmatic perspective almost inevitably comes in, although limited forms of non-pragmatic research remain possible (such as purely distributional studies of variable forms, or a descriptive account of the diachronic development of a specific linguistic form). Therefore, we can be extremely brief in this section, referring mainly to the available sociolinguistic literature. Language resources at the macro-level are basically what we have defined as **languages**, **codes** and **styles** (in section 4.1), keeping in mind – as any pragmatic perspective should – that those always show significant **variation** and are continuously subject to **change**. This final remark cannot be overstated. Adopting a radical (i.e. realistic!) pragmatic perspective could have saved a lot of people's energy that was spent on linguistic engineering, from Dr Esperanto, 'the one who hopes', all the way to Quirk's (1981) proposal to construct a 'Nuclear English'. From a pragmatic point of view, a 'universal language' is a paradoxical concept. The more universal a language is (i.e. the more widely it is spoken), the less universal it will become (i.e. the more it will diversify). Language may be the only commodity which is truly everyone's property (which may be why control over language is such a desirable totalitarian goal). Everyone uses language, there is no end to the variability of conditions of use, and language is essentially shaped by its use. Therefore, even the most modern tools to facilitate standardization cannot prevent diversification.

8.2 *Macro-processes in language use*

The following sections cover merely a random selection of topics, chosen on the basis of my own recent research interests. There will be no attempt to really define entire fields of pragmatic investigation, only to illustrate a pragmatic approach to certain topic areas (in sections 8.2.1 and 8.2.2) and to present some methodological considerations that follow from and feed back into the overall theoretical perspective (mainly in section 8.2.3).

8.2.1 Intercultural and international communication

Using the general pragmatic perspective sketched in this book, the principal guideline is not to look at phenomena such as intercultural and international communication as anything 'special', but simply as just another instance of linguistic behaviour, subject to the same types of influences and restrictions (though possibly with shifts of focus), consisting of the same sorts of structural patterns, and revealing similarly dynamic processes of meaning generation, taking place with varying degrees of salience. To the extent that things 'go wrong' in intercultural and international communication (just as things 'go wrong' in any other type of communicative event), and to the extent that what goes wrong is not simply a consequence of conflicts of interest or struggles for power (just as in many cases of intracultural interaction), the problem can often be reduced to a lack of attention for a basic pragmatic premiss (first introduced in section 2.2, and most recently reintroduced in section 8.1 above): the pervasiveness of variability. We will give two examples of intercultural/international communication, focusing on the way in which the metapragmatic framing of the Other's linguistic behaviour betrays a lack of understanding of, or respect for, communicative diversity.

Rocks – just layin' around

In January 1984, the Belgian radio and television broadcast a Swedish newsreel (in its 'Panorama' programme) devoted to the election campaign of the African American democratic candidate Jesse Jackson during the American presidential primaries. For 40 minutes, the Flemish audience was able to follow his trail from town to town, from state to state. Alternately, fragments were shown from interviews, press conferences, and political speeches and rallies. As always in The Netherlands and the Flemish part of Belgium, the original sound track – which did not contain any commentator's remarks, but only documentary data of the types mentioned – was kept intact, and the English was accompanied by Dutch subtitles.

The multiple layering of the linguistic behaviour involved should be quite transparent from the start. What we get is (i) Jackson addressing live audiences in the United States, (ii) Jackson addressing a wider US audience through the mediatization of his performances, (iii) a Swedish news crew making selections from Jackson's performances – with or without intermediary agencies – to inform a home audience about Jackson's role in the US primaries, and (iv) an incorporation of the materials selected by the Swedish journalists into an information-giving programme on Jackson's role in the primaries directed at a Flemish audience. What we will concentrate on is the way in which the introduction to (iv) – which is basically followed by an exact copy of the documentary content of (iii) – frames the events in (i), level (ii) being completely ignored, and level (iii) being mentioned only as the source.

In the introduction to the programme, Jackson is described, already in the title (shown in big letters as background behind the speaking journalist), as *een kleurrijk kandidaat*, 'a colourful candidate' (read: certainly fascinating, but a little out of place) with a considerable dose of oratorical talent. Part of the description is the statement in (1).

(1) Jackson weet met de media om te gaan.
(Jackson knows how to handle the media.)

This comment immediately follows the commentator's observation that Jackson was hardly known to anyone, until he went off to Syria and returned with an American pilot who had been kept prisoner. A judgment of demagoguery is not far away. Then we get a very explicit metapragmatic comment on Jackson's public appearances:

(2) Met typisch Amerikaanse predikantentruuks weet hij zijn volgelingen in vervoering te brengen.
(With typically American evangelistic tricks, he manages to bring his followers to a state of ecstasy.)

What this comment alludes to is a form of mass hysteria brought about by means of demagogical trickery reminiscent of the rhetorical style of religious cult leaders. This is supposed to be descriptive of the fragments of campaigning that the television audience will be offered a glimpse of. We should immediately ask, then, to what extent this description captures real characteristics of (i), i.e. Jackson's appearance in front of live audiences in the United States. The question is threefold. First, are we confronted with something *typically American*? Second, what is *evangelistic* about the reported speech events? Third, in what sense are we witnessing the use of *tricks*?

Even a superficial analysis allows us to see that what we get is not 'typically American' in any general sense. Considering the variety of English spoken by Jackson, we note that sometimes he uses a version of Standard American English, and sometimes a typical form of Black English. In some fragments, there is a clear break between the two varieties, as when (3) introduces a long rhetorical episode in Black English.

(3) Well, I done a li'l observin' now.

This instance of code switching (already referred to in section 4.1; see also section 6.4.1) is a textbook example of how the alternating use of different codes can serve a clearly symbolic function to reinforce identification and solidarity with the African American community (members of which make up most of the audience). When testing the reactions of Flemish students about a year after the broadcast, moreover, we noticed that exactly those passages that led most strongly to visions of demagoguery also showed most properties of Black English. It is hard to avoid the question, then, whether such visions were not largely induced by a defective familiarity with stylistic, if not linguistic, properties of language use common among African Americans. That impression is further strengthened by the observation that in recent years Flemish students seem to have less trouble with Jackson's 1984 style than their colleagues did in 1985, probably as a result of heightened exposure through popular music, movies and television. Speaking of typically American rhetorical practices, therefore, may stretch interpretation in undesirable directions.

What passes for Jackson's 'evangelistic' style, furthermore, may simply be an ethnic style – if a label can be put on it at all. As shown by Kochman (1981) or Gumperz (1982) and many other researchers, a system of socio-culturally determined norms and conventions separates African American language use (in its most distinct manifestations) from that of the white majority (though, strictly speaking, they communicate in the same language and many can switch with ease between varieties). The language of Black preachers in its most typical form is just one instance of a Black communicative style, which also characterizes political rhetoric, whether the politician is himself a religious leader or not. One of the basic characteristics of the modern African American 'sermon' is 'a dramatic interchange between speaker and audience' (Gumperz 1982: 189).

> By systematically modulating his performance, sometimes alternately singing and speaking, or, more frequently, shifting style, the minister speaks with, alternately, his own voice, that of the Lord, and that of the congregation. (Gumperz 1982: 189–90)

In all this, the active participation of the audience is of the utmost importance and 'can materially affect the course of the service' (Gumperz 1982: 190).

The most visible aspect of the Black orator's modulation of his speech is the symbolic switching from styles using Standard American English to a Black English 'folk style' (phonologically, lexically, grammatically, and prosodically distinct). Partly because the broadcast on Jesse Jackson's campaign did not show any speech completely, partly because the emphasis was entirely on the most captivating passages in a typical 'folk style', the symbolical value of the switching could not be appreciated by the average viewer. As a result, the ethnic (or group-specific) character of Jackson's style became even less conspicuous than it would already have been otherwise for an audience insufficiently familar with it. It is quite understandable why such a European audience, without compelling reasons to regard Jackson's communicative style as anything other than typically American rhetoric, would judge his performances in terms of values prevalent in mainstream European societies. Interpreting his style of performance in the light of the foregoing remarks, however, we must conclude that it can hardly be called 'typically American', and that the ethnic basis and the tradition to which it belongs are done an injustice by referring to it as an 'evangelistic' style.

We are left with the question whether we can talk in an unqualified manner of 'trickery' and demagogical means. We should not be naïve, and we can simply admit that all public rhetoric is full of strategies and tricks to reach specific goals. Beyond this general observation, however, there are some aspects of the communicative style in question which cast doubt on the suitability of this description. There is the already mentioned interactive nature of the religious and (closely related) political public performances. The audience participates in the event. That participation rarely takes the form of mechanical repetition, unless in the case of a clear and meaningful motto (e.g. *I am somebody*, meaning 'I may come from the ghetto, but I am an equally worthy human being') or for the sake of the humouristic effect, as when Jackson asks all those who have registered to vote to raise their right arm and to repeat (4) (where three dots indicate the time left for repetition):

(4) I . . . (state your name) . . . swear . . . that I am . . . a registered voter. . . . If . . . I am lying . . . I hope . . . that my right arm . . . will never come down.

Spontaneous comments from the audience are very frequent. Though the recordings were not at all aimed at registering those interventions, they were constantly to be heard. A sampling is given in (5).

(5) 1. **That**'s allright!
2. Now, **did** you, **real**ly?
3. Think of that!
4. **Bi:g** thing!

As long as interventions would have to express agreement, the interactive nature of public performances would not form a guarantee against manipulation. As appears from (5), however, at least some healthy scepticism can be voiced openly in the interventions that form the background. That reactions of this kind are essential to the event type appears most forcefully from speeches delivered to a different kind of audience. For instance, in the same programme Jackson's rhetoric can be seen to lose its force in one performance in front of a predominantly American Indian audience that reacts with silence and occasional applause.

In a most gripping campaign speech in Bakersfield, California, Jackson refers to Ronald Reagan as 'the Goliath of this day'. He continues:

(6) ... [he] won Illinois in 1980 by 300 000 votes ... there were 800 000 unregistered blacks ... rocks, just layin' around.

After a long enumeration of similar facts, always ending in the same words, and building up towards a climax by increasing speed and loudness, lengthened sibilants, and the like, he concludes:

(7) Pull your head high Bakersfield. Pick up your slingshots ... use your rocks ... let's sling them ... rocks, rocks, rocks, just layin' ... around.

It would be hard not to appreciate the aesthetic quality of the metaphor. Flemish viewers, however, whose reactions we can reasonably assume to be at least partly represented in the words of the commentator and in the judgments of university students (who tended to evaluate Jackson positively in terms of personality traits but quite negatively as a presidential candidate), did not seem ready to cope with the task of evaluating a political–communicative event taking place in a specific English-speaking community, in spite of their good or even excellent knowledge of the English language. Knowledge of the language used may create a false sense of easy intelligibility, leading to unreflective, habitual interpretation choices which are entirely based on group-dependent norms of communicative behaviour that are handled as if they would be universal rather than infinitely varied.

In this example, English becomes an object of misunderstanding. Let us now examine a case in which English – again by means of metapragmatic framing – serves as a medium of misunderstanding in an intercultural/international context.

Who exploded that land mine under the conference?

The event in question was the political incident following the shooting down over Soviet territory of an American U-2 spy plane on 1 May 1960. The study reported here (and presented at length in Verschueren 1985c) analyses all reports in *The New York Times* related to this event and its consequences from Friday, 6 May (when the first reports were published, the day after Khrushchev's public announcement of what had happened) to Friday, 20 May (a few days after the resulting abortive four-power summit in Paris). The focus of attention is the set of metapragmatic terms and expressions (and especially those of a metaphorical kind) employed to describe the language used by Soviet and American government officials, including Nikita Khrushchev and Dwight Eisenhower, in their verbal shaping of the incident. Briefly summarized, the framing of the incident as a political–communicative event looked as follows.

On the first day after Khrushchev's announcement that an American plane had been shot down over Soviet territory, the metapragmatic framing of the events tends to indicate that *The New York Times* attached less credibility to the details of Khrushchev's announcement (according to which the plane had willfully violated Soviet air space for reasons of espionage) than to the US explanation that a NASA weather-observation plane of the U-2 type might have strayed across the Turkish–Soviet border after having reported trouble with the oxygen equipment. This lower degree of credibility is partly established by the newspaper's factual (content-centred) and detailed reporting of the official American explanation (in which neutral linguistic action verbs such as *said*, *denied*, *observed*, *explained*, etc. figure prominently), and partly by its choice of linguistic action verbs focusing on emotionality, hostility and bad manners when reporting on Khrushchev's reactions. Thus there is a tendency to side with the quoted judgement of Senator EL Bartlett that Khrushchev's remarks were *crude*, *rude*, and *provocative*. Facing this attitude, America is said to have *reacted with restraint*, thus implying that there might have been good reasons for an angry, unrestrained, response.

On the second day of newspaper coverage, a new element is introduced. Emotion-oriented descriptions of Khrushchev's utterances are framed in such a way as to suggest demagogical calculations behind them rather than expressive value. Not only does the reporter of one article explicitly mention, as in (8), that 'Moscow encouraged the Soviet people [. . .] to express their "wrath".' But *set the public tone* in (9) offers the same information more implicitly. And so does *deliberate* in (10), suggesting that the expression of anger is strategic rather than spontaneous.

(8) With the summit meeting less than a fortnight away, Moscow *encouraged* the Soviet people today to express their 'wrath' over the incident in which it was charged that Soviet territory was violated by an unarmed United States plane on May 1.

(9) Premier Khrushchev *set the public tone* for his Government yesterday *in a bitter speech* to the Supreme Soviet.

(10) *More deliberate but still angry comment* about the incident *was given* today by most of the seventeen speakers who followed him to the rostrum.

Thus the revelations are presented as a pre-summit manoeuvre.

On the third day, after the US admission of spying (prompted by the Soviet announcement that the pilot of the plane, Francis G. Powers, had been captured alive and that the wreckage had been found), details of Khrushchev's revelations are no longer cast in a doubt-provoking mould. But his style of message delivery becomes the focus (especially an aspect of exaggeration which underscores the possibility of manipulative intent), thus diverting the attention from the American fabrications on the previous days. Just consider (11) (already quoted in section 6.4.1):

(11) Mr Khrushchev *made his account a story of high drama and low skulduggery interspersed with bitingly sarcastic remarks* about Washington's contention that the pilot was on a regular weather reconnaissance mission and had probably gotten lost during a blackout due to the failure of his oxygen equipment.

(These implications, however, are counterbalanced by a single article by James Reston which clearly offers the US Government's duplicity as a distinct possibility, not only with respect to the first official statement, but even with reference to the new version disclaiming President Eisenhower's personal responsibility.)

This general picture remains unchanged until the summit in Paris. The main new fact is an announcement by President Eisenhower in which he takes full responsibility for the espionage activities. This message is metapragmatically provided by the newspaper with a frame of emotionlessness and rationality, as in (12) and (13).

(12) *In a carefully worded statement* read at his news conference the President *said* that the Soviet 'fetish of secrecy and concealment' was 'a major cause of international tension and uneasiness'.

(13) *There was neither regret nor apology in* President Eisenhower's *statement* of the case *nor in the firm, measured tones with which he read it.*

Meanwhile, the defence of espionage activities (as in (12)) is given close attention, and on occasion American duplicity is slightly palliated by presenting the US as the victim of Soviet scheming:

(14) The United States Government, many members of Congress and much of the press *had been mouse-trapped into premature denials*.

But there is a clearly critical stance, not so much against the fact of espionage (except for the timing of the abortive flight – just two weeks before the summit meeting, and on the Soviets' major holiday) but against the Government announcements.

Finally, there is the communicative exchange, in Paris, which constitutes the climax of the conflict. Consider the following descriptions.

(15) [Front-page title] US–Soviet *clash* disrupts summit talks.
(16) President de Gaulle made a speech of welcome and then Premier Khrushchev *embarked on his tirade.*
(17) Mr Khrushchev's *savage attack was responsible for* this transformation [from criticism directed against Eisenhower to sympathy for him].
(18) Nikita S. Khrushchev, Premier of the Soviet Union, had *levelled a charge of* 'treachery' against the President of the United States.
(19) The Soviet Premier *bluntly told* the United States President that he would not be welcome if he went to the Soviet Union on his proposed visit next month.
(20) His denunciation of the United States and his imposition of conditions *were capped by the brutally frank announcement that* in the circumstances General Eisenhower's visit must be postponed.
(21) After Mr Khrushchev *threw out his thunderbolt* at the Elysée Palace this morning, [. . .].
(22) Some form of internal pressure may have compelled the Premier to come to Paris and *explode this land mine under the conference,* British diplomats said.
(23) At the end of *his blistering speech,* the system of high-level consultation and negotiation seemed *wrecked.*
(24) Mr Khrushchev's *speech was a devastating and explosive performance.*
(25) The reaction of a few experienced and detached diplomats who *were not blown over* by Mr Khrushchev's *storm* [. . .].

Thus the exchange at the opening session of the summit meeting (during which Khrushchev demands condemnation of the U-2 flights, their immediate cancellation, and punishment of those responsible) is presented as a clash for which the Soviet Premier's hostile attitude and bad manners are held entirely responsible. Metapragmatic metaphors are heavily relied on to establish this impression. Though the other partner in the exchange, Eisenhower, is said to have *exploded with fury* in private after the meeting, during the meeting he *kept his temper in check* and *responded in a 'statesmanlike and restrained manner'.* British Prime Minister Macmillan is quoted saying that he thought his 'old friend' had 'reacted with disregard for "face" that one would not find in lesser men coming from lesser countries'. Hence the burden of guilt is clearly placed on Khrushchev's shoulders: he is the one who *exploded a land mine under the conference.*

This placement of guilt is achieved by means of the metapragmatic framing of Khrushchev's and Eisenhower's verbal behaviour, without violating any standards of accuracy, but by focusing on aspects of speaking style in such a way that they are automatically subject to evaluation on the basis of norms that are handled as if they would have universal validity. Though this universality is not asserted, it is heavily implied by neglecting to allow for variability. Thus, when Khushchev is reported, quite accurately, to have 'exploded' in public, such behaviour is likely to be judged by the readership of *The New York Times* in terms of their own culture-specific standards of behaviour which dictate that explosions are permissible in private but not in public. Those standards shape the typically Western concept of diplomacy in which only unemotional, detached debating and negotiating is acceptable – irrespective of what one may feel. Therefore, Eisenhower is clearly evaluated as a 'real' diplomat because he *kept his temper in check*, though his emotions may have been visible in different ways during the meeting. In fact, Bohlen (1973, p. 468) notes that 'As Khrushchev talked, Eisenhower's bald head turned various shades of pink, a sure sign that he was using every bit of will to hold his temper', adding that 'When Eisenhower spoke, he gave no sign of the intense anger that he had obviously felt a few minutes before.'

8.2.2 Discourse and ideology

Communicative events or phenomena at a macro-level are hard to detach from processes that one could call 'ideological'. That is why we focused the discussion of the above examples of intercultural and international communication (both of which clearly transcend the here-and-now of face-to-face communication) on aspects of *language ideology* or, if you wish, communication ideology, as reflected in metapragmatic descriptions. In this section we will broaden the discussion to the general relationship between discourse and ideology. To that end, we will focus exclusively on the editorial introduction to *The world in 1996*, bits and pieces of which were discussed at length when introducing some of the common topics in pragmatics such as deixis (in section 1.1.1), when illustrating processes of sentential utterance building (in section 4.4.1) and suprasentential utterance building (in section 4.4.2), and when dealing with indicators of metapragmatic awareness (in section 6.4.1). For ease of reference, we bring the different portions discussed so far together in (26).

(26) (a) 1996 will be a year of prosperity and peace. (b) The world will move another notch away from the conventional wisdoms of the previous generation. (c) The American presidential campaign, which runs from the snows of the New Hampshire primary until November 5th, will be the setting for the political ideas that will hold sway for the rest of the century: less tax, less government interference, a drastically reduced welfare state. (d) These are themes that will be taken

up on the hustings in Spain, Russia, India and Australia. (e) (In 1996 over a billion people will go to an election booth, proof that democracy is energetically kicking dictatorship from the ring.) (f) Watch out for the European Union's inter-governmental conference, which starts in Italy in the spring, as the last place where the old nostrums of political interference and subsidy have credence.

(g) For this folly, Europe will be rewarded with a slow rate of economic growth in 1996, although Britain, at last, is surprisingly well placed. (h) The United States will enter its sixth year of growth, the longest period of uninterrupted expansion since the war. (i) It is towards Asia, however, that the world's wealth and influence will ratchet one more turn in 1996. (j)Year after year, East Asia achieves a growth rate about three times that of the West. (k) Most of the 90m extra people in the world in 1996 will be Asian. (l) They will be born poorer than the average reader of this article. (m) They will die richer. (n) The tilt of the world towards the East is scarcely beginning.

(o) The world will be a peaceful place in 1996. (p) Europe's civil wars will finally be over. (q) A Middle East settlement will fall into place, despite attempts by bombers and bigots to disrupt it. (r) A nuclear test ban treaty will be signed. (s) Armies, except in China and Africa, will be standing down.

[Two paragraphs omitted.]

(t) These are some of the trends and ideas you will find in *The World in 1996*, which will appear in 80 countries and in 12 languages. (u) This is our tenth year of publication: put all our mistaken predictions together and we could probably produce another edition. (v) But along the way much has been right and, I hope, most of it interesting.

For the present purposes, we define an **ideology** as any constellation of fundamental or commonsensical, and often normative, beliefs and ideas related to some aspect(s) of (social) 'reality'. The commonsense nature of the beliefs and ideas is manifested in the fact that they are rarely questioned, within a specific group of people in a given society or community, in discourse related to the 'reality' in question, often across various discourse genres. Their not being questioned means that the beliefs and ideas in question are often (though not always and not exclusively) carried along implicitly rather than to be formulated explicitly. Rhetorically constructed or supported ideological webs serve the purpose of framing, validating or legitimating attitudes and actions in the domain to which they are applicable. Such activities of framing, validating or legitimating, however, always take place in an environment characterized by **heteroglossia**, the constant interplay between different socio-ideological languages competing for dominance or **hegemony**. The normativity involved in discursive manifestations of ideology, therefore, is partly a function of reflexive awareness (of social and linguistic norms alike, which function in processes of **identity** construction), and partly projective (reaching for control over the Other's present as well as one's own future).

With this definition in mind, let us have a look at (26). As always in pragmatic research, the central concern should be with the dynamics of meaning generation. Our question is, then, *what patterns of unquestioned meaning emerge from the text?* In order to get to rephrasings of and answers to this question, let us first briefly 'locate' the speech event.

Spatially and socially, (26) is *about* 'the world', at the same time a form of communication *in* that same world. Temporally, it is situated *in* 1995, while it is *about* 1996, which makes the activity by definition predictive. The referential extension of *the world* is narrowed down by the fact that this is about 'the world from a (conservative) British perspective'. This fact, however, is left completely implicit. At the surface level, *the world* is dealt with in its most general sense. The implicit level is 'marked' by (or inferrable from) the plain contextual fact that the publisher is *The Economist*, which – however abstract in some ways – is the real source of the communication. That source is represented by the utterer, editor Dudley Fishburn, whose personal authority is established by means of an identification that tells the interpreters that he is a Member of Parliament for Kensington and on the Board of Overseers of Harvard University. The world of interpreters, the audience, is also presented at first sight as almost completely universal: as (26)t. has it, the text is distributed in 80 countries and in 12 languages. Of course, the real readers are restricted to an extremely small subset of a potential universal audience, a subset that is largely defined in socio-economic terms. The nature of the source, together with the target audience, impose further restrictions on content: the text is not really about *the world* as such, even as seen from a (conservative) British perspective, but mainly about economic and political aspects.

Structurally, the basic utterance unit we are looking at is a self-contained single-authored *text*. It is, however, embedded in a wider publication belonging to a well-defined activity type, the reporting of news. Its intertextual relations with portions of this wider publication are hierarchical: (26) provides an 'editorial introduction', thus sketching a perspective for all other texts. Both of these aspects define the genre to which (26) belongs. Given that the right amount of time and space could be devoted to it, (26) should be analysed at every level of structure from the text downwards. At the same time, it would have to be analysed in its coherence with the wider discourse of *The Economist* in general and even of competing publications. For the former task we will have to be happy with what earlier chapters have already revealed, adding only a few analytical observations directly relevant to the topic of this section. For the latter, we can only shed some light on what it would take to be carried out (in the form of the methodological observations in section 8.2.3).

As to salience, writing for publication (especially as editor of a magazine) involves a highly conscious process of choice-making. The author does not only think of propositional content, but is constantly modelling an audience and trying to express ideas in a way appropriate to the imagined or constructed interpreters. Yet, in view of our definition of ideology, some of the more interesting processes of meaning generation may be situated at the level of what the utterer takes so much for granted that it does not kindle any questions, or that he could not imagine his interpreters to disagree.

The main question on meaning-generating processes in a text such as (26) may be *how a text of this kind generates its own context*, for instance by narrowing down 'the world' that is at issue in a way that is compatible with the pre-existent restrictions that have already been contextually imposed. Consider, for instance, the way in which *prosperity* and *peace*, which (26)a. predicts in quite general terms, get narrowed down – apparently without further thoughts – in the paragraphs that exemplify them, (26)g.–n. and (26)o.–s., respectively. Whose prosperity is at stake? Only Europe, Great Britain, and the United States seem worth mentioning, though a warning is added that a comparison between the traditionally rich and Asia may shift in favour of Asia. Eagerness to compare leads to some questionable statements. Though it is no doubt true that most of the 90 million extra people, many of whom will be Asian, *will be born poorer than the average reader of this article* (line (26)l.), the author is probably overstating his case when claiming that *they* (all of them, or even most of them?) *will die richer* (in (26)m.). Similarly, to whom will the world be a peaceful place? Only Europe and the Middle East are really thought about (in (26)p.–q.). True marginalization is the fate of China and Africa, whose armies, which are not expected to 'stand down', cannot take away the expectation of global peace.

Beyond these matters of referential scope, an unmistakable and unquestioned economic and political world view permeates the text and explains its major tenets. I will leave it to the reader to trace those systematically.

8.2.3 The pragmatics of wide societal debates

Let us move, finally, to the level of a publicly accessible social and political debate of which the present author's linguistic work (a pragmatic analysis of the debate itself, in particular Blommaert and Verschueren 1992a, made accessible in English as Blommaert and

Verschueren 1998) happens to be one of the ingredients. The issue is the presence of what is perceived to be large numbers of foreigners (in particular foreigners with roots in the Maghreb and Turkey, usually referred to as 'migrants') in Belgium. This Belgian (and more specifically Flemish) 'migrant debate' is only one representative of the much wider European approach to the so-called migration problem. A synthesized version of the overall structure of the debate – not to be confused with a specific instance of real linguistic interaction that ever took place – is given in (27), where ER stands for the position taken by the extreme right, TM for what we call the 'tolerant majority', and JB&JV for Blommaert and myself. Note that the utterances in (27), though they do not match literal turns in a real-world exchange, are not stereotyped hypothetical ones. They represent real data in the sense (i) that they adequately summarize positions taken in the debate, and (ii) that each of them can be found in the discourse corpus we investigated.

(27) a. ER: Migrants should be sent back to their countries of origin.
b. TM: Migrants should integrate themselves into our society.
c. ER+TM: We respect other people's identity.
d. JB&JV: Neither ER nor TM accept fundamental forms of diversity.
e. TM: JB&JV just don't understand.

To understand the problem we want to address, it is important to keep the social, cultural and political context in mind. One ingredient that might lead to confusion is the context-specific usage of the verb *integrate* in (27)b. Whereas in the American debate on multiculturalism the term 'integration' usually refers to minority members' full participation at every level of social life, its Belgian–Flemish equivalent basically refers to a model of assimilation focusing on the non-natives' having to prove their being worthy of participation.

The problem, in relation to the pragmatics of meaning generation, is the following. Sentence (27)d. summarizes the conclusion of a pragmatic analysis of a discourse corpus with a time depth of roughly three years, collected from mainstream sources (i.e. avoiding overt extremism in any direction), and consisting of news reports on the 'migrant problem', moderate political policy statements, highly mediatized social scientific research reports, and a government training programme directed mainly at police officers. The question is: how is it possible to reach this conceptual, attitudinal or ideological conclusion in spite of the facts that (i) it is *not at all overtly represented in the linguistic form* of (27)a. and (27)b., nor in the texts which (27)b. (and to a certain extent even (27)a.) summarizes, and (ii) it *contradicts* the explicit claim to an attitude made by both ER and TM, as in (27)c.

A number of steps have to be taken in the search for a solution to the problem. In our highly communicative society, we are led to expect a high degree of transparent meaning. But in order for (27)d. to be correct as a research conclusion (especially in connection with discourse coming from the tolerant majority which, of course, makes every possible attempt to profile itself as open to diversity), we must assume that what is textually transparent, the literally encoded meaning, the explicit 'on record' communication about which the sources of the discourse would readily agree that it corresponds to their meaning intentions, does not exhaust the meaning of what is said. This is the easiest step to take, since it has been one of the premisses of pragmatics ever since its inception that one can never *completely* say what one means (see section 1.1.3). Communication is not possible without invoking a world of knowledge or assumptions, supposed to be at least partly shared between interlocutors, into which utterances can be anchored.

Background assumptions, however, may in principle be fully transparent to all participants, which is why they may be actively used in the build-up of context (as discussed in relation to earlier examples, e.g. in section 5.4). Therefore, a further step is needed. We must also assume that some conceptual patterns or meanings show a relatively low degree of salience. They may simply reflect conceptualization habits, whether rooted in conscious ideas or not.

The realm of habits of cognition which contribute to the less salient ingredients of the meaning of utterances does not only include aspects of conceptualization but also whatever conventional types of intentionality there may be. Moreover, non-salient types of meaning may, when made conscious, match what the language users would have meant or understood. A final step is needed, then, for (27)d. to be a possibly valid research conclusion in a context where (27)c. may (at least as far as the tolerant majority is concerned) be the honest expression of an attitude matching consciously intended meaning. That step is to assume that the lack of salience of the processes involved may go as far as to create a complete gap between the meaning corresponding more or less in a one-to-one fashion with the linguistic form of expression at the transparent, literal or explicit level on the one hand, and additional types of meaning or conceptual structures on the other.

This leads, first of all, to a sharper formulation of the problem. In cases where there is a gap between deeper conceptual and overt linguistic representations, how can the meaning be recovered with any degree of certainty? Certainly, it is not possible to ask the utterers what they meant, since they could only paraphrase their original words, representing the already overtly encoded intentions. Yet, in order for scientifically justifiable interpretation to be possible at all, there must still be a link between meaning and form, a bridge across the gap. A solution to the problem is now within reach since a bridge is clearly provided by the very phenomenon that made us take the first step away from what is textually transparent: the realm of *implicit meaning*, including, but not restricted to, most of the areas traditionally designated with terms such as background assumptions, common ground, presupposition, and implicature. What remains, then, is an assessment of the methodological and theoretical status of the study of implicit meaning in a body of publicly accessible discourse.

Let us turn to methodology first, and let us begin by situating the investigation referred to in general pragmatic terms. The contextual correlate with which linguistic forms of expression and processes of expressing are seen to be interadaptable in this case can briefly be described as an ideology bearing on group relations, in particular the basic attitudes towards diversity in society. The term 'ideology' is used here as in section 8.2.2. The locus of the study is further defined in terms of different structural levels at which relevant linguistic indicators of implicit meaning patterns are to be found. The processes under investigation involve various aspects of social and communicative dynamics (with at least as many strategic uses as forms of straightforward meaning encoding, because of the aspects of power involved in majority–minority interaction), and they take place with various degrees of salience.

The search for forms of implicit meaning bearing on latent attitudes towards diversity is, of course, only one aspect of an overall pragmatic methodology to study the types of discourse under investigation. Two aspects of the positioning of our present topic within a wider enterprise are worth emphasizing. First, most messages are built up in the dynamic combination of explicit and implicit aspects of meaning. The same goes for the communication we are dealing with now, but a significant peculiarity is that we observe a conflict between the explicit and the implicit, so that the implicit can be seen to undermine the explicit – if made explicit itself – rather than to combine with it in a relatively straightforward manner. Second, for communicative genres such as news reporting, and especially political rhetoric, it usually makes sense to ask which aspects of implicit meaning simply represent the substance of the world view which the speaker/author assumes he/she shares with the audience, and which ones constitute the (strategic) communication of new information. In the present case, however, the conflict between explicit and implicit meaning entails that the implicit meaning we are dealing with represents supposedly common background knowledge at a level which may be insufficiently conscious to be voiced explicitly at all. Since ideology is also a combination of implicit and explicit views, we can conclude, on the basis of these observations, that we are dealing with the deeper, generally unformulated premisses of an ideology.

It goes without saying that a methodology hinging on the search for implicit meaning is highly interpretive. The main concern must be, in order for the interpretation to provide the bridge across any potential gap between the deeper conceptual and the transparently presented worlds, to clearly **separate interpretation from speculation**. In spite of the existence of a long tradition dealing with similar issues, as in social psychology and critical linguistics or critical discourse analysis, too many sins have been committed against this principle to allow us to ignore it. Most of the ingredients of our methodology will not be 'news' to the readers of this book. We will try to demonstrate, however, that basic insights from (traditional) linguistic pragmatics, reinterpreted to allow for higher degrees of dynamics and for complex processing beyond a straightforward intention–interpretation link, can be combined with the concerns of critical linguistics and principles of sound ethnographic work to penetrate some of the most evasive realms of meaning.

On the level of face-to-face interaction it is not so difficult to demonstrate that there is a relatively clear distinction between interpretation and speculation. To take a trivial example, consider a job applicant who is waiting for an interview and asks the receptionist, *Could you tell me where the bathrooms are?* As the old literature on indirect speech acts tells us, a wide range of interpretive steps have to be taken for the receptionist to arrive at an appropriate answer. Though the literal form of the question inquires after the receptionist's ability to tell where the bathrooms are, the yes/no response which the form itself invites would not be appreciated as sufficiently cooperative. Moreover, as the literature on conversational implicatures would have it, the response *Just around the corner to the right* can only be appropriate if the bathrooms the location of which is described are available for use, since it can be assumed that the applicant would not be asking for their location simply out of curiosity. These phenomena have been described in much more detail elsewhere (see also Chapter 1). The point is that, because of a combination of conventional forms of expression with communicative habits and principles governing linguistic behaviour, an entire world of meanings which are not transparently expressed in the linguistic form of utterances is open to perfectly legitimate interpretation, even though one must keep in mind that tricky types of variability may be involved, that established practice is permanently negotiable, and that actual usage may be adapted to a vast array of strategic purposes which may warp the patterns of the expected. As a result, there is a relatively clear line where the boundaries of legitimate interpretation are crossed into mere speculation, as when the receptionist would conclude, merely on the basis of the utterance and without additional behavioural evidence, that the applicant is nervous. Note that the products of speculation may even be true. But they cannot be justified on the basis of a linguistic pragmatic methodology. And because the distinction between demonstrable meaning and speculative meaning can be drawn, what we are dealing with really are 'hard facts', if such things exist at all within the realm of what is human. The claim really is that the 'facts of meaning' we are dealing with, if they are investigated from the perspective of 'acts of meaning', provide us with harder data than many other endeavours in the humanities and social sciences.

In order to avoid unwarranted, i.e. speculative, conclusions when inferring implicit meaning from a discourse corpus on a wide societal level, more is needed than scrupulous attention to each individual lower-level inference drawn from details of the data – though such scrupulous attention is definitely the first requirement. There are several additional *requirements for data to count as evidence in the search for ingredients of an ideology.* Keeping in mind the working definition we have already provided for 'ideology', we must add that ideologies usually are hegemonic in the sense that they are supported by a (variety of) source(s) of societal power, and that they are dependent for their success (in terms of an influence that dominates social–political life and public debate) on the extent to which they are experienced by (a significant segment of) the population as representing the 'normal' views. Therefore, the set of methodological requirements must be able to establish **coherence**, both in terms of *conceptual connectedness* and *patterns of recurrence*. Though the requirements in question will be mostly formulated with reference to aspects of the 'data' in the following discussion, they bear more on the *scientific approach* than on, for instance, matters of data selection *per se*. Also the emphasis on 'coherence', though dictated by properties of the object of investigation, is in the first place a matter of scientific approach. It is not meant to imply that ideologies themselves have to be coherent. Evidently, if what we are investigating is a gap between the overtly represented norm of tolerance and a deeper lack of openness to diversity, we are dealing with a fundamental form of incoherence. More subtle incongruities may emerge as well. But in order for us to account for them, we must be able to 'place' them in a overall pattern which allows us at least to formulate hypotheses for an explanation. Any phenomenon that cannot be placed in this way must be regarded as an idiosyncratic fact until further evidence can be adduced.

The following presentation of methodological requirements will be reminiscent of principles established in critical linguistics and of some traditional ethnographic methods. However, looking at the way in which so many currently available studies tend to jump to conclusions, thus undermining the credibility of the field, their importance cannot be overemphasized.

First, the **types of data** have to be varied, both horizontally and vertically. The requirement of horizontal diversity in the data refers to the fact that it is desirable for different types of discourse (reporting, political documents, etc.) to be investigated simultaneously with the same kind of implication-oriented methodology. This will help to prevent potentially misguided conclusions based on the specificity of one type of utterer designing messages geared towards only one type of audience.

The requirement that the data should be varied along a vertical axis is more crucial. It refers to the demand for converging data derived from the analyses carried out at different layers of linguistic structure. This is so important because it helps us to detect (and thereby to avoid biased conclusions based on) potential self-monitoring on the part of the utterers of the analysed messages, utterers rarely being able to carry out such self-monitoring at many different levels of structure at the same time.

Let me illustrate the principle with reference to the main levels of discourse structure at which an analysis was carried out leading to conclusion (27)d. The conclusion represents the following diagnosis concerning the dominant ideology – which we call homogeneism – in terms of which diversity is thought about in a Flemish context: social homogeneity (in terms of history, descent, ethnicity, language, culture) is seen as 'normal', diversity as an aberration and hence, by definition, as a problematic state of affairs; therefore, negative reactions to diversity (say, racism or xenophobia) are also normal; hence, the solution to 'the migrant problem' is to be found in a rehomogenization of society, either by removing the foreign elements (the position of the extreme right) or by eliminating the differences as much as possible through a process of 'integration' (the position of the tolerant majority). This conclusion is only valid if ingredients of this ideology can be found systematically at different structural layers. In what follows, we shall point at four types of phenomena, to be situated in relation to different layers of structure. Many more types of examples could, of course, have been given. But the following ones have proved to be exceptionally relevant in the course of our investigation.

Patterns of word choice constitute one of the obvious structural loci for traces of habitual patterns of thought. At this level, even the term *migrant*, and the way in which it is used, already reflects the described attitude. The term did not occur in Dutch dictionaries at the time when it came to replace 'guest worker'. Though it was not a morphologically unlikely formation, the choice was marked in a variety of ways. First, it was not at all in common use, so that hardly any connotations were associated with it. Therefore it could be introduced as a relatively neutral term, replacing one that had become loaded with negative meaning – a fact that provides us with a first indication of negative attitudes towards the designated population group which is seen to be problematic. Second, it was marked because a perfectly common alternative was available: *immigrant*. This alternative, moreover, was definitely more accurate at the time when *migrant* was introduced, since it had become very clear that most of the foreigners referred to would stay in the country. The fact that *migrant* was chosen in spite of this, literally describing a person in a migration process rather than as someone who has completed a one-way migration (as in the case of *immigrant*), indicates that the need was felt to leave the return option open. A somewhat bizarre result is that it is now common to speak of second- and third-generation migrants, even though the designated group has never undergone any process of migration. (Note that these remarks bear only on the Belgian Dutch terms, not on their direct equivalents in other languages.) Third, in spite of its much wider applicability the term is reserved almost exclusively for Moroccan and Turkish immigrants, a group which is singled out and depicted as utterly problematic. This problematization is to a large extent a function of wording strategies, as when migrant demonstrations are not called 'demonstrations' but 'riots' (in contrast to 'farmer demonstrations', even if the latter may wreak more havoc), or when highly metaphorical dramatizations of immigration are evoked (as in a respected political commentator's question of despair, 'Can a dam-burst still be avoided?', in the face of 'waves' of immigration which put 'the European' in danger of 'becoming an extinct race').

A different structural layer of adaptability to which implicit meaning is attached consists of a wide variety of *implication- and presupposition-carrying constructions*. To give just one example, if a symposium is organized under the title 'Toward a viable multicultural community', the combination of the processual 'toward' and the description as 'viable' of the end product of the process, clearly implies that a multicultural community is seen as inherently problematic and that special measures are needed to make it 'viable'.

Further, *interaction profiles* may be particularly instructive. Consider the following exchange between a member of the extreme right and a member of the tolerant majority, taken from a televised debate:

(28) a. ER: It must be possible to revise naturalization procedures which have been completed since 1974.
b. TM: Also for those who have adapted themselves?

In this exchange, the member of the tolerant majority accepts the premiss that, in principle, revising naturalization procedures is something that can be considered (even though it is clearly self-contradictory to talk about the *revision* of processes that have been *concluded*). He only counters with the formulation of a condition under which revision should not be possible: if the foreigner has demonstrated enough adaptability to minimize the difference and to make his or her presence, therefore, less problematic.

Finally, *global meaning constructs*, such as patterns of argumentation (some of which will, of course, also manifest themselves in the types of interaction we referred to in the preceding paragraph), are of the utmost importance. On that level we find an unmistakable abnormalization of the foreigner: their characteristics are consistently described in evolutionary terms, with outspoken emphasis on a mostly rural area of origin (with which, in reality, they have at best flimsy ties left), and on a version of Islam conceived in terms of fundamentalism (disregarding completely the present practice of Islam in urban Belgium). Similarly, the normalization of racism is not hard to find: racism is explained away in terms of socio-economic uncertainty; or its causes are made compelling and objective rather than subject to personal responsibility in the search for a so-called 'threshold of tolerance', the proportional level of diversity that is acceptable in a society before it starts to produce really serious problems. Thus the rhetoric allows the tolerant majority to say (29) and the extreme right (30).

(29) TM: The Flemish may be 90% xenophobic, but there is only a small minority of racists.
(30) ER: We are not racists. We only want to guarantee a peaceful and safe life for our people.

(29) is a clumsy attempt to exculpate the masses, even if it takes replacing a specific accusation (racism) with a much broader one (xenophobia) which almost necessarily includes the specific. Both (29) and (30) take the focus away from the harm done by forms of discrimination; whereas (30) does so by openly justifying the giving of priority to 'one's own', (29) achieves the same effect in a more subtle way by playing on the connotational semantics of racism versus xenophobia with implicit reference to the attribution of intentions that are supposed not to be all that bad. Finally, respect for other people's identity is openly professed by both sides (see (27)c) and linked with their respective solutions to 'the problem', as in (31) and (32).

(31) ER: In order for them to be able to keep their own identity, migrants should be sent back to their countries of origin.
(32) TM: Migrants should integrate themselves, but they should not give up their identity.

The open violation of migrant rights in (31) thus contrasts less with the granting of equal rights than with a defence of a clearly – even if implicitly – discriminatory and repressive 'integration' process which, in the specific socio-political context of the discourse under investigation, has little to do with full participation for 'migrants' but everything to do with vague measures that are unidirectionally imposed on the migrant population; it is not at all obvious which aspects of identity may be preserved and which ones have to be altered in the light of this underspecified integration concept.

A second additional requirement for data to count as evidence in the search for ingredients of an ideology is concerned with the **amount of data**. This is not a trivial aspect of method, but it is grounded in an important theoretical consideration. Just as it is impossible to say everything one means fully explicitly, it is also impossible to mean (even in a non-intention-centred view of meaning) absolutely everything that is somehow implied by what one says implicitly. This means that conclusions should never be drawn from single examples; isolated examples can at best serve the purpose of formulating hypotheses or illustrating earlier findings. Patterns of recurrence, either in the form of occurrence or in the form of systematic absence, should be found across a wide range of data. In the case of the Belgian migrant debate, this requirement was satisfied by looking at four different types of discourse over roughly a three-year period of time.

Third, the **quality of the data** should be carefully heeded. This requirement, obvious as it may seem, means that data should be selected on the basis of criteria warranted by the research goal (in our case, the study of ideology). One could ask, for instance, why we paid attention to statements by politicians but barely to 'letters to the editor' in newspapers. The reason is that we needed discourse coming from people trying to get a message across to a wide audience, hence trying to avoid alienating this audience, and hence trying to maximize common ground. Politicians do not want to estrange their electorate, newspaper editors want to keep their readership, social scientists are concerned about funding, but individual letter writers mainly care about expressing their personal opinions and the uptake usually has no consequences for them at all. Therefore, discourse coming from the former categories can be regarded as more in tune with widely accepted habits of speaking and thinking about socio-political issues.

Fourth, **counterscreening** is a fundamental requirement. In other words, a systematic search is needed for potential implications contradicting the ones on which the research conclusions are based. This is why, in the case of the research summarized in this section, we had to look carefully throughout the corpus (i.e. in order to satisfy the recurrence requirement) and at different levels of linguistic structure (i.e. in order to have a sufficiently varied database) for implicit expressions of a fundamentally positive attitude towards diversity as well. Unfortunately, they could not be found with any degree of regularity.

These four requirements (bearing on the types of data, the amount of data, the quality of the data, and counterscreening) combine into the methodological concept of **coherence** (without, as stressed before, implying that the world of meaning under investigation would itself have to be coherent in a strict sense). To the extent that coherence can be established across structural layers and across a wide range of qualitatively adequate data in the sense that a systematic application of the same methodology does not yield contradictory findings, there is a valid empirical basis for conclusions. Coherence of this type serves as a criterion to avoid misinterpretations (as was also argued by Eco 1990: 60).

Methodology having been clarified, this leaves us with a theoretical question. Why is more importance attached to the implicit than to the explicit in the interpretation of attitudes and in the search for an ideology? In principle, the explicit should be as important as the implicit. And indeed, it *is* as long as there are no systematic discrepancies between the two. As soon as discrepancies appear, and especially if contradictions emerge which force us to dissociate implicit meaning from intentions, as in the case just summarized, the habitual world of reference represented at the level of implicit meaning carries more weight for the interpretation of patterns of thought. The reason for this is simply to be found in the nature of self-presentation. At the explicit level of meaning there is a conscious concern with positive self-presentation. This means that, predictably, one is inclined to refrain from ascribing to oneself opinions or attitudes that one knows will meet with general condemnation. This is why, at the explicit level, the extreme right and the tolerant majority, to stay with our example, share (27)c and that the extreme right is forced to reject allegations of racism as in (30). To describe oneself in terms associated with negative value judgements is conceptually and socially equivalent to passing a negative value judgement on oneself, which is by definition incompatible with any attempt at serious self-description (unless the negative terms in question have been moved to a meta-level as a result of possibly culture-specific strategies or re-negotiations). This phenomenon at the discourse level is almost completely parallel to what has been described at the level of speech acts in terms of restrictions on performativity (see section 7.1.2). Why is it possible to say *I promise to love you forever* but not *I threaten to kill you*? Simply because *to promise* is not associated with value judgements whereas *to threaten* describes a similar commitment to a future course of action which is not generally acceptable and therefore judged negatively. As a result, *to threaten* requires an evaluative distance between the act performed and its description, so that it cannot be used fully self-referentially without committing what Zeno Vendler (1976) described as illocutionary suicide.

How does all this feed back into pragmatic theory? Section 5.4 and Chapters 7 and 8 show that brief conversational exchanges as well as complex discourse domains transcending an immediate face-to-face context, when approached from a pragmatic perspective, create empirically identifiable forms of meaning the content of which is not restricted to what can be described in terms of individual intentionality. Methodologically, the empirical identifiability of such forms of meaning was shown to depend, in the cases at hand, on the traceable dynamics of context-building processes and on observable coherence at the level of implicit meaning. From a theoretical point of view, the examples also show that the non-Western cases which Rosaldo (1982), Du Bois (1987) and Duranti (1988) provide in support of their claims regarding the excessive attention paid to individual intentionality in Gricean and Searlean pragmatics, can easily be supplemented with Western instances of processes which point in the same direction. Therefore, to the extent that an intention-centred approach to meaning could be said to be ethnocentric, what is involved is at least ethnocentrism combined with an incomplete understanding of verbal interaction in general, most probably due to a specific Western philosophical tradition which is hard to break away from.

Of major theoretical importance is the fact that a pragmatic approach, especially with reference to its superordinate concern with the actual functioning of language, was thus shown to enable us to return to the question **What is the meaning of expression X in context Y?** It is no longer necessary to scrupulously restrict pragmatic investigations to the Gricean question *What does the language user intend X to mean in context Y?* Answers to the more daring question have to take into account speaker intentions where applicable, but should never limit the interpretation to intentions alone, even in cases where obviously strategic types of usage are at issue. What is involved as well is the entire range of widely divergent contextual ingredients of the speech event (including culture-related conceptualization habits and socialization processes), interadaptable with language at different structural layers of linguistic behaviour, permanently subject to interactional dynamics and negotiability, and characterized by vastly different degrees of salience ranging from fully conscious manipulative strategies to highly automatic processing.

There is certainly more to be said about the status of 'meaning' in a theory of pragmatics. But it should already be clear that a pragmatic return to meaning pretending to do full justice to the central role of meaning in human reality, whether cognitive, social or cultural, definitely requires that linguistics join forces with neighbouring disciplines such as psychology, anthropology, sociology, philosophy and even history. Pragmatic empirical research and theorizing, from this perspective, has important contributions to make to an understanding of the relationship between individual and society, or between cognition and culture, and the role which language and meaning play in the construction of that relationship. However elusive such a topic may seem, it is possible to approach its manifestations in methodologically justifiable ways by optimizing systematic attention for those phenomena that enable us to re-attach meaning to language in the scientific approach while recognizing a high degree of detachment between the two from a theoretical point of view. This approach even lets us address issues of extreme social and political importance, in addition to all that is involved in relatively simple small-scale interactions. In other words, the pragmatic return to meaning in its full complexity, indeed allows us, as Duranti (1994) suggests, to go from grammar to politics. Or, to say it with Lakoff's words, 'pragmatics is, and ought to be, the area of study that tells us what we really want to know' (1993: 367) – at least some of the things we really want to know about the functioning of language.

8.3 *Summary and further reading*

This chapter has presented a further selection of topics which a theory of pragmatics, as sketched in this book, can be used to analyse: aspects of intercultural and international communication, the issue of discourse and ideology, and properties of wide societal debates. They are all to be situated at a macro-level of interaction, i.e. at a level that transcends the immediate here-and-now. As in Chapter 7, the approach was merely illustrative, rather than representative. Yet, important lessons can be drawn from these exercises in relation to the methodology of pragmatic research. Moreover, the methodological considerations feed back into pragmatic theory. In particular, it was shown that, with some give and take, pragmatics is capable of revealing some real 'facts of meaning' or aspects of the true 'functioning' of language in social life.

On language resources at the macro-level: Fasold (1984, 1990); and specifically in relation to the pragmatics of language change, Meeuwis (1991). On intercultural communication: Blommaert and Verschueren (eds) (1991), Gumperz (1982), Hinnenkamp (1995). On discourse and ideology: Bakhtin (1981), Bourdieu (1991), Chilton *et al.* (eds) (1998), Wodak (1995). On the pragmatic analysis of a societal debate: Blommaert and Verschueren (1998). An interesting view of the micro–macro distinction can be extracted from Sharrock and Watson (1988).

8.4 *Research topics*

1. Carry out the exercise formulated at the very end of section 8.2.2.

2. Return to the examples in sections 4.7, 6.6 and 7.4, and describe in detail what they reveal about discourse and ideological processes.

9

The pragmatic landscape

The foregoing chapters were an attempt to lead the reader into a straightforward understanding of what pragmatics is all about, avoiding wherever possible the distractions of who-said-what-when or of polemical disputes. The main concern was to sketch the landscape of current issues in pragmatics in a coherent way, so that, somehow, this book can be seen as one lengthy definition of the field. Chapters 7 and 8 deviate slightly from this goal by selectively presenting carefully chosen sample topics to demonstrate not only what kinds of research questions pragmatics may address, but also how it does (or should do) so. Many other types of issues could have been selected from areas of investigation such as **language acquisition** or **language pathology**. Pragmatic approaches to language acquisition date back to the earliest period of systematic linguistic interest in language use, i.e. the period when Hymes' (1972) suggestion that language use involved a **communicative competence** had made it respectable to focus on **parole** (in the Saussurian langue–parole dichotomy) or **performance** (in the Chomskyan competence–performance terminology). Witness Ervin-Tripp (1973), Bates (1976), Ochs and Schieffelin (eds) (1979; 1983). As to clinical issues, they have come to the foreground more recently (as with Smith and Leinonen 1992), but the field has been catching up, as appears from the publication of practical, pragmatics-based, therapy manuals such as Andersen-Wood and Smith (1997).

The aim of this chapter is to lend additional depth to the presentation by situating present-day pragmatics in the historical context of its formative traditions (in section 9.1). Then we will briefly return to the issue of delimitation (section 9.2), we will mention some precursors and parallels to pragmatics as a theory of linguistic adaptability (section 9.3), and we will point again at the necessity of an interdisciplinary perspective (in section 9.4). At the end of this chapter, then, it should be clear why this book was written the way it was.

9.1 *Formative traditions*

A number of traditions have contributed, individually and collectively, to the formation of the field of linguistic pragmatics. Allowing ourselves to associate the *tradition* of pragmatics with its *name*, any such discussion inevitably starts – as will have been clear from the introductory chapter – from the classical definition of 'pragmatics' by Morris (1938) as the study of the relationship between signs and their interpreters. Though the concerns that constitute the scope of pragmatics have a much longer history (see, e.g., Nerlich and Clarke 1996 for an excellent overview), pragmatics – as a notion – was born from an extremely ambitious project. It was in his attempt to outline a unified and consistent **theory of signs** or **semiotics**, which would embrace everything of interest to be said about signs by linguists, logicians, philosophers, biologists, psychologists, anthropologists, psychopathologists, aestheticians or sociologists, that Morris proposed the following definition of the field:

> In terms of the three correlates (sign vehicle, designatum, interpreter) of the triadic relation of semiosis, a number of other dyadic relations may be abstracted for study. One may study the relations of signs to the objects to which the signs are applicable. This relation will be called the *semantical dimension of semiosis*, [...]; the study of this dimension will be called *semantics*. Or the subject of study may be the relation of signs to interpreters. This relation will be called the *pragmatical dimension of semiosis*, [...], and the study of this dimension will be named *pragmatics*. (Morris 1938: 6)

This definition has to be placed in the intellectual context of the emergence of **semiotics** as a philosophical reflection on the 'meaning' of symbols, often triggered by the use of symbols in science and hence related to developments in the philosophy or theory of science but soon expanded to all other domains of activity involving what Cassirer calls 'symbolical animals', i.e. humans. In particular, there is a direct line from the American philosophical tradition of *pragmatism* (represented by Charles S. Peirce, William James, Clarence Irving Lewis, John Dewey and George Herbert Mead, whose student Morris was), which was concerned with the meaning of concepts in direct relation to definite human purposes and practical consequences (the name of the tradition having been inspired by Kant's use of *pragmatisch* in his *Kritik der reinen Vernunft [Critique of pure reason]*).

The very context of this definition already turns pragmatics into an eminently interdisciplinary enterprise. Morris's ambitious goals did not just reflect his personal ambitions. They formed an integral part of an emerging movement which tried to combine philosophical and scientific rigour in its approach, with the inevitable risks involved in an uncompromising attempt to understand all of human reasoning and behaviour. It is not surprising then, that the 'formative' traditions which can be observed as having shaped pragmatics as we know it today have their origins in many different disciplines. For one thing, Morris's discovery of the language user was not an isolated development. It paralleled, and had a direct link with, the discovery of the human actor in relation to language and cultural and social behaviour in the work of Mead, Malinowski, Boas and Sapir. The interdisciplinarity is so fundamental, that any attempt at neatly ordering the following brief survey along disciplinary boundaries would grossly oversimplify the historical process. Yet we cannot avoid the use of a few disciplinary labels.

Even if we were to ignore the philosophical basis of semiotics, it cannot be denied that philosophy has provided some of the most fertile ideas in pragmatics. In addition to the **Wittgensteinian programme** to relate 'meaning' to 'use' (Wittgenstein 1958; see also Birnbacher and Burkhardt eds 1985), the philosophy of language produced two of the main theories underlying present-day pragmatics. The first one (introduced briefly in section 1.1.2) is **speech act theory**, originally formulated by an Oxford 'ordinary language philosopher' (Austin 1962) and further developed by Searle (1969). The second is the **logic of conversation** (Grice 1975; see section 1.1.3). Together, they provided the frame of reference for the consolidation of the field of linguistic pragmatics, which had become a fact by the time Bar-Hillel published *Pragmatics of natural languages* (1971) and Davidson and Harman published *Semantics of natural language* (1972), two classic collective volumes with predominantly philosophical contributions, but with a marked presence of a few linguists (e.g. Fillmore, G. Lakoff, McCawley and Ross) associated – to various degrees – with the dissident movement of generative semantics. It was indeed by way of *generative semantics*, however shortlived it may have been, that a philosophically inspired pragmatics caught root in linguistics as a respectable enterprise (a history eloquently described by Lakoff 1989).

Speech act theory has exerted an influence which has persisted until today. It was the driving force behind the Anglo-American prominence in pragmatics. This does not mean that speech act theory itself has not been subject to various influences. It has clearly been shaped by interactions with and challenges from research reflected in work by Vanderveken (1988), Récanati (1981); Sbisà (1989), the Geneva school of pragmatics (e.g. Roulet 1980, and the annual *Cahiers de linguistique française*), not to mention Apel's **transcendental pragmatics** (1989), Habermas' **universal pragmatics** (1979), or Rehbein's (1977) and Ehlich's (1991) **functional pragmatics** (a term which would be tautologous in the context of this book).

The name Habermas, which stands for critical social theory, provides a link to a different strand of formative traditions: a complex of sociological, anthropological, psychological, and psychiatric endeavours. All these are found in combination in the **Batesonean programme** emanating from the Mental Research Institute in Palo Alto. This tradition did not only reintroduce Bartlett's (1932) concept of *frames* (as in Bateson 1972), adopted later in Fillmore's **frame semantics** (1975b), Goffman's sociological **frame analysis** (1974) which he also applied to the analysis of verbal interaction (Goffman 1981), and in **artificial intelligence** (Minsky 1977). Bateson's was in fact a general programme, not less ambitious than the semiotic one, aimed at a better understanding of human behaviour, including both mental and verbal activity. The best-known statement of its views on communication already had 'pragmatics' in its title: *Pragmatics of human communication: A study of interactional patterns, pathologies, and paradoxes* (Watzlawick *et al.* 1967).

Some other trends in sociology and anthropology, converging to various degrees with the Batesonean programme (with roots from long before Bateson's own involvement, and especially with its expression in Goffman's work), soon came to be associated with pragmatics as well. This was particularly the case for two traditions. First the anthropologically oriented **ethnography of communication** which, from its first formulations (as in Gumperz and Hymes eds 1972) through all its further developments, whether simply under the label of **sociolinguistics** (e.g. Hymes 1974) or more specifically **interactional sociolinguistics** (e.g. Gumperz 1982), has remained an attempt – sometimes more and sometimes less successful – to study language use in context, taking into account the full complexity of grammar, personality, social structure and cultural patterns, without lifting these different aspects out of the pattern of speech activity itself. Second, there was the sociological tradition of **ethnomethodology**, initiated by Garfinkel (see Garfinkel 1967), which produced the ever-widening field of **conversation analysis** (e.g. Sacks *et al.* 1974; Atkinson and Heritage eds 1984; see section 1.1.4). Again, in spite of the little details with which conversation analysis often occupies itself, the underlying question was far from modest: face-to-face interaction became the subject of investigation in view of the clues it provides for an understanding of the organization of human experience and behaviour.

The basic assumptions of both the ethnography of communication and ethnomethodology take us back, unwittingly, to a British philosopher in the Wittgensteinian tradition, Winch (1958), whose basic claim was that human behaviour cannot be understood without access to the concepts in terms of which those engaged in the behaviour interpret it themselves, and that language provides the necessary clues to those concepts (see also section 6.4.2). Given the similarity of the foundations, it is not surprising that the two traditions have converged significantly. What they have produced, in conjunction, is for instance a highly dynamic notion of *context* (Auer and di Luzio eds 1992; Duranti and Goodwin eds 1992; see especially section 3.4 above) which is destined to remain a major building block for theory formation in pragmatics in the years ahead.

Psychology and cognitive science had been involved all along. Bühler's (1934) theory of the psychology of language, especially by means of the distinctions it makes between various functions of language, has been directly or indirectly present in most pragmatic thinking. Suffice it to enumerate a few random observations on later developments. Winch's (1958) book on 'the idea of a social science' was published in a series called *Studies in philosophical psychology*, and indeed it had as much to say about the mind as about society. One of the classical collections of articles pertinent to pragmatics – even though its title was *Semantics* – was published by a psychologist and a linguist and was labelled *An interdisciplinary reader in philosophy, linguistics and psychology* (Steinberg and Jakobovits eds 1971). Clark and Clark's (1977) textbook introduction to **psycholinguistics** had already fully incorporated whatever knowledge about language use, comprehension, production and acquisition had been provided by pragmatics by that time, and it has had a thorough influence on much later work. Meanwhile, a clearly **cognitive tradition** was developing in endeavours as diverse as the study of patterns of metaphorization (Lakoff and Johnson 1980), enquiries into aspects of meaning generation at the sentence level and in discourse (Fauconnier 1985; Givón 1989; Talmy 1978), and the writing of cognitive grammars (Langacker 1987). Recently we were reminded that the real aim of cognitive science was 'to prompt psychology to join forces with its sister interpretive disciplines in the humanities and in the social sciences' to study 'acts of meaning' (Bruner 1990: 2), a quintessentially pragmatic concept. At various points in the process, the much older ideas formulated by Vygotsky (see 1986) on the relationships between individual cognition and society were revitalized, with or without reference to language acquisition. **Developmental psycholinguistics**, as pointed out at the beginning of this chapter, has been using and contributing to the growth of pragmatics for decades, and it is in Ochs' (1988) study of language acquisition in a Samoan village that we find one of the fullest examples of how the cognitive, the social and the cultural combine in matters of language and language use, a matter already dealt with a century earlier in von Humboldt's work, and closely related to the concerns of linguists and anthropologists such as Whorf, Kroeber, Haas and Emeneau.

So far we have not mentioned any formative traditions which have their roots in linguistics as such. There are at least three that cannot be ignored, though even these will be shown to have connections beyond the 'purely' linguistic study of language. First, there is a distinctly **French school of pragmatics** (closely related to the Geneva school already referred to), with roots in the work of Benveniste (1966) and with Ducrot (1972; 1973; 1980) as its most outspoken proponent. Benveniste's main thesis was fundamentally pragmatic: *Nihil est in lingua quod non prius fuerit in oratione* (roughly, 'There is nothing in language that was not first in language use'). His work was clearly influenced by British analytical philosophy, as is Ducrot's by the later developments of speech act theory. Influence in the other direction has been unjustifiably scarce, since numerous original contributions have been made: Benveniste's concept of 'delocutivity', further developed by Anscombre (1979) as a tool to explain the self-referentiality of explicit performatives; Ducrot's notion of the 'polyphonous' nature of utterance meaning, resulting from an illuminating distinction between producer, locutor and enunciator as distinct aspects of the speaker (with remarkable parallels to Bakhtin's 'voices'); Ducrot's recasting of speech act theory into the mould of a general theory of argumentation, in the context of which close attention is paid to the detailed study of the 'small words' which serve as argumentative structuring devices (an endeavour which the French and the Geneva schools have in common). Moreover, some of the traditional topics of linguistic pragmatics, such as presupposition, have been subject to highly insightful analyses in the context of this tradition (e.g. Ducrot 1972).

Second, **Prague school linguistics** (e.g. Mathesius 1928; Daneš ed. 1974; Firbas 1983; Sgall and Hajičová 1977) provided some key notions related to information structuring and perspectivization, which have acquired an established place in the pragmatic study of language, such as 'theme–rheme', 'topic–comment', and 'focus', not to mention the contributions it made to the study of intonation. The tradition was functionalist in the sense that language was viewed from the perspective of the goals it serves in human activity. Though much of the work was devoted to linguistic details, its foundations were linked to cybernetics with its notion of the goal-directedness of dynamic systems. Moreover, there was a stylistic component (e.g. Jakobson 1960) which brought the Prague school close to the concerns of semiotics in general. And the relationship with other disciplines was regarded as a highly relevant issue (as reflected, for instance, in Jakobson's 1970 account).

Last but not least, we should not forget the tradition of **Firthian linguistics**, hinging on a 'view of speech as a social instrument both for "sense" and "nonsense", work and play – practical, productive, creative' (Firth 1964: 15) and, following in Malinowski's footsteps, refusing to look at language outside of a 'context of situation' (see section 3.1). Today, most **functional approaches in linguistics** have direct or indirect historical roots in Firthian linguistics or the Prague school or both (e.g. Halliday 1973; Dik 1978; for an overview, see Dirven and Fried eds 1987). They have produced fully-fledged pragmatically oriented theories of grammar such as Halliday's (1985) **systemic functional grammar**, as well as, in a different line of development, entire traditions of **discourse studies** (e.g. Sinclair and Coulthard 1975) and **critical discourse analysis** (e.g. Fairclough 1989).

Many of the above trends have left an abundance of traces in the major works in mainstream linguistics, such as Bolinger's (1968) classical textbook, *Aspects of language*.

9.2 *The problem of delimitation*

In the course of its history, a large number of attempts have been made to come to terms with the problem of delimiting the field of pragmatics in a principled way, i.e. in such a way that there is some *topical* unity – the types of research questions asked – as well as a *methodological* one. A bird's-eye view of some of the major collective volumes, monographs, and introductory as well as advanced textbooks reveals the following picture.

In general, anything resembling topical and methodological unity is to be found only in work that restricts the scope of pragmatics to more or less bounded notions such as *speech acts*, minimally extended into the realm of dialogue or discussed in direct relation to logical or grammatical problems (e.g. Wunderlich ed. 1972; Schlieben-Lange 1975; Dahl ed. 1977; Searle *et al.* eds 1980), or *énonciation* (e.g. Récanati 1979; Kerbrat-Orecchioni 1980; Berrendonner 1981; Latraverse 1987). It is also to be found in work focusing on 'phenomena' eminently relevant to the study of language in use, whether or not in combination with a clear focus on the types of notions already illustrated, such as *appropriateness* (as in Verschueren 1978a, and about which Parret *et al.* 1981 somewhat naïvely claim that there seems to be 'some sort of general consensus' [p. 8] that it is of central importance), *implicitness* (as in Östman 1986; Ducrot 1972; Kerbrat-Orecchioni 1986), *'meaning derivation'* or *inferencing* (e.g. Cornulier 1985), or *'transphrastic'* units (Stati 1990), or – more importantly in the recent development of pragmatics – *relevance* (Blakemore 1992; Carston and Uchida eds 1998; Escandell Vidal 1996, Sperber and Wilson 1986).

Once the confines of such notions are left, aspirations towards topical and methodological unity are often translated into a view of pragmatics as a clear *component* of a linguistic theory, complementary to semantics and/or grammar. Thus Leech (1983: 4) claims

> [...] that grammar (the abstract formal system of language) and pragmatics (the principles of language use) are complementary domains within linguistics.

In Leech's terminology, semantics is part of grammar. Two other, quite straightforward formulations of such a view are Gazdar's (1979) statement that (formal) pragmatics is the study of meaning minus truth-conditions (semantics being confined to the study of meaning in terms of truth-conditions, as in Kempson 1975), or Cole's (1981: xi) contrast between semantics as 'involved in the determination of conventional (or literal) meaning' and pragmatics in 'the determination of nonconventional (or nonliteral) meaning'. Though critical of such definitions, Levinson (1983: 32) sides with them in a slightly reformulated fashion, after carefully reviewing a wide range of alternative proposals:

> The most promising [definitions of pragmatics] are the definitions that equate pragmatics with 'meaning minus semantics', or with a theory of language understanding that takes context into account, in order to complement the contribution that semantics makes to meaning.

This is the basis of the widespread definition of pragmatics as the study of *meaning in context*. This view is further modified, while remaining within the same general paradigm, by the distinction which Davis (1991: 11) introduces between a theory of satisfaction and a theory of pragmatics (see research topic 3 in section 2.6).

The clear separability of a pragmatic component is often denied, as when Guenther and Schmidt (1979: vii) say that 'we cannot hope to achieve an adequate integrated syntax and semantics without paying heed to the pragmatic aspects of the constructions involved'. This idea would be supported by most of the proponents of the component view of pragmatics, for whom the same observation often triggered their interest in pragmatics in the first place. The pragmatic component is even seen as a necessary component of an adequate theory of linguistic competence. Thus Levinson (1983: 33) argues for 'the need for a pragmatic component in an integrated theory of linguistic ability', and Davis (1991: 4) says: 'I shall regard pragmatics as part of a theory of competence and, as such, take it to be psychologically realized'. Whatever differences in theory there may be, adherents of this general type of view focus on a roughly shared range of pragmatic phenomena: deixis, implicature, presupposition, speech acts, conversational interaction, and the like – i.e. the ones we started out from in Chapter 1. What they also share, in spite of the obvious cognitive nature of the competence or ability under investigation (inferencing processes, for instance, being a major concern), and in spite of the social and cultural determinants of context, is a general fear of trespassing into the realm of sociolinguistics and psycholinguistics.

Bolder approaches speak of pragmatics as 'la science qui reconstruit le langage comme phénomène communicatif, intersubjectif et social' ('the science that reconstructs language as a communicative, intersubjective and social phenomenon') (Parret *et al.* 1980: 3). This is joined by a chorus of claims about the necessary interdisciplinarity of the field of pragmatics:

> 'Pragmatik' – gleich ob als linguistische Teiltheorie oder als neuartige Theorie sprachlicher Kommunikation – ist angewiesen auf enge Zusammenarbeit mit anderen Disziplinen wie Soziologie, Psychologie, Philosophie, Logik und Mathematik, Informations- und Systemtheorie, Jurisprudenz, Literaturwissenschaft etc.
>
> ['Pragmatics', whether as a component of a linguistic theory or as a new kind of theory of linguistic communication, has to rely on close cooperation with other disciplines such as sociology, psychology, philosophy, logic and mathematics, information and system theory, jurisprudence, literary science, etc.] (Schmidt 1974: 7)

In much the same way, van Dijk's (1978) introduction to pragmatics stresses its links with cognitive psychology, sociology, and anthropology, and Golopentia's (1988: 2) approach is said to lean on 'la sémiotique mise à part, la linguistique, l'ethnolinguistique, l'analyse textuelle, l'analyse conversationelle et la théorie littéraire' ('linguistics, ethnolinguistics, textual analysis, conversation analysis, and literary theory, in addition to semiotics') and on the work of not only Austin but also von Wright and Bakhtin. The same general orientation is to be found at the basis of many collective volumes of work on pragmatics (e.g. Verschueren and Bertuccelli Papi eds 1987). Similarly, intersections with the fields of text linguistics, narrative, discourse analysis, literary studies and stylistics almost invariably show a clear interdisciplinary slant (e.g. Chafe ed. 1980; van Dijk 1981; Hickey ed. 1989; Pratt 1977; Steiner and Veltman eds 1988), whilst applied forms of pragmatics are of necessity interdisciplinary (e.g. Blum-Kulka *et al.* eds 1989; Smith and Leinonen 1992).

Of course, not all interdisciplinary approaches cast such a wide net around all that is of interest for an understanding of the functioning of language. In an attempt to recapture unity of topic and method after the expansion across disciplines, tight restrictions are imposed, for instance, by **relevance theory** (Sperber and Wilson 1986) which limits pragmatics to whatever can be said in terms of a cognitively defined notion of relevance. Or, as Blakemore's (1992: 47) relevance-theoretic textbook would have it:

> [. . .] it is misleading to include phenomena like politeness, face-saving and turn taking together with the phenomena discussed in the following chapters [on explicature and implicature] under the general heading of pragmatics.

Though she does not reject socio-pragmatics (as defined by Leech 1983) as a valid endeavour, she does not accept the possibility of combining a cognitive and a social approach into one general theory of pragmatics. Rejections in the other direction are less common, but many authors who enter the domain of the social when defining pragmatics, leave out the cognitive. A recent example is provided by Mey (1993: 42):

> Hence, *pragmatics is the study of the conditions of human language uses as these are determined by the context of society.*

Thus Mey's book deals with all the 'common topics' of pragmatics, leaving out a detailed treatment of presuppositions, but adding a chapter on 'societal pragmatics', with distinctly critical overtones – as was to be expected of the author of *Whose language?* (Mey 1985). More or less ambitious combinations of the cognitive and the social aspects of language use are to be found in a number of recent textbooks such as Bertuccelli Papi (1993), Ghiglione and Trognon (1993), Moeschler and Reboul (1994), as well as in Givón's (1989) grand design of a functionalist theory with 'at its very core the notion of *context*, or *frame*, or *point of view*' (p. 1) in relation to the entire system of signs at every possible level of structuring, labelled the 'code', and emphasizing the role of the human 'mind' in the process of communication.

9.3 *Precursors and parallels to pragmatics as a theory of linguistic adaptability*

My use of the notion of adaptability does not appear in a vacuum, but could be seen as an instance of 'an emerging paradigm' (Van Parijs 1981) in the social sciences. In particular, *evolutionary epistemology* extends biological theory, and especially its natural selection paradigm, to all aspects of behaviour and socio-culture, including language, learning and science. Evolutionary epistemology views organisms as engaged in continuous problem-solving, positing behavioural and socio-cultural adaptations as the product of 'epistemic' processes, and interpreting human evolution in general as a growth of knowledge. Applied to language, the viability of such functional explanations may depend (as argued by Van Parijs) on a distinction between natural selection mechanisms in evolution (selecting or eliminating features through the selection or elimination of the entities which they characterize) and reinforcement mechanisms (selecting features directly), the latter being closer to what seems to happen in the shaping of languages and, by extension, in the functioning of language.

To the extent that evolutionary epistemology is concerned with learning, it is reflected in Piaget's psychological theories in which adaptation is a central notion (e.g. Piaget 1971), and in Vygotsky's (1978) views of mental development which allow him to talk about 'those means of adaptation we call signs'. Piaget's way of coping with the multidirectionality of adaptation is to define it as an equilibrium between assimilation (the integration of a new element into an organism's cycle) and accommodation (the organism's being modified as a result of the assimilation).

Even when disconnected from the more general attempt to extend biological theory to aspects of behaviour and socio-culture, as embodied in evolutionary epistemology, theories of *the origin and evolution of language(s)* show a strong tendency to refer to phenomena of adaptation. As far back as 1875, Whitney implicitly ascribed the origin and growth of language to an adaptive process by treating it as a gradually developing response to the need for communication (though he would not have subscribed to a continuity between *Naturwissenschaft*, roughly the 'sciences', and *Geisteswissenschaft*, roughly the humanities and social sciences, firmly placing linguistics in the latter category). Similarly, though strongly emphasizing that language is a cultural, rather than a biologically inherited function, and that 'Speech is not a simple activity that is carried on by one or more organs biologically adapted to that purpose' (in the sense that they would have been especially developed for language), Sapir claimed that

> It [speech] is an extremely complex and ever-shifting network of *adjustments* – in the brain, in the nervous system, and in the articulating and auditory organs – tending towards the desired end of communication. (1921: 9; italics added)

Reference to evolutionary adaptation of a biological kind, implying an extension of biology beyond the realm of 'nature' proper (and therefore not in contradiction with the earlier views as such), has become more explicit since. Thus, while recognizing the huge qualitative leap from 'zoosemiotic' to human speech, Jakobson (1970) argues that there is an evolutionary continuity and that, as far as human language is concerned, there cannot be a strict dichotomy between nature and culture. And the connection could not have been expressed more clearly than in the following remark by Lieberman:

> Human language could have evolved only in relation to the total human condition. There would have been no selective advantage for retention of the mutations that gradually resulted in the evolution of human language if language had not been of use in what Darwin in 1859 termed the 'struggle for existence'. (1975: 1)

Coming to the area of *language acquisition*, pragmatic aspects of this process have been approached by various students of child language under the label of 'ethology' (e.g. Becker 1984, Foppa 1979, Mahoney 1975). The idea that language acquisition can be described as a chain of adaptational steps resulting in adult language, is now sometimes used as a basic premiss (e.g. in Bernicot 1992). The complexity of the processes, however, including the fact that again there is no unidirectional adaptation of the child's behaviour to adult speech, should be clear from accounts of 'baby talk', representing the adult's adaptation (whether momentary or systematic) to the level of the child.

More *'local' adaptationist descriptions and explanations* have been offered for a diversity of more restricted linguistic phenomena. Thus the speech act type of requesting has been viewed in relation to its functioning in social groups, drawing attention to its adaptedness to ways of resolving the conflict between natural competitiveness and the need for co-operation (e.g. Becker 1984). Natural selection has been adduced (by Pawley and Syder 1983) to explain the differences between certain syntactic and morphological usages in conversational and formal written English. For instance, conditions of use are said to render *they, them, their* more suitable or adapted to conversational English for gender-neutral singular third-person reference than the conjoined *he or she*, which remains tolerable in writing. Ideophones (i.e. vivid representations of ideas by means of the sound quality of a linguistic form, whether spontaneously created, as in *gooey goulash*, or conventionalized as in *flimflam*) have been described (by Samarin 1978) as adaptations to the expressive function of speech. Sound symbolism in general has been related, for instance, to a biologically determined 'frequency code' which associates high acoustic frequency with the meaning of 'small vocalizer, therefore subordinate, non-threatening, etc.' and low acoustic frequency with the meaning of 'large vocalizer, therefore dominant, aggressive, threatening, etc.' (see Ohala 1984). And even the different voice qualities of men and women have been attributed to biological adaptation processes.

On the same 'local' level, it should be clear that a number of the pragmatic notions we reviewed in Chapter 1 are implicitly adaptationist. Remember, for instance, the notion of 'direction of fit' which was used as one of the criteria to classify speech acts, characterizing assertives as attempts to make one's words or propositional content match a state of affairs in the world, or directives as attempts to bring about a state of affairs corresponding to the spoken words. Furthermore, the entire apparatus of 'felicity conditions' can be said to bear on the adaptedness of speech acts to goals and circumstances. Similarly, 'background assumptions' bear on pre-existent, known or supposed, contextual circumstances to which forms of expression are adapted in such a way as not to have to express them literally or explicitly. In this context, different layers of adaptedness have to be distinguished. That is why the concept of 'presupposition failure' makes sense even when there is no 'communication failure' of any kind: if George did not come back, the presupposition in *When did George come back?* fails to be satisfied; however, the negotiability of meaning is such that this question can still be asked very successfully for very specific interactional purposes (e.g. to draw the attention to George's absence).The more general applicability of the notion of adaptability in the field of pragmatics, moreover, was already demonstrated by Bertuccelli Papi (1993), as well as by Givón (1989). Needless to say this overview is only illustrative, and can by no means be seen as representative of adaptationist views and concepts in the language-related sciences.

Inevitably the question will be asked as to the precise relationship between a pragmatic notion of adaptability and the concept of 'adaptation', with its necessary connotation of 'natural selection', in biology. One false impression that should immediately be eliminated is that using the label of adaptability, as a result of its parallel in biology, would promote language to the status of a natural species consisting of a member set of independently living organisms. The real idea is, of course, to view language, the development of which was made possible by certain evolving properties of living organisms (*Homo sapiens*), as one of a range of adaptive phenomena in the interaction between those organisms and their 'environment' or 'conditions of life'.

As was already pointed out in section 2.2 and repeated on many occasions since, any association of unidirectionality, suggesting a behaviouristic stimulus–response mechanism in which anything 'in the world' can act as a stimulus to provoke a linguistic response, should be dismissed vigorously. Note that adaptation, as observed in biology, is definitely not a unidirectional process either. Though goal-directed, it is not teleological in the sense of being goal-initiated and goal-determined, since 'natural selection is strictly an *a posteriori* process that rewards current success but never sets up future goals' (Mayr

1974: 22); in other words, there is no great 'design' as Dennett (1995) would put it. The ultimate function of adaptation always transcends its initial purpose. Every form of adaptation creates new possibilities. It could be claimed, for instance, that division of labour, as known amongst humans, would not have been possible without language; yet, division of labour was not the 'goal' of the development of language in humans. Similar examples could be given with reference to most biological phenomena of adaptation, which is why Darwin often used the term **co**adaptation and repeatedly focused on the multidirectionality of adaptation processes in the natural world:

> [...] how the innumerable species inhabiting this world have been modified, so as to acquire that perfection of structure and coadaptation which justly excites our admiration. Naturalists continually refer to external conditions, such as climate, food, &c., as the only possible source of variation. In one limited sense, as we shall hereafter see, this may be true; but it is preposterous to attribute to mere external conditions, the structure, for instance, of the woodpecker, with its feet, tail, beak, and tongue, so admirably adapted to catch insects under the bark of trees. In the case of the mistletoe, which draws its nourishment from certain trees, which has seeds that must be transported by certain birds, and which has flowers with separate sexes absolutely requiring the agency of certain insects to bring pollen from one flower to the other, it is equally preposterous to account for the structure of this parasite, with its relations to several distinct organic beings, by the effects of external conditions, or of habit, or of the volition of the plant itself. (1958 [1859]: 28)

Darwin further asks:

> How have all those exquisite adaptations of one part of the organisation to another part, and to the conditions of life, and of one organic being to another being, been perfected? (1958 [1859]: 73)

This question certainly forestalls restrictive interpretations of the directionality of adaptation. Add to this Lewontin's warnings against attaching to the metaphor of trial-and-error adaptation the implication 'that the world is divided up into pre-existent ecological niches and that evolution consists of the progressive fitting of organisms into these niches' (1982: 159). Or his claim that

> There is a constant interplay of the organism to the environment, so that although natural selection may be adapting the organism to a particular set of environmental circumstances, the evolution of the organism itself changes those circumstances. (1978: 159)

Or consider Waddington's (1959) and Bateson's (1980) belief that causality in biology is circular rather than linear. It should be clear, then, that when applied to language, the notion of adaptability would become entirely void if interpreted unidirectionally.

There are important lessons to be drawn from the biological parallel, both in terms of comparability and difference. On the one hand, when we look at language in general as a product of human evolution, its adaptability functions in precisely the way described above. On the other hand, looking at language in its day-to-day use among human beings, we have to take into account that part of human biological evolution has been the development of the specifically human mind, 'mind in society' as we have called it (Chapter 6), with its specific properties of reflexivity and intentionality, and with the capacity to design courses of action. There are good reasons why Nairne (1997) uses *The adaptive mind* as a title for his psychology textbook. We must resist the temptation, however, to overstate the role of those properties and that capacity – a mistake that was obviously made in those approaches to language use that place intentionality at its core. Much linguistic choice-making, as said before, is automatic and subliminal. And even when design comes in, resources are limited (even if in principle boundless) and force choices to be made which do not quite correspond to the intentions and which may score completely undesired outcomes. This is by no means a pessimistic view of either humankind or language. But if we ever want to understand language use, we have to move beyond illusions of an omnipotent free will, without denying that individual human actors can really make a difference.

9.4 *Interdisciplinarity revisited*

In section 9.2, approaches to the delimitation of pragmatics were presented as differing along the parameter of interdisciplinarity. No attempt was made anywhere in this book to hide a bias favourable to the more radically interdisciplinary side (remember the presentation in section 0.3 on pages 6–8, as well as the discussion of the notion of adaptability in the foregoing section). Moreover, in this chapter, the legitimacy of this preference was at least implicitly shown to derive from the nature of the formative traditions, practically all of which had a distinctly interdisciplinary slant. Yet, though approaches with a broad scope may be preferable (if for no other reason, at least because the narrower approaches have been largely unsuccessful in marking their territory in a fully principled – as opposed to an *ad hoc* – manner, i.e. they have not really brought about the kind of topical or methodological unity the search for which motivated narrowing down the scope), often they do not constitute 'better pragmatics' at all. Usually this is due to a lack of clarity and coherence, deriving from missing theoretical foundations and uncertainty about the methodological demands to be placed on empirical evidence. It is therefore easy to understand why some would say, with Davis (1991: 3), that 'The problem with this broad view of pragmatics [as defined by Morris] is that it is too inclusive to be of much use'.

Davis's point may be valid unless we combine a return to Morris (as advocated in section 0.2 on page 6), which would indeed demand that pragmatics should incorporate cognitive and social as well as cultural aspects, with a radical departure from viewing pragmatics as a separable component of a linguistic theory, and with a decision to stop thinking in terms of separable disciplines (or subdisciplines). This modification was not yet present in Morris's work. Though he speaks of *dimensions of semiosis*, his view is basically componential: 'Syntactics, semantics, and pragmatics are components of the single science of semiotic but mutually irreducible components' (1938: 54). These components, moreover, are ordered hierarchically:

> In a systematic presentation of semiotic, pragmatics presupposes both syntactics and semantics, as the latter in turn presupposes the former, for to discuss adequately the relation of signs to their interpreters requires knowledge of the relation of signs to one another and to those things to which they refer their interpreters. (Morris 1938: 33)

Note that a challenge to (sub)disciplinary thinking is becoming more widespread in the social sciences in general:

> All these new questions are being raised in the context of a disciplinary structure that is no longer very well suited to them. The social science disciplines were defined a century ago and despite the rash of multidisciplinary centers and programs in academia, departments are still divided along those traditional lines. . . . it's still true that the safest way to carve out an academic career is to publish in the traditional mainline concerns of your disciplines.
>
> Trouble is, traditional disciplinary boundaries are nowadays being blurred and bent almost out of recognition to accommodate torrents of new knowledge, to respond to the demand for socially relevant research by funding agencies, and to reflect the fact that the problems of greatest moment today have to be tackled by multiple approaches. (Holden 1993: 1796)

In order not to leave the humanities and social sciences in total chaos after abandoning adherence to disciplinary boundaries, they should be rethought in terms of *dimensions* of human reality to be approached from different *perspectives*.

The perspective view of pragmatics, which we took as our starting point in this book, has a long implicit, if not explicit, history. In their editorial introduction to the first issue of the *Journal of Pragmatics*, Haberland and Mey say:

> Linguistic pragmatics, ... can be said to characterize a new way of looking at things linguistic, rather than marking off clean borderlines to other disciplines. (1977: 5)

Even earlier, at a time when respect for pragmatics among theoretical linguists had only just started to spread, Weiser (1974) concluded her seminal paper on the problems of the 'performative theory' (treating every utterance as a single, classifiable act) as follows:

> Syntax, semantics, and pragmatics are a famous triad. It is perhaps natural to assume that the same relation holds between semantics and pragmatics as between syntax and semantics, but it [i.e. this assumption] is unwarranted. Our current view of syntax and semantics is that they are related as parts of a continuum, separated by either a fuzzy boundary or a nonexistent one. We have no justification for placing pragmatics on this continuum, or for assuming that a formal theoretical structure developed to handle language abstracted from performance can be adopted for the study of the communicative interaction of people in real-world situations. It has been shown more than once recently ... that pragmatic considerations have effects on syntactic transformations, but this does not mean they have to be written into syntactic trees. This is very important for us to realize. As theoretical linguists embarking on the study of pragmatics we are not just slightly widening our area of investigation, but we are *taking an entirely different point of view on language*. We must take care that we do not burden ourselves with theoretical constructs that are not appropriate to the new endeavor, or we will miss the opportunity to gain the fresh and revealing insights into language and human beings that pragmatics so temptingly offers. (p. 729; italics added)

It is unfortunate for pragmatics that her warning has not always been kept in mind.

Such an approach is not necessarily a prerogative of pragmatics. Recently, Berger made a very similar remark about sociology:

> Sociology is not so much a field as a perspective; if this perspective fails, nothing is left. Thus one can study the economy, or the political system, or the mating habits of the Samoans from perspectives that are quite different, one of which is sociology. The sociological perspective has entered into the cognitive instrumentarium of most of the human sciences with great success. Few historians have not somewhere incorporated a sociological perspective into their work. Unlike most other human scientists, sociologists cannot claim a specific empirical territory

> as their own. It is mostly their perspective that they have to offer. (1992: 18)

But the 'other human scientists' may not have their own 'empirical territory' either. Probably the time has indeed come for a complete reassessment of the human sciences as a network of converging and diverging perspectives on different dimensions of human reality rather than a collection of disciplines.

In a wider historical perspective, such a reassessment is not even new. Already in 1929 Sapir said that

> It is difficult for a modern linguist to confine himself to his traditional subject matter. Unless he is somewhat unimaginative, he cannot but share in some or all of the mutual interests which tie up linguistics with anthropology and culture history, with sociology, with psychology, with philosophy, and, more remotely, with physics and physiology. (1929: 208)

An advocate of interdisciplinarity *par excellence* he clearly viewed anthropology, sociology, and psychology, all of which were intertwined in his own work (witness collections such as Sapir 1966) in terms of perspectives rather than objects of inquiry (see Winkin 1981: 64–5). In this, as in many other respects, present-day pragmatics is somehow re-inventing Sapir's work. From the point of view of pragmatics we can only regret that a relative dominance of the Chomskyan paradigm seems to have interrupted the flow of Sapir's ideas in linguistics (in much the same way as Parsonian sociology can be said to have interrupted a development that, as Hilbert 1992 shows, had to be re-invented, for instance, by ethnomethodology). As shown by Thibault (1997), it is even worth going back to Saussure for pragmatically relevant ideas that have become obscured by later developments in linguistics.

Opting for an approach to pragmatics which requires it to be defined as a particular perspective on language, as described systematically in this book, necessarily results in *methodological pluralism* which allows for *various types of evidence*. A few general guidelines, however, should be kept in mind. Since pragmatics (in its different guises) basically studies language as a form of and in relation to behaviour, there are strong empirical demands to be imposed. At the same time, the behaviour is of interest only to the extent that it is related to the meaning it has for the people involved. Hence, the empirical orientation has to be combined with a clearly interpretive stance. And since cognitive processing is involved, evidence as to the psychological reality of the described phenomena is at least desirable. A tall order indeed, but one to which we hope to have brought linguistics closer by the writing of this book.

9.5 *Further reading*

Most of the references in this chapter are recommendations for further reading. However, here are a few more on specific topics that were brought up for discussion. For some of the basic writings of pragmatism, see Thayer (ed.) (1970). For detailed discussions of the relationships between pragmatics and semiotics, see Parret (1983) and Deledalle (ed.) (1989). The role of philosophy in the formation and further growth of pragmatics is not restricted to the major traditions listed in section 9.1; vastly divergent contributions have indeed been made by philosophers throughout; just compare Dascal (1983), Heringer (1978), Kates (1980), Martin (1979), Montague (1974), or Barwise and Perry (1983). For a succinct and insightful account of the Batesonian tradition, see Winkin (1981). Valuable ideas on how to approach language as a social 'reality' are to be found, amongst many other sources, in Bourdieu (1982). For a coherent attempt to combine cognitive and social issues in the study of language use, see Marmaridou (1995). For warnings concerning the applicability of methods common in the social sciences, such as survey research, see Cicourel (1982) and Briggs (1986). Finally, for warnings against a misuse of an adaptationist perspective on cognition (and hence also on language), see Varela *et al.* (1991).

Bibliography

Abraham, W. (ed.) (1991). *Discourse particles: descriptive and theoretical investigations on the logical, syntactic and pragmatic properties of discourse particles in German*. Amsterdam/Philadelphia: John Benjamins.

Andersen-Wood, L. and Smith, B.R. (1997). *Working with pragmatics: a practical guide to promoting communicative confidence*. Oxon: Winslow.

Anscombre, J.-C. (1979). Délocutivité benvenistienne, délocutivité généralisée et performativité. *Langue française* 42: 69–84.

Apel, K.-O. (1989). Linguistic meaning and intentionality. In G. Deledalle (ed.) (1989: 19–70).

Atkinson, M. and Drew, P. (1979). *Order in court*. Atlantic Highlands, NJ: Humanities Press.

Atkinson, M. and Heritage, J. (eds) (1984). *Structures of social action: studies in conversation analysis*. Cambridge: Cambridge University Press.

Auer, P. (1995). Context and contextualization. In J. Verschueren, J.-O.H. Östman, J. Blommaert and C. Bulcaen (eds) (1995). (loose-leaf contribution).

—— (ed.) (1998). *Codeswitching in conversation*. London: Routledge.

Auer, P. and Di Luzio, A. (eds) (1992). *The contextualization of language*. Amsterdam/Philadelphia: John Benjamins.

Austin, J.L. (1962). *How to do things with words*. Oxford: Oxford University Press.

Bakhtin, M.M. (1981). *The dialogic imagination*. Austin: University of Texas Press.

—— (1986). *Speech genres & other late essays*. Austin: University of Texas Press.

Bar-Hillel, Y. (1971). Out of the pragmatic wastebasket. *Linguistic Inquiry* 2/3: 401–7.

Bar-Hillel, Y. (ed.) (1971). *Pragmatics of natural languages*. Dordrecht: Reidel.

Bartlett, F.C. (1932). *Remembering*. Cambridge: Cambridge University Press.

Barwise, J. and Perry, J. (1983). *Situations and attitudes*. Cambridge, MA: MIT Press.

Basso, K.H. and Selby, H.A. (eds) (1976). *Meaning in anthropology*. Albuquerque: University of New Mexico Press.

Bates, E. (1976). *Language and context: the acquisition of pragmatics*. New York: Academic Press.

Bateson, G. (1972). *Steps to an ecology of mind*. San Francisco, CA: Chandler.

—— (1980). *Mind and nature*. London: Fontana.

Becker, J.A. (1984). Implications of ethology for the study of pragmatic development. In S.A. Kuczaj (ed.) (1984: 1–17).

Benveniste, É. (1966). *Problèmes de linguistique générale*. Paris: Gallimard.

Berger, P.L. (1992). Sociology. *Society* 30: 12–18.

Bernicot, J. (1992). *Les actes de langage chez l'enfant*. Paris: Presses Universitaires de France.

Berrendonner, A. (1981). *Eléments de pragmatique linguistique*. Paris: Editions de Minuit.

Bertuccelli Papi, M. (1993). *Che cos'è la pragmatica*. Milano: Bompiani.

Biggs, B. (1969). *Let's learn Maori: a guide to the study of the Maori language*. Wellington: A.H. & A.W. Reed.

Birnbacher, D. and Burkhardt, A. (eds) (1985). *Sprachspiel und Methode*. Berlin: De Gruyter.

Blakemore, D. (1992). *Understanding utterances: an introduction to pragmatics*. Oxford: Blackwell.

Blommaert, J. and Verschueren, J. (1998). *Debating diversity: analysing the discourse of tolerance*. London: Routledge.

Blommaert, J. and Verschueren, J. (eds) (1991). *The pragmatics of intercultural and international communication*. Amsterdam/Philadelphia: John Benjamins.

Bloor, T. and Bloor, M. (1995). *The functional analysis of English: a Hallidayan approach*. London: Edward Arnold.

Blum-Kulka, S., House, J. and Kasper, G. (eds) (1989). *Cross-cultural pragmatics*. Norwood, NJ: Ablex.

Bohlen, C.E. (1973). *Witness to history, 1929–1969*. New York: W.W. Norton & Company.

Bolinger, D. (1968). *Aspects of language*. New York: Harcourt Brace Jovanovich.

—— (1986). *Intonation and its parts*. Stanford: Stanford University Press.

Bourdieu, P. (1982). *Ce que parler veut dire*. Paris: Fayard.

—— (1991). *Language and symbolic power*. Cambridge: Polity Press.

Briggs, C.L. (1986). *Learning how to ask*. Cambridge: Cambridge University Press.

Briggs, C.L. and Bauman, R. (1992). Genre, intertextuality, and social power. *Journal of Linguistic Anthropology* 2: 131–72.

Bronowski, J. (1973). *The ascent of man*. Boston/Toronto: Little, Brown & Co.

Brown, P. and Levinson, S.C. (1987). *Politeness: some universals in language usage*. Cambridge: Cambridge University Press.

Bruner, J. (1990). *Acts of meaning*. Cambridge, MA: Harvard University Press.

Bühler, K. (1934). *Sprachtheorie*. Jena: Fischer.

Button, G. (ed.) (1991). *Ethnomethodology and the human sciences*. Cambridge: Cambridge University Press.
Button, G. and Lee, J.R.E. (eds) (1987). *Talk and social organization*. Clevedon: Multilingual Matters.
Carston, R. and Uchida, S. (eds) (1998). *Relevance theory: applications and implications*. Amsterdam/Philadelphia: John Benjamins.
Chafe, W. (ed.) (1980). *The pear stories: cognitive, cultural, and linguistic aspects of narrative production*. Norwood, NJ: Ablex.
—— (1994). *Discourse, consciousness, and time: the flow and displacement of conscious experience in speaking and writing*. Chicago, IL: The University of Chicago Press.
—— (1996). Consciousness and language. In J. Verschueren, J.-O.H. Östman, J. Blommaert and C. Bulcaen (eds) (1995). ff. (loose-leaf contribution).
Chilton, P., Ilyin, M.V. and Mey, J.L. (eds) (1998). *Political discourse in transition in Europe 1989–1991*. Amsterdam/Philadelphia: John Benjamins.
Churchward, C.M. (1953). *Tongan grammar*. Oxford: Oxford University Press.
Cicourel, A.V. (1982). Interviews, surveys, and the problem of ecological validity. *The American Sociologist* 17: 11–20.
Clark, H.H. (1996). *Using language*. Cambridge: Cambridge University Press.
Clark, H.H. and Carlson, T.B. (1982). Hearers and speech acts. *Language* 58: 332–73.
Clark, H.H. and Clark, E.V. (1977). *Psychology and language*. New York: Harcourt Brace Jovanovich.
Clark, H.H. and Haviland, S.E. (1977). Comprehension and the given-new contract. In R.O. Freedle (ed.) (1977: 1–44).
Cole, P. (ed.) (1978). *Syntax and semantics 9: Pragmatics*. New York: Academic Press.
—— (1981). *Radical pragmatics*. New York: Academic Press.
Cole, P. and Morgan, J.L. (eds) (1975). *Syntax and semantics 3: Speech acts*. New York: Academic Press.
Coleman, L. and Kay, P. (1981). Prototype semantics: the English verb *lie*. *Language* 57: 26–44.
Comrie, B. (1981). *Language universals and linguistic typology*. Chicago, IL: The University of Chicago Press.
—— (1985). *Tense*. Cambridge: Cambridge University Press.
Cornulier, B. de (1980). *Meaning detachment*. Amsterdam: John Benjamins.
—— (1985). *Effets de sens*. Paris: Editions de Minuit.
Coulson, S. (1995). Cognitive science. In J. Verschueren, J.-O. Östman and J. Blommaert (eds) (1995: 123–40).
Coulter, J. (1990). Argument structures. In G. Psathas (ed.) (1990).
—— (1991). Cognition in an ethnomethodological mode. In G. Button (ed.) (1991).
Coupland, N. (1995). Accommodation theory. In J. Verschueren, J.-O.H. Östman, J. Blommaert and C. Bulcaen (eds) (1995: 21–6).

Cranach, M. von *et al.* (eds) (1979). *Human ethology: claims and limits of a new discipline*. Cambridge: Cambridge University Press.
Cushing, S. (1994). *Fatal words: communication clashes and aircraft crashes*. Chicago, IL: The University of Chicago Press.
Dahl, Ö. (ed.) (1977). *Logic, pragmatics and grammar.* Göteborg: Göteborg Univ., Dept. of Linguistics.
Daneš, F. (ed.) (1974). *Papers on functional sentence perspective*. The Hague: Mouton.
Darwin, C. (1958 [1859]). *The origin of species by means of natural selection or the preservation of favoured races in the struggle for life*. New York: Mentor Books.
Dascal, M. (1983). *Pragmatics and the philosophy of mind 1*. Amsterdam: John Benjamins.
—— (ed.) (1985). *Dialogue: an interdisciplinary approach*. Amsterdam/ Philadelphia: John Benjamins.
Davidson, D. and Harman, G.H. (eds) (1972). *Semantics of natural language*. Dordrecht: Reidel.
Davis, S. (ed.) (1991). *Pragmatics: a reader.* Oxford: Oxford University Press.
Deledalle, G. (ed.) (1989). *Semiotics and pragmatics*. Amsterdam: John Benjamins.
Dennett, D.C. (1995). *Darwin's dangerous idea: evolution and the meanings of life*. Harmondsworth: Penguin.
Dijk, T.A. van (1978). *Taal en handelen*. Muiderberg: Coutinho.
—— (1981). *Studies in the pragmatics of discourse*. Berlin: Mouton de Gruyter.
Dik, S. (1978). *Functional grammar.* Amsterdam: North Holland.
Dirven, R. and Fried, V. (eds) (1987). *Functionalism in linguistics*. Amsterdam: John Benjamins.
Dittmar, N. (1995). Register. In J. Verschueren, J.-O.H. Östman, J. Blommaert and C. Bulcaen (eds) (1995). (loose-leaf contribution).
Dixon, R.M.W. (1972). *The Dyirbal language of North Queensland*. Cambridge: Cambridge University Press.
Dorval, B. (ed.) (1990). *Conversational organisation and its development*. Norwood, NJ: Ablex.
Downing, P. (1977). On the creation and use of English compound nouns. *Language* 53: 810–42.
Dressler, W.U. and Barbaresi, L.M. (1994). *Morphopragmatics: diminutives and intensifiers in Italian, German, and other languages*. Berlin: Mouton de Gruyter.
Drew, P. and Heritage, J. (eds) (1992). *Talk at work: interaction in institutional settings*. Cambridge: Cambridge University Press.
DuBois, J.W. (1987). Meaning without intention: lessons from divination. *IPrA Papers in Pragmatics* 1: 80–122.
Ducrot, O. (1972). *Dire et ne pas dire: Principes de sémantique linguistique*. Paris: Hermann.
—— (1973). *La preuve et le dire*. Paris: Mame.
—— (1980). *Les échelles argumentatives*. Paris: Minuit.

—— (1996). *Slovenian lectures/Conférences slovènes.* Ljubljana: ISH.
Duranti, A. (1988). Intentions, language, and social action in a Samoan context. *Journal of Pragmatics* 12: 13–33.
—— (1994). *From grammar to politics: linguistic anthropology in a Western Samoan village.* Berkeley/Los Angeles, CA: University of California Press.
Duranti, A. and Goodwin, C. (1992). *Rethinking context.* Cambridge: Cambridge University Press.
Eastman, C.M. (1995). Codeswitching. In J. Verschueren, J.-O.H. Östman, J. Blommaert and C. Bulcaen (eds) (1995). (loose-leaf contribution).
Eco, U. (1979). *The role of the reader.* Bloomington, IN: Indiana University Press.
—— (1990). *The limits of interpretation.* Bloomington, IN: Indiana University Press.
Edwards, D. (1997). *Discourse and cognition.* London: Sage.
Edwards, J.A. and Lampert, M.D. (eds) 1993: *Talking data.* Hillsdale, NJ: Lawrence Erlbaum Associates.
Eelen, G. (1998). *Ideology in politeness research: a critical analysis.* University of Antwerp Ph.D. dissertation.
Eemeren, F.H. van and Grootendorst, R. (1992). *Argumentation, communication, and fallacies.* Hillsdale, NJ: Lawrence Erlbaum Associates.
—— (1995). Argumentation theory. In J. Verschueren, J.-O.H. Östman, J. Blommaert and C. Bulcaen (eds) (1995). 55–61.
Ehlich, K. (1991). Funktional-pragmatische Kommunikationsanalyse: Ziele und Verfahren. In D. Flader (ed.) (1991).
Errington, J.J. (1988). *Structure and style in Javanese.* Philadelphia, PA: University of Pennsylvania Press.
Ervin-Tripp, S.M. (1973). *Language acquisition and communicative choice.* Stanford: Stanford University Press.
—— (1976). Is Sybil there? The structure of some American English directives. *Language in Society* 5: 25–66.
Escandell Vidal, M.V. (1996). *Introducción a la pragmática.* Barcelona: Editorial Ariel.
Everett, D. (1985). Dialogue and the selection of data for a grammar. In M. Dascal (ed.) (1985: 247–63).
Fairclough, N. (1989). *Language and power.* London: Longman.
Fasold, R. (1984). *The sociolinguistics of society.* Oxford: Basil Blackwell.
Fasold, R. (1990). *The sociolinguistics of language.* Oxford: Basil Blackwell.
Fauconnier, G. (1985). *Mental spaces.* Cambridge, MA: MIT Press.
Fielding, N.G. (ed.) (1988). *Actions and structure.* London: Sage.
Fillmore, C.J. (1971a). Verbs of judging: an exercise in semantic description. In C.J. Fillmore and D.T. Langendoen (eds) (1971: 273–90).
—— (1971b). Types of lexical information. In D.D. Steinberg and L.A. Jakobovits (eds) (1971: 370–92).
—— (1975a). *Santa Cruz lectures on deixis, 1971.* Bloomington, IN: Indiana University Linguistics Club.
—— (1975b). An alternative to checklist theories of meaning. *Proceedings of the 1st Annual Meeting of the Berkeley Linguistics Society,* 123–31.

Fillmore, C.J. and Langendoen, D.T. (eds) (1971). *Studies in linguistic semantics*. New York: Holt, Rinehart & Winston.
Firbas, J. (1983). On the concepts of scene and perspective in Fillmore's approach and in that of functional sentence perspective. In S. Rot (ed.) (1983: 101–7).
Firth, J.R. (1964). *The tongues of men [1937] and Speech [1930]*. Oxford: Oxford University Press.
Flader, D. (ed.) (1991). *Verbale Interaktion: Studien zur Empirie und Methodologie der Pragmatik*. Stuttgart: Metzler.
Foolen, A. (1996). Pragmatic particles. In J. Verschueren, J.-O.H. Östman, J. Blommaert and C. Bulcaen (eds) (1995). ff. (loose-leaf contribution).
Foppa, K. (1979). Language acquisition: a human ethological problem? In M. von Cranach *et al.* (eds) (1979).
Foucault, M. (1966). *Les mots et les choses*. Paris: Gallimard.
Fraser, B. (1996). Pragmatic markers. *Pragmatics* 6: 167–90.
Freedle, R.O. (ed.) (1977). *Discourse production and comprehension*. Norwood, NJ: Ablex Publishing Corporation.
Fretheim, T. and Gundel, J.K. (eds) (1996). *Reference and referent accessibility*. Amsterdam/ Philadelphia: John Benjamins.
Fuentes, J. (1960). *Diccionario y gramática de la lengua de la Isla de Pascua: Pascuense–Castellano, Castellano–Pascuense. Dictionary and grammar of the Easter Island language: Pascuense–English, English–Pascuense*. Santiago de Chile: Andres Bello.
Gal, S. (1979). *Language shift: social determinants of linguistic change in bilingual Austria*. New York: Academic Press.
García, O. and Otheguy, R. (eds) (1989). *English across cultures; cultures across English: a reader in cross-cultural communication*. Berlin: Mouton de Gruyter.
Garfinkel, H. (1967). *Studies in ethnomethodology*. Englewood Cliffs, NJ: Prentice-Hall.
Gazdar, G. (1979). *Pragmatics: implicature, presupposition and logical form*. New York: Academic Press.
Ghiglione, R. and Trognon, A. (1993). *Où va la pragmatique? De la pragmatique à la psychologie sociale*. Grenoble: Presses Universitaires de Grenoble.
Giles, H. and St. Clair, R. (eds) (1979). *Language and social psychology*. Oxford: Oxford University Press.
Givón, T. (1989). *Mind, code and context: essays in pragmatics*. Hillsdale, NJ: Lawrence Erlbaum Associates.
Gladwin, T. and Sturtevant, W. (eds) (1962). *Anthropology and human behavior*. Washington, DC: Anthropological Society of Washington.
Gnerre, M. (1987). The lexicalization of linguistic action and its relation to literacy. In Verschueren, J. (ed.) (1987: 11–25).
Goffman, E. (1974). *Frame analysis: an essay in the organization of experience*. New York: Harper & Row.
—— (1976). Replies and responses. *Language in Society* 5: 257–313.
—— (1981). *Forms of talk*. Philadelphia, PA: University of Pennsylvania Press.

Golopentia, S. (1988). *Les voies de la pragmatique*. Anma Libri.
Goodwin, C. (1993). Recording human interaction in natural settings. *Pragmatics* 3: 181–209.
—— (1994). Professional vision. *American Anthropologist* 96: 606–33.
Green, G.M. (1989). *Pragmatics and natural language understanding*. Hillsdale, NJ: Lawrence Erlbaum Associates.
Greenberg, J.H. (ed.) (1978). *Universals of human language*. Stanford: Stanford University Press.
Gregory, M. and Caroll, S. (1978). *Language and situation*. London: Routledge & Kegan Paul.
Grice, H.P. (1957). Meaning. *Philosophical Review* 67: 377–88. Reprinted in D. Steinberg and L. Jakobovits (eds) (1971: 53–9).
—— (1968). Utterer's meaning, sentence-meaning, and word-meaning. *Foundations of Language* 4: 1–18.
—— (1975). Logic and conversation. In P. Cole and J. Morgan (eds) (1975: 41–58).
—— (1978). Further notes on logic and conversation. In P. Cole (ed.) (1978: 113–28).
—— (1979). *Studies in the way of words*. Cambridge, MA: Harvard University Press.
—— (1981). Presupposition and conversational implicature. In P. Cole (ed.) (1981: 183–98).
Grundy, P. (1995). *Doing pragmatics*. London: Edward Arnold.
Grunig, B.-N. and Grunig, R. (1985). *La fuite du sens: la construction du sens dans l'interlocution*. Paris: Hatier-Credif.
Guenther, F. and Schmidt, S.J. (eds) (1979). *Formal semantics and pragmatics for natural languages*. Dordrecht: Reidel.
Gumperz, J.J. (1982). *Discourse strategies*. Cambridge: Cambridge University Press.
—— (1996). The linguistic and cultural relativity of conversational inference. In J.J. Gumperz and S.C. Levinson (eds) (1996: 374–406).
Gumperz, J.J. and Berenz, N. (1993). Transcribing conversational exchange. In J.A. Edwards and M.D. Lampert (eds) (1993: 91–121).
Gumperz, J.J. and Hymes, D.H. (eds) (1972). *Directions in sociolinguistics: the ethnography of communication*. New York: Holt, Rinehart & Winston.
Gumperz, J.J., Jupp, T. and Roberts, C. (1979). *Crosstalk*. London: Centre for Industrial Language Teaching.
Gumperz, J.J. and Levinson, S.C. (eds) (1996). *Rethinking linguistic relativity*. Cambridge: Cambridge University Press.
Gunnarsson, B.-L., Linell, P. and Nordberg, B. (eds) (1997). *The construction of professional discourse*. London: Longman.
Haberland, H. and Mey, J. (1977). Editorial: linguistics and pragmatics. *Journal of Pragmatics* 1: 1–12.
Habermas, J. (1979). *Communication and the evolution of society*. Boston, MA: Beacon Press.

Halliday, M.A.K. (1973). *Explorations in the functions of language*. London: Edward Arnold.
—— (1985). *An introduction to functional grammar.* London: Edward Arnold.
—— (1989). *Spoken and written language*. Oxford: Oxford University Press.
Halliday, M.A.K. and Hasan, R. (1976). *Cohesion in English*. London: Longman.
Hanks, W. (1990). *Referential practice: language and lived space in a Maya community.* Chicago, IL: The University of Chicago Press.
—— (1995). *Language and communicative practices*. Boulder, CO: Westview Press.
—— (1996a). Exorcism and the description of participant roles. In M. Silverstein and G. Urban (eds) (1996: 160–200).
—— (1996b). Language form and communicative practices. In J.J. Gumperz and S.C. Levinson (eds) (1996: 232–70).
Heinemann, W. and Viehweger, D. (1991). *Tekstlinguistik: Eine Einführung.* Tübingen: Niemeyer.
Heller, M. (1995). Bilingualism and multilingualism. In J. Verschueren, J.-O.H. Östman, J. Blommaert and C. Bulcaen (eds) (1995). (loose-leaf contribution).
Heringer, H.J. (1978). *Practical semantics: a study in the rules of speech and action*. The Hague: Mouton.
Hickey, L. (ed.) (1989). *The pragmatics of style*. London: Routledge.
Hilbert, R.A. (1992). *The classical roots of ethnomethodology.* Chapel Hill, NC: The University of North Carolina Press.
Hinnenkamp, V. (1991). Talking a person into interethnic distinction: a discourse analytic case study. In J. Blommaert and J. Verschueren (eds) (1991: 91–109).
—— (1995). Intercultural communication. In J. Verschueren, J.-O.H. Östman, J. Blommaert and C. Bulcaen (eds) (1995). (loose-leaf contribution).
Holdcroft, D. (1979). Speech acts and conversation. *Philosophical Quarterly* 29: 125–41.
Holden, C. (1993). New life ahead for social sciences. *Science* 261: 1796–98.
Horn, L. (1984). Toward a new taxonomy for pragmatic inference: Q-based and R-based implicature. In D. Schiffrin (ed.) (1984).
Hoye, L. (1997). *Adverbs and modality in English*. London: Longman.
Hymes, D. (1962). The ethnography of speaking. In T. Gladwin and W. Sturtevant (eds) (1962: 13–53).
—— (1972). On communicative competence. In J.B. Pride and J. Holmes (eds) (1972: 269–93).
—— (1974). *Foundations in sociolinguistics: an ethnographic approach*. London: Tavistock Publications.
Irvine, J.T. (1995). Honorifics. In J. Verschueren, J.-O.H. Östman, J. Blommaert and C. Bulcaen (eds) (1995). (loose-leaf contribution).
—— (1996). Shadow conversations: the indeterminacy of participant roles. In M. Silverstein and G. Urban (eds) (1996: 131–59).

Jacobs, G. (1997). *Preformulating the news: an analysis of the metapragmatics of press releases.* University of Antwerp, Ph.D. dissertation.

Jakobson, R. (1960). Concluding remarks: linguistics and poetics. In T.A. Sebeok (ed.) (1960: 350–77).

—— (1970). *Main trends in the science of language.* New York: Harper & Row.

—— (1971). Shifters, verbal categories, and the Russian verb. In *Selected writings II*, pp. 130–47. The Hague: Mouton. [1957]

Janssen, T.A.J.M. and van der Wurff, W. (eds) (1996). *Reported speech: forms and functions of the verb.* Amsterdam/Philadelphia: John Benjamins.

Johnson-Laird, P. and Wason, P.C. (eds) (1977). *Thinking: Readings in cognitive science.* Cambridge: Cambridge University Press.

Karttunen, L. (1974). Presupposition and linguistic context. *Theoretical Linguistics* 1: 3–44.

Kates, C.A. (1980). *Pragmatics and semantics: an empiricist theory.* Ithaca: Cornell University Press.

Kempson, R.M. (1975). *Presupposition and the delimitation of semantics.* Cambridge: Cambridge University Press.

Kerbrat-Orecchioni, C. (1980). *L'énonciation.* Paris: Armand Colin.

—— (1986). *L'implicite.* Paris: Armand Colin.

—— (1990/92/94). *Les interactions verbales* (3 vols.). Paris: Armand Colin.

—— (1997). A multilevel approach in the study of talk-in-interaction. *Pragmatics* 7: 1–20.

Kiefer, F. and Verschueren, J. (eds) (1988). Metapragmatic terms. Special issue of *Acta Linguistica Hungarica* 38: 1–289.

Kienpointner, M. (1997). Varieties of rudeness: types and functions of impolite utterances. *Functions of Language* 4: 251–87.

Kochman, T. (1981). *Black and white styles in conflict.* Chicago, IL: University of Chicago Press.

Koschmieder, E. (1935). Zu den Grundfragen der Aspekttheorie. *Indogermanische Forschungen* 53: 280–300.

Krupa, V. (1982). *The Polynesian languages: a guide.* London: Routledge & Kegan Paul.

Kuczaj, S.A. (ed.) (1984). *Discourse development.* Berlin: Springer Verlag.

Kurzon, D. (1986). *It is hereby performed . . . : Explorations in legal speech acts.* Amsterdam: John Benjamins.

Lakoff, G. and Johnson, M. (1980). *Metaphors we live by.* Chicago, IL: University of Chicago Press.

Lakoff, R.T. (1973). The logic of politeness: or minding your p's and q's. *Proceedings of the Ninth Regional Meeting of the Chicago Linguistic Society*, 292–305.

—— (1989). The way we were. *Journal of Pragmatics* 13: 939–88.

—— (1993). Lewis Carroll: subversive pragmaticist? *Pragmatics* 3: 367–85.

—— (1995a). Conversational logic. In J. Verschueren, J.-O.H. Östman, J. Blommaert and C. Bulcaen (eds) (1995: 190–8).

—— (1995b). Conversational implicature. In J. Verschueren, J.-O.H. Östman, J. Blommaert and C. Bulcaen (eds) (1995). (loose-leaf contribution).

Lambrecht, K. (1981). *Topic, antitopic and verb agreement in non-standard French*. Amsterdam: John Benjamins.
Langacker, R. (1987). *Foundations of cognitive grammar*. Stanford: Stanford University Press.
Latraverse, F. (1987). *La pragmatique*. Brussels: Mardaga.
Lee, J. (1991). Language and culture. In G. Button (ed.) (1991).
Leech, G.N. (1983). *Principles of pragmatics*. London: Longman.
Levinson, S.C. (1983). *Pragmatics*. Cambridge: Cambridge University Press.
—— (1992a). Primer for the field investigation of spatial description and conception. *Pragmatics* 2: 5–47.
—— (1992b). Activity types and language. In P. Drew and J. Heritage (eds) (1992: 66–100).
Lewontin, R.C. (1978). Adaptation. *Scientific American* 239: 156–69.
—— (1982). Organism and environment. In H.C. Plotkin (ed.) (1982: 151–70).
Lieberman, P. (1975). *On the origins of language: an introduction to the evolution of human speech*. New York: Macmillan.
Linde, C. and Labov, W. (1975). Spatial networks as a site for the study of language and thought. *Language* 51: 924–39.
Lucy, J.A. (1992a). *Language diversity and thought: a reformulation of the linguistic relativity hypothesis*. Cambridge: Cambridge University Press.
—— (1992b). *Grammatical categories and cognition: a case study of the linguistic relativity hypothesis*. Cambridge: Cambridge University Press.
—— (ed.) (1993). *Reflexive language*. Cambridge: Cambridge University Press.
MacKay, A.F. and Merrill, D.D. (eds) (1976). *Issues in the philosophy of language*. New Haven: Yale University Press.
Mahoney, G. (1975). Ethological approach to delayed language acquisition. *American Journal of Mental Deficiency* 80: 139–48.
Malinowski, B. (1923). The problem of meaning in primitive languages. Supplement to Ogden, C.K. and Richards, I.A. (1989: 296–336).
Mann, W.C. and Thompson, S.A. (eds) (1992). *Discourse description: diverse linguistic analyses of a fund-raising text*. Amsterdam/Philadelphia: John Benjamins.
Markovà, I. and Foppa, K. (eds) (1990). *The dynamics of dialogue*. New York: Harvester Wheatsheaf.
Marmaridou, A.S.S. (1995). *Cognitive and social aspects of pragmatic meaning: a contribution to experiential realism*. Athens: University of Athens.
Martin, R.M. (1979). *Pragmatics, truth, and language*. Dordrecht: Reidel.
Martín Rojo, L. (1994). The jargon of delinquents and the study of conversational dynamics. *Journal of Pragmatics* 21: 243–89.
Mathesius, V. (1928). On linguistic characterology with illustrations from modern English. *Proceedings of the 1st International Congress of Linguists*, 56–63.
Mayr, E. (1974). Teleological and teleonomic: a new analysis. *Boston Studies in the Philosophy of Science* 14: 91–117. Reprinted in H.C. Plotkin (ed.) (1982: 17–38).

McCawley, J.D. (1977). Remarks on the lexicography of performative verbs. In A. Rogers *et al.* (eds) (1977: 13–25).

McCormack, W.C. and Wurm, S.A. (eds) (1978). *Approaches to language: anthropological issues*. The Hague: Mouton.

McGregor, G. (1986a). *Language for hearers*. Oxford: Pergamon.

—— (1986b). *The art of listening*. London: Croom Helm.

—— (1990). *Reception and response*. London: Routledge.

Meeuwis, M. (1991). A pragmatic perspective on contact-induced language change: dynamics in interlinguistics. *Pragmatics* 1: 481–516.

—— (1994). Nonnative–nonnative intercultural communication: an analysis of instruction sessions for foreign engineers in a Belgian company. *Multilingua* 13: 59–82.

—— (1997). *Constructing sociolinguistic consensus: a linguistic ethnography of the Zairian community in Antwerp, Belgium*. University of Antwerp, Ph.D. dissertation.

Meeuwis, M. and Östman, J.-O. (1995). Contact linguistics. In J. Verschueren, J.-O.H. Östman, J. Blommaert and C. Bulcaen (eds) (1995: 177–82).

Merritt, M. (1976). On questions following questions in service encounters. *Language in Society* 5: 315–57.

Mey, J.L. (1985). *Whose language?* Amsterdam: John Benjamins.

—— (1993). *Pragmatics: an introduction*. Oxford: Blackwell.

Miller, G.A. and Johnson-Laird, P.N. (1976). *Language and perception*. Cambridge: Cambridge University Press.

Minsky, M. (1977). Frame-system theory. In P.N. Johnson-Laird and P.C. Wason (eds) (1977: 355–76).

Moeschler, J. (1996). *Théorie pragmatique et pragmatique conversationnelle*. Paris: Armand Colin.

Moeschler, J. and Reboul, A. (1994). *Dictionnaire encyclopédique de pragmatique*. Paris: Editions du Seuil.

Montague, R. (1974). *Formal philosophy*. New Haven: Yale University Press.

Morris, C. (1938). *Foundations of the theory of signs*. Foundations of the unity of science: Towards an international encyclopedia of unified science, I, 2. Chicago: The University of Chicago Press.

Munitz, M.K. and Unger, P.K. (eds) (1974). *Semantics and philosophy*. New York: New York University Press.

Nairne, J.S. (1997). *Psychology: the adaptive mind*. Pacific Grove, CA: Brooks/Cole.

Nerlich, B. and Clarke, D.D. (1996). *Language, action, and context: the early history of pragmatics in Europe and America, 1780–1930*. Amsterdam/Philadelphia: John Benjamins.

Nunberg, G. (1993). Indexicality and deixis. *Linguistics and Philosophy* 16.

Nuyts, J. (1992). *Aspects of a cognitive–pragmatic theory of language: on cognition, functionalism, and grammar*. Amsterdam/Philadelphia: John Benjamins.

Nuyts, J. and Verschueren, J. (1987). *A comprehensive bibliography of pragmatics* (4 volumes). Amsterdam/Philadelphia: John Benjamins.

Ochs, E. (1988). *Culture and language development*. Cambridge: Cambridge University Press.

Ochs, E. and Schieffelin, B.B. (eds) (1979). *Developmental pragmatics*. New York: Academic Press.

—— (1983). *Acquiring conversational competence*. London: Routledge & Kegan Paul.

Ogden, C.K. and Richards, I.A. (1989). *The meaning of meaning: a study of the influence of language upon thought and the science of symbolism*. New York: Harcourt Brace Jovanovich. [1923]

Ohala, J.J. (1984). An ethological perspective on common cross-language utilization of F_0 of voice. *Phonetica* 41: 1–16.

Östman, J.-O. (1981). *'You know': a discourse-functional approach*. Amsterdam: John Benjamins.

—— (1986). *Pragmatics as implicitness: an analysis of question particles in Solf Swedish, with implications for the study of passive clauses and the language of persuasion*. Ph.D. dissertation, University of California at Berkeley, CA.

Ortony, A. (ed.) (1979). *Metaphor and thought*. Cambridge: Cambridge University Press.

Palmer, F.R. (1986). *Mood and modality*. Cambridge: Cambridge University Press.

Parijs, P. Van (1981). *Evolutionary explanation in the social sciences: an emerging paradigm*. Totowa, NJ: Rowman & Littlefield.

Parret, H. (1983). *Semiotics and pragmatics*. Amsterdam: John Benjamins.

Parret, H. *et al.* (1980). *Le langage en contexte*. Amsterdam: John Benjamins.

Parret, H., Sbisà and Verschueren, J. (eds) (1981). *Possibilities and limitations of pragmatics*. Amsterdam: John Benjamins.

Pawley, A. (n.d.) Verb reduction in the Kalam Pandanus language. MS.

Pawley, A. and Syder, F.H. (1983). Natural selection in syntax: notes on adaptive variation and change in vernacular and literary grammar. *Journal of Pragmatics* 7: 551–79.

Piaget, J. (1971). Functions and structures of adaptation. In J. Piaget (1971). *Biology and knowledge*. Chicago, IL: The University of Chicago Press, pp. 171–77. Reprinted in H.C. Plotkin (ed.) (1982: 145–50).

Plotkin, H.C. (ed.) (1982). *Learning, development, and culture: essays in evolutionary epistemology*. New York: John Wiley & Sons.

Pratt, M.L. (1977). *Toward a speech act theory of literary discourse*. Bloomington, IN: Indiana University Press.

Price, S. (1996). *Communication studies*. London: Longman.

Pride, J.B. and Holmes, J. (eds) (1972). *Sociolinguistics*. Harmondsworth: Penguin.

Prince, E. (1981). Toward a taxonomy of given-new information. In P. Cole (ed.) (1981: 223–55).

Psathas, G. (ed.) (1990). *Interaction competence*. Lanham, MD: University Press of America.

Quirk, R. (1981). International communication and the concept of Nuclear English. In L.E. Smith (ed.) (1981). *English for crosscultural communication*. New York: St. Martin's Press, pp. 151–65.

Récanati, F. (1979). *La transparence et l'énonciation*. Paris: Editions du Seuil.

—— (1981). *Les énoncés performatifs: contribution à la pragmatique*. Paris: Editions de Minuit.

Reddy, M. (1979). The conduit metaphor: a case of frame conflict in our language about language. In A. Ortony (ed.) (1979: 284–324).

Rehbein, J. (1977). *Komplexes Handeln: Elemente zur Handlungstheorie der Sprache*. Stuttgart: Metzler.

Rogers, A., Wall, B. and Murphy, J.P. (eds) (1977). *Proceedings of the Texas conference on performatives, presuppositions and implicatures*. Arlington, VA: Center for Applied Linguistics.

Rosaldo, M.Z. (1982). The things we do with words: Ilongot speech acts and speech act theory in philosophy. *Language in Society* 11: 203–37.

Rosch, E. (1977). Human categorization. In N. Warren (ed.) (1977: 1–49).

Rot, S. (ed.) (1983). *Languages in function*. Budapest.

Roulet, E. (1980). Modalité et illocution. *Communications* 32: 216–39.

Roulet, E. *et al.* (1985). *L'articulation du discours en français contemporain*. Berne.

Rudzka-Ostyn, B. (1995). Case and semantic roles. In J. Verschueren, J.-O.H. Östman, J. Blommaert and C. Bulcaen (eds) (1995). (loose-leaf contribution).

Sacks, H. (1992). *Lectures on conversation* (2 volumes, ed. by Gail Jefferson). Oxford: Basil Blackwell.

Sacks, H., Schegloff, E. and Jefferson, G. (1974). A simplest systematics for the organization of turn-taking in conversation. *Language* 50: 696–735.

Samarin, W.J. (1978). Linguistic adaptation to speech function. In W.C. McCormack and S.A. Wurm (eds) (1978: 595–614).

Sapir, E. (1921). *Language: an introduction to the study of speech*. New York: Harcourt Brace Jovanovich.

—— (1929). The status of linguistics as a science. *Language* 5: 207–14.

Sarangi, S. and Slembrouck, S. (1996). *Language, bureaucracy & social control*. London: Longman.

Sbisà, M. (1989). *Linguaggio, ragione, interazione*. Milan: Il Mulino.

—— (1995a). Analytical philosophy. In J. Verschueren, J.-O.H. Östman, J. Blommaert and C. Bulcaen (eds) (1995: 28–36).

—— (1995b). Speech act theory. In J. Verschueren, J.-O.H. Östman, J. Blommaert and C. Bulcaen (eds) (1995: 495–506).

Schank, R.C. and Abelson, R.P. (1977). *Scripts, plans, goals and understanding*. Hillsdale, NJ: Lawrence Erlbaum.

Schank, R.C. (1982). *Dynamic Memory*. Cambridge: Cambridge University Press.

Schegloff, E. (1990). On the organisation of sequence as a source of 'coherence' in talk-in-interaction. In B. Dorval (ed.) (1990: 51–77).

Schiffrin, D. (1994). *Approaches to discourse*. Oxford: Basil Blackwell.

Schiffrin, D. (ed.) (1984). *Meaning, form and use in context: linguistic applications*. Washington, DC: Georgetown University Press.
Schiffrin, D. (1988). *Discourse Markers*. Cambridge: Cambridge University Press.
Schlieben-Lange, B. (1975). *Linguistische Pragmatik*. Stuttgart: Kohlhammer.
Schmidt, S.J. (ed.) (1974). *Pragmatik I: Interdisziplinäre Beiträge zur Erforschung der sprachlichen Kommunikation*. München: Fink.
Schudson, M. (1978). *Discovering the news: a social history of American newspapers*. New York: Basic Books.
Searle, J.R. (1969). *Speech acts: an essay in the philosophy of language*. Cambridge: Cambridge University Press.
—— (1975a). Indirect speech acts. In P. Cole and J.L. Morgan (eds) (1975: 59–82).
—— (1975b). A classification of illocutionary acts. *Language in Society* 5: 1–23.
—— (1983). *Intentionality: an essay in the philosophy of mind*. Cambridge: Cambridge University Press.
—— (1989). How performatives work. *Linguistics and Philosophy* 12: 535–58.
—— (1992). *The rediscovery of the mind*. Cambridge, MA: MIT Press.
Searle, J.R. *et al.* (1992). *(On) Searle on conversation* (compiled and introduced by Herman Parret and Jef Verschueren). Amsterdam/Philadelphia: John Benjamins.
Searle, J.R., Kiefer, F. and Bierwisch, M. (eds) (1980). *Speech act theory and pragmatics*. Dordrecht: Reidel.
Sebeok, T.A. (ed.) (1960). *Style in language*. Cambridge, MA: MIT Press.
Senft, G. (1995). Phatic communion. In J. Verschueren, J.-O.H. Östman, J. Blommaert and C. Bulcaen (eds) (1995). (loose-leaf contribution).
Sgall, P. (1995a). Prague school. In J. Verschueren, J.-O.H. Östman, J. Blommaert and C. Bulcaen (eds) (1995: 429–35).
—— (1995b). Functional sentence perspective. In J. Verschueren, J.-O.H. Östman, J. Blommaert and C. Bulcaen (eds) (1995). (loose-leaf contribution).
Sgall, P. and Hajičová, E. (1977). Focus on focus. *Prague Bulletin of Mathematical Linguistics* 28: 5–54.
Sharrock, W. and Watson, R. (1988). Autonomy among social theories: the incarnation of social structures. In N.G. Fielding (ed.) (1988: 56–77).
Sherzer, J. (1987). A discourse-centered approach to language and culture. *American Anthropologist* 89: 295–309.
Shibatani, M. and Thompson, S. (eds) (1995). *Essays in semantics and pragmatics*. Amsterdam/Philadelphia: John Benjamins.
Silverstein, M. (1976). Shifters, linguistic categories, and cultural description. In K. Basso and H. Selby (eds) (1976: 11–55).
—— (1993). Metapragmatic discourse and metapragmatic function. In J. Lucy (ed.) (1993: 33–58).
Silverstein, M. and Urban, G. (eds) (1996). *Natural histories of discourse*. Chicago, IL: University of Chicago Press.

Sinclair, J. McH. and Coulthard, R.M. (1975). *Towards an analysis of discourse: the English used by teachers and pupils*. Oxford: Oxford University Press.
Škrabec, S. (1903). Zum Gebrauch der Verba perfectiva und imperfectiva im Slovenischen. *Archiv für Slavische Philologie* 25: 554–64.
Slembrouck, S. (1995). Channel. In J. Verschueren, J.-O.H. Östman, J. Blommaert and C. Bulcaen (eds) (1995). (loose-leaf contribution).
Smith, B.R. and Leinonen, E. (1992). *Clinical pragmatics: unravelling the complexities of communicative failure*. London: Chapman & Hall.
Smith, H. (1976). *The Russians*. New York: Ballantine Books.
Sperber, D. and Wilson, D. (1986). *Relevance: communication and cognition*. Oxford: Basil Blackwell.
Stalnaker, R.C. (1974). Pragmatic presupposition. In M.K. Munitz and P.K. Unger (eds) (1974: 197–214).
Stati, S. (1990). *Le transphrastique*. Paris: Presses Universitaires de France.
Steinberg, D.D. and Jakobovits, L.A. (eds) (1971). *Semantics: an interdisciplinary reader in philosophy, linguistics and psychology*. Cambridge: Cambridge University Press.
Steiner, E.H. and Veltman, R. (eds) (1988). *Pragmatics, discourse and text*. London: Pinter.
Stroud, C. (1992). The problem of intention and meaning in code-switching. *Text* 12: 127–155.
Talmy, L. (1978). Figure and ground in complex sentences. In J.H. Greenberg (ed.) (1978: 625–49).
Tannen, D. (ed.) (1982). *Spoken and written language*. Norwood, NJ: Ablex Publishing Corporation.
Tax, S. (ed.) (1959). *Evolution after Darwin*. Chicago, IL: The University of Chicago Press.
Thayer, H.S. (ed.) (1970). *Pragmatism: the classic writings*. New York: Mentor.
Thibault, P. (1997). *Re-reading Saussure: the dynamics of signs in social life*. London: Routledge.
Thomas, J. (1995). *Meaning in interaction: an introduction to pragmatics*. London: Longman.
Travis, C. (ed.) (1986). *Meaning and interpretation*. Oxford: Basil Blackwell.
Ungerer, F. and Schmid, H.-J. (1996). *An introduction to cognitive linguistics*. London: Longman.
Vanderveken, D. (1988). *Les actes de discours*. Brussels: Mardaga.
Varela, F.J., Thompson, E. and Rosch, E. (1991). *The embodied mind: cognitive science and human experience*. Cambridge, MA: MIT Press.
Vendler, Z. (1976). Illocutionary suicide. In A.F. MacKay and D.D. Merrill (eds) (1976: 135–45).
Verschueren, J. (1978a). Reflections on presupposition failure: a contribution to an integrated theory of pragmatics. *Journal of Pragmatics* 2: 107–51.
—— (1978b). *Pragmatics: an annotated bibliography*. Amsterdam: John Benjamins.
—— (1980). *On speech act verbs*. Amsterdam: John Benjamins.
—— (1981). The pragmatics of text acts. *Journal of Literary Semantics* 10: 10–19.

—— (1983a). Review article on speech act classification. *Language* 59: 166–75.
—— (1983b). On Bogusławski on promise. *Journal of Pragmatics* 7: 629–32.
—— (1985a). *What people say they do with words: prolegomena to an empirical–conceptual approach to linguistic action*. Norwood, NJ: Ablex Publishing Corporation.
—— (1985b). Review article on G.N. Leech, *Principles of pragmatics*, and S.C. Levinson, *Pragmatics*. *Journal of Linguistics* 21: 459–70.
—— (1985c). *International news reporting: metapragmatic metaphors and the U-2*. Amsterdam/Philadelphia: John Benjamins.
—— (1987). *Pragmatics as a theory of linguistic adaptation* (= IPrA Working Document 1). Antwerp: International Pragmatics Association.
—— (1988). The study of language on language: methodological problems and theoretical implications. In F. Kiefer and J. Verschueren (eds) (1988: 211–34).
—— (1989a). English as object and medium of (mis)understanding. In O. García and R. Otheguy (eds) (1989: 31–53).
—— (1989b) Language on language: toward metapragmatic universals. *IPrA Papers in Pragmatics* 3: 1–144.
—— (1994). Meaning in a theory of pragmatics. *Proceedings of the Twentieth Annual Meeting of the Berkeley Linguistics Society*, 553–62.
—— (1995a). Linguistic pragmatics and semiotics. *Semiotica* 104: 45–65.
—— (1995b). The pragmatic return to meaning: notes on the dynamics of communication, degrees of salience, and communicative transparency. *Journal of Linguistic Anthropology* 5: 127–56.
—— (1995c). Metapragmatics. In J. Verschueren, J.-O.H. Östman, J. Blommaert and C. Bulcaen (eds) (1995: 367–71).
—— (1995d). The conceptual basis of performativity. In M. Shibatani and S. Thompson (eds) (1995: 299–321).
—— (1995e). The pragmatic perspective. In J. Verschueren, J.-O.H. Östman, J. Blommaert and C. Bulcaen (eds) (1995: 1–19).
Verschueren, J. (ed.) (1987). *Linguistic action: some empirical–conceptual studies*. Norwood, NJ: Ablex Publishing Corporation.
Verschueren, J. and Bertuccelli Papi, M. (eds) (1987). *The pragmatic perspective*. Amsterdam: John Benjamins.
Verschueren, J., Östman, J.-O.H., Blommaert, J. and Bulcaen, C. (eds) (1995). ff.: *Handbook of pragmatics*. Amsterdam/Philadelphia: John Benjamins. (One bound volume 1995, loose-leaf contributions 1995 onwards.)
Vygotsky, L.S. (1978). *Mind in society: the development of higher psychological processes*. Cambridge, MA: Harvard University Press.
—— (1986). *Thought and language*. Cambridge, MA: MIT Press.
Waddington, C.H. (1959). Evolutionary adaptation. In S. Tax (ed.) (1959: 381–402). Reprinted in H.C. Plotkin (ed.) (1982: 173–93).
Walter, B. (1988). *The jury summation as speech genre: an ethnographic study of what it means to those who use it*. Amsterdam/Philadelphia: John Benjamins.
Warren, N. (ed.) (1977). *Studies in cross-cultural psychology*. New York: Academic Press.

Watson, D.R. (1987). Interdisciplinary considerations in the analysis of pro-terms. In G. Button and J.R.E. Lee (eds) (1987: 261–89).
Watson, J. and Hill, A. (1997). *A dictionary of communication and media studies* (4th ed.). London: Edward Arnold.
Watzlawick, P., Bavelas, J.B. and Jackson, D.D. (1967). *Pragmatics of human communication*. New York: Norton & Company.
Weiser, A. (1974). Deliberate ambiguity. *Papers from the Tenth Regional Meeting of the Chicago Linguistic Society*, 723–31.
Whitney, W.D. (1979). *The life and growth of language*. New York: Dover Publications. [1875]
Wilson, D. and Sperber, D. (1986). Inference and implicature. In C. Travis (ed.) (1986: 45–76).
Winch, P. (1958). *The idea of a social science and its relation to philosophy*. London: Routledge & Kegan Paul.
Winkin, Y. (1981). *La nouvelle communication*. Paris: Editions du Seuil.
Witkowski, S.R. and Brown, C.H. (1983). Marking reversals and cultural importance. *Language* 59: 569–82.
Wittgenstein, L. (1958). *Philosophical investigations*. Oxford: Basil Blackwell.
Wodak, R. (1995). Critical linguistics and critical discourse analysis. In J. Verschueren, J.-O.H. Östman, J. Blommaert and C. Bulcaen (eds) (1995: 204–10).
Woolard, K. (1989). *Double talk*. Stanford: Stanford University Press.
Wunderlich, D. (ed.) (1972). *Linguistische Pragmatik*. Frankfurt am Main: Athenäum.
Yule, G. (1996). *Pragmatics*. Oxford: Oxford University Press.

Index

MANAGING PEOPLE IN EDUCATION